"A soulful coming-of-age memoir ... Dawson has become a graceful, even lyrical, writer.

    —SETH MASIA, president, International Skiing History Association

"Lou Dawson has led the kind of adventurous life that most people only imagine. *Avalanche Dreams* tells the story of how he helped shape modern ski touring, and also tells the tangled story of his family and how he overcame substantial challenges to become a husband, father, and successful professional. His memoir accomplishes what few do, integrating his passion with profound insight about facing one's demons and triumphing with love."

    —DAVID J. ROTHMAN, author of *Living the Life: Tales from America's Mountains and Ski Towns*

"An honest narrative that stands as a stellar snow crystal amid the pantheon of adventure literature."

    —JON WATERMAN, author of *Into the Thaw,* and *National Geographic's Atlas of the National Parks* and *Atlas of Wild America*

"This is Lou Dawson at the top of the form that has made his landmark book, *Wild Snow,* such must reading, and the eponymous website a clearing house for all things backcountry. There is a code as well as cadence to his writing that illuminates every story, beautifully taking us places we didn't necessarily know we needed to be, much like skiing itself."

    —JAY COWAN, author of *Going Downhill Fast,* and *The Best of the Alps*

"Against the backdrop of wind-scoured alpine ridges and icy summits, *Avalanche Dreams* emerges as a riveting exploration of the human spirit's eternal quest for adventure and self-discovery. Strap in for an unforgettable ride that will take you to the heights of mountain peaks and the depths of the human experience."

    —ERIC BLEHM, *New York Times* bestselling author of *Fearless, The Last Season*, and *The Darkest White*

Author, powder day, 1984

©Michael Kennedy

AVALANCHE DREAMS

A Memoir of Skiing, Climbing, and Life

Louis W. Dawson

BEST PEAK

Disclaimer: This book is a work of creative nonfiction. All herein is based on the author's memories, journals, notes, interviews, correspondence, and family archives—including Patricia Dawson's journals. The correspondence, journal excerpts, and dialog are paraphrased and/or recreated, not literal, and may be conflations of past writings and verbal communication. While autobiographical in nature, this book is not a blow-by-blow narrative but rather an approximation of the author's lived experience—it is not an autobiography. Several individuals' names and identifying characteristics are changed to protect privacy, and several pseudonymous individuals are conflated characters: Keith Wilson, Eva Breton, and others. While the sequence of events is, for the most part, factually chronological, and known historical events are presented in their correct timing, on occasion the author summarizes details and alters the timeline for narrative flow. Regarding the above, other than commonly known events described herein, the reader should not consider this book anything other than a compilation of memories and emotional impressions.

The avalanche account sections written as if from Bob Limacher's point of view, are based on interviews, subsequently fictionalized as narrative.

To avoid copyright issues, song lyrics are paraphrased.

Several chapters include revised content based on the author's previous writings. See the chapter notes for attributions.

Avalanche Dreams / Louis W. Dawson.—1st ed. (105)

ISBN 979-8-9863385-4-5 (case-laminate hardcover)
ISBN 979-8-9863385-1-4 (paperback)
ISBN 979-8-9863385-2-1 (ebook)
ISBN 979-8-9863385-3-8 (audiobook)
ISBN 979-8-9863385-7-6 (IngramSpark jacketed hardcover)

Editing by Ivey Harrington Beckman, Lisa Dawson, Manasseh Franklin, and Catherine Lutz
Proofreading & copy editing by Ken Pletcher
Layout by Best Peak Press
Cover design by Art Burrows, Ajax Design
Cover background, Dawson collection: Looking NE from Harper Glacier, Denali, 1973
Front cover author portrait by Don Peterson: Winter climbing in Canada, 1974

For Lisa

Invisible wings.
Your laughter sings.

He dreamt the dream.
The setting was the same as always:
a thin ridge of rock, a dome of snow,
and, beyond the dome,
the blue and gleaming emptiness of the sky.
But whereas, before, he had invariably been alone,
there were now others with him.

– James Ramsey Ullman,
Banner in the Sky, 1954

AVALANCHE

A falling, churning mass of snow that occurs when the snow's weight overcomes its attachment to an angled surface.

On average, 41 people die by avalanche every year in North America. Most of these avalanches are triggered by the victim or those in their party.

The human body is denser than avalanching snow, making burial likely.

When an avalanche stops, it thickens and settles, entombing the victim as if buried in concrete.

Most victims suffocate soon after burial; the rest perish from trauma caused by the violent, fast-moving snow.

CONTENTS

COLUMBIA ICEFIELD, 1995

Lou: LINKED BY A safety rope and straining against the weight of our overloaded sled, my wife Lisa and I inch our way up Canada's Athabasca Glacier. Above us is the vast Columbia Icefield, where tonight we'll sleep on ice a thousand feet thick, surrounded by nothing but the cold wild of the Rocky Mountain alpine. And tomorrow, if all goes according to plan, we'll ski Snow Dome—said to be one of the easiest yet most aesthetic summits of the region.

Judging from the map's open contour lines, the "Dome" is as mellow a climb and ski descent as its name implies. Still, we have to navigate a glacier to get there. And there's the weather.

As the sun nears the ridge above us, a cloud bank pushes in from the south. There's no time to waste—we need to make camp. But first, we need to pass below an icefall that drops random avalanches on the Athabasca ascent route.

That morning, a park ranger had given us a spiel worth heeding: "Speed through the section exposed to the icefall. It calves once a week ... When that happens, you don't want to be there. And it's due ... Hasn't gone big in a while. You can take a winding route around the danger zone. Lots of crevasses that way. Travel roped. If you fall in a hole without a cord, you'll end up a statistic."

It's a classic mountaineering dilemma: falling ice, over which we meager humans have no control, or bottomless crevasses where skillful navigation saves lives—in theory.

Over the years, I'd made many such choices. This time is different. I'm married. We have a five-year-old child. Lisa is an exuberant athlete, game for every adventure. Yet, in my selfish quest for summits, was I leading us to peril? It wouldn't be the first time I'd made such a move.

....

Lisa: *We enter the icefall danger zone. Chunks of shattered blue ice scatter the glacier, some the size of a suitcase, others as bulky as our living room couch. Knowing that random death can fall from above is a scary part of mountaineering, something I don't want to think about.*

Without speaking, Lou swerves and enters the crevasse field. We ski past dark fissures, sometimes a few feet from the edge. They vary in size from boot-width cracks to chasms that could hide a locomotive. "Make sure there's no slack in the rope," Lou cautions.

After an hour of crevasse wandering, then a final gut-busting climb up a steep pitch, we're on the vast, snowy playa of the Columbia Icefield. We erect our tiny, pyramid-shaped tent five miles from our morning start.

....

Lou: In the evening twilight, the clouds lift like a stage curtain. We crawl from the tent and stand shoulder to shoulder. A full moon bobbles over massive peaks that ring the eastern horizon like theater walls. Banner clouds flag from Mount Andromeda and other matterhorns of grim north faces and rugged ridges—the sons and daughters of the roiled glaciers. The Rockies' soul tightens around my heart. What union is this? Man and mountain; the human animal in its place. A taste of primitive joy? Or do I attach innuendos for simple chemistry?

I follow Lisa back into our shelter. Whether it's the endorphins or the mystic, our pasta dinner tastes five-star—even the prepackaged, artificially enhanced cheese sauce is a tingling delight.

....

Lisa: *When Lou suggested a road trip, I envisioned another honeymoon: romantic decadence, lightly stirred Canadian adventure. Perhaps a few days at the Lake Louise hotel, lounging around the pool after a sunny morning ski tour. Camping on an oversized ice cube in a six-by-eight-foot tent with no floor—to save weight—is more Lou's style. My sweet man cooks me dinner, and the steaming cocoa pairs perfectly with a foot rub. At bedtime, we pull our double sleeping bag over our heads. Lou's arm brings me near—I'm warm and safe. The sound of our luffing tent brings me close to sleep.*

"Wild wind out there," I say.

"Up here, there's always wind," he replies.

Lisa, Icefield camp, 1995 ©Dawson

Lou: The next morning, a four-inch layer of snow covers nearly every-thing we own, including our sleeping bags. The wind had found the three-inch gap at the bottom edge of our tent. Our bags are water-resistant, and our organized gear is easy to find. But how does this look to Lisa? She's now had ten winters in the Colorado mountains, but there's also a beach girl in there. Warm sand is one thing; a snow-covered bed is quite another.

....

Lisa: *The interior of our tent looks like a giant powdered donut, which I wish I had, as Lou hands me a bowl of dry granola and the plastic spoon he'd grabbed at a convenience store during our drive north. "It'll save weight," he'd said as we both laughed, but I wasn't sure he was joking.*

....

Lou: I unzip the tent door and poke my head outside for a weather report. There's nothing but white on white—no sky, no texture in the snow. It's a total whiteout. If the weather spoke, it would say, "Welcome to the northlands. Be ready."

Snow Dome might be Canada's most relaxed ski peak, but not today. Instead, it's a vivid reminder of my two prior Alaskan climbing trips, one an abject failure, the other almost so.

While sipping Darjeeling, I sketch bearing lines onto our map and tweak the rotating dial of my compass. The summit is two miles away, 1,800 feet up.

Visibility varies with the snow squalls and shifting clouds, from a ski length to 300 feet. I'm confident we'll find the summit—it's a big target—but if we rely solely on our compass, we could miss our tent on the return. We have twenty-five marker wands; we need three or four times that to mark a reversible route.

"Maybe the clouds will lift during the climb," I say, shooting for optimism. "That way, we can space the wands farther apart—then we'll have enough."

Lisa zips her orange parka to her chin and says, "Let's go."

We tie a full rope length between us. I hold the compass in front of my chest. Every ten steps, I line my skis up with the dancing magnet, trying to ski a straight line. One rope length from the tent, about 150 feet, I stab my first wand into the snow. After that, each time Lisa reaches a wand, she shouts, and I place another, thus using our cord as a measure.

....

Lisa: *As Lou struggles with route finding, he's a phantom, fading in and out of the murky white. The only thing of distinction is the faded purple rope blurring into nothingness. I wait for a muffled shout, then follow the floss into the swirling haze.*

....

Lou: Suddenly, in front of my ski tips, a crevasse yawns through the custard air; an eerie and terrifying experience when you've got no sense of scale or points of reference. Five feet wide? Or thirty?

"Tighten the rope," I shout. "I'm backing up!"

I take a few strides rearward, plop in a wand, and then ski alongside the maw, searching for a way across. It soon appears—the beast choked by a plug of snow the size of a compact car. I stab another wand into the glacier and ski across the bridge while probing with my ski pole to check for hollow weakness.

As we continue, I break wands in half to stretch our supply, but I soon place our last. At that moment, the whiteout breaks, and reveals Mount Columbia. Then, before I can howl in delight, the shroud closes again, like someone raking dry cotton balls over my eyes.

Today, there'd be nothing easy; we must mark our trail. Can we leave items of gear along the way? I poke a Snickers candy wrapper into the snow.

It blows out of reach. I deploy my shovel and excavate a twenty-four-inch snow block, stand it on end, and tie a spare sock around it. Good. Another rope length. I hack another mini-edifice, clip a carabiner off my harness, and jab it on top. One, ten, thirty times, I bend over and cut a block from the wind-packed snow between my skis. I mark each cairn: hats, spare gloves, a pen jabbed through my blue bandana—anything to make our markers visible in the soup.

My biceps feel like wet cement; fire shoots through my elbow tendons. Our emptied packs sag like deflated party balloons, but we still have our essentials: extra layers, first-aid kit, emergency food. My altimeter says we're close. We stop, gulp the final dregs from our shiny stainless-steel thermos, and then jam it in the snow as a final marker.

A catchy pop song loops through my mind, the Talking Heads' "Once in a Lifetime." I shuffle my skis to the beat as David Byrne's voice acknowledges a beautiful wife and asks the existential question: How did this happen?

Byrne's query can be answered in countless ways, unique to every individual on this planet—we all have our journey, our story. This is mine.

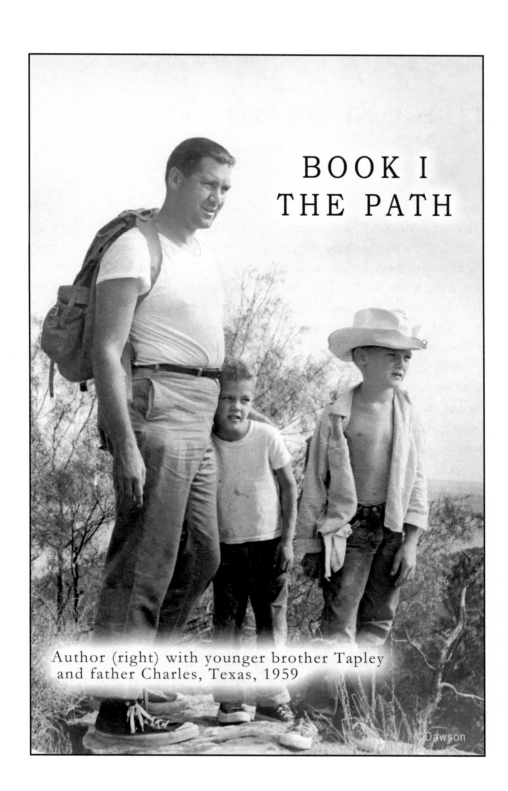

BOOK I
THE PATH

Author (right) with younger brother Tapley
and father Charles, Texas, 1959

1 | BEGINNINGS, 1950-1965

I HAVE MANUFACTURED A memory. It's 1950, two years before my birth. Yet seeded by my mother's elopement honeymoon journal—the scrawled text, the tiny snapshots, her stories told in later years—I picture myself as a small boy slouched in the Ford station wagon's cavernous back seat. My mother drives. She wears her outdoorsy cloche pulled low over her brow.

In front of me, my twenty-five-year-old father brings his right hand to his face and drags on a Marlboro. The smoke swirls, stings my eyes. I draw a breath through my nose because I like the smell of my dad. He flicks the cigarette out the window, unfolds a road map over the dashboard, and presses the map with one hand as it flutters in the breeze from the fin vent. With his other hand, he points to a dashed line, an unpaved road traversing the New Mexico mountains.

"Let's take a look at this one."

My mother strengthens her grip on the steering wheel and snaps a side glance at her man.

"Just tell me where to turn, darling."

That evening she journals: "Drove miles on the damnedest bumpy road we could find. Finally, pavement again ... Charles balanced the camp stove on his lap and warmed our supper in a can ... Dinty Moore beef stew."

NOW, SEVEN DECADES AFTER the honeymooners' 4,000-mile road trip from New Jersey to the Grand Canyon and back, I've eaten too many canned dinners of my own, and just like my father in his younger days, I've said, "Let's take a look" so many times it's engraved on my vocal cords. In my life of adventure, such utterances usually came with a smile, though it wasn't unusual for that smile to evaporate as certain other body parts clenched in mortal terror.

My mother Patricia, honeymoon car camp, 1958
©Dawson

IN 1957, WE MOVED from New Jersey to Dallas, Texas. As a five-year-old, I was still just along for the ride. But around age ten, as I began to fit the things of life together in my mind, I asked my mother why we'd moved.

"Your father had trouble with business, and he's got a better job here," she said. "And I like being near my brothers, especially your uncle Frank."

I never learned exactly why my maternal grandmother had migrated with her four sons to Dallas from New Jersey in the early 1950s, some years before my parents. My uncles were smart, likable fellows. Frank, the oldest, with his U.S. Air Force-inspired haircut and Texas-suntanned skin, owned and operated a thriving powerboat dealership.

Dad's story regarding our family's move: "New Jersey was too uptight."

I knew enough about intolerance by this point to have an inkling of what he meant. My mother, an avowed antiracist even then, had been quick to hop Texas churches when I told her the latest Sunday school topic was "white, the color of good." As for my dad, he never clarified what he meant by "uptight"—something about politics and hairstyles were my best guesses. In any case, the Texas geographical cure was a mixed blessing. The man never seemed happy with the day-to-day, merely existing, working as a planner for a housing developer, fiddling with garden projects.

And yet there was something more, something beyond humdrum homelife, something his new locale provided in abundance. My father found his joy in the backcountry. And Texas—as large as France yet with about one-third the population—had plenty of it. From the Rio Grande River, 500 miles north to the Panhandle, he thrived in the Lone Star outlands and shared the joy with his wife and four sons: me, the eldest, birthed in 1952, followed within three years by Craig and Tapley, then Tomas, born in 1960.

Our Texas-based adventures live in my mind as a black-and-white highlight reel:

Caddo Lake, paddling a canoe around the cypress trees protruding from the blackwater swamp. "Those spikes sticking up through the water are cypress knees," my father said. "That's how the tree breathes with its roots underwater."

In Big Bend National Park, chatting up a skinny Mexican fellow as he dumped water from his cowboy boots after wading across the Rio Grande.

Closer to home, hunting fossils on roadside scarps, where we picked and shoveled like tomb raiders and scored a spiraled nautilus the size of a small bicycle wheel. "We can sell it," our leader proclaimed.

Home from adventures, my brothers and I spent summer days running with the neighborhood pack, popping slingshots, and crashing bicycles. We explored jungle-smelling creeks where we flipped rocks to find hidden coral snakes, their skin painted with black, bright red, and yellow rings. Their neurotoxin venom could kill a boy in minutes. We hopped and giggled while the beasts slithered away.

My mother dabbed her brood's poison-ivy blisters with pink calamine lotion that dried to a flaky crust. "Don't scratch. You'll get an infection. They'll chop your leg off." Healed in minutes, we dusted our ankles with handfuls of yellow-sulfur chigger powder from the paper sack next to the door, then rushed outside to chase armor-plated armadillos or toss Black Cat firecrackers at each other's feet. I didn't whine about the tetanus shots; they came with the lifestyle.

AROUND 1961, MY FATHER surfaced his affection for beat culture and anti-establishment philosophy. He grew a thick beard—the Texas equivalent of dying his hair florescent green—and began spending much of his time in cafés and hip nightclubs. (At least what there were of such clubs in prehistoric Dallas.) He told me later that he'd always rolled with the hipsters, hanging out in Manhattan jazz clubs in his early twenties, tracking Kerouac readings and such. That explained at least part of his internal conflict: beatnik versus worker drone. But there was more. I was too young to intellectualize all this, but as my former trailblazer dad retreated into himself, my world spun like summer tornadoes we sometimes spotted in the distance, dragging their mud-gray fingers across the grasslands. What *was* going on with him?

As red-blooded American boys often did less than two decades past World War II, I obsessed over the cigar chewing, craggy faced, unbuckled-helmet-wearing comic book war hero Sgt. Rock. So came the inevitable question.

"Was Dad in the war?" I asked my mother.

Long pause.

"He rebelled against the army. Got out somehow. He doesn't like to talk about it."

I wanted to ask more, but the subject was closed.

My father's beard grew longer, his sideburns bushier. He quit his job, sold our brick-faced suburban tract home, and built a house from recycled construction materials in an undeveloped area outside Dallas known as Crazy Acres—for good reasons. Our neighbors on one side lived in a house built with discarded automobile batteries. On the other side lived what might have been the only gay-and-out couple in Texas: musicians, soon enlisted for my brothers' music lessons.

When the Cuban Missile Crisis threatened fiery obliteration, my father built a closet-sized, earth-covered bomb shelter in the backyard. He equipped the refuge with a hand-cranked fan attached to a stove vent, and a cheap plastic-stocked .22-caliber rifle he told me was "for self-defense."

I joined a Boy Scout troop. The tall, chain-smoking, stick-thin scoutmaster, whom we were required to call *Mister* Ellis, was a neighbor friend of my parents. Instead of the complete uniform, I tucked the official khaki shirt into jeans, cinched with the official belt with its insignia-embossed brass buckle. The official red neckerchief was neatly folded and snugged under my chin with the official slide-clasp.

For my first merit badge, I chose poultry management. With my father's help, I constructed a backyard chicken run, bought a dozen poults at the feed store, and was in business. The full-grown rooster guarded his harem, and their eggs, with his life. To defend against his weaponized beak, I wore beefy leather gloves, a barn jacket, and my brother Craig's football helmet.

After a few meetings, the local Scouting Council excommunicated our troop from the meeting hall. I didn't know why—maybe Mister Ellis' son's affection for homebrew explosives? Though this being Texas, such proclivities might have rated a merit badge ...

For our next gathering, Mister Ellis came equipped with a pipe wrench the length of his arm, twisted the knob off the meeting hall door, and kicked it open.

While my joining the only outlaw Boy Scout troop on earth clearly had something to do with my later behaviors, its primary effect was to continue my evolution as an outdoorsman. (I never took to animal husbandry.) During the cooler months, our troop embarked on multi-night backpacking junkets through enormous private ranches. We waded chocolate-colored creeks and camped in enchanted oak groves where hand-sized tarantulas rustled through the grounded autumn leaves. Mister Ellis stood still as a tree while a hairy one scuttled over his bare foot.

"Don't bother them. They won't bother you."

In the Texas backcountry, I learned how maps link your spirit to the land and how you can travel unhitched, carrying everything you need on your back. For an inquisitive boy with a folding knife clipped to his belt and a pair of sturdy shoes on his feet, nirvana.

The outlands could have molded me into a southern-style outdoorsman—bass fisher, deer hunter. I'd have liked that, but it wasn't going to happen. Instead, it was mountains.

Following their creative inclinations, my parents filled our home with books: large-format art tomes, essential Kafka and Kerouac, and my father's mountaineering literature collection. His copy of *Mountain World*, published in 1955, was perfectly designed to entice an adventurous boy. On page 79, a sketch depicted a futurist aircraft designed to land on and launch from the flanks of Himalayan giants. In later pages, men sported thick jackets and hats, coiled ropes, ice axes, and bug-eyed dark goggles worn because up in the mountains, you needed such things. The book lived in my bedroom, and there my love of the written word began—as well as a fascination with mountaineering.

That Christmas, my parents gave me James Ullman's *Banner in the Sky*, a fictional boy's adventure based on the Matterhorn's first ascent. Ullman's protagonist mountain boy, Rudi Matt, was obsessed with climbing what the adult mountain guides of his village deemed impossible: The Citadel, the last unclimbed peak in the Alps—"cliff upon cliff ... tower upon tower."

I read *Banner* at night by flashlight when I was supposed to be sleeping, covers tented over my head, sweating in the heat of my breath. Animated by my boy-mind, Rudi's exploits floated off the pages as a virtual reality: the metallic swirl of cold snow on my tongue, the bitter wind so strong I pushed against it like a fence, my team lurching uphill, chuffing like pack horses in the brittle air of altitude. Musky wool, stiff wet canvas backpacks, their oiled leather shoulder straps stretched so thin over muscle and bone they looked to snap.

From page one to the end, I wanted to be Rudi, "only looking up—as the great mountain world unfolded before him," as Ullman wrote.

IN HIS PERPETUAL SEARCH for countercultural, meaningful work—and to satisfy his outdoor adventure urgings—my father started a side business: hauling eight-to-twelve-year-old kids on camping trips in the alpine mountains closest to upper Texas, which were those in Colorado. As the oldest child, much to my delight I was always included. We hiked, explored mine ruins, and cooked pancakes on a clever shelf that folded from the side of the plywood camping trailer my dad had built. It was outdoor education before outdoor-ed was cool.

At age nine, I climbed my first peak during those Colorado trips: a 12,000-foot grassy bump in the otherwise high and massive Sawatch Range, where fifteen peaks top 14,000 feet. Lacking a backpack, I tied my jacket around my waist and carried a quart of water in an army surplus aluminum canteen hung on my belt. It banged my thigh with every step, as if a puckish elf were thumping me with his fist. The water smelled of the green canvas cover and left a metallic aftertaste.

At the top, two of us donated our makeshift walking sticks, from which we lashed up a cross. We piled rocks into a cairn and planted the cross on top. We thought that's what you did when you climbed a mountain.

My father's snapshot told the story: Four spunky boys gathered around the symbol of our conquest, our clothing a ragtag assortment of plaid shirts and unzipped barn jackets, my face shaded under a dome-topped straw cowboy hat, one kid with a band-aid on his forehead. Unknown to us, the bulky mountain in the photo's background was 14,200-foot Mount Yale, the 21st highest of Colorado's fifty-four "fourteener" peaks—the renowned monarchs that would define future chapters of my life.

First mountain, 1961
author second from left

My smooth-soled Keds tennis shoes skittered on the gravely trail as we hiked down that Sawatch bump. I fell on my butt and bloodied my palms. *Who cared?* We were climbing—that made everything perfect. Or almost. After every trip we were too-soon back in Texas, where the usual amusements paled. Yet the prairie still had its appeal, and vipers topped the list.

IN WHAT WAS PROBABLY an attempt to live his artisan-hipster dreams, my father dabbled in professional photography. As I learned many years later, you don't just buy a sack of glass and start making a living as a pro. It's a long, drawn-out process, and the expense-revenue equation can be absurd. That's how it was for my father. But the would-be Ansel Adams tried, and while he didn't seem any happier, he went after it harder than I'd ever seen him work. He spent hours, days, in his darkroom and almost always had a black-and-silver Nikon dangling from his neck.

As I entered my pre-teens, my father let me slosh prints through the acrid-smelling liquids and towed me along on the shoots: cattle roundups replete with sun-pinched Texan cowboys, portrait sessions with western artist Kelly Pruitt, and, topping all, the Sweetwater Rattlesnake Roundup, held in the railroad cowtown of Sweetwater, about four hours west of Dallas.

Billed as the "largest snake hunt in the world," the Roundup was something you'd find only in the state where everything is bigger. Several hundred pistol-strapped, Stetson-crowned hombres showed up with their snake sticks, six-foot poles with hand-sized hooks on the ends. Wielding garden sprayers, the men squirted gasoline into rock piles and crevices. When the addled reptiles slithered into daylight, the hunters slipped their hooks underneath, raised their sticks into the air with the beasts dangling like ropes, and transferred their live catch to throbbing burlap sacks.

Back at event headquarters, the men dumped their prey into a dry, family-size portable swimming pool. High-booted snake wranglers waded into the writhing mass. They snatched snakes by their necks bare-handed, and milked the rattlers for their venom by jabbing their fangs into rubber membranes stretched over mayonnaise jars. Pharmaceutical labs used the harvest to manufacture antivenom. The organizers gave out prizes for the most pounds of snakes, the longest, and the snake-eating contest.

My father burned film while a milker snagged me six live serpents. We hauled them home in our camp cooler, after punching air holes into the lid with our firewood hatchet.

A WEEK LATER, MY school teacher announced a show-and-tell. I thought show-and-tell was silly, and it gave me stage fright, standing in front of thirty fidgeting kids and mumbling about my latest pocketknife—"Eight blades ... Um ... This one's the can opener"—or introducing my hamster. But it wasn't silly this time, and my pets were not hamsters. Instead, I brought the fabled beasts that any child of Texas feared and thus obsessed on: three venomous rattlesnakes in a fish aquarium with a slab of warped plywood for a lid.

Word spread like a grassfire. During morning recess, the entire student body mobbed my classroom. I was the master of ceremonies. "Flick the glass. Watch them *strike*. They can swallow a hamster whole, cuz their bones stretch!"

With each tap of a fingernail, the rattlers slammed their needle-filled jaws against the glass, leaving smears of pale-white venom, which bore an uncanny resemblance to something we pubescent boys were coming to know well.

The ceiling loudspeaker broke the melee: "Evacuate the building, evacuate ... An unsafe situation exists!"

The local sheriff swaggered into the room. His holstered, black-gripped, Texas-sized revolver hung low, the muzzle just about grazing his kneecap. His beige uniform pants were tucked into his stovepipe cowboy boots.

"Git them danged buzzworms outta here!"

My dad laughed as we slid my serpentarium into the back of his station wagon. "Typical Dallas," he said with a smirk. "What's wrong with snakes? I wish I'd been there with my camera."

With a pet, 1964

2 | ASPEN LIFE, 1966

I FIRST HEARD THE word "existentialism" when I was fourteen years old. My father and I were sitting at the kitchen table after dinner, talking—just the two of us, a rarity. He had switched off the air conditioning to save on the overdue electric bill, and the 105-degree Texas day lingered like a slow-cooling oven. Occasional shrieks of pain filtered through the open windows, my brothers tormenting each other with stick swords and spear-grass darts.

"Existentialism means you decide what life is to you," my father said about the term I could barely pronounce. "You make your own way. That's how to live."

As a young teen, high-toned philosophizing was beyond me. But it didn't take a savant to see how my father's actions reflected his ideals: the eclectic work history, the beatnik grooming, the crazy house in Crazy Acres, John Coltrane's soul-searing improvs sifting into my bedroom as I slept.

I wanted to learn more about my father, this "living your own way," and his army experience, which I sensed were related. But he was done talking about it, especially the war part.

A few days later, I queried my mother as she drove me to school.

"Mom, what happened to Dad during the war?"

Her shoulders tensed, and she tilted forward in her seat.

"He joined the 10th Mountain Division, the soldiers who snow skied. Then he deserted from Camp Hale, that Army training place in Colorado. He went to prison."

Hearing the word "deserted" conjured thoughts, no doubt from popular culture, of getting shot for the offense. And the word "prison" blew my mind.

"How long was he in jail?"

My mother glanced left at the countryside flowing by and said nothing.

"Mom, how long was he in jail?"

"About a year and a half. Grandpa got him out early. He knew some politician or something."

My paternal grandfather lived in New York City, where he headed up a large insurance corporation and enjoyed the fruits of his toil: the tailor, the tony apartment bordering the greenery of Central Park. But Grandpa wasn't just another drone of the concrete canyons. As my father faltered, my grandfather became our family's bedrock. He accomplished this by modeling his work ethic, writing scores of thoughtful letters, visiting occasionally, and flying me and my brothers east for summer vacations. He was an avid reader and loved gifting us with books, hundreds over the years, always inscribed: "With Love, Grandpa and Grandma."

As fathering sometimes does, much of Grandpa's positive character had skipped his son. Not only was there the military debacle, but my father was so financially irresponsible he failed at every business endeavor—more than once taking a partner down with him. He never made much of a living and devoted his financial energies to scheming for Grandpa's occasional handouts. Even as a young boy I sensed the pitifulness of this.

To make ends meet, my mother worked an almost full-time job at a Dallas community center, while dredging up the energy to raise us four boys as well as obey her creative impulses: silkscreening, ceramics, and painting. I didn't comprehend how strong she was until much later in life, when I realized that those years of hardship in Dallas underpinned her success as an artist.

Still, my mother was only human. The constant strain of financial troubles and an ailing marriage bred a bottomless pool of delirium under her fragile shell. I saw this in the frequent screaming fits she directed at us brothers and the maniacal way she pushed a vacuum cleaner, as if it were a lethal weapon: "Die, dust bunnies!"

The situation led to extreme permissiveness, which my father passively supported—especially when it came to his version of Dr. Spock childcare. We were allowed to do almost anything: roam the Dallas countryside like stray dogs, build homebrew gunpowder bombs, and so on. It's a miracle none of us were drowned in the creeks, snatched by a pedophile, or blown to bits.

And yet, the loose life of Crazy Acres had its positives: the expansive worldview it gave me, the willingness to explore and take physical risks. But our freedom was based on dysfunction, which would later segue into neglect, especially with my youngest brothers.

THROUGH 1965, MY FATHER's emotional abandonment continued. As we became something of a single-parent family, my mother's scolds traveled with ease through the scanty wooden walls of Crazy Acres.

"You spend all day reading junk paperbacks and smoking in those coffee shops. We can't live on my meager wages and your father's Christmas cash. You need to work."

Dark-suited, neck-tied strangers appeared at our front door. During their muttered conversations with my mother, some lines stood out, even to a youngster:

"When can you pay?"

Even if he'd wanted (he didn't), my father couldn't stroll out and land a job with a steady paycheck. His bearded beatnik look—not to mention his attitude—fit the Texas milieu about as well as a nudist streaking the Southern Baptist church across the freeway from our house.

Still, with parents such as mine, there was always something interesting on the horizon.

DESPITE THE TEXAS MADNESS, my father had continued leading his Colorado youth camping trips. While doing so, he spent much of his time in and around Aspen, where he had a close friend from his and my mother's New Jersey high school days. George Parry was about my father's age, married with three kids. He was tall, active-lifestyle lean, and seemed to have no other jacket but his blue ski-instructor parka. In addition to teaching skiing, he owned and operated the town laundromat, raced sailboats on a nearby reservoir, and built houses—a typical mountain-town denizen.

We went into town often to grocery shop, visit the doctor for the inevitable boy-wounds, and see George and his family. I loved walking the dirt streets, inhaling the flinty dust of mine tailings the town used as road base. I pictured the network of hand-hewn tunnels under my feet, where fist-sized silver nuggets gleamed under miners' helmet lights.

One afternoon we stopped in at Aspen Hardware. The old counterman wore faded denim overalls and a collared shirt with rolled sleeves. A retired miner? My father needed a specific nut and bolt to repair our car. Overalls turned in one motion to a wall of small wooden bins and extracted the exact pieces as if by telepathy.

Aspen was still a blue-collar mining town. But it was fast becoming more. Throughout the 1950s and up to the present, the ski boom and the town's reputation as a "cool" place had attracted a diaspora of artists, athletes, beatniks, thrill seekers, and just plain seekers. Puffy goose-down vests and scuffed leather mountain boots were standard street attire. Ski instructors and carpenters drank with intellectuals and celebrities. And when the celebs came, so came their wealth to underpin the town's economy. A progressive vibe hummed, scented with adventure.

I hardly noticed Aspen's countercultural aspects—I was too young and too interested in the mountains—but my father did. To him, the permissive paradise must have made Texas look like the gulag.

There was only one choice.

My father sold our Texas digs and, with financial help from Grandpa and a moderate inheritance, bought land three miles outside of Aspen up narrow, glacier-carved Castle Creek Valley. He purchased a chainsaw, hired George Parry, built a wooden timber bridge across the creek, and broke ground on a two-story rectangular house that fit the terrain as if it sprouted between the spruce and aspen trees.

A month or so after beginning construction, in June 1966, he rented an apartment at the gingerbread-trimmed Cresta Haus Inn one-quarter mile east of town, and relocated our household within two weeks.

I was soon smitten with our new hometown, wandering through the aspen forest behind the Inn, riding my bicycle, exploring. Yet other things were not so wonderful.

During conversations with George (who knew of my father's wartime history), I'd learned that Aspen was chockablock with military veterans, specifically those of the 10th Mountain Division. George explained that many of them had visited the town during the war, fell in love with the place, and returned to operate much of the town's ski industry and various other endeavors. Learning of this kept me questing for more of my father's story, which, in bits and pieces, my mother delivered.

My AWOL father hadn't made an innocent mistake, like passing out drunk and not showing up the following day. Instead, he'd bolted like a rabbit with no intention of returning. Hence the jail sentence rather than a week of potato peeling.

I wanted to respect my father, gauge myself against him, and find something solid on which to hook the tape measure. Instead, in the muddled thinking of a fourteen-year-old, I feared he was a coward. If so, was he ashamed, or at least embarrassed? Or was he so existentialist, so cool, he cared not that one of the local 10th Mountain Division vets might notice his last name? After all, there couldn't have been that many Hale men who ended up in prison. I imagined witnessing the results, and the imagining was torture.

"Dawson? I knew a Dawson at Hale. Yellow-dog deserter. Any relation?"

DESPITE OBSESSIVE WORRIES ABOUT my father's past, I relished his newfound focus. My creator-explorer dad was back—and this time, the adventure was in making something with our hands.

I had my own nail apron, tri-square, and hammer, and I was helping my dad and his two carpenters build a house from the ground up in the mountains.

After a few weeks of ditch-digging and concrete forming, we assembled the first-floor walls flat on the concrete slab foundation. My brawny father could slap the four-inch framing nails to the head with one blow of his waffle-face framing hammer.

The entire crew gathered to raise the walls, first prying them up a few inches with our hammer claws as we kicked lumber scraps into the gaps to hold a space for our hands. The process resembled folding up the sides of a flattened cardboard box. "One, two, three, lift!"

During breaks, I soaked up stories of George and the other carpenter's mining-turned-resort-town lifestyle: hunting, teaching tourist "turkeys" how to ski, and mountaineering adventures.

At least for a while, my father was a builder—a good one. And, when we completed our house, might he thrive in his discovered utopia?

As for me, I had a revelation.

While working on the Castle Creek house, now and then I'd pause, holster my hammer, tilt my head back, and lose myself to the snow-patched sawtooth ridges and the sky. I'd fill my lungs, and savor the alpine—an odor without an odor, nostrils dilating in its purity. I wanted to breathe it forever. After the books, after my dreams of Rudi, I had to climb. How to start?

Charles Craig Dawson & George Parry, Castle Creek house, 1966

My father hired lanky teenager Chris Landry as a construction laborer. While Chris would later become known for his near-impossible extreme skiing descents, in 1966 he was just a smart, quiet kid two years older than me, with one essential difference: he climbed. As we shoveled ditches and humped lumber, he told of scrambles on precipitous 14,130-foot Capitol Peak—nearby in the Elk Mountains, the hardest fourteener of all—and rock climbs on the scruffy granite crags of Independence Pass above Aspen.

Was Landry my key to the kingdom?

One day, after we picked up Chris on the way to work, I got the guts to pop the question. He sat in the passenger seat of my father's white Ford pickup while I nestled in the back next to a keg of nails and a spare hammer.

"Can you teach me how to climb?" I asked.

Landry glanced back over his shoulder. The "no" came swiftly, with a hint of condescension.

I voiced a faint "oh" as my throat closed and my eyes watered. What of the alpine brotherhood in my books? And didn't the Code of Boys dictate sharing perilous fun?

Not all was lost with the finality of Landry's answer. There were fish. I grabbed my spin rod almost every summer afternoon, and attached a shiny silver lure. Behind our house, I waded snowmelt-chilled Castle Creek in shorts and canvas sneakers without socks. As I squinted through the water, sometimes I spotted a trout, head upstream, its gray body waving like a flag in the wind. The lure twirled through the tumbling water, glittering in the sunlight until my prey darted through the riffles and hit it like a missile.

My mother froze the fish. Each time the count topped a dozen, she served them for dinner. Two each for everyone.

IN THE FALL OF 1966, I began my freshman year at Aspen High School. For the first few months, a clique of alpha males teased me without mercy, calling me "Texas," punching, kicking, shoving. Almost every day, a rancher kid stole my lunch and pawed through it in front of a dozen sniggering students.

I'd soon had enough. One morning I grabbed the dishwasher soap from beneath our kitchen sink and made the rancher a tasty Texas sandwich—*extra mayo!* He disappeared for a few hours that afternoon. The thievery ceased, as did the harassment once my classmates saw I'd defend myself, and was nothing more than another befuddled teen with an equally 'fuddled family.

In more important matters, my stylin' Beatles haircut helped things along. More than one girl said I was cute. But they didn't know I couldn't ski. That was worse than being a Texan expat; it was the Aspen equivalent of being paralyzed from the waist down.

In October, my father hauled his six-member tribe to Aspen's annual ski swap. With George as our advisor, we barged into the riot of deal seekers. We outfitted ourselves with battered wooden skis and black leather lace-up boots a few years behind current models, which were incorporating ever more plastic. I chose a pair of boards that were slathered with red house paint—someone's makeshift style statement. The red was flaking off like confetti, but George said they were "good ones," priced low because of their appearance.

Patricia Dawson, 1970,
throughout it all, she loved to ski   ©Dawson

From the miles of clothing racks, my mother scored a dark blue, upper-thigh-length, nylon-shelled parka belted at the waist with an H-shaped metal clasp—her skier look for the next twenty years. Dad told my brothers and me to ski in our jeans and school parkas.

We moved into the Castle Creek house a month later, and the ski lessons commenced. Learning to ski was hard, not having been born with planks on my feet like everyone else in Aspen. Yet I loved every minute of it, gaining a new skill directly tied to my dreams of mountaineering—and of girls.

By my second season on the slopes, I was playing the skiing version of hare-and-hounds with female classmates. It seemed they were always ski racers, with headbanded hair and patterned sweaters. If I caught up, it was a miracle. Yet sometimes, my involuntary coaches waited. When they did, the chairlift rides were sensational.

3 | ASHCROFTERS, 1967

As the climbing life eluded me, fantasy filled the gap. Before the night's sleep, I pictured myself in my lug-soled mountain boots, kicking for grip on rock and snow. I left dog-eared catalogs open on the living room table, with products circled and labeled. During family dinners, I chattered ad nauseam about gear—*Kelty pack, forty dollars, good deal*. Hints had little effect. Action spoke.

Highland Peak cut the sky nearly a mile overhead to the southwest of our Castle Creek home. Above a vast reach of aspen and conifer forest, its bare, above-timberline summit glinted with patches of last winter's snow as if daubed with white paint. One cloudless, late spring day, around noon, I stuffed a canteen and three chocolate bars into my daypack and embarked on the hike. In my books, boys scaled greater mountains. How tough could Highland Peak be?

The ascent began with a lengthy trudge through steep aspen forest, on a network of elk and deer paths that wandered without human purpose, often sideways instead of upward. More than once, I glimpsed the summit through the treetops and found I'd strayed too far to the left or right, climbing toward the crest of a ridge. I worried these ridges would lead me into the wrong drainage, in danger of becoming lost. If I'd been more mountain savvy I'd have known that ridges are often the best path to the top. Instead, as long as my chosen game trails stuttered upward, I used them until they faded, then wandered uphill a few hundred feet to the next likely path for ascension. From a bird's-eye view, my route probably resembled that of a madman.

There were worthy distractions: snack stops, sitting on my backpack in the noisy silence of my solitude, the hollow *thock-thock-thock* of a woodpecker, the squall of a hawk. Deep in the timber, I scented my first elk, a musky mix of garden mulch and wet dog fur—you never forget it. By instinct, I slow-stalked through the aspen thickets, yet caught no glimpse of the beasts. I knew them only by the thud of their hooves as they stampeded away.

Later, a wild turkey the size of a small dog erupted from its perch in a spruce eight feet above my head, loud as a helicopter, startling me into a chest-scrunching adrenaline rush.

As I stumbled over the last rocks and tundra hummocks to the summit, the sun kissed the stacked ridges to the west, and a cooling breeze hinted at night. I hadn't packed a flashlight. After a one-minute celebration, I turned and dropped into the fast-darkening timber—without a clue about my return route.

Lost? Go downhill, said my books. So I blundered downland through the conifers and aspen trees, hopping over elk-muddied creeks. Moonless dark had fallen when I met the paved road, a half-hour starlit stroll from home.

I strutted into our house like the stud I thought I was, headed to the kitchen for a glass of water. My mother, her face pinched with panic, stood near the black telephone mounted on the wall next to the refrigerator.

"Lou, you told us you were just hiking around and would be back soon. You scared us. They're getting a search party together. Sheriff said fifty men!"

MY PARENTS GOT THE message: If not initiated into the alpine arts, I would disappear for good in the rugged wilderness sprawling untold miles in nearly every direction. The solution seemed predestined. Near the upper end of the Castle Creek Valley, nine miles from our home, outdoorsman Dave Farny operated his Ashcrofters Mountaineering School boys' camp.

Farny was a typical 1960s Aspenite, instructing skiing in the winter, working multiple gigs, and even attempting to develop a ski resort from scratch. Regarding the Ashcrofters, he presented himself as an alpine guide. I suppose he was—though not to the extent of more broadly experienced professionals, such as the Exum guides of the Wyoming Tetons. While climbing and hiking, he favored a peaked Tyrolean-style "alpi" hat. In a PR photo, he sported a coiled climbing rope looped over one shoulder, imitating iconic images. His somewhat hyperbolic—and convincing—school brochure oozed with self-confident actuation: "A five-week program at the Ashcrofters is a rare experience, an important part of a young man's life."

Dave Farny, 1967
©Tony Gauba

TWO WEEKS AFTER my Highland Peak escapade, I was unpacking my duffle on the bottom bunk in one of the Ashcrofters' brown, twelve-by-sixteen A-frame cabins.

The school's base camp sat a few hundred yards off the valley's dirt road, tucked into an aspen grove at 9,500 feet—where deciduous forest transitions to gray-green conifers. During windless mornings, the swimming pond beside the dining hall mirrored the serrated ridges above. Foot trails ducked into the forest near our cabins, leading into the Elk Mountains, where six 14,000-foot peaks ruled over 200 square miles of glacial lakes, dark timber, and snow, always snow.

The fun began with the pond. A wood-burning sauna perched on a nearby hillside, from where a zipline dropped 200 feet to the water—the mountain equivalent of an amusement park ride. We climbed the hill, baked in the sauna, monkey-hung from the whizzing zip-wheel, and screamed to a royal splash. Stimulated to a frenzy, we darted about in our sagging-wet underwear, slimed with green algae from head to feet, and repeated our zip runs, over and over, until Farny wolf-whistled his savages in for dinner.

I'd arrived at the camp with my proud Beatles' haircut grown to a shoulder-length sun-bleached shag. A few days later, after a rowdy zipline session, Farny singled me out.

"Lou, you need a haircut. That mop will tangle in the climbing ropes. Besides, you look like a girl. Sit on my porch chair; I'll get my clippers." When my parents visited the next day, my mother fumed about Farny's above-the-ear trim. But I liked Farny's structure, his certainty. And now I could zipline without algae strands trailing from my coiffure. Though I liked girls, not looking like one was okay, too. The only question: If this is a "mountaineering" school, when do we go mountaineering?

A FEW DAYS INTO the program, we trucked to a campground near Independence Pass, east of Aspen, and set our tents twenty yards from a rope-length-high granite wall (about 150 feet).

We rock climbed every day for a week, learning how to jam our hands in cracks, tie knots, and control the quivering calf muscles that ejected our boots from the footholds like a bulldog was chewing our heels. And the rappels: staggering backward over rock overhangs where we dangled from our pencil-thin cords, spinning free as we squeezed our hands so tight on the rope our forearms spasmed.

All our practice climbs were "top-roped." This involved someone sitting at the top of the cliff (accessed via a short hike) and rope belaying the climber coming up.

Top-roping was the ideal learning tool for beginner climbers. But I'd learned from my books that lead climbing—leading—was the essence of the sport. I wanted so badly to lead I'd have bribed the instructors with my lunch candy. But learning lead climbing in the 1960s was complicated and dangerous—not in the sport plan for us kids. My learning would come later, under different circumstances. Instead, Farny had other adventures on tap.

GRADUATING THE ASHCROFTERS REQUIRED what Farny called the "survival," a solo night in the woods, equipped with a dozen matches and a knife—no food, sleeping bag, or tent. Having never overnighted more than twenty feet from another human, nor alone in the wild, I should have been afraid or at least concerned. *What if it rained? Can you build a teepee with a pocket knife?* Instead, I double-checked my canister of waterproof matches, then jumped from the drop-off vehicle like I was going for pizza.

I spent the afternoon exploring the nearby forest and gathering firewood. As instructed, I scraped out a shallow hole, kindled a blaze, then covered the fire with dirt to create the wilderness equivalent of a heating pad. Good idea, but my execution was lacking. I'd built too small a fire, ending up with a patch of warm dirt just large enough to fit my upper back.

As night fell, I shivered, pumped sit-ups, and didn't sleep. Which was okay. There were shooting stars, and the nearby creek sang me the song first heard during my fishing sojourns: low notes, hissing highs, volume modulating as the air moved. I'd never heard it so clearly. Soothed by the liquid lullaby, girded by my introversion, and nourished by the wild, I barely felt the hunger pangs.

Can I do it again?

After a few days back at base camp—more zipline laps, soccer in a field of grapefruit-sized stones with pairs of cow pies as goal markers—we loaded six days worth of backpacking food and set off through the lush aspen forest behind the dining hall. Within 200 feet, our cleat-soled mountain boots were scuffing wilderness dirt, headed for the peaks. Intense alpine sunlight filtered through the canopy, projecting blotchy patterns on the ground. Knee-high ferns sagged over the trail and brushed my bare legs. Mosquitoes and biting flies homed in on our unwashed boy scent like radar-guided missiles, provoking a constant chorus of hand slaps and curses.

We broached a high pass and skittered two miles down the rockiest trail I'd ever hiked. Then, we camped near timberline at Conundrum Hot Springs, nestled deep in the Maroon Bells-Snowmass Wilderness. The rock-ringed bathing pool was the size of a hot tub, surrounded by alpine tundra sprinkled with pale gray granite boulders and purple lupine flowers.

Unlike hotter springs that soon had you heat-struck and dizzy, the Conundrum waters were just above body temperature. Here you could soak all night. And we nearly did.

We languished for hours, dozing, squeezing mud between our toes, lulled by the sound of trickling water. Now and then, I looked up at the bulk of 14,279-foot Castle Peak, the highest in the Elk Mountains. We'd climbed it from the other side a few days earlier; a long hike up a low-angled valley. Here, the mountain swooped upward a few hundred yards away, an impenetrable castle wall.

As the day waned, the disappearing sun threw an orange glow over the sawtooth ridge to our west. And when the stars came alive, it was like the planetarium I'd visited as a kid: brighter than reality, the Milky Way a blurred path across the dome.

The hot spring waters lapped our shoulders and stifled the chill of the night breeze. In hushed tones, the adults spoke of climbs done and yet to do, and wilderness winters.

"Does anyone ski here?" I asked.

"Sometimes. Snow gets deep. People die in avalanches."

TWO HIKING DAYS LATER, we set our tents at the base of Pyramid Peak, a fractured, cliffy fourteener that looks like a fantasy mountain when seen from a distance and a scree-covered earthen tumor up close. When climbers fell off Pyramid—not uncommon—rescue teams returned from the mountain with tales better left untold.

Instead of using the standard Pyramid Peak west flanks climbing route, which took a complex line to avoid cliffs and nearly unclimbable scree, we scrambled up a dirty, boulder-studded scarp and halted at the base of a near-vertical wall. I assumed our guide was taking a better line, more direct. Years later, I'd realize he'd lost the route—or didn't know it. Unperturbed, he dropped his pack to the ground, opened the top flap, and pulled out a rope. "Already so steep here you could trip and take a nasty tumble. But now, the real stuff."

The "cliff" above was a near-vertical rubble pile. Rocks, from toaster to refrigerator-sized, teetered as if stacked by a Zen stone gardener in a fit of delirium. As we took turns on the rope, nothing more than the brush of a boot sole or mislaid hand dislodged the stones, which emitted thunderous booms and harsh cracking sounds as they struck edges and outcrops below us. A flinty fragrance wafted through the air, like a burning match.

Here you smelled the danger, even tasted it. Yet the possibility of death and dismemberment hardly glimmered. As we took our turns on the rope, just one thing mattered: This was no hike.

4 | MOUNTAIN HIPPIES, 1967

LITTLE MORE THAN A year after we'd moved from Texas, the hippie movement went full bloom in Aspen. The town was a longhair's utopia: natural beauty, free camping on vast public lands, liberal culture. With few exceptions, people here didn't care about male hair length or shaving habits; anyone could find a job. And if you didn't work (a noble attribute for a hippie), or worked at an alternative profession such as supplying your friends with recreational substances, the only people who objected were the dwindling cadre of conservative town residents and the cowboy sheriff they supported.

While most hippies drifted in from afar, more than a few locals possessed the worldview to qualify, my parents included. By summer 1967, Charles and Patricia Dawson were strutting paisley-patterned clothing, puffing pot, and dropping acid with the best of them.

When the hippie times came, my brothers and I knew little of recreational drugs, but the adults soon moved past wine. Almost every night after bedtime, we sat on the bottom tread of our living room stairs and listened to the hissing inhales, cackling laughter, and weird conversations.

"You guys see any UFOs out here in the wilderness?" a party guest asked during one of our eavesdropping sessions.

"We've seen far-out stuff," Dad replied. We could tell he was yanking their chain. "Freaky lights in the sky. You think they're aliens?"

After a few more nights of spying on these faux Aquarian confabs, my brother Craig and I were fed up. We'd spent plenty of time outside at night and seen nothing weirder than the moon, heard nothing more sinister than a hoot owl. *Aliens? Like the ones I read of in the coffee-stained sci-fi paperbacks I snitched off the dashboard of my dad's truck?*

"Let's play a joke on these guys," Craig whispered.

We retreated to our downstairs bedroom. It had a window view, the same as upstairs. Craig had snagged my father's photography strobe for a school project. He held it to the window and flashed it, illuminating the trees outside.

"Did you see that?" came from upstairs. "Wowwww!"

Craig again triggered the strobe.

"Unreal—maybe a visitation," a stoner said. "See what happens when we direct our consciousness to an evolved entity?"

Another flash. My father laughed. "Hey, you kids, I can see the flash coming up the stairs. I know that's you with my strobe."

The stoners went mute and soon left the house in search of bonafide entities.

Guido's Swiss Inn, Aspen, 1968

©Aspen Historical Society

My father blended his counterculture persona with his efforts at professional photography. He sculpted his furry black sideburns to Elvis proportions and proved his hipster cred by getting kicked out of the only restaurant in Aspen with a "No Beatniks Allowed" sign. He was quite proud of this, as were my brothers and me. *Our father stands up to prejudice!*

Enabled by the hippie ethos, my slim, energetic mother found free expression in her appearance: flowing peasant dresses she sewed herself, natural brunette hair parted in the middle under a beaded headband. She purchased Michel Abehsera's book, *Zen Macrobiotic Cooking*, and shelved it next to her *Betty Crocker*. Brown rice became a staple, but thick, sugary chocolate cake wasn't unheard of. Whatever the creed of the moment, she loved cooking—and along with my father, she loved ganja.

It's tragic that recreational drugs defined the times as much as the good stuff: love and creativity. And more tragic still was how cavalier our father was with introducing his young teens to the green kindling of the sixties. Delaying this a few more years (or avoiding it entirely) would have been healthier for young minds. But such concerns were far in the future. Our parents were having the chemical time of their lives; some of our young friends were too, and we wanted in on the action. It wasn't like we said, "Hey, Dad, we want to smoke pot." Instead, the culture and circumstances made it almost natural, albeit with an adventure-dad twist.

A few weeks after my stint with the Ashcrofters, my father, brothers Craig and Tapley, and I attended an impromptu outdoor music jam in a sunny alpine valley south of Aspen.

After the concert, we joined my father's friend Kent, a barefoot quintessential hippie with a pine-bark tan and hair down to his rear. We ducked into a dense thicket of waist-high willows next to a trickling brook. From a beaded-leather shoulder pouch, Kent brought forth a soapstone meerschaum pipe and rubbed it with a cloth he dampened in the creek. He packed the bowl with ganja pinched from a plastic bag, struck a stick match, and held the pipe to his lips. After a barrel-chested inhale as loud as a vacuum cleaner, Kent looked into my eyes and pressed the meerschaum into my hand.

While the coughing was embarrassing, the process wasn't rocket science. A few intakes and I was so high even the flies glowed. Then the real weirdness began. As I floated on my cloud of mild enlightenment, Kent stripped off his shorts and underwear, kinked his knees into a lotus seat, and reached for his pipe. After another enormous hit, smoke swirled around his head as he bent forward at the waist and placed his forearms on the ground. Still with yoga-pretzeled legs, buck naked, he rocked forward, curled up to a headstand, then bent backward at the waist, nearly double. I tried not to stare.

BEFORE KENT'S INITIATION TO the way of weed, I was a muddling, confused teenager—trying my best to sort out the significant from the mundane.

While riding the ganja, everything was significant. I loved the rebel lifestyle, the high, the stoner folk (other than the peculiar ones). I remained a muddling teenager, but now I didn't know it.

It was all so innocuous at first, so fun. "If it feels good, do it ... Open your mind!" Individuals such as Timothy Leary—who coined the motto "turn on, tune in, drop out"—babbled about alternate pharmaceuticals freeing your consciousness from the enslavement of "reality."

How did this look in real life? The era's culture did produce wonderful things, especially the music. But as I'd realize later, much of the 60s was theater of the absurd. Double so for Aspen High School.

As I began my sophomore year, at fifteen, it seemed a third of the students floated through the halls with slack smiles and bloodshot eyes—including me. The staff looked to be powerless, in denial, or was it ignorance? A future famous entrepreneur made regular visits, wearing love beads over his fringed sarape, selling LSD. He was not a student. I bought a hit, popped it on the spot, and went to math class. It was there I first experienced being a legend in my own mind. It wouldn't be the last.

My grades tanked. Except for biology class—my thriving collection of alpine pond organisms garnered straight A's.

For a while, I was one of the craziest stoners at school. But it didn't matter how well I maintained my perma-high, how many classes I skipped, or how many nubile classmates I chased—I hated the place. I called the circular buildings the "sewer plant," alluding to the similarly shaped structures of Aspen's wastewater treatment facility. When I actually attended class, I sat at my desk and stabbed my fingertips with my pencil just to feel something. Later, I dug at the graphite with the spike of my geometry compass, leaving a few black-filled tattoos that somehow linked me to the trees and mountains outside.

The halcyon times had their moments. We lived in a wonderland, seemingly a thousand miles from what we sometimes called the "real world." But it all was a little too loose, a little too fun, and genuine joy was always a little over the horizon. As for the dope, I'd fade in and out of sobriety a few times over the years and trim a few points off my IQ. Yet my true, unrecoverable addiction was the mountains—and that's where I sought my sanity.

Patricia and Charles Craig Dawson, outside Crested Butte, 1969

5 | MY FIRST TIME, 1968

IT WAS JANUARY 1968; I'd just turned sixteen. After the Ashcrofters, the idea of a snow-cloaked Conundrum Hot Springs had become an earworm blaring in my head, with no volume control. Not a day went by that I didn't envision soaking in that winter oasis, embraced by sulfur-scented steam and the soft sound of trickling water. It was time to make it real.

Castle Peak, 14,279'

Head of Conundrum Creek, hot springs circled   ©Dawson

My father owned a pair of army surplus backcountry skis, thick seven-foot slabs coated with white paint, gouged in places where grainy-brown hickory showed through. I'd previously pried my hiking boots into the steel cable bindings and used the planks for clumsy ski tours near our house. They'd do for Conundrum.

More dad-gear rounded out the kit: soot-blackened aluminum cookpot, thick goose-down Holubar sleeping bag, a pouch of ski wax, and a three-mile ride to the trailhead in his truck. After I dragged my skis and backpack from the pickup bed, my father leaned his head out the window, voiced a preoccupied "be careful," and left me standing in the fast-dissolving cloud of snow crystals kicked up by his tires.

Feeling the pull of adventure, I filled my lungs with the pristine air of the snow-slathered Elk Mountains, stepped into my skis, and began my first-ever wilderness ski trek—alone as a single drop of rain on the surface of a frozen lake.

Near noon, I'd been working for two hours, pushing my touring skis through a foot of new snow, bent under my thirty-pound backpack. The friendly morning sun was now a white-hot orb glaring from empty sky, its radiant heat amplified by the trillions of tiny snow-crystal mirrors sheathing the valley walls. Despite the sub-twenty-degree air, sweat drenched my undershirt and sweater. I could smell my body odor, and figured every carnivore within five miles smelled it too. The heat of my Texas summers didn't have anything over this.

As I squinted behind my sunglasses—cheapos I'd found in the ski swap free-box—a dull ache drilled from my eyes to the back of my skull. I knew of snow blindness. Were my shades dark enough? If not, I'd soon be wandering blind, my eyesight reduced to vague blotches of dark and light. The searchers would find me in spring—after the coyotes gnawed away the tasty parts.

Seeking shelter from the searing rays, I turned my skis toward the shady forest a few hundred yards away, where Forest Service crews maintained a summer trail to the hot springs. Couched in the youthful optimism otherwise known as stupidity, I continued. Six miles of gently ascending terrain lay ahead; how hard could it be? Winter soon answered.

Six feet of snow smothered any hint of a path. Burdened branches tangled with those of neighboring trees, their drooped tips trapped in the snow-pack, blocking the way as sure as a fence. As if this joke from the timber gods wasn't enough, fallen trees lay everywhere, like a colossal game of pick-up sticks.

An awkward clamber over horizontal tree trunks was often the sole option for progress. To accomplish this, I stood parallel to the log with my skis, shifted my hips a quarter turn, and sat on the rough bark. I leaned back, lifted both skis into the air until the tips hovered over my head, spun further—and set both skis down on the other side of the trunk, pointing the opposite direction from the start. If the acrobatics worked, I finished upright. If not, I fell over the log in a tangle of skis, poles, and backpack, ending with my head punched deep in the snow, sputtering curses. Sometimes, it was easier to just barge through the thickets while crawling on my knees, skis in each hand.

At sunset, after five hours of brawling, I'd gained a scant two miles.

As THE SUN SLIPPED behind the peaks, I dropped my backpack between two scraggly evergreens, stomped out a nest in the powder snow, and prepared for my inaugural night in the winter wild, alone or otherwise.

Dinner was supposed to be easy: melt snow to a boil, add a bouillon cube and the instant rice I'd packed in a knotted plastic bag. I kindled a handful of twigs, placed my cookpot on the flames—and watched the fire melt a sixteen-inch-diameter, slush-lined tunnel down through the snowpack. I was soon kneeling with my face in the smoke, reaching for my meal down a tube the length of my arm while coughing like a chain smoker.

After slurping the lukewarm slop, I took out my frustration by kicking snow into the fire hole, staunching the hypoxic blaze.

Without fire, moonless night closed in—the miles of snowy wilderness between me and home seemed as wide as the Atlantic Ocean. I stared into the dark timber next to camp. A surge of loneliness and fear tightened my jaw. This was not the Ashcrofters solo, this was winter survival.

I can't ski back until morning. Over there, in the trees, what's that freaky noise?

Under the starlight, I tied a string between the two trees to support my nylon tent-tarp, and staked my skis and poles into the snow to anchor each corner. I rolled out my bedding and lay wide-eyed in the Elk Mountains wilderness. My father's puffy sleeping bag was so warm that I opened the zipper to my waist, closed my eyes, and invited slumber. Yet I remained awake as my thoughts swirled in a whirlpool of teenage worry: drugs, girls, grades, life, my father's past and his present weirdness.

I FINALLY DOZED, RESTLESS, waking as the night grew colder and moon-beams filtered through the spruce branches above me. I cinched the sleeping bag hood around my head with just my eyes and nose bared, welcomed the moon, and slipped into my dreams. It was the deepest I'd slept in months.

Morning came, with sky so blue it was almost black. Exhaling breathy clouds into the alpine chill, I wriggled from my cocoon. Breakfast was a handful of crackers and chunks of frozen cheese I thawed in my mouth.

Thinking I knew the route from my summer hike with the Ashcrofters, I'd not packed a topographic map. So I continued my wander through the deadfall and thickets, plowing lead-footed through the snow, crushed under my cargo like an overloaded packhorse.

Enhancing the misery, I'd waxed my skis with klister, a tacky, tooth-paste-like concoction you squeezed from a tube and smoothed over your ski bases with a small plastic trowel. I'd chosen a klister formulated to glide on warmer, somewhat slushy snow. It had worked well in the sunny areas. But as I gained elevation and traveled deeper into the shady forest, the cold, fluffy snow stuck to the klister, forming six-inch stilts under my feet, adding torturous weight and eliminating every vestige of glide. Skis should slide; otherwise they're snowshoes, if that.

The only way forward was to stomp along while lifting my snow-caked planks like a man walking through a backyard littered with dog poop. Every six steps, I attempted to remove the wads of snow by scraping one ski over the other in a pigeon-toed parody. No luck, and I could think of no other way to remove the klister.

The open terrain I'd shunned the day before remained available a short distance away. Enduring the heat would be worth having functional skis, but not without another price: the route crossed dozens of treeless gullies and chutes—the avalanche paths my Ashcrofters instructor had mentioned.

I knew as much of slide-hazard prediction as I knew of Latin, which, other than the first line of the Lord's Prayer, was zero. So I engaged the ever-effective decision-making technique of rationalization—*no avalanches happening*—and got on with it.

My skis slid on the warmer snow as if greased, and the open terrain was easy to navigate. As for snow slides, the hills held their silence. But not without reminding me who ruled. In the gut of a V-notched avalanche gully, I shoved a ski tip into a bush and executed an exquisite over-the-head forward roll. As I lay on my side, pinned by my backpack straps like a moth in an insect collection, I stared up the chute and listened for the gut-liquifying roar—it would begin far above, a ten-second warning—and then the afterlife. Not today. Yet, as I wallowed, I sensed the sword of Damocles hanging 3,000 feet from the summits above, whispering: *Rocks, snow, people—all fall.*

AN ABANDONED ONE-ROOM LOG cabin stood 400 yards below the springs. I staggered over a pile of wind-driven snow clogging the half-open door, threw my backpack onto the tamped dirt floor, and surveyed the scene. The last minutes of daylight leaked through the cracked, fly-specked window. A three-legged cast-iron woodstove leaned in one corner, its crooked vent pipe suspended from lengths of baling wire nailed to the walls. On the floor, rodent pellets and shredded dreck hinted at a caretaker: likely a housecat-sized packrat. Most old Colorado cabins had one lodging in the attic or inside the walls.

The cabin filled with the stink of a dumpster fire as I chucked my tubes of klister wax into the woodstove blaze. I held my ski bottoms an inch from the stove's cherry-hot walls, which softened the goo, and sponged it off with my wax pouch, which in turn fed the fire. Saturated with petroleum products, it burned hot.

Under the glow of a rising moon, I left the cabin and skied to the hot spring. It looked almost the same as when I'd been there with the Ashcrofters, the grass and flowers now blanketed by wind-rippled snow. I danced out of my musty clothing and stood naked, arms akimbo, head rotating as I eyed the summits silhouetted against the heavens. A breeze slung a sting of powder snow against my shins, where it seemed to sift through my skin.

I splashed into the warm water. *Ecstasy.* As the moon bloomed from the alps above, the moment etched my future: I would climb, ski the wild snow, and return to Conundrum, in flesh and spirit, for the rest of my days.

6 | PETZOLDT, 1968

AFTER THE POWERFUL EXPERIENCES I'd had over the past few years, I craved all the mountains could give: the athletic, the spiritual—and a proper night's sleep.

Despite their drug-fogged minds, my parents saw my passion as healthy for a teenager. Yet when they'd given me a rope and ice axe that previous Christmas, they had failed to consider how mountaineering—especially for an obsessed novice—might be a path to self-destruction. Did they expect me to ask around, find a random partner, and climb something?

I'd tried the partner thing with Landry and a few other teenage friends. It wasn't working.

Grandpa visited. He was breaking seventy. A halo of thinning hair circled his bare pate, and his New York overcoat fit Aspen's rugged style like a silk smoking robe. Still, his gravitas was undeniable.

Led by my ever-hipper father, our family's counterculture disregard for education and conventional work must have driven our patriarch batty. So he latched onto anything with the faintest whiff of normalcy. In my case, these were the alpine aspirations I made sure to voice, thinking he'd at least buy me a backpack.

While his outdoor experience was limited to casual fishing, Grandpa knew mountain climbing involved commitment and the pursuit of excellence. Moreover, in his worldview learning was as crucial as doing. So within weeks, he'd gone beyond gear shopping and determined that Paul Petzoldt's National Outdoor Leadership School (NOLS) was the place for my continued education. He paid the tuition and even sprung for the army-green, aluminum-framed Kelty backpack I'd been eyeing. As things progressed, I was sure he regretted both.

Paul Petzoldt was a mountaineering legend. At age sixteen, he'd
made his name as the youngest person to climb Wyoming's Grand Teton.
Later, in 1938, he'd reached a record-high 26,000 feet on then-unclimbed
K2, the second highest mountain in the world. During WWII, as a 10th
Mountain Division soldier of the U.S. Army, he taught climbing to the
recruits—likely to my father.

In 1963, Petzoldt helped establish the Colorado branch of Outward
Bound. Other than necessary survival skills, the Outward Bound pedagogy
avoided didactic education. Instead, it focused on character-building challenge experiences.

Outward Bound accomplished its mission, albeit with one nagging
problem: a shortage of what Petzoldt felt were qualified instructor-guides.
And so it was that, in frustration-inspired genius, Petzoldt founded NOLS in
Lander, Wyoming, in 1965. His plan: meld Outward Bound style adventure
with leadership and skills training in the nearby Wind River mountain range.

Paul Petzoldt holding forth, NOLS, circa 1968

IN JULY 1968, my father drove his gangly, sixteen-year-old son seven hours north to a campground near Lander. While we didn't talk much, the confluence of him at the wheel and me next to him on the pickup's crackly plastic bench seat was warm—a rare feeling of security. Dinner time, we sat at the government-brown Forest Service campsite picnic table. He heated our canned stew on the same pump-up gasoline stove he'd impressed my mother with during their honeymoon.

It was a glimmer of my erstwhile adventure dad. I cherished the moment.

After scraping my bowl clean of mushy potato chunks, I took a walk along the Popo Agie River. The torrent's organic scent reminded me of home—the good parts, anyway: fishing, hiking, riding my beloved Peugeot ten-speed bicycle to and from school—and most of all, the prospect of mountain climbing.

I paused, balancing on the rounded Wyoming river stones under my feet, and let the water open my mind—*something extraordinary was coming*.

THE FOLLOWING DAY, IT began. Now a barrel-chested, white-haired man of sixty years, Petzoldt had cobbled an outfitting facility from a ramshackle pumphouse eight miles west of Lander in Sinks Canyon. As the new students arrived, the staff divided us into coed patrols of twelve or so.

Our patrol's instructor, Burt Redmayne, was a chiseled, fair-haired, twenty-something who also worked as an Exum guide in the Teton mountains out of Jackson, Wyoming. *A real climber!* I hung on his words like he was the second coming.

Redmayne handed each of us a gear checklist and a pencil. "First, grab your backpack. Go through the line and fill it up. We'll equip you from socks to hat if necessary."

I needed everything except for my lug-soled boots, Kelty, Swiss Army knife, toothbrush, underwear, and Christmas-gifted ice axe.

I'd figured NOLS clothing was specialized for alpinism, so I anticipated a sartorial transformation. Instead, the gear room's makeshift plywood shelves sagged under stacks of pre-owned sweaters, woolen pants, gloves, and assorted other rags. An eye-watering thrift shop odor oozed from the walls. It looked insane. Yet reason supported the madness.

Petzoldt's philosophy dictated that outdoor equipment be ultra-afford-able, so he'd stocked a plethora of army surplus items, along with heaps of used clothing harvested from Goodwill stores as far away as Denver. Because these were the days before synthetic layers and waterproof-breathable fabrics, other than our cotton underwear and a rubber-coated nylon rain poncho with the breathability of a plastic bag, every clothing choice was wool.

"Wool, it's warm when wet," Petzoldt intoned. "Cotton kills!"

Consider the trousers: cotton jeans were standard attire for 1960s wilderness recreators. Not here. Instead, you fit up a pair of World War II military uniform pants, 100 percent wool. You labeled the fuzzy brown trousers with your name and placed them on a teetering stack next to seam-stress Thelma Young. She and her production line of beehive-coiffed Lander housewives sewed on a butt reinforcement patch scissored from a trashed overcoat and installed drawstrings in the hems so you could shut out insec-toid pests or "knicker up" into a semblance of mountaineering high style. In all, an ingenious garment costing pennies.

Despite the promise of knickers, the ensemble's upper half shattered any remaining hope for alpinist frippery. Enter the "double sweater," an oversized wooly with the lower half of a second donor sweater sewn to the hem, thus dropping over your butt.

As I'd later learn, while the customized sweater was unflattering in nor-mal conditions, add a sprinkle of rain (common during any afternoon in the Wyoming mountains), and boys and girls alike soon sported sagging mini-dresses. The attire never stopped looking silly on us guys. As for the girls, who knew a hiking-sculpted female derriere could so deliciously fill the bottom half of the Petzoldt double sweater? So said testosterone, anyway.

I'd brought my father's goose down bag, the one I'd used for Conun-drum—it seemed more than adequate and it was a light four pounds. "Leave that behind," an instructor said. "Take a NOLS Dacron 88 bag instead."

The synthetic insulated bag weighed about seven pounds and, due to its lack of compressibility, required a stuff sack the size of a couch pillow. I thought this was downright weird, until a few hours later, when Petzoldt cleared up the mystery:

"Get caught in a storm, and tent in a wet down bag," he explained. "You might as well be naked in the rain. You'll get hypothermia. In a few hours you're pissing yourself, then you die. Dacron doesn't matt down when wet, still provides some warmth."

Redmayne and his cohorts completed our kits by dividing us into tenting pairs, to which he handed an eight-by-ten-foot nylon tent-tarp, a dented aluminum frying pan, and a repurposed coffee-can "billycan" cookpot. Next, food rationing.

Nurtured by my mother's healthy cooking, the NOLS rations horrified me. Sure, there were raisins and nuts, and the small plastic jars of the spice kit held their ten promises: pepper to nutmeg. Yet the school's foundational ingredients were white flour, bulk macaroni, sticks of yellow lard-based margarine stuffed into small wide-mouth plastic jars, and bricks of store-brand orangish-yellow "cheese" that leaked grease like a roasting pig.

"Is there any brown rice?" I asked an instructor.

"You eat the NOLS way until you shit as orange as the cheese."

I laughed. He didn't.

"What about protein?" I said.

"Fishing, man. There's no place up there where you can't catch a trout."

I packed my share of everything into my Kelty. "Everything" included a quarter-ounce of cheap, lung-searing marijuana rolled tight in a plastic bag, secreted inside the hollow aluminum backpack frame. Against the rules, and illegal, but I wasn't giving up all my hippieness, at least not yet. I attached a wire to the contraband for retrieval—clever me.

THE STAFF LOADED OUR herd of wool-clad wanderers into the back of a slat-sided stock truck and wheeled us to a nearby trailhead. As we traveled the two-lane Wyoming asphalt, the Wind River Range peaks jutted in the distance. They were by and large a granitic gray, yet every so often, the white swatch of a glacier shone through the bluish haze. I was familiar with the Colorado mountains; these were different: wilder, farther, steeper—a little scary. My new compadres chattered. I just stared, not at them, but at the Winds. It was like meeting that special someone you just know, beyond thought, will be in your life forever.

DURING HIS PRIOR YEARS of involvement with outdoor education, Petzoldt had determined that the Wind Rivers were an ideal learning environment, nothing less than a wilderness classroom. Covering ninety miles in a skinny, north-south strip, no part of the Winds is more than a two-day hike from a trailhead. Compared to more deep-cut mountains, the range juts in moderate vertical relief from a lofty plateau—easier on backpackers' knees and back muscles. The weather is neither wet nor excessively dry. And the relatively solid granite of the Wind River peaks is safer for climbing, in stark contrast to rockfall-prone mountains such as most of those in Colorado.

Yet despite their more human-friendly aspects, the Winds held challenges aplenty. Backpacking, 1960s style, involved rough, undeveloped trails and huge loads that often topped sixty pounds. Abundant climbing routes asked of every ability. Biblical-scale mosquito swarms, wildlife food thievery, and foot blisters completed the picture. And, in these days before cell or satellite phones, our companions were the only option for timely help in the event of an accident.

THE TRUCK DROPPED US off on the edge of a sagebrush prairie next to a grove of cottonwood trees. We spent the afternoon learning how to set up our tarp-tents, build fires, and stay cool (without success) in our wool clothing while roasting in Wyoming's low-altitude summer heat.

The following day, we woke to clanking cookware and the acrid smell of cottonwood smoke. Petzoldt was teaching the finer points of oatmeal gastronomy.

"Say you're feeding four. Fill a billycan one-third full of water, get it boiling. Throw two drinking-cups of oats and a quarter-cup of raisins in there. Don't forget salt. Out here you need more salt; you're working and sweating."

After we'd packed our bellies with gooey oats, our instructors gave a quick tutorial on blister prevention: "Wear two thick socks on each foot, and wash them every chance you get."

Wondering how one washed their socks in the Wind Rivers, we climbed back into the truck, wheeled a half hour to the trailhead, and the backpacking commenced.

Our agenda: move through the high country, mastering disciplines such as the amalgam of empathy and compromise they called "expedition behavior," map reading, and self-care. I especially liked the natural history and soon memorized a raft of flower names—favorites: bistort (edible) and silky phacelia (pretty like its name). Glacier geology also compelled me: how they flowed as deep rivers of ice, tooled with embedded boulders that pulverized the valley bedrock like slow-motion jackhammers. I loved all of it, but never stopped thinking about climbing.

While human against cliff is always a conflict, NOLS climbing in the 1960s was a flat-out battle. We climbed in our clunky mountain boots rather than the slipper-like rock shoes that gained popularity a few years later. Likewise, we used a type of rope soon relegated to the trash bins of history: 3/8-inch thick, yellowish nylon Goldline. The Goldline cord was weak (and cheap) compared to other types of synthetic ropes coming on the scene, and it stretched like a rubber band. If you took a leader fall on it, the elongation added so much distance to the fall you stood a good chance of impacting a ledge or the ground before the rope came tight. Hence, Petzoldt and his instructors often spouted a firm edict: "The leader shall not fall."

What they meant was, "The *climber* shall not fall," because even while top-roped, you could plunge far enough and fast enough to smash bones. We anticipated the rope stretch, planned for it. But plans fail. One student broke his ankle, and not a climbing day passed without a scare.

Belaying was hairy as well. Modern belaying incorporates mechanical rope-gripping devices. At NOLS in 1968, we used our hands and waists for a "hip belay." This comprised passing the rope behind our backs and holding on for dear life if the belayed climber fell. In essence, we used our bodies as friction pylons, like the bollards you wrap boat-docking ropes around. Pain was part of the bargain as the rope always found a patch of bare skin between shirt and pants. If the tortured belayer let go, the boat sailed. Fast.

When we fumbled a hip belay, the instructor punched us in the arm, hard enough to bruise. I welcomed corporal punishment. While climbing safety is nearly always binary (mistake equals death), every aspect of this primitive mountaineering technology was extra ruthless. Perfection required.

All told, the challenge and discipline of vintage rock climbing made it an exceptional foundation. Years later, on climbs where falling was not an option, I thanked my NOLS instructors for the life-saving habits they had baked into my brain.

WE SETTLED INTO A routine defined by weekly ration resupplies delivered via pack horse, climbing days, and hard miles under heavy packs. Petzoldt often kept to himself—he was writing a book—but he wandered from campfire to campfire during mealtimes. While poking our cooking fires with a stick, he'd say something instructive like, "Let's move these logs—the fire will smoke less," or a gentle, "You guys doing okay?"

Petzoldt was more than a mountaineering teacher. While gruff, and strict, he was kind, with a knowing glint in his eyes that showed he got more from the hills than primal challenges. He seemed at total peace, perhaps even in bliss, as he hiked with his trademark ambling pace, his long, ash-shafted NOLS standard ice axe gripped in his right hand, *tap-tapping* the ground like the cane of a nobleman. We all held our ice axes precisely as he did, and I wished he were my father.

Yet I wasn't all in. Early on, I snuck into the forest and lit a joint—more from a habit of rebellion than anything else. A few days later, my stash dropped from its hiding place to the trail behind me. An instructor found it. He said nothing as he handed it back. That night I tossed the ganja on my campfire. Not that some of our youthful instructors didn't enjoy a toke now and then; it was about the overall vibe.

Early in the course, during one of his campfire lectures, Petzoldt seemed to stare into my eyes as he pontificated on drugs and youth culture.

"Young people are going to get adventure one way or another," he said. "The wilderness is one way. It's better than LSD or marijuana. Kids are constantly preached to by their parents, at school—everyone telling them how they should think. Out here they can relax, discover themselves, and learn by doing things, sometimes dangerous things."

While my parents had never been fond of lecturing as a form of child rearing, especially not recently, I was as familiar as any teenager with adults telling me how to think.

And chemicals, despite my being a user, I was already aware of the lie. Back home, I'd witnessed the ganja-scented fog as but a patina over an inauthentic void, like termite-hollowed wood that appears normal on the surface yet collapses under the press of a finger. Petzoldt was right. In the wild, drugs paled in the face of just about everything. What that would mean when I returned home, I didn't know. For now, there were mountains, and fish.

TROUT THRIVED IN THE Winds' cool, oxygenated lakes and brooks, where they gorged on aquatic larvae and great swarms of mosquitoes. For harvesting the protein bounty, the school issued each of us a nifty combination fly-spin rod.

While spin-casting a plastic or metallic lure was easier for novices, fly-fishing with a fake insect and a less mechanically complex reel was the way and the truth of Wind River life. It was ethically superior—a fair chase—and fun once you learned it.

Most days after dinner, I grabbed my rod for a final session. One such evening I was shore-fishing on a lake next to camp. My quarry taunted me with their rising and splashing as they dined on floating insects a few feet beyond my wet-spaghetti casts. How could something with a raisin-sized brain be so smart? Trying for distance, I whipped my rod like I was driving a racehorse, succeeding only in hooking the willow bushes behind me.

Petzoldt, dinner rounds complete, ambled to my spot on the lake. "What are you using?" he asked while waving a hand at the mosquitoes attacking his bare face like a bee swarm. I was glad for my headnet; it hid my embarrassment.

"Black ant fly—the right thing?"

Petzoldt nodded approval, explaining how ants drop off lakeside rocks, then float out to where the big fish are—the "whales" that don't go near shore. "You need to throw your line farther out. Here, let me help you."

Petzoldt moved behind me into the classic fly-cast teaching position. He wrapped his huge paw over my hand on the rod grip and worked my arm and wrist, drilling the neuromuscular motion of fly-casting into my nerves: Rod tip to twelve o'clock vertical, no farther back, quail for a microsecond so the line curves out behind, bring it forward. Repeat.

As Petzoldt coached, the setting sun backlit hordes of mosquitoes hovering over the lake. The splash of rising trout punctuated the click-track of stripping line and the burble of cascading water melting from the blue-ice glaciers above. That simple exchange, Petzoldt teaching a rail-thin, grubby sixteen-year-old how to cast—one human showing another how to use a tool—meant more to me than all the great man's sayings, jokes, and charisma. At that moment, I idolized him, the third man in my paternal trinity: my dad, my Grandpa as the voice of reason, and now Petzoldt showing me how to navigate the gaps in my life with the mountains as my bridge. In a letter home, carried out by the horse packers, I wrote:

> Dear everybody, Today we made fish jerky in a smoke oven we built from mud and willow branches. We've learned twenty-five plants, survival skills, hiking, fishing, cooking, climbing. I love it.

Cooking was essential to Petzoldt's curriculum—right up there with fishing and climbing. At first, I thought this ridiculous. All from scratch, fiddling with a dozen variations on mac-and-cheese (with lots of pepper to help the faux cheese). Were we not here to climb mountains? Wasn't a bag of M&Ms and a box of crackers enough?

And yet, the peace and empowerment of cooking surprised me. After a few days of practice, my oatmeal was world-class: enough brown sugar and salt to border on the appeal of cookie dough, yet not so sweet you couldn't eat enough to stretch your belly. With the basics mastered, we moved on to making yeast-risen bread; a soul-centering primal craft. I now understood why my mother baked bread every week, no matter how bizarre her life was.

"You need to eat plants for vitamin C," Petzoldt lectured while he nibbled on a leaf. "Scurvy is real ... Your teeth fall out ... This has as much C as a vitamin pill. And someday, you might have to survive on plants."

Heeding the guru's words, we scrambled on hands and knees through nearby vegetation, plucking and chewing like a flock of chickens. Sweet wild huckleberries were my favorite. It took ten minutes to pick a tablespoon's worth. The mini strawberries were the bonus, hidden under fringed leaves close to the ground. I ate these one at a time. Each hit my tongue with a puckering detonation beyond any candy I had ever known.

MIDWAY THROUGH THE COURSE, we camped at The Cirque of the Towers, a magnificent array of glacier-polished granite spires, arete ridges, and finned summits surrounding Lonesome Lake, a glacial tarn just under a half-mile long. As I studied the guidebook that instructor Redmayne hauled around like a religious relic, I found the Cirque was a place of incantations, words that conjured climbers' dreams: Shark's Nose, Warbonnet, Pylon—and the icon, Pingora, a 150-floor skyscraper rising some 2,000 vertical feet from the stony shore of the lake.

After we pitched our tents and snacked, Petzoldt called a late-afternoon class. Such confabs almost always involved a massive fire. This time was no exception. On a flat rock outcrop, the great man and his cohorts had kindled a blaze topped by an enormous, partially rotted conifer stump. Three billycans teetered on the tree remnant, one brimmed with fluorescent yellow macaroni, the remaining two steamed with cowboy coffee boiled to the consistency of thin mud.

The lecture was probably a geology lesson and details for the next day's Pingora climb. All I remember is Petzoldt standing next to his hearth, his bushy white eyebrows glowing under the rim of his black beret, his large hand wrapped around a blue enamel mug as the stump billowed smoke like a warehouse fire.

OUR GROUP OF SEVEN—FIVE students, Redmayne and his assistant—summited Pingora as darkness fell. There were a few flashlights stashed back in camp, none with us. The chalky light of a quarter moon would have to do. A vertical section of the descent required a rappel, for which we used the archaic Dülfersitz technique (named, of course, for a European climber named Dülfer). This was as harsh as it was simple. While facing the mountain, you looped the rope in an S-curve through your crotch and over a shoulder. It was just you, the cord sliding around your body, and friction. Boys carefully positioned the rope lest they lost their ability to father children, and the girls were equally cautious.

The rope burned my shoulder like a blowtorch as I spouted slack through my brake hand, inch by stuttering paranoid inch. When the angle went vertical and my total weight was on the rope, the looped cord folded me double until my face was a foot from my knees. Several students froze, dangled, and whimpered. Redmayne talked them down.

The following day, we moved camp. I liked how the suppurating rope burn on my left shoulder stung under my backpack strap.

FOUR NIGHTS BEFORE OUR scheduled return to civilization, Redmayne and the other instructors strutted through camp after dinner, shouting like town criers: "Meet at Paul's fire. Bring every crumb of your food."

As we stood together, Petzoldt and Redmayne tossed our plastic-bagged rations on their bonfire, leaving us nothing more than our spice kits and a few tablespoons of our willow-smoked fish. Teenage stress? Watching your food burn, with the nearest grocery store as far as the moon, has to top the list.

"Imagine you were in a plane crash and had to hike out," lectured Petzoldt while fanning at the polyethylene smoke churning from the fire. "Pick leaders from among yourselves. We'll assign you a backpack route to a trailhead, where we'll pick you up in four days. Live on fish and plants, practice leadership and expedition behavior. Learn about yourself, learn what food really is, and how to do without. You'll gain self-confidence for the rest of your lives."

After going over the maps, Petzoldt and his instructors hiked away with a cheery "see you at the trailhead."

My books said humans could function for three days or more without food—so long as they stayed hydrated. But the prospect of going without regular meals scared me.

Would I collapse on the trail, waiting for the real mountaineers to save me?

Before we began hiking, our crew of survivalists attacked a nearby lake as if it owed us money. We stuck the trout, small ones, on willow whips and cooked them like marshmallows. When we left, I swung my backpack to my shoulders using one arm. Empty of food, it weighed nothing.

By the second day, I was so hungry the mere thought of our incinerated cheese opened my salivary glands like a faucet. Hiking and resting took most of our time; fishing was an afterthought. At best, we consumed a few mouthfuls of trout, chased by a sprig of leaves from an aquatic plant known as miner's lettuce. With nearly zero calories in my tank, each step along the trail felt like walking through shin-deep mud.

More than once, I tripped on a tree root and fell on my face.

Despite the dizzying hunger and brutal hiking, a straw-haired student named Marcy had my attention—proving, once again, the inconsolable power of teenage libido. It was nothing more than risk-induced romance, like those disaster movies when the protagonists discover each other in the bilge of a capsized cruise liner. But it was real enough. We spread our sleeping bags together, kissed, rolled away, and fell fast asleep. She tasted good: willow smoke with a hint of fire-roasted trout.

The next day, our final five miles into Sinks Canyon felt like a hundred-yard victory march, eyes up and ahead as our ice axe spikes *tap-tapped* in syncopation on the rocky trail. Our newfound energy was the pride of accomplishment, not to mention the donuts and orange slices we knew the instructors had waiting at the trailhead—but it was more. Even before the first blast of sugar scrubbed the fuzz from my neurons, I knew—and figured we all knew—that the NOLS Survival trek had been the transcendent limit-busting event of our young lives.

At the graduation banquet, we stretched our walnut-sized stomachs on budget Wyoming cafeteria offerings: grayish mystery meat, mashed and buttered spuds. The luminous, paprika-decorated mac-and-cheese went untouched. Petzoldt passed out frame-worthy diplomas. I was now an alpinist with the certificate to prove it.

I was also homeless.

7 | ENTER CHAOS, 1968

WHEN I RETURNED TO Aspen from NOLS in August 1968, my parents had sold the Castle Creek house and set up camp on a vacant parcel of land in the nearby mountains. We didn't call ourselves homeless, just something like, "We're camping for the summer until Dad builds a house." Good fun until monsoonal rains forced the six of us under the ten-by-eight-foot kitchen tarp for five days straight. After that, we packed into a two-bedroom apartment in Aspen.

At the time, neither parent was working a paying job. I wondered briefly where the money came from. Yet at sixteen, mind occupied with girls, bicycles, and mountain climbing, I just figured *whatever*. Years later, I learned that my father had mortgaged the Castle Creek house not long after building it, spent much of the proceeds on day-to-day expenses, and then sold the house to repay the loan—his usual process of wealth destruction.

What funds remained went toward a hillside, riverfront lot on State Highway 82, a mile east of Aspen. With the help of a friendly banker, and the land as collateral, the Charles Dawson financial cycle began anew.

As autumn shifted to winter, my father and a small crew brought a two-story structure out of the ground with a T-footprint reminiscent of our Crazy Acres house. When snow stuck to the ground and the ski lifts began their yearly spin, we moved into the unfinished basement to save on high-season apartment rent. My brothers and I slept in our sleeping bags, with our thin camping pads between us and the icy concrete floor. The utility room served as the kitchen, with a shower curtain for a door.

Six weeks after moving into the basement, I was packed shoulder-to-shoulder with my brothers and father in the "kitchen," waiting for breakfast. A lunchbox-sized electric heater with a rattling fan kept the room just above freezing; it was the warmest place in the house. My mother cracked ten eggs into a family-sized skillet. The hand-pump Coleman camp-stove sputtered, then gushed with blue, yellow-tipped flames that wrapped around the sides of the pan. The stench of burnt eggs filled the room. Mom slammed the skillet onto the fold-up camping table that served as our kitchen counter. Her face flushed scarlet with rage.

"Look at the eggs, Charles. I can't cook the eggs ... I can't live like this!"

My brothers and I stared at the floor, as did my father, saying nothing. The situation could have been fun, an adventure. But a darkness was creeping in from the edges. It wasn't until years later that I realized my mother was inches from a stint in the rubber room at Aspen Valley Hospital.

As he dried up the construction loan, my father made the upper floors livable, and we moved into what passed as a home: heat, kitchen, and electricity from wall outlets instead of extension cords. The splintery plywood floors, unfinished walls, and missing bedroom doors were clear signs of our family's troubles. Yet I found such things comforting as well. After camping in a concrete basement, a room with painted walls and carpet might have given me nightmares.

And beyond the crude, unfinished nature of the place—or perhaps enhanced by it—my parents manifested their knack for imaginative design. Such was the other side of 60s hip, the good side, the artistic side. Maybe the drugs tapped my parents' souls, or the drugs and libertine culture were just excuses for creative risk. I didn't know. But at first, what we came to call the "82 House" was nothing short of magical.

To the rear, a long, narrow deck cantilevered over the bank of the Roaring Fork River—the place for yoga in the hot afternoon sun. Around front, a twelve-foot-high, windowed entry looked out to quiet, two-lane Highway 82, where a twenty-minute drive reached the rock climbing and alpine hiking of Independence Pass. My father suspended plant baskets from bare-wood roof beams using chains we'd scrounged from abandoned mines. He hung a pair of thick manila ropes from which he fashioned a whimsical swing. Now in a better mood, nesting, my mother wood-burned flowery designs into the wooden swing seat. When pandemonium reached inhumane levels, you could withdraw to the swing and pendulum your stress away.

I loved coming home. I'd open the tall front door to the scent of wet planting soil and walk four strides to the combination dining room and kitchen. After raiding the fridge, I'd head for the split-level living room, where my mother had integrated a bright-red shag carpet with two burgundy wing chairs. Somehow, this potentially nauseating color combination was just right.

82 House entry, 1971   ©Dawson

The vinyl record collection was on the floor, five feet long, book-ended with pumpkin-sized chunks of silver ore we'd scrounged from nearby mine tailings. I sat cross-legged and pulled out the Beatles' *Sgt. Pepper's* album. I held the black disk by its edges, pressed between the flats of my hands, and lowered it onto the Marantz turntable. Careful not to scratch the plastic, I set the needle on the shiny track-band demarcating my favorite number, and sank into the carpet. The song was "Getting Better."

For a year, maybe two, despite our underlying family dysfunction, hippiedom was a hoot for us teens.

During summers, my two oldest brothers and I were never without our musical instruments. I noodled on a Honer blues harmonica. Craig, in his middle teens, paddled a pair of conga drums at home and tapped out a beat on any convenient surface when he roamed. Tapley carried a silver concert flute in a beaded leather case slung from his shoulder. During our hikes and alpine picnics, he perched like an elf on a creekside rock, improvising melodies to accompany the burbling water. Most summer days, he sported a dark-brown domed fedora with a feather in the band. Unless it was cold enough for a ski cap, I went hatless. I'd forgone my Ashcrofters trim and again let my hair grow to my shoulders. I loved the feeling of it flying mountain-kid free, and though I'd never admit it, I pictured myself as the straight haired, blond frontman of a rock band. I felt special, part of something, running about the valley in my headband and flowery shirt pinned with "Make Love not War" and "Ban the Bomb" buttons.

Tin can bread loaf   ©Dawson

Once or twice a week, the 82 House filled with the aroma of my mother's homemade bread. She took pride in the cylindrical loaves, cooked in #3 "tall" size tin cans, 4x7 inches, large enough for her to reach inside. Each of her half-dozen cans was special, with the top removed in such a way as to leave a smooth edge, and a brown interior patina that loosed the loaves like magic. Five minutes after they came out of the oven, my brothers and I would cut the brown mushroom-shaped heel from the hot loaves, soak them with butter and wildflower honey, and feast.

AND THERE WAS WINTER, when our world-class ski mountains boasted their tapestries of white, there for the taking. And take we did, which in my case involved an extra dose of adventure.

During my summer NOLS course, I'd learned of a unique—radical is a better word—yearly expedition led by Petzoldt. The goal: climb Wyoming's famed Grand Teton in winter, preferably on New Year's Day. This was the perfect next step from my Conundrum trek.

When I arrived in Lander during the last days of December 1968, the weather had sunk into midwinter Wyoming cryogenics; daytime temperatures hovered around forty below zero. While walking to the grocery store, I wore my woolen face mask and wondered how one might climb a mountain in such weather, hands muffled by mittens, feet numb with incipient frostbite. Would we need goggles to prevent our eyeballs from freezing?

For ski touring gear, the school outfitted us in typical Petzoldt budgetary fashion: thick wooden army-surplus planks with rusty steel cable bindings, low-cut square-toed leather "Frankenstein" boots large enough for three pairs of thick wool socks, and climbing skins: strips of furry fabric you buckled to your skis for uphill traction.

Years later, I realized this kit was identical to the gear my father had used during his stint with the ski troops—a coincidence that enlightened me about how tough his military ski days had been, and helped me understand his life choices. Unless you were world-class, you didn't ski this gear; you survived it. None of us were world-class.

After an unheated bus ride north to Jackson Hole, we gathered at the Garnet Canyon trailhead and set off for the cold unknown. With seventy-pound backpacks compressing our spinal disks to near failure, we followed leader Tom Warren as he stomped a knee-deep trench into the snow. Here, my first time "skinning" was a revelation. The skin-equipped skis took steep angles with ease and eliminated the hassle of waxing.

We set camp midway up the mountain and waited out a two-day storm. The night after the clouds cleared, it was so cold the nylon fabric of my jacket crinkled like desiccated cake frosting. I heard the instructors laughing from their nearby tent, saying, "I'm not kidding. Look at my thermometer. It's 58 degrees below zero!"

Funny, until it wasn't. Near 60 below is too cold for climbing, let alone cooking. Our tent filled with steam and gasoline fumes as we tried to boil freeze-dried noodle soup on a dinky Svea one-burner gasoline stove, which refused to fully self-pressurize because of the extreme cold. As we fiddled, we knocked over the billycan of gruel. It flowed like toxic sludge under our sleeping bags, where we sponged up the flood with a pair of spare socks. During the confusion, a leaky sack of garlic powder tangled in my bag liner. I slept with the aroma of perfectly spiced pizza for the remaining nights of the trip.

The avalanche danger was too high, the weather too cold. After four nights on the mountain, we retreated. On the descent through Garnet Canyon, Warren said, "Go for it, Aspen, turn 'em loose." And I did—only to endure the howls of my mates when my skis sank like rocks into the zero-density, cold-ravaged snowpack, causing me to flip forward and punch my head three feet deep into the powder, with the help of my backpack as a pile driver.

Back in Lander, most students said they'd never try anything like that again. Yet for me, skiing to a significant climb was an eye-opener. Two boards, an ice axe, a big peak, and a dose of winter, this was mountaineering to its fullest. As to the garlic, for years after, the smell of pizza brought memories of that night on the Grand, our tangled sleeping bags, the brightest sky of stars I'd ever seen and maybe ever would.

The Tetons were my version of the Beatles' "Getting Better." Back home, things had taken a turn for the worse.

THE DRUG USE AND general insanity of the 60s and 70s exacerbated my father's inability to do paying work. He gained the nickname "Space Carpenter," and my mother transformed as well. On the surface, she presented a liberated, fun-loving demeanor that her many friends enjoyed. Yet her beloved interior decorating had waned, and she'd long ago quit any significant work as an artist. When I paused my obsessive roaming long enough to pay attention, I sensed she teetered on the cusp of two eras: the post-Victorian of her upbringing, and the whacky counterculture. More than anything else, her dancing revealed the conflict.

Zeppelin's pounding kick drums and Clapton's staccato guitar notes had already molded my weed-softened mind and those of my teenage peers. Free-form rhythmic dancing came naturally to us. Yet my mother never got the knack. Instead, she swayed and shuffled without keeping time, occasionally waving her hands as if signaling a taxi. I found this embarrassing, especially when my friends witnessed it. Yet there was a sweetness, a girlish innocence, Patricia breaking open the shell of her 1930s childhood, reveling in self-expression.

"What kind of dancing is that?" I asked during one of our carnival-like house parties.

"I'm Isadora Duncan, the inventor of modern dance. I love to boogie," my mother said as she twirled her peasant-style sundress, eyes blazing with lysergic acid.

My mother remained slim and lovely, with an uncanny ability to combine odd clothing pieces into world-class hippie attire: ankle-length handmade dresses, paisley printed blouses, beaded sheepskin vests. A skilled seamstress, she delighted in outfitting the men in her life, including her sons, with blousy armed Renaissance-style shirts we wore almost as uniforms.

MY PARENTS' FREAKY LIFESTYLE exacerbated their financial issues. My mother wasn't working, and aside from a few photography gigs, my father worked at nothing more than kiting bank loans and scamming handouts from Grandpa. They needed day-to-day cash for food, gasoline, and incidentals. So my mother stepped in again as the breadwinner and rented the beds of our 82 House to a revolving tribe of 1960s characters: the future film industry insider, the thief, the dilettante fond of my mother's handcrafted shirts, the writer, the drug dealer(s), a photographer or two, and others.

We operated as a sizable family—"commune" was mentioned. When we gathered for holiday meals, my mother set out her heirloom china and silver, contrasting the rustic decor and her irreverent, stoned-out dinner guests. The main course was often a one-pot vegetarian stew my mother called Hungarian goulash, heavy on tomatoes and sweet corn she stripped off the cob. Desserts were brown-sugary concoctions, often made from fruit we picked in the lowland orchards an hour or so west of Aspen.

Boarding house, Aspen, 1969

On the surface, the Dawson boarding house was a merry free-for-all. Friendships happened, and memories were forged. A half-century later, some still extol the experience and venerate my mother. They have a point, but they'd not seen the Patricia I'd seen as her sensitized child: the tight-wound discomfort hidden behind the parties, the drugs, the serial lovers, the manic energy burbling under the surface of the carefree ski days.

And it got crazier. Friends of friends of friends "hung out," sampling whatever recreational substances came to hand. We slept two or three to a bedroom, eight residents sometimes sharing one half-finished bathroom.

One evening, as my mother's inebriated dinner guests clowned like lunatics, she paused beside the table while holding a five-quart glass casserole brimming with goulash. She opened her hands. The dish shattered on the floor, leaving long chunky streaks. Without a word, she stalked back to her kitchen. Under a soundtrack of giggling stoners, four scrappy dogs snarfled their tongues around the glass shards.

Too much loud music. Too many diseases of the intimate sort. Not long after my mother cracked, someone stole the communal grocery money from the pouch on the kitchen counter.

I wanted out, from the chaos, from the stultifying grind of high school. So began the extraction.

8 | DROP OUT, 1969-1970

AS A HIGH SCHOOL senior in the fall of 1969, the self-reliance and moun-taineering training I'd gained from Farny and Petzoldt didn't mesh with reg-imented education, nor with much else of my life. I still saw mountaineering as a path and was dabbling in roped climbing. Yet the seduction of drugging, combined with teenage brain fog, kept me bouncing between healthy jaunts in the hills and the aspen forest escape-zone behind the sewer plant, aka school—where my primary activities were rolling joints, napping, reading.

I followed my father's example and burned through paperback sci-fi: Herbert's *Dune*, Crichton's *Andromeda Strain*. And I continued reading climbing books—his and those from the town library. Obsessed with Ul-man's teenage protagonist, Rudi, I'd imagine the pitons, the ice axe, the rope tied at my waist. I'd lead my team to the summit, where we'd have a bird's-eye view of the village below. And I'd disdain the words of those who'd warned us not to go, that the climb was too treacherous.

Hiking the wilderness trails surrounding Aspen got me close to the peaks. Riding my bicycle up the steep, curving roads of the Castle Creek and Maroon Creek valleys burned adolescent energy that might otherwise incinerate my brain. School? Algebra class was about gazing out the win-dows at the woodlands and beyond, where the mountains promised future adventure.

Meanwhile, the chaos of the 82 house grew like the weeds we took for a lawn. To wit, the *Aspen Times* featured the place as their Blight of the Week, stating:

> The tipped-over Jeep and upside-down American flag enhance the overall winning appearance of this home.

The *Times* write-up only made things worse. After the column came out, we dialed up our outdoor music until the amplifier smoked. Led Zep' loud as sin—let your freak flag fly. *Take that and stick it in your ears, uptight neighbors!* It's a miracle I can still hear.

The Jeep was a battered green 1947 CJ-2A Willys flat-fender, purchased by my father while we still lived in Texas. The old dog had wheeled our family through many fine adventures, from Big Bend National Park to the trails of Colorado. I'd learned how to drive in it, racing about Aspen in a cloud of fumes from the dripping gas line under the seat, pumping the brake pedal three times before anything happened by way of stopping. Now with a blown engine, the relic was rolled on its side for eventual repairs, much to the annoyance of our neighbors.

In the family Willys during its better days, 1966

The day reality trumped innocent hippie fantasy, I was with two of my school friends the first time they shot heroin into their veins. As I lay on the floor, cooked on weed and deafened by Steppenwolf's "Born to be Wild" blasting from the stereo speakers I'd planted a foot from each ear, my friends began their demise. I thought about joining them for the new adventure, but the needle revolted me. The dividing line was no thicker than that. As the years rolled, I'd learn that both guys lived longer than one might expect, but had nonetheless died by the paw of the monkey.

I SOON QUIT DRUGGING, thanks to the aversion therapy provided by my smack-shooting friends, Paul Petzoldt's positive influence, and my interest in athletics. Yet even without a buzz, I still loved the aspen forest behind Aspen High, loved grooving with my friends and brothers under the sunlight dappling through the rustling leaves. A few other kids lived clean, but the hardcores were still smoking enough marijuana back there to support the entire economy of Acapulco. Until the sheriff showed up.

It was a sunny Indian-summer September morning in the aspens. As I watched with my brother Craig and a dozen fellow students, four Pitkin County sheriff's cars rolled in and parked next to the school, sirens burping, roof lights flashing like they were responding to a murder. Led by Sheriff Carrol Whitmire, the cowboy-hatted posse exited their vehicles and filed through the school's double front doors. We hid behind bushes and trees, not sure what was happening.

It turned out to be a drug raid. The deputies searched every locker for suspicious substances. Hunt completed, they used the outdoor loudspeaker to call us educational reprobates from our refuge. Later, they claimed to have found nothing. One would assume that busting a kid and losing the parental vote wasn't conducive to reelection.

As we marched through the grass near the entryway sidewalk, the deputies singled out Craig, shoved him into the back seat of a cruiser, and hauled him away. When my father arrived at the sheriff's office to retrieve his detained son, he lost his temper, verbally abused the redneck deputies, and came close to experiencing a dagger-pointed cowboy boot or two.

After the non-bust bust, the school principal ruled our wildwood refuge off-limits. Suddenly, I had no escape zone. Or did I?

TWO WEEKS AFTER WHITMIRE put the scare on Craig, I laid out my plan at the dinner table. "I'm quitting school. I just want to do stuff in the mountains, to climb."

My mother gasped. "Really, Lou? Is that all there is to it?"

"I'm searching for God, too. I can't do that in school."

That was a stretch. Despite dabbling in yoga and meditation, the only religion I sought was that of rope and rock.

"If it feels good, do it," my dad mumbled as he sparked another joint—the Space Carpenter was proud of his son.

Quitting felt right, sort of. The mountains were my school, my home, my everything. As for God, he'd always be there. Nonetheless, when I cleaned out my locker for the last time, the migraine throbbing in my left temple was like a railroad spike hammered into my skull.

Back in Texas, whenever I'd brought home a report card filled with Cs and Ds, my mother responded: "You want to end up like the greasy man pumping gas?"

By the time we got to Aspen, my parents were saying little to nothing about my grades, but Mom's words echoed from the past. The possibility of life as a grimy worker drone scared the heck out of me—as did my grandfather's inevitable disappointment. NOLS was cool, but it wasn't Cornell Law School, Grandpa's alma mater, and his vision for my matriculation. Yet, other than telling me I was making a mistake, he continued writing his loving letters, the rock on the shore of our family storm.

Maybe I'd pump gasoline for a living, but I had become a self-certified existentialist. I also had a draft card.

NEARLY EVERY WEEK, THE Vietnam War was producing body counts in the hundreds. Over 11,000 US soldiers were lost in 1969, their flag-draped coffins the bleeding lead on TV news.

Along with the carnage, came the draft. By force of law, the US government was snatching boys, such as me and my friends, and sending them off to the jungle with eight weeks of training, a rifle, and a steel hat. Per the law, I had registered for the draft a few weeks before my 18th birthday. I had some time to await my fate; the lottery date for my birth year was August 1971.

After NOLS that previous summer, I thought I'd seen my destiny in rocks and snow. Could it become bombs and blood?

There was a college-student draft deferment. But college wasn't happening for me and most of my carousing cohorts. Some proclaimed they'd move to Canada. Others, including me, applied as conscientious objectors. (You'd still serve, with the steel hat, though without the weapon—and likely return home in a box anyway.)

An older friend went through the enlistment medical exam. To fake illness, he injected builder's caulk into his anus and shat it out during the physical as he raved like a lunatic. The military rejected him as mentally unfit because he wasn't pretending.

JANUARY 1970. I WAS standing next to the black cast-iron woodstove in our Aspen home, warming my back after cross-country skiing. The Rolling Stones had recently released their tenth album, *Let It Bleed*. Tapley pranced up the three steps to the living room, dropped the needle on side one, track one, spun the Pioneer amplifier dial to eleven, and "Gimme Shelter" rocked the house like a sonic tsunami.

The anti-war anthem melded with 'Nam—yet spoke to me not of war but of life. Jagger snarled about fading away. That was me, faded, with about as much agency as the field mice our house cat gutted.

After the intro, as Jagger and gospel singer Merry Clayton surged into their spine-tingling crescendo duet, Mother handed me the letter. It was not from the Draft Board.

The missive was from NOLS: handwritten address, crooked stamp. I put my cup of honey-sweet peppermint tea on the hot woodstove and tore open the envelope: "Dear Louis, we invite you to attend the inaugural NOLS instructor certification course."

Would the mountains be my shelter?

BOOK II
NOLS YEARS

Denali, Harper Glacier, 1973

9 | EDUCATED, 1970-1971

PAUL PETZOLDT LAUNCHED THE first-ever NOLS instructor course in early summer 1970. His staff included some of the school's best instructors. Quiet, college-degreed naturalist Jim Halfpenny was said to know more about Wyoming wildlife than just about anyone, and was a climber. Tom Warren (who'd taught on my student course) was the archetypical Wyoming outdoorsman, Pendleton sleeves rolled up on his brawny arms, good at everything. Also present was my first-course patrol leader, Exum guide Burt Redmayne, his hair sun-bleached by countless days outdoors. Capping the diverse mix, Outward Bound England graduate Rob Hellyer, Petzoldt's right-hand man, was set to trudge through the entire program with his wife, Martha, carrying their infant child in a mosquito-netted homemade baby pack. I was impressed. Who knew you could teach a NOLS course while parenting a baby?

The staff also included an outlier. Don Peterson had never worked for the school nor been a student. As a reputed Yosemite climber, he was there to share the nuances of modern gear and technique. He was a muscled, six-foot-tall man with a clean-shaven face, his hair slightly long, yet ivy-league. Word was Peterson climbed Yosemite's tallest cliffs: "Fourth ascent of El Capitan's Dihedral Wall in 1968, set a speed record." Somehow, perhaps by his looks and concise way of speaking, you knew this was an intellect as well as an athlete.

The staff's eclectic mix of outdoorsy generalists and specialized climbers portended something unique, a melding of hook-and-bullet outdoor skills with 1960s self-improvement culture—the reinvention of "wilderness adventure." I was there for my love of climbing—and was excited for Don Peterson's tutelage—though open to anything Petzoldt and his mountain mentors cared to share. Much of this would repeat my experience as a student: NOLS philosophy, basic climbing, cooking. I was expecting all that, but one thing hadn't occurred to me: why was NOLS suddenly operating an instructor mill?

Petzoldt soon explained during a campfire lecture that NOLS had experienced a modicum of success, graduating around a hundred students a year. But that was changing, fast. Millions of baby boomers had come of age. They sought outdoor recreation and had the leisure time for it.

"This summer, we'll handle nearly a thousand students," Petzoldt said, "and eventually tens of thousands. You people will make this transition safe and effective."

Was I up for this? What would become known in NOLS history as the Boom Years? I'd turned eighteen a few months earlier. Was I ready for actual *students*, some older than me?

THE THREE-WEEK INSTRUCTOR COURSE, structured around a backpacking trip up trail-less Bull Lake Canyon into the heart of the Winds, was nothing less than an advanced degree in alpinology.

In the evenings, after crossing the scree fields and wading the rivers, I memorized everything from advanced first aid to a thorough natural history: weather prediction, geology, the behavior of noble elk as well as the tiny, rodent-like pika that scurried under their hooves, hard at work, elfin farmers harvesting sprigs of grass for the coming winter. Human sanitation was a detailed topic, with Petzoldt devoting an entire lecture to preventing "Toilet paper blowing around ... Hanging from the bushes. And wash your hands!"

I spent a good part of each day over a campfire, learning backcountry culinary specialties such as cinnamon rolls and fish chowder. "Plenty of pepper and salt in the soup," Petzoldt commanded.

We even learned ways of redeeming the official NOLS low-budget cheese. My favorite: make a basic flour and water dough, palm out a tortilla, sprinkle with cheese and trout meat. Per the Petzoldtian way: salt until your blood pressure redlined just from looking at it. Bake into a pizza by tending a stack of coals on the lid of a "fry-bake" frying pan.

We ate most of our mistakes. The carbonized substances were said to help with the gaseous effusions we blamed on the cheese.

Cooking was fun. So was fishing. But every waking moment, and often in my dreams, climbing remained my purpose. Thus, a contradiction. During practice climbs, I scampered up moves many students struggled with, but nobody was impressed. I hadn't quite gotten the message: NOLS wasn't about Yosemite muscle-flexing; it was "wilderness leadership education."

I pushed it anyway, practiced bouldering alone after dinner, and was always first to volunteer for climbing sojourns.

AFTER A FEW DAYS in Bull Canyon, Petzoldt declared a two-night stop, to allow for a day of climbing. He and his instructors camped in a verdant meadow, next to a rock slab that resembled the hearths they'd enjoyed during my time as a student in 1968. The standard inferno was soon kindled. Above our tents, the canyon's grey walls rose steep, topped by serrated ridges.

The next morning, we were called to our first climbing lecture. As seemed to be the NOLS way of things, the billycans were again balanced on a smoking tree stump, and we gathered upwind from the acrid plume. The sun burned through a clear sky. The usual Wind River mosquitoes darted about, seeking patches of skin that lacked the insect repellent we slathered like Maybelline moisturizer.

Petzoldt picked up a coil of our stiff Goldline rope. He untied the kinky weave and piled it loosely on the ground, a process known as "flaking out," intended to provide use of the rope without it tangling. Essential with Goldline.

"Coiling," Petzoldt proclaimed with a rasp of gravitas. "It's the basic part of rope management. There's one good way of doing it. Watch."

Petzoldt grabbed a cord-end from the ground, wove the rope into a tight oval coil, finished it by wrapping an end six times, then slung it over his head onto a shoulder. The bundled strands now matched the shouldered rope Dave Farny featured in his Ashcrofters brochure photos: the standard fashion of alpine hero shots worldwide.

Coiling a rope the NOLS way was already imprinted on my neurons as sure as walking. And yet, was it the best way? Paul was sixty-three years old, a climber of the previous generation. Were his methods current?

Enter Don Peterson.

Standing by the fire in a tight white T-shirt, his buffed arms crossed, Peterson patted a bicep with the fingers of one hand—as if gauging his strength for the next world-renowned Yosemite crack he'd jam his way up. In his other hand, he held a V-shaped spring-loaded grip exerciser. It squeaked faintly as he squeezed, slow and deliberate. The tendons on the back of his hand moved under his skin, veins bulged. You knew the workouts never stopped, just paused.

Petzoldt handed the coiled rope to Don. "Let's see how you do this."

Don began his teaching with a line from his resume: "There's a new route on Half Dome I climbed with Royal ..."

In my view of early 1970s mountaineering, Royal Robbins was the most famous rock climber in the world and maybe the best. He'd put up a bunch of Yosemite first ascents, and was a key individual in the Valley's evolution as the epicenter of modern rock-sport. Was Don the second best? I sat cross-legged on the meadow grass, looking on like a puppy eye-begging for chopped beef.

Don hung his exerciser from a pocket, grabbed Petzoldt's photogenic construct, and began pulling it apart.

"The old way of coiling doesn't work for big climbs," Don said as he yanked strands of rope, causing us rookies to know that the walls of Yosemite were *big* while the walls we practiced on with NOLS were not. "This way is better," he continued, laying the rope in a butterfly pattern over one arm. "You can hold it on your lap while perched in sailboat rigging—or in a cramped position on a climb. To carry it, you lash it together, sling the ends over your shoulders, tie them around your waist, like this."

Don deftly slung the bundled rope behind and knotted both ends around his waist, forming a backpack-like configuration. It was fast and efficient.

"Ridiculous. That'll tangle the rope," grumbled Petzoldt.

There beneath the Bull Canyon walls began a clash for the ages. Don Peterson and Paul Petzoldt dodged stump smoke and argued about everything from rope storage to belay techniques. Even the gymnastic style of modern rock climbing came under Petzoldt's attack. At one point, he called Don a "rock monkey" to his face.

In my view, the rock monkey won the debate. His rope-coiling method made sense, and after all, he climbed with Royal.

Later, I obsessed on showing Don my developing talent as his fellow granite-enabled primate. I came close to falling off the hardest of our practice routes, but suppressed my hyperventilation and hid my quivering muscles.

"You've got potential," Don said.

It took all my will to wipe the dumb grin off my face. When I returned home that summer, I bought a hand exerciser. A pair of them, actually.

JUST BEFORE THE COURSE completed, Rob Hellyer hired me as an assistant instructor. I liked to think my potential as a climber was the reason, but my fireside mac-and-cheese and bug-eyed enthusiasm had more to do with it.

The life-changing climbing would have to come later. And it did.

I was hiking with Redmayne during the last day of the course, heading for our vehicle pickup at the designated exit trailhead.

"Want to come up to Jackson Hole?" Redmayne said. "I'll take you rock climbing—Guides Wall. It's where I teach for Exum."

The Guides Wall access trail threaded through the same conifer trees and huckleberry groundcover I knew from the Wind Rivers. Pebbles crunched under my rubber-cleated mountain boots. Flinty dust bit my throat. I smelled my sun-heated leather daypack straps and wool trousers. It was another of a hundred similar trails, yet today, the sounds were crisper, and the smells demanded attention—all somehow anew.

Redmayne flowed up the cliff like rising water, his body upright and relaxed, gripping each handhold without hesitation. He paused only to clip carabiners and thread the rope through the pre-placed pitons. Soon came the call, "On belay, climb." As I followed, he held the rope taut and offered gentle hints: "Keep your hand in the crack ... From the ledge you're standing on, it looks hard, but there's a hidden hold, just reach ..." When we met on the belay ledges, as was the way of climbers, we discussed the route ahead as we checked knots and organized the tools of ascension: satiny aluminum carabiners, blue nylon slings we slung over our shoulders like bandoliers.

We paused together below an easier section. "You should lead this part," Redmayne said. "Follow the crack. Clip every piton. When you're near the belay spot, I'll shout so you know where to stop and belay me up."

Leading is climbing's essence. It demands skill, provides danger, and brings the hormonal trance that some liken to a religious experience. The process involves coordination between the leader, tied to the rope's end and trailing it behind, and a belayer, who lets it out from below. The leader periodically installs temporary gear (or uses fixed gear) known as "protection," and passes the rope through a carabiner attached to the protection. In the event of a fall, the leader drops past the protection until the rope—held by the belayer—comes tight. If the leader falls from five feet above their last protection, the total fall is ten feet (plus rope stretch and slack). Once the leader reaches a stopping place, (often dictated by the rope's length), he belays the second climber, who ascends while top-roped. If the climb is taller than a rope length, the sequence is repeated until the top.

I'd climbed easy leads back home and during the instructor course. This was different: vertical, smaller handholds and footholds, not what smirking climbers called a "ladder." I trembled with nervous anticipation as I pulled in a slow breath, reached for a handhold—and it all flowed like the sweet river in the canyon below. At that, I was welcomed into the cult of stone.

Teaching, NOLS, 1972   ©Dawson Collection

That summer I worked two NOLS courses, the second as full instructor. They went well—nothing more exciting than a student stumbling off a ledge while making a privy call in the dark (cuts, bruises, purple-black eye). I returned to Aspen and spent the winter working nights as a dishwasher while hardening myself with long days of skiing and technically easy yet cold, stormy, physically ferocious winter climbs up the Elk Mountains' peaks.

GRANDPA MAILED ME A book stuffed with a note he'd penned on his matte-finished, pale yellow stationery: "Lou, I enjoyed reading this, but I remain concerned."

The patriarch had purchased and read James Ramsey Ullman's climbing novel *And Not to Yield* (Ullman had authored *Banner in the Sky*, the fomenter of my mountain dreams). The narrative began with fifteen-year-old Rick Venn taking his pigtailed junior sister climbing near Aspen and watching her fall to her death. After that, Ullman spun a tale of Venn's troubled soul, a Sherpa woman, and a mountain as enchanting as its name: Dera Zor.

I imagined Grandpa reading Ullman's tale, his alarm growing as he realized his namesake grandson—whom he'd taught to tie his shoes—was involved in the same sort of dicey alpine activities. Near Aspen, no less.

Reading *Yield* got me thinking of relationships—*was combining love and climbing even possible*? As for the danger, it didn't register. I was now a trained guide; wouldn't I be the last guy to let a girl fall off a mountain? Grandpa wasn't so deluded. And it wasn't just the climbing that concerned him. The Dawson family's entire scene grew weirder by the week.

Out of the blur, one event stood in my mind as a marker of the times. That previous autumn of 1970, writer Hunter S. Thompson had used our Aspen house for a "campaign meeting" during his storied "gonzo" run for county sheriff. His entourage included my father.

My brother Craig and I watched as the man of mania dangled on our entryway swing, swigged from a bottle of Wild Turkey, and spouted such zingers as: "No drug worth taking should be sold for money."

Craig and I locked eyes and lifted our brows. Thompson wasn't talking about aspirin. Dope had brought us more darkness than light. Despite our own experiences with ingestion, we knew there were no recreational drugs truly worth taking.

In an oft-published photo taken during the campaign, my headbanded father sits next to Thompson. You could interpret Charles's pinched brow and dagger eyes as powerful disgust with the "establishment." But I saw his scowl as nothing more than his drug-burned soul.

Thompson lost the contest by 173 votes to incumbent sheriff Whitmire—he of our high school quasi-bust. Sir Gonzo should have given away more drugs—or maybe he gave away too many?

Hunter S. Thompson (center)
Charles Craig Dawson (right)
Thompson's sheriff campaign, 1970   ©Bob Kruger

BY LATE SUMMER 1971, I'd graduated from two instructor courses and spent two summers in adult responsibility: teaching mountaineering and leading NOLS expeditions through some of America's most beautiful alpine wilderness.

Yet all was not alpenglow and gorgeous Wind River granite—there remained that little bugbear known as *the draft*.

On August 5, I joined a somber gathering of nineteen-year-old boys, parents, and curiosity seekers amidst the Victorian furniture of Aspen's Hotel Jerome lobby. The cursed lottery was broadcast from Washington, D.C., on a wall-mounted set. A dark-suited, jowly congressman stood in for the Grim Reaper, drawing plastic capsules from a glass bucket as if conducting the rituals of a sinister cabal.

Each capsule contained a birthdate. The drawn dates were assigned a sequential number starting with one. Men with lower numbers would be drafted first, with the high-number cutoff dictated by the Vietnam War's current need for cannon fodder. The more wounded and killed, the higher the number, a barometer of the taken.

Extrapolated from the previous year's conscription, we figured 200 was the approximate breakpoint; a call-up of higher numbers was unlikely.

The Reaper read his numbers in an evil monotone. I edged closer to my father, until my arm pressed against his. He was tense, glancing from side to side, checking out the other teens and their parents, maybe planning his route to the door, back to the comfortable fog of hippiedom.

Later, I realized that standing in front of that television, helpless to protect his child's safety and right to self-determination, must have cut my dad to the core.

As the Reaper opened the capsules, my birth date continued to push ahead. When capsule 200 came, still without my birthday, my eyes wet, and I felt as if I were melting into the floor.

Capsule 228 was mine. Barring a third world war or alien spaceships filling the sky, I was entirely out of mandatory service range.

My high number was nothing more than chance. But it felt preordained, as if the universe supported my passion. No steel hat. No rifle. No hunting humans—or being hunted by them. It was time to stalk ice and stone, time to climb mountains. And so I reveled in the power of young muscle and bone, now in the prime of my manhood.

As the climbs grew in difficulty and the mountains in size, my adventures grew closer to the heroics of my father's books.

What could go wrong?

10 | AVALANCHES, 1971

BEFORE MOVING TO ASPEN, I had read about snow avalanches. On the grasslands of Texas, they were bookish abstractions—nothing more than grist for Ullman's fictive Rudi, who was buried by a slide and dug himself out with his bare hands. Impossible.

During our first winter in Colorado, avalanches had soon become more than abstractions. Sixty miles as the crow flies from Aspen, on Loveland Pass, a man was teaching a group of Denver teens how to snow climb. He chose a 200-foot road bank for a practice slope. It slid and buried three boys, only one of whom would survive.

Sun., Jan. 8, 1967   Fort Collins Coloradoan   3

Three Dug Out Of Loveland Pass Avalanche

DILLON, Colo. (AP) — Three teenage boys from Denver were buried for 30 minutes in a snow- utes of external heart massage and mouth-to-mouth resuscitation by Patrolmen Keith Hagan

A few weeks after the Loveland accident, I was riding a chairlift with George Parry. He'd been comping us free ski lessons on the sly and was still helping my father put the final touches on our Castle Creek house.

"Did you hear about that Loveland Pass avalanche?" I asked. "Any bad ones around here?"

"We've been lucky the last few years," George answered, his normally tenor voice dropping a notch. "But there was one, I think it was in 1961—really sad."

I pulled my goggles up and squinted at George as he told the story.

"A former schoolteacher, Loretta Thorpe, was skiing Aspen Mountain, a patch of powder in the trees above Gretl's [now Bonnie's] Restaurant," George said. "One minute she's skiing, not even thinking about avalanches, next minute she's gone. Ski patrol usually keeps things safe. They missed a spot. The slide was tiny, about a hundred feet long. But she suffocated—buried three feet deep."

George explained how the accident had impacted the community: The widowed ski-instructor husband. The four young children. The entire town grieving for a gregarious, beloved lady.

"The oldest kid was around six," George said. "She'd be about thirteen now. I see her and her sisters in the lift lines."

Sad for people I'd never met, I pulled my goggles down and said nothing.

TWO YEARS AFTER MY conversation with George, I was sitting at my desk on the second day of my junior-year algebra class (a redo, I'd failed it the previous year).

As teacher Mr. Orcutt chalked equations on the blackboard, a pretty girl strolled through the door and took the seat behind me. I caught a hint of perfume and turned around. Her thick chestnut-brown hair was woven into an over-shoulder French braid. Emerald-green eyes, a large, expressive mouth—and, only partially disguised by a sweater, curves that made me notice.

Orcutt focused on the girl who had captured my attention. "Kristina, how do we solve the first equation?"

"I'm—not—sure," she replied.

The girl hit me with a grin as we gathered our books after class. I liked how her greens crinkled into an eye smile as if she was enjoying a secret joke. A hint of flirtation sparked between us—but my shyness nixed it. Something about this girl belied her youth—self-confident body language, an aura. There were less enigmatic female schoolmates to pursue.

Come winter of 1970–71, long after I'd dropped out of high school, Kristina had befriended my brothers, Craig and Tapley. She'd taken to the scene at the 82 boarding house, which to an outsider was nothing more than chaotic fun—at least at first.

Keith Wilson, one of our renters, was a curly-blond, twenty-four-year-old Adonis. He and Kristina had a springtime fling when she had just turned seventeen. While Craig and I had reservations about older men seducing our female peers, those concerns paled in light of something else: Keith and my mother, fifteen years his senior, had been lovers for around a year. As Keith continued his relationship with my mom, he was making time with a girl seven years his junior.

I tried to repress, or at least hide, my confusion with the musical beds and age spreads. I wasn't a prude—I was a 1960s teenager. Still, having had a few puppy romances, I was well acquainted with the confusion of polyamory and the sting of jealousy. I saw it all over my mother, in her short temper, in the tight-faced way she looked at Keith and his teenage minx.

Enhancing the muddle, my father was in the mix as well, still sleeping with my mother now and then, along with bedding one of my brother's girlfriends. My brother was not impressed. Sixties-style love might have been "free," but the attendant emotions were not.

Kristina tagged along on many of our climbs. She was a natural athlete and, on the surface, appeared to enjoy technical climbing. But not once did she say, "Let's go climbing." And I observed more than one screaming fit when, stuck in the middle of a cliff, her calves shaking with the strain of standing on her tiptoes to compensate for her petite stature, she lunged for handholds her tall, male friends had grabbed with ease. Anyone could see that her heart wasn't in it, that she liked tamer mountain pursuits: peak scrambles, backpacking, skiing. Later, I realized she climbed steep, technical rock only because her friends and lovers were climbers.

AROUND THIS TIME, I had a brief conversation with Kristina about the avalanches that haunted the memories of most Aspenites. I'd known for a while that she was the daughter of Loretta Thorpe, whom George Parry had mentioned on that chairlift ride, but we'd never spoken about it.

"A ski instructor told me about your mom's slide," I said. "He said it was so small nobody could believe it, buried her three feet, she suffocated?"

"That's what happened," she replied. "When my dad finally came home, alone, he sat my four-year-old sister and me down and said, 'Your mother's gone away.' My first thought was she'd gone to Paris. But when my father said 'she's not coming back,' I knew she was dead."

While asking Kristina about her mother wasn't pleasant—and I resisted the temptation to dig for details—she seemed to appreciate my attention.

As for Keith, though I counted him as a buddy, I was never sure what to think of him. He was fun most of the time, yet with a cynical streak and quick to pick at people's faults. Most importantly to my single-minded focus, he was a strong climber—a natural fit for our cadre of Aspen crag rats.

BEFORE I HEADED TO NOLS for another instructor course in the summer of 1971, Keith invited me to join him and Kristina on a springtime road trip to Yosemite Valley. It would be our first visit to the epicenter of rock climbing. None of us had the skills to do the place justice. But, there's a first time for anything, and for us, the Valley topped that list.

1947 Chevrolet Fleetmaster
©BestPeak

Keith's ride was a scarred-black 1947 Chevrolet Fleetmaster two-door coupe—five years older than my nineteen years. When I asked why he'd bought such a thing, he rapped his knuckles on a rear fender the size of a horse's rump and said something like, "Check this solid steel. Only cost me a hundred twenty-five bucks."

We yanked out the Chevy's rear seat and stuffed the space with gear and Keith's black-haired mongrels: Dope and Frog. I squeezed through the passenger door, behind the front seat, and into a divot between duffle bags and backpacks. Lying down, I pushed my feet against the trunk lid and snuggled beside Frog. With a coiled climbing rope for a pillow and a stack of paperback novels within reach, I wanted for nothing—at least for the first few hours.

Keith told us he'd do all the driving. "I know how to baby this thing so it'll make it."

"Babying" meant Keith piloted his junker at a top speed of thirty-seven miles per hour—barely faster than a peloton of bicycle racers. We were on the road for three days. During fuel stops, I oozed from my lair, brushing off tufts of dog hair while exuding a pungent cloud of road sweat and canine stink. I paced the cramps out of my legs until Keith ushered me back to my burrow, slammed the massive side door behind me, and began another four-hour, 150-mile crawl.

OUR FRESHMAN YOSEMITE VISIT was far from a milestone. We were so inexperienced we could hardly determine what climbs to try, thus ending up on a handful of novice routes on smaller, vegetation-festooned outcrops. When I topped one such cliff, I gazed in awe at the 3,000-foot eastern ramparts of El Capitan—the real walls of Yosemite. The Captain laughed. Anything up there required Yosemite Decimal System (YDS) 5.9 climbing skills as a minimum, along with high-level use of hardware and ropes.

As we'd become involved in the climbing scene, the YDS difficulty ratings had become part and parcel of our lifestyle. Free climbs (those that involved the use of natural hand and foot holds) with a prefix of "5" usually required the use of a rope, and those above 5.5 or so required practiced technique. The hardest climbs were rated 5.10. The hardest route we'd tackled so far was a 5.8, and said by the locals to be an easy one at that.

That night, Keith parked on the road shoulder to avoid the National

Park campground fees, and we unrolled our sleeping bags in the bramble. At daybreak, we cooked breakfast while Dope and Frog chased squirrels and yapped like they owned the place.

As we finished our tea, a law-enforcement ranger pulled up in his white, green-accented Park Service truck. He climbed out, put his flat-brim hat on his head, and walked over to where we'd set our cookstove on a rock. "There's a leash law in the Park. And camping outside of designated areas is illegal."

"Hey, my dogs obey," Keith said. "And we're not camping. See any sleeping bags?"

I cringed, knowing the park cop had just seen Frog, followed by Dope, launch like rockets after a squirrel who had dared sprint across open ground. And it was obvious we'd camped.

"You guys are banned from the Park—leave immediately," the ranger said, hand resting on his pistol grip.

A few hours out of Yosemite, the ancient Fleetmaster engine gave it up with the clatter of a thrown rod. We had the car towed to a repair shop and found lodging at a friend of a friend's house in Merced. I was still a babe when it came to relationship dynamics, but it felt plenty peculiar when Keith and I phoned my mother to borrow money for the repair.

As we waited for the wire transfer and engine rebuild, the air between Keith and Kristina became downright frosty—and warmed between her and me. We laughed often; easy words flowed between us, smiles. We'd become friends—maybe more than friends—though nothing romantic happened. Back in Aspen, we partnered for a few climbs. Then I was off to Wyoming as a NOLS instructor.

I WAS NOW UNDER the spell of Petzoldt and NOLS. But I was lonely. Maybe Kristina was still with Keith, or maybe with another guy, but why not get her on a course I was instructing, let the Wind Rivers work their magic, and see what developed? Perhaps we'd go no farther than sharing a time in these amazing mountains. But I hoped for more. With a bit of backroom dealing, Kristina was approved for a full scholarship—on my course.

The moment I heard the news, I jogged to Mr. D's grocery store with a pocket of dimes for the pay phone.

Don't sound too eager. Play it cool. What if she's not really into me?

"Guess what!" I blurted like I'd won a sweepstakes. "We got you on a course. I'm teaching it. You'll be in my patrol!"

So much for cool.

"Fantastic!" Kristina replied with a lilt in her voice I'd not heard before. "Keith and I broke up right after we got back from Yosemite. What gear should I bring?"

It was now up to me—and the Winds.

Two weeks into the course, things heated up. When Kristina needed help tying into the climbing rope, I stood behind her in the position we used to teach the bowline knot: my arms extended around her waist to mimic her tying the knot herself. I resisted the temptation to lean in and see how much body contact I could get away with. I need not have cared. She leaned back.

ONE DAY, WHILE SITTING on a rock ledge in the alpine sun, belaying practice climbers, we spoke of families and children.

"Life is crazy back in Aspen," Kristina mused. "The married couples we know seem so unhappy. Your parents, my dad and stepmother, they don't get along. I wonder if it ever works."

Marriage was as far from my reality as planet Neptune. Yet random thoughts of matrimony did pop up—usually while I was stuck in one place, tied to a cliff and belaying Kristina. And, I'll admit, while sneaking peeks down her shirt. My internal monologues always ended with one conclusion: *Marriage and children would nix my life as an alpinist faster than a bad result in the draft lottery.*

Nonetheless, vivid images skittered through my mind as I yarded the rope and shouted the belay signals. Me and a girl—maybe this one?—together for life.

That was a long shot at best. I had no idea what kind of woman, or for that matter, what kind of relationship, it would take to overcome the psychic scrap heap of hippie insanity. Maybe an angel on an extended vacation from heaven?

Two weeks into the course, we moved above timberline to a tundra camp a quarter mile from Peak Lake, a high-alpine tarn surrounded by cliffy granite peaks with dozens of climbing routes. The unclimbed northerly face of Stroud Peak caught my immediate attention—a perfect day trip, about a thousand feet, sheer yet with plenty of obvious hand-and-foot lines—climbable. I convinced my assistant to take our students practice climbing while Kristina and I snuck away for a first ascent.

The weather was perfect: clear sky, morning chill warming fast. We hiked to the climb in our T-shirts.

Kristina deftly managed the rope as I raced up each pitch, barely needing protection gear. We were united, in sync with each other and the vertical world.

Back at the lake after an easy hike-off descent, we sat on a shoreline boulder and snacked on fry-baked bread we'd saved from breakfast.

"That was ultimate," I said, pointing to the route. "Thirteen pitches. A couple of them five-eight. You're great at this stuff."

That we'd just climbed a 5.8 in clunky mountain boots instead of slip-per-like climbing shoes made the climb a 5.9—a proud accomplishment, a wilderness alpine route.

"I like mountaineering, Lou. But I don't care what we do out here—it's so beautiful, anything is okay."

For a moment, I forgot about 5.8s and mountain boots. She climbed. She was born with skis on her feet. Shoot, she even looked good in a double sweater. Was all that enough? Thinking about relationships was like navigat-ing an avalanche zone—all those neurons firing at once, flooding my brain with more data, more chains of cause and effect than a chess master could handle. So I zenned out and savored the moment. And when I looked ahead, all I saw was the soaring granite walls of Yosemite Valley.

11 | YOSEMITE ROUND TWO, 1971

Spring 1970. A friend and I were stumbling about the base of Gold Butte, a popular climbing spot on the outskirts of Aspen. As we brushed deer ticks off our socks, we wondered how one might climb the more demanding routes.

An older guy showed up, late thirties at least—prehistoric compared to my eighteen years. Along with his sun-beaten face, his torn plaid shirt and knee-patched jeans brought to mind a bum, or to be kinder, a prospector who'd spent a lifetime grubbing for gold. We watched the oldster lead a climb. This guy was no bum. He had skills: every move deliberate, using his hands like scrub brushes to clean the dust off holds, placing plenty of protection along the way. In turn, the man watched us struggle up a route most climbers could do in their sleep.

Later, we gathered at the cliff base. Knee Patches introduced himself as Harvey Carter. Our jaws dropped.

This guy was the legend who'd put up almost every climbing route near Aspen and hundreds in the Utah desert—and recently founded Climbing *magazine?*

"I'll take you guys out tomorrow, show you some stuff," Harvey said. So began a mentorship. And, for a while, a friendship.

Eighteen months later, fall, Harvey was in the mood for Yosemite. He said we'd take his camper van, and my girlfriend was welcome to join.

"The valley won't be too hot ... I'll teach you how to climb some of them chimbleys." Harvey pronounced the word "chimney" in his own alternate dialect. No one ever knew why or from where.

When I invited Kristina, she was hesitant. We both knew she'd do little, if any, climbing—for her, it was just a road trip. "Harvey is kind of strange," she said. "Does he climb in Yosemite much?"

"He says he's been there enough," I replied. "He's exaggerating, but still, he's making big climbs in the Utah desert. I bet we'll get up something."

In truth, Harvey's climbing skills were a generation behind the Yosemite rock jocks who were reinventing the sport. But I rolled with it. Whatever his experience, it was far beyond mine—and he was willing to teach. Might Yosemite round two make up for my round-one scrum?

The morning after our late night arrival, we headed for a climb. The route's crux feature was a bomb-bay chimney. Picture the bomb exit in the belly of an aircraft: an inverted funnel slot with a good bit of air below. I'd climbed a few easy chimneys. This one was different. When I tilted my head back and stared into the maw, I was clueless, feeling as if I'd materialized mid-flight into the pilot seat of one of those bombers.

I grabbed the guidebook from my pack and flipped to the climb description. "I don't know, Harvey, it's rated five-eight. I've climbed a few chimneys, but nothing that looked like this thing. Can we pick something easier?"

"You can do it," Harvey said. "Five-eight, good practice. Anything worth climbing in the Valley is at least five-eight. Just put in plenty of protection."

The first part was easy, sixty feet of 5.6 moves up and over chockstones wedged in the back of the chimney. After that, the crack pinched closed and forced me out toward the cliff face, into the narrowing portion of the inverted funnel—still about three feet wide.

Harvey had told me to brace my back against one wall and wedge my knees and feet against the other to "wriggle upward." His suggestions worked—with one problem: Lacking expertise and opportunity, I'd placed none of his mandated protection. And three feet above me, the funnel stem began—a twenty-inch-wide slot, the squeeze chimney, the 5.8 crux. With no intervening gear lodged in cracks or otherwise installed, the rope arced from my waist seventy feet down to my friends. Should I slip, I'd crater before their eyes.

I considered wriggling back through the chimney and downclimbing the chockstones. But I'd led plenty of 5.8 climbs. How severe could this be?

Ten feet later, the squeeze had forced me into a stretched posture, as if lying in bed, only I was vertical, using every speck of strength in my adductors and abdominals to pull my legs up and forward, to keep my knees pressing the rock, to gain what little friction I could. Which was essentially none. The rock was smoother than that of Independence Pass or the Wind Rivers, with fewer resting places. "Sustained difficulty," climbers called it—one strenuous move after the other, no letup.

I was miles past my limit as a climber.

For added purchase, I forced my palms against the wall, demanding every ounce of strength from my fried triceps. Brute force gained me another fifteen feet up the squeeze. Below me, the rope traced my path of ruin.

My legs quivered and shook like a jack hammer. Denim tore, and then skin, as my right knee slipped five inches down, streaking the rock with blood. I pressed my hands harder against the wall in front of me, but my back and butt continued sliding toward the ground, inch by creeping inch.

Seconds before I plunged through the bomb bay, I edged a shoe on a pencil-eraser sized nubbin. This move helped, but unless I used every ounce of strength, my foot popped off the hold as if coated with bacon grease.

Gravity continued its evil pull. My bleeding knee smoldered. My entire body trembled. My grunts mixed with the agonal bleats of a torture victim. Bile burned my throat.

"Climb sideways. Find more holds!" Harvey yelled, his tone dripping with disgust.

Tears oozed from my eyes. "I ... can't hold on," I moaned. "I might fall!"

"What the hell are you waiting for? Brace your back and knees and go!" Harvey bellowed.

I tried harder. Quivered harder. Nothing worked. I panicked, thrusting my feet in a mad parody of a bicycle sprinter.

My pants ripped over the other knee—flesh against granite—more dark-red fast clotting blood.

Looking down past my climbing shoes, I watched Kristina stand, look up with a pained expression, and march into the nearby forest without a backward glance. It didn't take a mind reader to know she was repelled by the possibility of her boyfriend splatting at her feet.

"Lou ... Lou!" Harvey shouted. His voice had changed, booming, yet somehow gentle. He was standing closer to the cliff base, clenching the rope with both hands raised to chest level as if willing strength and skills to transmit through the cord from his muscles to mine.

"Calm down. Stop moving."

I paused, hanging by threads of flesh and denim. Harvey was directly below me. I'd seen him play softball; he was a pretty good catch. *Could he cushion the impact of my fall?*

No, I realized. If he tried, if I let go, we'd both die.

Harvey, still gentle, with an edge of concern: "Find small footholds for your feet before you move. Slow, steady."

The words of my mentor sank past my gasping breaths and the sweat dripping into my eyes. A peace came over me, knowing that my only option was to try my best and accept what came of it: fall and die or make upward analytical progress. My breathing slowed. My legs stopped shaking.

In the calm, I studied the rock like Sherlock Holmes examining hair follicles. Though much of it was the same polished tile, I spotted the spoon-shaped depressions, the quartz crystals, the nooks where the toes of other climbers had rubbed away the dust.

Pressing my feet and hands against nearly invisible holds, I pushed upward. One inch, then another, and inches became feet. Pain lashed my knees like I was kneeling in a barbeque pit. Yet my mind was still.

"That's it, Lou! Can you work your way to the back of the chimbley now?" Harvey yelled, still with atypical tenderness.

Continuing my tedious yet effective mini-moves, I progressed upward and sideways. I soon reached the back of the slot, where more chockstones provided footing for a hands-free rest—and I found a solid placement for protection gear.

When I snapped my rope through the protection's carabiner, it was like slipping into a warm bath. Now, instead of a terminal flight to the ground, a fall would, at worst, bang me up. When I emerged from the shade and placed my hands on the sun-warmed belay ledge, it felt like freedom after ten years of prison. I anchored in and yelled, "On belay, come on up!"

"I'm not sure why we chose this godforsaken chimbley," Harvey snarled as he lurched from the crack and sat beside me. One of his pant knees boasted an eight-inch tear, and was that a hint of blood?

We left for Colorado that night.

At about three a.m., something prodded me awake in the van's passenger seat. Harvey was straddling the center line of the two-lane road. He explained that if he dozed off, straddling the line gave him time to recover rather than crashing. After that, I rode shotgun and didn't sleep a wink, instead keeping my left arm in position to grab the wheel.

OVER THREE YEARS, HARVEY and I climbed dozens of days together. Building on my NOLS foundation, he instilled a safety mindset and a dose of climbing philosophy: "Two anchors are almost always the rule; one might as well be none. Fear the rappel, that's how most climbers die. They get sloppy and rap off the end of the rope. When you're leading, don't skip the rest spots. And always, find those first ascents."

One morning we groveled up an obscure, mossy cliff near Aspen—*first ascent!* Afterward, I found myself in Harvey's study—a cramped spare bedroom in his Aspen home. Stacks of books and magazines teetered on every horizontal surface. A bundle of battered carabiners hung from the door handle, some made from rust-speckled steel rather than aluminum, relics from before my time.

"What a worthless climb," I grumbled as I moved a rope off his guest chair. "Climbing is about ultimate flow, it's like yoga or something. I don't care who was up there first, especially on a pile of junk."

"You know, Lou," Harvey said in his clipped southern Colorado accent. "Any first's important, short or long, quality climbing or not. It's the history of the sport. The firsts give it meaning. Get it?"

I did not get it. Sure, first ascents were cool—such as Stroud Peak during NOLS. It was fun to explore; maybe brag a bit. Yet for me climbing was existentialist expression, in my father's sense of the word. The physical act—every bicep twitch, the self-determination of fate—was my thing, an in-the-moment experience. Despite the mountaineering books that launched my life as a climber—those stories of firsts in the great ranges and the men with the vision to accomplish and write about them—the historical context of firsts meant little to me.

Harvey grabbed his current journal from a stack of black-spined ledger books. He opened it on his desk.

"See here, Lou," he said, as he ran his scarred fingers over pages of tiny penciled hieroglyphics—hundreds of his climbs, often first ascents. "You've gotta record your climbs, especially your firsts. If you don't record one and eventually report it, you're not doing the first, you're not contributing to the sport. And whatever the climb, write it down, and you'll never forget it."

At that moment, the spirit of mountaineering leaped off Harvey's journal pages and permeated my soul: the metallic scent of a piton hammer slamming steel, the scratch of dusty eyes, battered fingers seeking grip on rock never touched, skis carving places never skied. There was no need for further didactics. I got it.

That same day, I bought a blue ledger book with the word "Record" printed on the spine in gold lettering.

At first, I only journaled climbs when the mood hit. Another trip to Yosemite changed that. For the next seven years, I scribbled almost all my climbs—including many first ascents—on the pages of what became the tattered, spine-broken record of my seminal years as a mountaineer.

Along with Harvey's enlightenment regarding firsts and journaling, the chimbley epic shifted my climbing career from wannabe to devotee. I'd learned strength and technique were essential, yet tricky climbs were more than physical. To succeed as a mountaineer, I'd need the flow, that zone where fear evaporated, where only the solitary mattered: a single flake of rock, an ice crystal, the toothpick-thin steel edges of my skis. I'd found that place once. Would I again?

12 | UNRAVELING, 1972

IF I POSSESSED ANY remaining illusion regarding the transcendence of the counterculture, winter of 1971-72 crushed the mirage.

Hippie cult leader Charles Manson was on trial. During a multiple-murder spree, Manson's disciples had painted the Beatles' song title "Helter Skelter" in human blood on their victims' refrigerator door.

I'd loved that tune—good and rowdy rock 'n roll. But after the murders, every time I heard McCartney scream-singing like demons hooked their claws in his face, all I could think of were Manson's minions hacking Sharon Tate and her unborn baby to death.

In the song, McCartney yells the proverbial two-word warning, the prelude to countless disasters: watch out!

We should have listened.

That winter, nineteen-year-old champion Hawaiian surfer Tomi Winkler landed in Aspen to try a stint as a ski bum. He found a surrogate family in the Dawson compound and rented a bunk in Craig's room. As much as he relished skiing and surfing, Tomi savored the party.

It happened during first light on a clear February morning. Yet I remember it as a time of shadows flitting through a damp mist.

I woke to loud voices and clomping feet. Doors slammed. Someone was sobbing.

"Grab all the drugs. Bury the stuff in the yard, or flush it. The cops are coming!"

My mother flung open my bedroom door. "Tomi. He's dead!"

Adrenaline catapulted me from bed. Tomi was ten feet away, in Craig's room, on the other side of the wall.

I pulled on my jeans, threw a scruffy blanket over my bare shoulders, and bolted out the front door. The scene was surreal. Police bubble lights flashed a blue-white-and-red light show on the snowy driveway and the house's outside walls. An officer in a bulky black jacket stood toe to toe with my father, grilling him. I gripped my blanket and pulled it tighter against the winter morning.

I was in one of my clean-living phases—nothing to hide. Yet, here I was at the Dawson "blight" house, with a dozen stoners the local constabulary knew well. Thinking there was no way out of guilt by association, I stood stunned and silent. *Were they going to haul us to jail?*

The ambulance rolled up, and soon, the county coroner. The wheeled cart exited our house, bearing the sheeted Tomi. Downers and alcohol had teamed up to do their worst.

None of us ended up behind bars. Tomi wasn't a minor, and the drugs were flushed or hidden. Yet the dark had overcome the light.

My parents' marriage was over. Every day, a menagerie of stoned freaks lay about what had become nothing less than a flophouse, most with no visible means of support, snacking on my mother's homemade bread and whatever else they could scrounge. Keith incessantly teased my two youngest brothers, calling sixteen-year-old Tapley "pube" and making raunchy jokes at his expense. I said not a word in his defense.

I had no clue how to handle the rot of hippiedom. So, inspired by my father's edict, "Make your own way," I again headed for the hills to seek the best climber I could be.

13 | THE PITON, 1972

ON A SUNNY MORNING in 1972, our gang of Aspen climbers gathered for a day on the cliffs. Someone had invited a new guy, Michael Kennedy, a neck-bearded, lanky fellow visiting town for a photography workshop. He'd begun his rock climbing career in Ohio, but it was in Aspen where he'd experienced the sport as the self-actualizing lifestyle it was for so many of us. He'd move to town that next summer, 1973, to eventually become a famed alpinist and the owner-publisher of *Climbing* magazine.

Something attracted me to Michael—perhaps the creative glint in his eyes, perhaps a fellow in fanaticism. In conversation, I gathered he was a cerebral climber; planning, and thinking things through, were essentials to his process. I was the opposite in temperament, climbing from the gut, taking mortal, sometimes unnecessary risks. After finding my flow that previous season with Harvey, I lusted for the lead, far above my protection, the rope dangling below me, my mind and muscles the only things between me and death. Some called me stupid, but it was pure zeal.

Accordingly, that first summer of our acquaintance, I gave Michael—and myself—a little more than we might have expected from the Aspen climbing scene.

AS THE 1970S MARCHED on, rapid technological progress was the norm. Microwave ovens, automobile tape players, the seeds of personal computing, space probes, a tornado of what, in a broader sense, you could call "gear." Rock climbing was no exception. Thanks to innovations like controlled-stretch dynamic rope and purpose-engineered equipment, old edicts and standards, such as, "The leader must not fall," had given way to the new era. Leader falls were now okay, so long as you didn't slam into something hard, like rock, before your protection gear and your buddy's belay caught you.

While Michael and I had both had dropped a few feet now and then, neither of us had taken a substantial leader fall, what climbers called a "screamer."

No doubt, it was time to scream.

"Nice new rope you've got," I said to Michael one morning as we loaded gear into his crumpled (something about a deer) red Fiat 500. I suggested doing Grotto Wall via Intelligentsia, a route Harvey had established a few years prior. "With that primo rope in case of a fall, maybe I can free climb the upper section. That'll be a first."

As budding climbers of the 1970s, we'd bought into an important code of the era: the division between "aid" and "free" climbing. If climbers used installed gear for upward progress, pulling on it or otherwise, they were aid climbing. In contrast, when climbers installed gear just for fall protection, and used natural hand and foot holds for ascension, they were free climbing. Michael and I sought to master all forms, but free climbing was the ideal. It was a matter of purity, of athletic idealism—mind and body superseding technology. Thus, the *first-free* ascent was the ultimate in creative expression. And in my case, I didn't mind the bragging rights.

What better location for a first-free than Aspen's most popular cliff, Grotto Wall, 300 feet high, just a few steps from the Independence Pass road? Maybe Harvey would be watching.

HALFWAY UP THE SECOND pitch of Intelligentsia, I reached a bent, rusted piton we knew Harvey had driven several years prior. Unlike the pitons he normally installed—the ones he beat into the rock until they resembled a rusty mushroom—this one protruded two inches.

"Got Harvey's piton," I shouted as I snapped the rope through a carabiner. "But it's cracked, sticking out too much—maybe can't hold a fall." Pause. "There's another piton fifteen feet up. Should I go for it?"

Michael was belaying from a tiny ledge just wide enough for his feet.

He leaned back on his tie-in slings, which allowed him to look up without putting a permanent crick in his neck. "Yeah, I've got a solid belay. Good anchors. Good rope. Go for it."

After a few lurching moves, I hooked my left-hand fingertips into a shallow crack, pulled myself a few feet higher, and stood with both shoe toes fighting for room on a polished, sloping hold about the size of a playing card. I paddled my feet, hunting for grip, but the rock just got slicker. My left forearm burned as my fingers uncurled and began to slide out of the crack. My breath burst in and out. If I fell, Harvey's janky piton might fail. In that event, I'd crater on a ledge a few yards below Michael, mangle body parts, maybe sample the permanent sleep. I needed protection. I needed it fast.

I laser-focused on the piton above. Within reach? I raised my right arm, pushing, striving upward with every muscle fiber from fingers to torso. Touched it!

With that, I should have grabbed a carabiner from my shoulder sling, snapped it through the piton, then clipped the rope so a fall was a matter of inches instead of a skydive. Not to be. The moment I moved my right hand toward my gear sling, my feet oozed off the foothold. Without thought, I reached like a dunking basketball player and stabbed my index finger through the piton's eye hole.

"I've got my finger in the pin," I yelled. "I can't get my feet to hold. I might fall!"

Any basic climbing class will teach you the eye of a piton is for a carabiner, not a finger. The pain was intense.

"Aaaaa, my finger!" I screamed. "I can't hold. Take rope. Fallingggggg!"

Out popped my finger. I went ballistic, backward, dropping like a boulder, whipping past the terror piton. Then, after a spine-bending jerk, I dangled on the rope, level with Michael and fifteen feet to his right.

Michael held the rope in a white-knuckle grip, wrapped across his waist like a gunslinger setting up for a cross-draw. It was probably dried sweat that moussed his shaggy hair into a crown of porcupine quills, but it could have been fear. "You okay, Lou?"

"I think so," I panted. "Banged my elbow, not too bad."

Michael shook his head. "You took a thirty-foot screamer. Scared the shit out of me. That stupid piton held!"

I vibrated with residue fear as I hung from the rope and brushed my feet against the cliff. The tunnel vision eased. I studied the route above. *Should I try it again?* The rope leading from my waist up to Harvey's manky piton was not inspiring.

"Let's bail," I said.

I swung into Michael, and we rappelled to the ground, leaving a carabiner dangling as a talisman of failure. While coiling the rope, we noted a ten-inch section of friction-fused nylon sheath where it had rubbed across the fall-catching carabiner. During the drive home, I repeatedly ran my fingers over the melt-hardened surface, as if it were a rosary.

My desperate mistake of hanging from a piton with one finger might have scared off most climbing partners. But Michael must have seen some potential. A decade later, after our many climbs together, a writer of a climbing book quoted Michael's take on my style: "A very bold climber with lots of natural ability and a bit of a crazy streak."

I don't deny the part about a crazy streak. As for my ability, as the years progressed it was more about devotion than genetics—I clocked the requisite 10,000 hours on the cliffs and practice boulders, studied the books, and submitted to the mentors. The bird bones I'd inherited from my stick-thin mother were the "natural" part of the equation; because strength-to-weight ratio is everything to a climber.

14 | CADAVERS, 1972

SUMMER OF 1972 WAS to be my debut as a full-on NOLS instructor. Fifteen weeks in the high Wind Rivers, three courses. And to top it off, Kristina had enrolled in the instructor course. The plan: she'd get hired, and we'd co-instruct. It seemed like alpine heaven was just around the corner.

Heaven didn't happen.

For reasons unclear, NOLS didn't hire Kristina. Faced with our lost summer, she found a job and a place to live in Lander. We played house between my courses, and she hiked into the Winds a few times for visits.

During one such reunion, she floated the "L" word. I was still more in love with mountaineering than with the thorny work a relationship demanded—work I had no clue how to do. Yet I wasn't ready to sever the rope—was there a way to have it all? I considered sneaking her onto my next course. If we convinced the course director to keep the secret, she could pretend to be a student, or even join me as a co-instructor.

Yet in the end, it was good that Kristina stayed in Lander, and not just because her bootlegging a course would have gotten us both excommunicated. As she'd long known, and I'd soon learn, the dark side of the mountain was never far away.

IT WAS THE END of August, my last NOLS course of the summer. Dave Neary and I were leading our patrol on a three-day, above-timberline glacier traverse, orbiting cliffy Gannett Peak—Wyoming's highest at 13,804 feet. Neary had been an asset throughout the entire course: smart, with a considerate, soft-spoken style of instructing I tried—and often failed—to emulate. A mountain-mannish beard accentuated the effect.

I loved the glacier environment and made it my mission to transfer that love to our students. There was something mystical about the starkness, the sensory isolation. No trees. No grass. No green whatsoever. Shining granite cliffs jutted from the ice, decorated with dark streaks of snowmelt water. Little splashes of color—the dull red in a plaid shirt, the brown of a wooden ice axe shaft—all hit your eyes like the oversaturated hyper-reality landscape photos in tourist-town galleries.

On most summer days, sun-loosed water was everywhere, squishing under your feet, trickling, gurgling. The air smelled clean, with occasional hints of watermelon-scented musk from microscopic chionophile organisms growing in summer-warmed snow. All sprinkled with a spice of danger: crevasses, rockfall, thousand-foot-deep slick-sided water funnels known as moulins.

My charges got it: absorbing my geology talks, improvising snow camps with their summer backpack gear, and with the day's busyness behind, sipping after-dinner tea while looking around in awe at the glacial environment. Yet two days on the nieve were enough. We were sunburnt and foot wet, ready for dry ground.

We spent the morning of our third day climbing the Minor Glacier to a saddle on Gannett's south ridge, the standard route to the summit. I gathered everyone. "We'll climb Gannett from here, then descend Gooseneck Glacier at night for an ultimate adventure." When I told them we'd sleep on dry ground at Floyd Meadows—with campfires, fry-bake bread, and the chance to dry our spongy boots—the excitement was palpable.

GANNETT'S SUMMIT RIDGE VARIED from wide, easy hiking sections to narrows where tripping on a shoelace would dump you over a cliff. Ever safety aware, we strung fixed ropes across the dangerous areas.

All was well until Sally, a slim student who kept her short brown hair tucked under a stocking cap, unclipped from the safety line and view-shopped within inches of a precipice.

I tried to hide my frustration, but it was impossible. "Damn it, Sally!" I shouted, gesturing for her to clip back in. "I've been telling you guys for weeks how careful we need to be ... How long it takes to get help."

From my first days in the Wind River Mountains, I'd both lamented and mostly loved the remoteness of civilization. The closest trailhead was often a twelve-hour-plus march over a mountain pass or two. And if you needed a telephone, you had to find a ride to a ranch or town.

"It seemed safe to me," Sally replied, as she grabbed the rope. She didn't see what I saw as a guide, how easy it was to stumble from the edge of a cliff.

Was I too young for this? I wondered. *Would I ever be the mountain guide some other instructors were?*

WITH GANNETT PEAK CHECKED off, we tied five ropes together to connect everyone for the glacier descent. I designated sixteen-year-old tent mates David Clark and Dick Neilson as our leaders. I was third on the rope, with Neary behind me and seven following him.

As we dropped from the ridge to the glacier's upper reaches, the sunset rake light revealed an unnatural groove scored in the snowfield below us. The mysterious feature appeared about three feet wide, snaking downhill some 500 feet before disappearing over a humped transition.

"I can't figure out what made a mark like that," I said as I helped a student tie his knots. "Maybe a boulder rolled all that way? We'll see when we're down there."

AS WE DESCENDED, KICKING our feet into the snow for traction, dark fell like a blanket. Moonrise was an hour away. We had no flashlights or head-lamps. We moved in slow motion as if crossing a minefield, often pausing to let the person ahead continue and keep the rope snug. The cord was our protection should one of us plunge into a hidden, snow-bridged crack. Neilson and Clark disappeared over a roll, pulling the rope with sporadic jerks, taking their time to find the best route.

Then the rope stopped moving.

I grabbed the cold, wet cord with my bare hands and pulled. In came sheaves of slack, which I piled on the snow in front of my boots. "Hey," I yelled into the shadows. "Can you move ahead? I've got too much rope here.

You guys behind me, stop, don't make more slack. It'll be all over if someone falls into a hole with this loose rope."

A few lazy "okays" floated from above.

From below, silence.

What now? I speared my ice axe into the snow, flung my pack off my back, and bayed with every decibel my lungs could muster. "What the hell are you guys doing down there?"

Clark's shouted reply punched through the still night air. "Someone is lying on the snow. He's sleeping, hurt, or dead!"

"You think those guys really see something?" I blurted to Neary, spooked. "Maybe a man-sized hunk of snow? They're freaking in the dark?"

Neary was calmer than I, almost aloof. "Yeah, we need to get everybody safe. There might be crevasses down there. Maybe a guy fell into a hole, and somebody pulled him out and left him."

I paused, picturing the students roped behind us. "Everyone, back up and tighten the ropes between you. Sit and plant your ice axe. Wait 'till we check things out."

Neary and I re-rigged our ropes and downclimbed into what was a few moments earlier a peaceful glacier under an orb of winking stars—now a pit of mystery.

We soon reached Clark and Neilson. In the starlight, two yards away, the elongated shape commanded attention.

As we crept toward the object, the night-hardened snow crunched under our boot soles, loud as gunshots. A rancid odor stirred my stomach. My vision squeezed through a dark tube between me and the man. Definitely a man. He lay on his back, face upturned, still as the mountain above us. Rucked-up shirt, jeans—*not a NOLSie*. His arms were folded over his chest, fingers clenched into claws. Random loops of rope draped his waist and torso.

"You alright?" I muttered as I touched his cheek. Cold, clayish—crusty with dried blood—no need to check for a pulse.

Just then, the moon rose over the ridge behind us and blazed over the man's face. His lips were pulled back from glowing white teeth in a macabre grin. His wide-open eyes caught my gaze as if he'd reached behind my head and was pulling me in for a kiss. I froze.

"Man, oh man," Neary whispered, easing me back from the abyss.

Could we not continue walking under the pretty stars, leave this behind as a bad dream? Why a dead guy in the middle of a glacier? Why the rope?

Fearing unusual hazards hidden by the darkness, Neary and I concluded we'd stop and set up camp. But first, we could not leave this poor soul lying uncovered, staring at the moon with that grisly expression on his face.

We spread a tent-tarp next to the corpse. Neary grabbed the feet and lifted. In full rigor, the man rose as a log. Averting my eyes, I held his shoulders, and we shifted him to the tarp. When we tightened the fabric into a makeshift body bag, the paper-thin nylon made a form-fitting, moonlit mask over his prominent brow, nose, and chin.

The four of us rejoined our fellows. I erected my tent while the students spread their ground sheets and sleeping bags on the glacier snow nearby. Any other night, an uncomfortable yet happy adventure.

"What do you think happened to that guy?" Neary asked as we sat on our sleeping bags.

"I don't know." I hugged my knees to my chest. "There's nothing steep here, and any crevasses are obvious—in daylight. The tangled rope, weird."

I shivered, thinking the man's ghost floated over our tent, under the night sky, listening.

Summoning a gram of courage, I poked my head through the half-zippered door of our tent. The fat moon painted the glacier with white-cold fire. Above us, mysteriously shadowed fissures punctuated Gannett Peak's ribs and ridges. A student's muffled sobs drifted through the library-still air.

Well past midnight, we zipped into our sleeping bags. As I tossed, sleepless, a scream rent the silence. It was Clark. "Nooooooo, get away from me!"

"Clark! Clark!" I sat up, bag over my shoulders, shouting through the tent wall. "You ok? What's going on?"

"I'm ... I'm fine. I'm awake now. I dreamed the dead man was looming over me, in my face."

Morning came with sweltering glacier-reflected sun. We packed in fifteen minutes, eager to flee the scent of death. Roped together in forty-foot intervals, we marched past the tarp-wrapped corpse as though for a funeral viewing. His face, perfectly defined in its clinging nylon mask, was turned to the sky. He could have been napping.

Two hours later, we stepped from the glacier's toe to the land of life. The meadow grass was a green ocean, seeming to vibrate when I held my eyes in any one spot. The thick air swelled my lungs, redolent of wood smoke, wetland, and dirt. Mosquitoes hummed.

The next day, I took a pair of students climbing on a granite outcrop above our camp. While lounging on a sun-soaked belay ledge, we watched an outfitter lead a pack horse along the trail below us. It was like a movie scene from an old Western, the tarp-wrapped corpse draped belly down across the saddle, bouncing.

When my students wondered, I explained that a rescue team had brought the body down, and the packer was transporting it to a helicopter landing spot or perhaps to a trailhead. "Let's quit talking about it," I said.

A few days later, I sent Kristina a note with a horse packer, letting her know when I'd be at my exit trailhead and asking if she'd pick me up—a self-absorbed move on my part, given the unstable terrain of our relationship. But she was there.

THE DAY AFTER MY students returned from their survival trek, I was in the NOLS gear shed, helping them clean and return their equipment. Kristina walked in. She looked at the stacked ropes with a dubious, closed-mouth smile—a facial expression that usually made me laugh. Not this time.

"I'm not liking this lifestyle one bit," she said as my students watched, keyed in on the romantic drama. *How did mountain-guide heroes operate in the arena of love?*

"I can't stand being apart," I said. "I'm a climber. And I love being in the mountains—with you."

"I don't know ..." Kristina said.

"I'm headed to the Valley. Let's go together."

Of course, we already knew the polished cracks of Yosemite were not her scene. But it seemed like the thing to say, even though I could feel our relationship fraying from too much tension, too many tugs in the wrong direction.

"Maybe," she replied.

I nodded, then turned back to my students.

15 | VALLEY CLIMBER, 1972

I wasn't sure why we gave the Valley another go as a couple. It was more emotional than anything else—sharing the driving, camping together, and joining the Yosemite climber culture. I also relied on Kristina's support; she had a car, I did not, and I was desperate for Sierra granite.

Once in the Valley, we tapped a handful of easy routes—"easy" being a relative term. Church Bowl Chimney was rated just 5.6, yet demanded the nonintuitive techniques for which the smooth-sided Valley cracks were famous. Kristina was happy to continue her escape from the Aspen scene—in this, we were of one mind—but she didn't have her heart in Valley climbing, struggled, and soon left.

I missed her. Yet I had my rocks: arcs and slabs of firm granite, "sinker" cracks that engulfed my hands in the vertical dance, tendon-scourging finger cracks, and the dreaded offwidth slots no body part fit securely, thus requiring an outlandish mix of technique, pain tolerance, and power.

And power I had. Training was no mystery to me—it was just a matter of lifestyle and the will to see it through. Work three NOLS courses in a row. Carry a hundred-pound backpack, spend an hour or two a day on the Winds' ubiquitous boulders, sneak away to ropeless solo a few climbs—usually rock—but strap on the crampons and run a few icy couloirs in the evening while my students ate dinner. I was now a climbing machine: six percent body fat, 135 pounds with pants on.

The previous spring had been my Yosemite graduation. Aspen-based climber Steve Kentz and I had bagged our first multiday Yosemite wall (we weren't total klutzes, but it was best nobody was watching) and proved our crack-climbing skills in the squeeze chimneys and cracks of the storied Steck-Salathé route on Sentinel Rock.

Now flush with cash from my NOLS work, and romantic pursuits on hold, there would be no messing around.

First order of business: a two-day direct-aid wall route with Rich Jack on the face of Leaning Tower, an overhanging line of about eight 150-foot rope lengths.

Rich was another Aspen-based climber. He was tall; his six-foot-seven-en-inch frame caused him to walk with a slight hunch to avoid door jambs and such, yet it was an advantage for rock climbing. He often made climbs a grade easier by skipping one or two normal-height moves. And while direct-aid climbing, he could reach past manky gear placements for better options. Enhancing his unusual stature, his shoulder-length, ruler-straight blond hair was so bright it lit a room. We'd become fast friends, both in climbing and in life. There were many cliffs in our future.

Though we were Yosemite big-wall novices, things clicked for us on Leaning Tower. I discovered I had a talent for the technical, gear-intensive nature of aid climbing. Years of physical work had a lot to do with it—my hands were strong and skilled from construction—yet more important were my fitness and lack of fear. With little thought to the airspace below, I could stand tall in my foot slings and reach high for each gear placement.

Rich and I were not fast—speed being a metric of wall-climbing talent—yet we executed Leaning Tower without a blip. No falls, no dropped gear, adequate food and water. I loved it, especially the problem-solving: Which piton fits this crack? How to eat without dropping my spoon onto a climber's head 400 feet below?

ON A SUNNY MORNING, a few days after Leaning Tower, Rich and I sat for breakfast at a picnic table in Camp 4, the Yosemite climbers' campground. I stirred a pot of oatmeal; Rich sorted the carabiners and pitons for our next climb. He was a gear freak, a valuable attribute for a climber.

Forty feet away, a husky mesomorph and his female partner cooked pancakes and bacon on the tailgate of their sagging Rambler station wagon.

Pork smells better than oatmeal. I wanted to meet those guys.

"That's Ray Jardine over there," Rich gushed. "I know him from when I was in school in Boulder. He's an amazing climber."

I turned off my stove, and we moseyed over to meet our neighbors.

At nearly thirty years old, Ray Jardine had been seriously climbing for about a decade. His build showed it: basketball-shaped shoulders, veined forearms, his back hunched by strength-training pull-ups—"a thousand a day during rest days," Rich claimed. Ray's light-brown hair hung to his neck, enhancing the outlaw effect of a bushy beard that reminded me of my father. A pair of Buddy Holly eyeglasses intellectualized his deep-set eyes. On his table, an open Bible big enough to span the Rambler's steering wheel hinted at someone seeking more than cliffs.

"Hey," Rich said, "This is Lou. He's a hot climber from Aspen."

My cheeks flushed. There were other competent climbers in Aspen—and this was Yosemite Valley, not my piddly Independence Pass backwoods, where the longest climb was three pitches, maybe four if you used your imagination. But I suppressed a swell of pride; I was only human.

"We did Leaning Tower a few days ago," Rich continued. "He's been leading some hard free-climbs too."

Ray eyeballed me from head to toe. "Rest day today, an easy five-eight climb to stay loose. Why don't you guys come along, see how you do?"

I wasn't too worried about making it up a 5.8; I'd already climbed 5.9 pitches in Aspen that our crew quietly admitted were 5.10 (in climbing culture, downrating was better than being accused of braggadocio). And things were moving fast. The climbing world was now abuzz over ascents of the Valley's first acknowledged 5.11s: New Dimensions and Hourglass Left. I was far from ready to touch the sacred handholds of such climbs—and didn't know if I ever would be. But I thought of those routes nearly every day.

Rich and I flashed Ray's "rest" climb like we were hiking.

THE NEXT DAY'S CLIMB was our final exam, 5.10-d Twilight Zone. Our guidebook described the crux as a "steep and very strenuous 60-foot jam-crack in a flared corner," yet said nothing of this climb's storied history. It didn't need to, because any climber worth their rope knew the tale by heart:

Valley hardman Chuck Pratt had made the first lead of Twilight Zone in 1965, when offwidth crack-climbing, Yosemite style, was esoterica along the lines of forbidden magic.

The Zone was one of the earliest climbs that deserved a 5.10 rating. And now, despite being established seven years earlier (an eon in climber time), we knew it to be one step in difficulty from the fabled grade of 5.11. My fingers tingled when I brushed a hand over the rock at the base of the climb. It was as if Pratt had compressed the time-space continuum.

As Ray worked the Twilight Zone crux, I obsessed on his masterful technique: stacking one foot over the other to create a heel-toe jam, nesting two fists together for a move, and the "arm-bar." The latter involved pressing a hand against one side of the crack while pressing an elbow against the opposite side with no more help than a bicep contraction, creating friction for purchase.

I climbed as Ray's second, breathing hard, making the moves. With the toprope extending from my waist to Ray's belay above, I could experiment with no fear of falling.

"Throw an arm-bar in there," Ray shouted as he looked down, his head silhouetted against the sky. "Pull with your other hand on the crack's edge so your shoulder gets friction. Use your whole body. Whatever works."

Sections of the climb's smooth granite were reminiscent of my bomb-bay chimney nemesis. This time, I found the traction. I could have led it.

Back on the ground, coiling our ropes, Ray said, "Let's partner for some climbs. Put you on the lead."

YOSEMITE WAS NOW A huge part of my life; I was spending over two months a year there. Yet the highlands also had my affection—the ice, the snow. When I returned to Aspen from Yosemite, Kristina and I wanted to live together. So we looked for options at my parent's 82 house. But the bedrooms were filled with renters, the drugs and chaos unbearable.

I had the brilliant idea of shoveling a hobbit house in the four-foot-high dirt-floored crawlspace under the kitchen, to create our special nook. After a few days on our knees, our backs nuked from pushing a loaded wheelbarrow while bent at the waist, we'd carved out a plot the size of a picnic table.

"Are we seriously going to build a room in there?" Kristina asked. "Concrete, frame walls, and stuff?"

"I hadn't thought much about that," I answered, true to my impulsive nature. "Aren't a couple of sleeping bags enough?"

That fall, we found a place in town.

Now living away from my family, concentrating on climbing, I hardly noticed when a red-lettered for-sale sign sprang up amid the firewood piles and assorted car parts on the 82 house's scraggly lawn. It sold fast.

My mother packed her belongings and purchased a twenty-by-forty foot, one-bedroom 1800s miner's shack—she called it a "cabin"—in Crested Butte, a funky, more affordable ski town on the south side of the Elk Mountains, twenty-five miles from Aspen as the crow flies. Her down payment was $500 (about $3,500 today). Along with Keith and my two younger brothers, she relocated in October.

©Dawson

Patricia's cabin, Crested Butte, 1972

WHEN I VISITED THE CABIN early that winter of 1972-73, I expected something small and rough. But not that rough. As with most such structures built in the 1800s mining camps, the place lacked a foundation and had settled into the ground. You needed sea legs for the humped and dipped floors. The exterior walls, doubtless uninsulated, leaned noticeably out of plumb. The interior walls were paneled with splintery local-milled spruce planks, aged to dirty gray. Condensation fogged the single-glazed windows, dripping down to nourish the mold on the sills. To reach their attic beds, my brothers climbed a wooden ladder through a rough-cut semi-rectangular hole in the ceiling.

Later, I learned that when the plumbing froze solid, everyone used the toilets at the bars down the street.

On the surface, Crested Butte looked like hillbilly poverty, something for social services. But my mother loved Keith, and she loved her children. Love makes a home. She hung her artwork, cooked her bread, and turned her two cats loose on the mice, creating a peaceful nest from the dust and splinters. While there remained plenty of friction between Keith and my brothers, the overall vibe was the polar opposite of the Aspen chaos. When I sat in her armchair next to the glowing woodstove and picked up a book from the side table, I wanted to live there, too.

My father moved to the 'Butte a few weeks later. This had little, if anything, to do with my mother. He was just another Aspen expat hippie, of which there were many who'd fled the legendary ski town's skyrocketing property values and barnwood-paneled fern bars, the beginnings of a long, downward spiral of glitzification.

Years later, my mother explained what had occurred while I'd been away for the summer: Her feelings for Keith had dissolved any remaining shred of her marriage, and the financial picture was bleak. She and my father agreed to sell the 82 house, pay off the loans, and split what little was left.

"You were grown up and off teaching climbing," she explained. "I was thinking about your younger brothers, providing a roof over their heads, how they'd get along with Keith."

By this time, seven years out of Texas—it felt like twenty—my brother Craig and I were now the only members of our clan still residing in Aspen.

16 | SPIN THE WHEEL, 1972

FOUR YEARS HAD PASSED since I'd lost my backcountry innocence in the wintery Conundrum valley. During that time, I'd read *The Snowy Torrents*, a compilation of all fatal avalanche accidents in the United States, 1910 through 1966: from the devastating 1910 Stevens Pass incident, 96 people lost, to construction workers who stood too close to dynamited snow cornices, to Loretta Thorpe skiing her small patch of Aspen powder. Along with book study, I'd taken a ski touring guide certification class. Hidden under Colorado's legendary powder snow, time bombs were ticking. And I knew it.

Yet despite my training and gleaned knowledge, I climbed and skied in denial, sheltered under fantasies of crystal blue skies and powdery snow where skis seemed to turn themselves. How could I and my mountain companions, who danced over the hills like superheroes, incur such wrath?

But the truth was there, and the truth was spoken in many ways.

On a dark midwinter afternoon in 1972, when we returned from skiing, I asked Kristina about a ring she wore, a splendid gold-flecked rainbow stone. She held her hand out for inspection, fingers spread.

"It's a snowfire opal my great uncle found, and my father had mounted. It was my mother's. She loved it. My father gave it to me a few years after she died ... in the avalanche."

Sorrow squeezed my throat closed like a pair of pliers. I stood silent, neck hairs tingling. I pictured her mother falling, the snow washing over her, packing against her face as she whispered her last goodbyes to her husband and daughters.

The story of Loretta was a warning flare for our mountain-adventure crowd. More than a few of us were fast becoming lab hamsters in an adrenaline-addiction experiment, spinning the run-wheels inside our cages, working off the high from our last hit. We ran, we spun, and sometimes we rode the wheel to a screeching halt in a cloud of acrid smoke from the burned-out axle bearings.

A couple of years earlier, Kristina had met Meta Burden, a worldly Vermonter who, along with her husband, was making a go of Aspen. Meta was outgoing and stylish, with dark brunette hair and the burnished face of a fashion model. During winter, she lived in her classic-patterned sweaters, topped by a fashionable parka. She skied well. And, like Kristina, she was an avalanche orphan; her father had perished in a snowslide in the Alps twenty years earlier. The pair became close friends, sharing a love of literature, Aspen culture, and the ski mountain rising above the town. There, the twosome ventured into the out-of-bounds, where cold-smoke powder washed over their shoulders—and avalanches lurked under their feet.

IT WAS DECEMBER 8, 1972, a month before my twenty-first birthday. I was manning the second-floor ski workbench at the Aspen Mountaineering outdoors store. The scent of burning tree sap swirled from the pine tar I was torching into a pair of wooden Nordic skis. Outside the window, rice-sized snowflakes spit from muddy, low-hanging clouds. As my mind drifted to the next day's skiing—*a storm, but not much pow*—the shop door crashed open, and Kristina sprinted up the stairs to my workbench like a dozen wolves were on her heels. Her tear-streaked face twisted in agony as her voice broke with grief. "Meta," she howled between sobs. "She's dead! Avalanche."

I stood frozen—a self-absorbed boy-man of twenty years with no significant life experience, no vocabulary of loss. All I could muster was a hug, and a glance into her tormented eyes. And honestly, what gesture or words could have consoled her when the white wave had obliterated her best friend—as it had her mother? Were the mountains so cruel?

After an argument with her ski patrol paramour, Tim Howe, Meta had embarked on a solo ski down one of Aspen Mountain's closed, out-of-bounds slopes. She triggered an avalanche that swept her to the bottom of the run, where she suffocated. Meta was as fine a skier as there ever was. Tim was the ski patrol avalanche expert. None of that mattered when it came to a layered, unstable snowpack.

17 | WINTER EPICS, 1973

A WISER, OLDER MOUNTAINEER might have taken pause after Meta's death. I was neither old nor wise. Despite the avalanches, I loved how winter morphed my home range, the Elk Mountains, into snowy monuments not unlike the great-range peaks of my climbing books. Out of Aspen, there were Mount Everests just a day's travel away. Irresistible.

"Let's do some *real* winter climbing," I proclaimed to Kristina during a ski tour. "It'll be *fun*."

That was an outright lie. Winter climbing isn't fun. You might see a nice sunrise now and then, and enjoy your friends, but mostly it's about constant suffering punctuated by moments of sheer terror.

"What climbs?" She asked.

"I'll let you know after we get you some winter boots."

WHILE KRISTINA WASN'T A die-hard winter mountaineer, she was comfortable with the winter wild and good with roped climbing. As for the risk, she'd gained a modicum of caution after Meta's accident. Yet rather than running from the mountains, Kristina held the hills close, honoring, perhaps replicating, her lost friend's alpine joy. And she hadn't lost her thirst for new experiences.

How spicy would she go? I never asked. Instead, I ordered a pair of size seven—the smallest made—Galibier Hivernale double-layer mountain boots. When I picked them up at the post office, the astringent smell of tanned leather seeped through the box—new shoes for new adventures. That afternoon, we tied the thick red laces, so French, and Kristina evaluated the fit by tromping about indoors.

"Feel okay?"

"I think so, but my feet are swimming ."

"You need the extra space for blood circulation, so your toes won't freeze off."

Despite allusions to impending peril, she didn't remove the boots right then, rebox, and return them. I took that as a yes, yet waited a few weeks to reveal the rest of my plan: climb 14,130-foot Capitol Peak—in deep winter.

Capitol is a steep-sided fin arete, about 3,000 feet from base to top, glacier-carved into something like the blade of a gargantuan spade. There are bigger mountains in the world. But in its context, Capitol looms plenty large—and it's the most technically difficult of the fifty-four Colorado fourteeners. A 150-foot section of Capitol's easiest route, Knife Ridge, necks down to inches wide at some points, with dizzying cliffs dropping from both sides. By now, I'd climbed Capitol a half dozen times—though only in summer. As for winter, local lore said climbers had summited Capitol just twice during the frozen season.

When I broached the idea of a winter climb to Kristina, I said little about Knife Ridge. Just: "I'll lead, make it safe."

There were maybe thirty mountaineers in the entire state qualified for this type of climbing. I wasn't sure we were members of that club, but I didn't dwell on it. Instead, I focused on the summit, and on the bond with my partner that such a thing would strengthen. Such was my mind for adventure.

ON A GRAY, OVERCAST mid-February day in 1973, we began breaking deep trail up the nine-mile ski approach to Moon Lake, where we'd stage our campsite for Capitol Peak. The trek soon became a sweaty, leg-burning grind under our forty-five-pound backpacks. We swapped leads, stopping often to sip water and discuss which break to follow into the next thicket of close-spaced aspen trees. The mood wasn't grim, but it wasn't bubbly. We needed a boost. The mountain brought it.

While crossing a ravine where West Snowmass Creek flowed under eight feet of snow, we spotted a slug of age-blackened words scraped into the creamy-white bark of an aspen tree. This was nothing out of the ordinary; as far as I knew, humans had been scratching tree-graffiti since the beginning of time. However, this inscription was special. They were the words we needed, carved unusually high above the ground: *Capitol, first winter ascent 12/1966, Wells, Arndt, Roos, Hamilton.*

In 1966, I was fourteen—my freshman year at Aspen High. I'd known nothing of this crew. Now, they were a presence. The sky brightened, our mood lifted—*Hello, sister and brother. It can be done!*

Five miles and four hours from the epigram, we set our green nylon tent next to ice-sheathed Moon Lake.

The following day, we loaded up with our climbing gear, left our skis tied to the tent, and hiked an hour of wind-packed snow to the start of Knife Ridge. Wind bursts blew skiffs of white over our feet, while mud-gray clouds scudded across the sun. I dropped my pack and pulled out our rope.

"Check your knot after you tie in," I said. "Cold-stiff rope, cold hands. It might not be tight. Could come undone."

Kristina belayed me as I crawled and otherwise navigated the Knife. I found footholds on exposed rock and leeward windrows of wind-deposited snow that had somehow stuck to the mountainside. Some of the snow was wide enough for a boot sole—empty air below. I installed a few pieces of gear along the way and snapped the rope through carabiners, so she could catch me if I slipped—and to protect her as she followed. The efficacy of this was questionable. Should either of us tumble off the ridge, we'd swing like a wrecking ball when the rope came tight.

I set up a belay where the Knife blended into bare, fractured rock. "Come across," I shouted. Kristina moved well—like she'd done this before, albeit within the limits of her stature. At one point, she couldn't extend a leg far enough to use my boot print in the snow windrow. She tilted her head up toward me. The scarf tied over her mouth blocked her speech and obscured her facial expression, but the ask was obvious: "What now?"

I resisted the urge to yell encouragement. With the wind and our hat-covered ears, any attempt at verbal communication would devolve into confused shouting. Some of our worst fights had occurred during climbs: me barking advice, the girl fed up with her know-it-all boyfriend. Better to keep my mouth shut and transmit supportive vibes through the cord. She struggled for a moment, then figured it out.

WITH THE KNIFE BEHIND us, we were 600 vertical feet below the top. Here the summer route deviated to the left, taking easy ground to bypass technical climbing on the ridge proper. Devoid of snow, it was a pleasant hike often decorated with flowers poking up between the rocks: bluish, aptly named sky pilot, maybe a few columbine, their bright yellow eyes rimmed by fluorescent-purple petals. Today, the summer route was a snowy avalanche slope, a dice game with the reaper, a no-go. Instead, I climbed to the right, up snowless rock, to a ledge where a fifteen-foot wall blocked access to the ridgecrest.

I stood below the wall, stymied, slow motion dancing from foot to foot in search of traction. Clad in my winter climbing boots, my fingers blunted by gloves, I was at my limit.

I pictured my fall trajectory: The rope would do nothing before I bounced off the granite outcrops below. And then Kristina would be alone, her frost-numbed fingers clamped around the taut nylon strand connected to her dead or dying companion. After that, the dilemma: attempt an impossible rescue, or leave and save herself? A broken rope was the preferred alternative.

The burgeoning wind spit ice crystals at my face. My breath quickened. She was down there, freezing in the wind. We needed to move. *There must be one crack, somewhere, that fits my gear.*

I balanced on my toes and reached so high my shoulder fired a jolt of pain. At the extent of my gloved fingertips, a one-inch wide fissure split the otherwise blank scarp. I unclipped a small aluminum wedge chock from my gear sling, reached again, fiddled it into the crack, and clipped the rope.

"I've got something in!" I yelled. "Watch me."

Kristina flipped the rope toward me in reply.

I hooked my left hand inside the chock sling, cupped a small handhold with my right, pulled, and flopped over the obstacle onto my chest. I found a stance and belayed Kristina up with a few tugs on the rope to ease her way.

On the final pitches, I fought through two more short cruxes and raced up the mellow parts, sometimes speed-crawling through snowbanks on all fours. I thought nothing of the void below, only what lay ahead: gear placements, every tug of the rope, boots finding footholds as though by psychic attraction. The books had spoken of alpine climbing transcendence. This was it.

At the summit, several feet of snow covered anything useful as a belay anchor. I sat facing the route, wriggled my butt into the snow, and pressed my boots against the stacked-rock summit cairn. With nothing attaching me to the mountain, we'd both plunge to our doom if my ropemate fell and my stance failed. I yanked the rope twice, signaling "climb!" The wind powdered my face with snow that melted on contact, then refroze and glued my beard to my woolen neck scarf. When I moved my head, the beard hairs tugged on the scarf, twinging like stabs of doorknob static.

Back home, while fitting Kristina's new climbing boots, I'd considered this climb a fun game. Instead, it was gritty, arctic, and risky as hell. When her snow-dusted blue knit hat bobbed above the rocks, I held back tears of relief. Ours was Capitol's third winter ascent and the first by a woman. None of that mattered. A climb is only successful once you're down.

I was in full mountain-guide mode now; keeping my companion safe, thinking little about myself, depending on my training. More than once, I remembered the teenage climber in the Ullman book, the neophyte who'd failed to prevent his little sister from plunging from a climb, her "pigtails spinning in the wind."

"Let's get moving. The descent is going to take almost as long as the climb."

Behind thickening clouds, the dropping sun was now a yellowish cryogenic glow. Rappelling the crux took a half hour. Reversing the Knife wasn't any faster. Our last food and water were long gone. We quaked with chills.

Darkness loomed as we hiked down the final snow slopes. Our camp wasn't visible from above, and the wind had erased our footprints. Should night fall, we might not find our tent. I moved fast, relying on instinct for direction. Aha! There in the dimming light was our pyramid-shaped nylon refuge, flapping in the wind. In a surge of survival joy, ready to say, "Finally," I spun around.

Kristina wasn't there.

Fighting panic—this could be fatal!—I reversed my footprints. Avalanche? Wandered and fallen through the ice into the lake? Five minutes later, I found her lying in a bathtub-shaped snow hole between two boulders. As I brushed the snow from her face, she mumbled through chattering teeth, "I broke through the snow into this hole. It's warm—I want to stay here for a while."

Darkness fell as I pulled her from the snow, threw her arm over my shoulders, and coaxed her to the tent. As she quaked with hypothermic shivering, we burrowed inside our sleeping bags. The storm wind roared through the rocks and ridges above—loud as a jet on takeoff. Her shivering calmed, and we slept the sleep of death denied.

A FEW WEEKS AFTER topping Capitol, our adventures found us well into a twenty-mile ski tour over the Elk Mountains from Aspen to Crested Butte. We intended to visit friends and surprise my mother. In the five months since she'd left Aspen, she had mellowed out of the hippie mayhem, and was showing the first hints of what I'd later realize was a remarkable transformation. Most notably, she was painting again—flowers ablaze with creative light, snowy landscapes. And she was skiing more than ever. It was as if the simple act of leaving Aspen had dissolved a cloak of darkness. Or maybe it wasn't a "leaving," but rather her homecoming, to Crested Butte.

Neither of us was keen on seeing Keith, but the last time I'd visited, he seemed to have mellowed too—though I sensed a continued tension between him and my two younger brothers.

My father was living in Crested Butte as well. I wasn't sure about dropping in on him. What good would that be? Unlike my mother, my father was stuck in the past. Every time I saw him, his long hair and hippie slang reminded me of a time I'd rather forget. I didn't intellectualize it until later, but I despised his lack of role modeling and his abandonment of my younger brothers. Over and over, I played the mental game of "nobody's perfect," but that was like throwing a pebble in the ocean. And when I looked inside myself, my father was there. Was my life as a footloose climbing bum all that different from his dysfunction? Or was the joy I received from the hills something I could thank him for?

From the trailhead near Aspen, we'd skied twelve miles to the barren summit of East Maroon Pass. Considering elevation gain as well as mileage, we'd made more than half the twenty-mile journey to Crested Butte. Kristina had broken her share of the trail, exhausting work. We made a rest stop in the wind shadow next to a waist-high snowdrift. I broke out a bag of trail mix and a water bottle I'd wrapped in my sweater to protect it from freezing.

"We could slog four hours back home from here," I said. "Or we can ski the short downhill to the Gothic summer cabins. After that, it's just three miles of flat, slightly uphill snow-covered road to the Crested Butte trailhead. Shouldn't take more than an hour or two."

Kristina grabbed a handful of peanut-raisin snack mix and took a drink. "I'm doing okay, Lou. I'm a little tired. Remember we don't have any camping gear. Nighttime pretty soon."

I stuffed the food and water bottle into my rucksack and hoisted it over my shoulders. We were both more than a little tired. I didn't want to admit it.

I stomped my feet to force blood into my freezing toes.

"Promise, the road is always packed by snowmobiles. We'll scoot along it like Nordic ski racers. You climbed Capitol. This is nothing."

Kristina clipped into her skis. "All right, let's keep going."

As we skied the road past the deserted summer cabins, I was still breaking trail through shin-deep powder. Snowmobiles had not packed a trail—this was *not* an easy "glide." Each stride required an energetic stomp—exhausting work after a full day.

While skiing behind the trail breaker is easier than leading, Kristina was still burning calories like a racehorse as she pushed through the snow. As night crept closer, she bundled into her red goose-down parka. Dressing so heavy is unusual for an active ski tourer in Colorado. A shirt and body heat are often all one needs. Her bundling should have clued me that her fuel tank was empty.

I ignored the message of her clothing choice and bent to my bullish agenda, what mountaineers jokingly called a "death march."

She wasn't in on the joke.

After a few minutes, I looked behind. Kristina had fallen sixty feet back.

"I can keep breaking trail if you can follow!" I yelled, while still moving my feet, stomp-kick-stomp-kick, making every second count. "We've got two more hours. It's okay if we ski the last part in the dark—it's a wide, obvious road."

"No way, Lou! I'm cold. You promised this would be easy."

"Mellow out, Kris, just keep moving. You're strong. No time to rest!"

I continued breaking trail, head down, thinking only of forward progress. Kristina dropped farther behind.

"You jerk. Slow down. Wait!" she yelled.

My eyes remained locked on my shambling black-leather ski boots.

"Shut up! I'm doing the work here. How could I know about the road, the snowmobiles? Follow me, don't stop!"

Kristina was fuming now, crying, pre-hypothermic. My temper boiled. *Skiing in my track was easy. Why couldn't she do it?*

"Lou—stop. We need to do something."

Those simple words, her plaintive tone—part desperation, part level-headed reason—flipped a switch inside my head. My anger evaporated. I quit my metronomic plod and turned. She had tightened her parka hood. Her cold-blanched face peered from the circular opening like a small mammal peeking from its burrow, checking for predators.

My tank is empty too. I'm as wasted as she. Can't believe I got us into this. We could die.

Nobody in Crested Butte expected us—we were on our own. The sun hung less than a hand-width from the ridge above us—an hour of daylight. I had a dozen waterproof matches, an extra wool sweater, no puffy parka. Could we overnight in the forest, in waist-deep snow, wallowing for firewood as frostbite worked its way from our toes to our knees?

"Okay," I said, "Let's head back to the cabins."

Kristina forced words through her frozen grimace, clearly exasperated. "You convinced me the road would be easy, and then you wouldn't wait. You wouldn't slow down. You were going to drop me!"

She was right—though my pride blocked an apology.

We crawled through a cabin's unlocked window and kindled the fireplace. The flames barely won over the uninsulated roof and walls, yet the situation was survivable. When dawn gleamed through the frosted windows, we ate the last of our raisins and peanuts, crawled outside, and continued.

We never heard the welcome whine of snow machines. But the sky was clear and the sun warmed us as we worked. Had we not stopped and sought refuge, we'd have ended up in a shelterless bivouac, lost fingers and toes, likely died. That would have been on me.

In Crested Butte, we dropped in on my mother. As we expected, she was surprised and delighted to see us. Keith being out of town was also a nice touch—no residual tension. The tiny cabin was still decrepit—it took me two tries to close the front door. Yet my mother's magic was strong. The air was warm from a crackling fire in the woodstove, and smelled of turpentine, oil paints. A brown, longhaired cat curled on a wicker chair three feet from the stove, front paws hanging over the cushion edge, reaching for heat.

We talked of my brother Tom's ski racing, his "fast" yellow parka, and the books she was reading: Jack London and Tolstoy. She fed us tea and homemade bread and drove us to the dirt airstrip outside town. We hopped a single-engine plane for the twenty-minute shuttle flight back to Aspen over East Maroon Pass. I enjoyed flying close to the ground, pointing out our ski tracks to the pilot, and naming the big Elk Range mountains. But it felt a little risky. *One motor? What if it threw a rod?*

As our plane touched down in Aspen, I realized we'd forgotten to drop in on my father. Or at least that was the lie I told myself, because I'd not forgotten. Denial had done its work. If my dad was content perpetuating the hippie ethos, so be it. I'd moved on. Though in the years to come, the party days of 1960s Aspen were never far behind—and more than once, they seemed to be gaining on me, if not bowling me down like a Wind Rivers rockslide.

SPRING CAME. ROCK CLIMBING was, for me, more than a sport now; it was a way of life, a meditation. The odor of it: dry lichen powdering off as I moved, a hint of smoky flint from falling rock, acrid bat guano, the pungent bay leaves of Yosemite. Even the rope had a scent, a baked textile fragrance that triggered an involuntary inhale, like when you pull a freshly laundered and sun-dried shirt over your head.

High on a climb, I sometimes wedged my hand in a tapered crack so faultless it seemed created for the human anatomy. While so embraced, falling was impossible, and I became one with the cliff, the mountain. From my perch in the sky, I'd survey the lands spread below, a monarch over his realm.

And yet, the cliffs of summer paled.

OVER THE PAST WINTER, along with eight other climbers I'd been planning a climb of 20,310-foot Denali, the highest peak in North America.

For me and almost every alpinist I knew, Denali was on the checklist or already scribbled in the résumé. Beyond the legends, the look of the thing was enough: 156 square miles of glaciated blue ice, glow-white snow and wind-abraded stone jutting from central Alaska like a fist punched from the planet's core. By measure of its prominence from bottom to top, some 18,000 feet, Denali exceeded Mount Everest's verticality.

There was no better place to test my fitness, ski skills, and climbing expertise—no better place to find myself as a mountaineer. And my résumé had a blank line.

I was in charge of the Denali equipment list, which had ballooned to 114 lines. The Monopoly game seemed frivolous, but I rolled with it. Could be handy if we were stormed in.

Denali, irresistible, 1973   ©Dawson collection

Two weeks before my planned departure for Alaska, I was squatting in a twelve-foot-diameter canvas teepee my brother Craig had erected in a grassy meadow on a friend's land above Aspen. If you ignored the mice, such things were a 1970s solution to the town's perpetual housing shortage.

Kristina visited. Our rainbow had dimmed since the fight on Gothic Road. But we were still seeing each other—not quite down to the "friends" level, but close. She spent the night in a spare sleeping bag.

The dark hours seemed to stretch forever as images of our past two years swirled through my mind. Our elusive tent on Capitol, the boulder next to Peak Lake, avalanches. A life well lived, or way too intense?

In the morning, I stepped outside in the lingering chill of dawn to greet the day with my yoga routine. Robins and warblers sang their songs of spring. Sunlight fringed through the greening aspens while patches of snow glowed from the shaded forest floor.

I was in my third cycle of surya namaskar, the sun salutation. Kristina ducked through the unpainted, splintery plywood door flap.

"Will we get together when you're back from Alaska?" she said. "Or is climbing all you really love, all you want?"

There was no drama in her question. She already knew the answer, knew who—or in this case what—I loved. Something was missing from our relationship, something to fill a void in my heart, and hers, that our dance-with-death adventures never touched. Could I ever tone down my fanaticism, find the thing our parents had started and never finished, build a normal future? Maybe some day ...

Kristina voiced a flat "Goodby," slung her blue nylon rucksack over a shoulder, and headed down the mile-long foot trail to town. Two weeks later, I left for the northlands, chasing after a mountain bigger than the world.

18 | DENALI WAS ALIVE, 1973

ALASKAN BACKPACKING. SOUNDS LIKE fun, right? It may be that, in certain places at certain times. But the twenty miles and nine days of tundra and brushy hills leading to Denali's Muldrow Glacier were not fun. We waded rivers so dark with glacial silt they resembled flowing concrete, got uncomfortably close to a grizzly bear, and fought incipient trench foot caused by the constant splashing through swampy muskeg—all while relaying hundred-pound loads.

To paraphrase Jack Kerouac: You hike and hike toward the Muldrow, and tomorrow night you're still stumbling through the muskeg.

So the moment was sweet when I finally shrugged off my pack and lowered it to the sterile, rocky side-moraine of the Muldrow. A hundred feet from my boot toes, the ice river splayed nearly flat, a mile-wide expanse of rumpled white, patched with gray ice where the May sunshine had melted the covering snow. Above, bluish haze hid the summits of 11,000-foot peaks rising a vertical mile. And beaming beyond even those grand spires, Denali's gravity pulled me to a mountain so large that thinking about it sometimes struck me speechless.

During our first night on the glacier, I left the tent door open and lay with my head and shoulders out of my sleeping bag. The moist air falling from the heights smelled odd, yet familiar, an ancient bouquet of rock and ice, untouched by man. I didn't feel like sleeping, but I needed rest, needed escape from the night-sun. So I rolled onto my side, pulled the quilted nylon over my head, and pressed my ear into my sleeping pad. After that, it wasn't just the sun keeping me awake. From the deeps, the ice spoke: faint rumblings, booms, whale-speech chitters. The living Muldrow ice could not rest under its own inconceivable pressure.

I never really slept.

THE PREVIOUS SUMMER, I'd befriended charismatic NOLS course director John Whisnant. With his brown ringlets, preppy demeanor, and aesthetic sensibility—he was never seen in a double sweater—Whisnant won the NOLS style contest hands down. He had an attractive female tent-mate during the course we worked together, and cut a figure as he hiked with his mate at his side, his two-foot long Chouinard "piolet" ice axe balanced in one hand like a scepter. I envied his insect-proof tent and its curvy contents. And I respected his ability to facilitate thirty people working together for a month in the Wyoming wilderness.

While Whisnant and I dodged cookfire smoke one evening in Wyoming, I broached the Denali idea.

"We'll invite the best mountaineers we know. Use our skills on the real deal—see if we're any good against that mountain. And you should lead us."

"What route?"

"Northern, Muldrow Glacier." I jabbered the rest of the itinerary that I'd mapped out in my head. Relaying loads of supplies through the bush would take at least a week, to reach the glacier. Then, an eleven-mile, low-angle ski ascent of the glacier, while dodging deadly crevasses. After that, the steep work of traversing Karstens Ridge, followed by four miles on the Harper Glacier to Denali Pass. And then the summit attempt, about 2,000 vertical feet from the final camp. "About a month," I concluded. "It'll be ultimate."

I didn't mention that, six years earlier, a storm had killed seven Denali climbers on the route I was suggesting. Maybe Whisnant had read the book. In that case, no need to remind him.

Whisnant looked into my eyes and nodded. "Let's do it."

I tossed a log on the fire, fanned mosquitoes from my face, and told him the other part of my plan. "We should make skiing a serious part of the trip. Maybe we can ski from the summit—a first."

I explained that the National Park Service had been against using skis since two skiers lost their lives in a crevasse in 1932. But skis would distribute weight on the crevasse snowbridges, making the glacier travel safer and faster.

"You don't have to convince me skis will be useful, especially with climbing skins," Whisnant said. "But the climbing will be involved enough without trying to ski from the top."

Whisnant was wise. The compromise ski equipment of a Denali expedition—loose-fitting, flexible mountaineering boots rather than ski boots, 1950s-style cable bindings—made the somewhat steep and possibly icy ski from the summit an iffy proposition. There was no chance we'd tally nine men who could pull it off, and truth told, I might not have had the ski skills myself.

I acquiesced, knowing that not everybody on the trip would be the expert skiers I'd invite. "We'll bring skis, use them for skinning up the glaciers, toss them in a glacier crack if they're a hassle. No big skiing agenda."

A lie. Skiing from the summit of Denali was, despite my doubts about my ski skills, still the bold-faced all-caps numero uno entry on my bucket list. I said nothing more.

Kendall Williams, 1973   ©Dawson collection

I invited my Colorado-based climbing and backcountry skiing partners Tom "Cardo" Merrill, Kendall Williams, and Robert "Pimmy" Pimentel (a family friend). Kendall recruited his buddy, Nordic ski instructor Tim Lane. Whisnant conscripted climber Jim Burton, the only man in our crew with a spouse. I found that intriguing, as few climbers in their twenties were married. Then, bringing the count up to nine, Whisnant invited stout NOLS instructor Mark Caffrey—"He can carry the heaviest pack I've ever seen"—who'd bring his friend Allan Ward.

In these early days of Alaskan expeditionary climbing, there was strength in numbers. So I liked our nine-count—with one worry: the first time most of us met was a few weeks before our start date, when we gathered for final preparations at Whisnant's house in California. It was unrealistic to expect a group of individualistic mountaineers to march in perfect unison, but our common goal—the top of North America—was powerful glue. Despite minor clashes and posturing, we managed to hold it together.

Still, I couldn't help but wonder how we'd get along while sardined in a snow cave—the smells, the guy next to you snoring into your ear.

During our final prep, a top issue was how much food we'd haul. Five weeks' worth seemed to be the consensus, about seventy pounds per person—an enormous amount. When combined with thirty gallons of stove fuel and team gear such as shovels, stoves, boot repair kits (quantity two, containing epoxy, a can of waterproofing, assorted nails, and a small hammer), we were looking at two or three portages of a hundred-plus pounds each. The total load per man would diminish as we consumed food and fuel. But other than the last leg to high camp, we'd each need to relay at least two carries between camps.

WHILE SHOPPING FOR LAST-MINUTE groceries in Alaska, Whisnant met Bill, a soft-spoken local who offered us lodging. That evening the nine of us spread our sleeping bags on his concrete basement floor, like soldiers commandeering someone's home for a wartime bivouac. A four-foot-high stack of skin magazines teetered in a corner. I grabbed the one on top. The cover presented acres of puffy flesh amidst strategic charcoal-black leather. I hoped there was something more to my taste, somewhere in the stack—maybe a copy of *Climbing* magazine? Not a chance.

"The ratio of men to women in Alaska is around twenty to one," Bill explained as he watched me rooting through his library. "Those mags are as essential as snow shovels."

It took a week for our food and gear-filled shipping crate to arrive. Bill seemed a little too friendly as we lounged on his front lawn and whipped up breakfast eggs in the kitchen. I figured he was seeking rent money. That wasn't going to happen. Our expedition bank account was zeroed out, and our wallets were so anemic Ward had pawned his camera.

The next day, Bill joined us for sandwiches at his dining-room table. After a short preamble regarding Alaskan weather and moose meat, he got down to business. "I'm into Sikh chanting," he said as if sharing his preference for checkers over chess. "You repeat the '*Ek Ong Kar*' enough times, you get rich. Best as a group."

It was time to pay the rent. Once a day for the rest of our stay, we circled with Bill on the carpeted floor of his musty television room. There we wailed, moaned, and otherwise voiced the litany.

"*Ek ong kar sat nam siri wahe guru*" was the correct wording. Correct pronunciation was another matter. My version went something like: "Heck on car what bam weary jolly who-you." The other guys performed about the same. Several of us tried to harmonize. The result was somewhere north of the Beach Boys enhanced by an off-key "Jesus Christ Superstar."

During one exceedingly Gregorian session, I cheated a glance through squinted eyes.

Caffrey was the most reserved of our chanters. He'd somehow folded his tree-stump legs into a half lotus. His lips barely moved, his shoulders hunched. Ward followed along, quietly. He was the enigma of our group, the hardest to get to know. *Was he was already cynical about the climb, wondering what he'd gotten himself into?*

My Aspen-based friends, Cardo, Pimentel, and Kendall, sang like they were born to it. These fellows would do anything required for the climb.

Whisnant answered my glance with half-open eyes and a secret smile. Team collaboration boded well for the future.

THE MANTRA OF EK brought us blessings—we kept our sleeping quarters and the associated library. Along those lines, Bill was right; the northlands did produce lonesome men. So I gave him my last twenty for the toll and called the girl.

"I've been missing you," I mumbled, at the limit of my verbal skills. "I'm not sure about what I said that morning at my teepee."

"I've been thinking too," Kristina said, her words breaking through the scratchy analog phone connection. "What about making a life other than climbing? Would you marry me?"

A marriage proposal? After all the fights, after all I'd put her through? A surge of anger tightened my chest—outrage, frustration at having to choose between relationships and mountains.

"Not going to work. I'm climbing until I die," I replied.

Kristina was quiet for a long moment. "Okay, now I know how you feel. Be careful."

"Sure," I said, dropping the handset into its cradle with a fatalistic clack. At that, for me it was over.

The next morning, we hopped a bush flight to the gravel airstrip where we'd begin our trek to the mountain.

THE ROUTE DESCRIPTIONS WARNED that climbing the Muldrow Glacier required miles of low-angle slogging—and implied that boredom would never be a problem. Among glaciers used as climbing routes, the Muldrow is one of the most convoluted in the world, riven by countless crevasses—bottomless cracks, pits, and holes that are perfect traps for unwary climbers.

Crevasses vary in width from inches to yards. Yet they have one thing in common: Most are hundreds of feet deep, the equivalent of skyscraper elevator shafts. Should you fall in without the safety of a rope, you greet the hereafter—and even with a rope, the outcome is uncertain.

Our crevasse safety system relied on roped climbers functioning as human anchors. Best case: In the event of a teammate's fall, you're pulled off your feet and left lying safely on the glacier's surface, the fallen climber suspended below. Unhurt, the climber can then use various techniques to climb the rope back to the surface. But there's a good chance a crevasse-fallen climber will be injured, in need of a complex rescue. And, if you're having a really bad day, the falling climber drags you and other roped companions into the maw. Thus, while a Muldrow crevasse fall was, in theory, survivable, avoiding a plunge into the icy-dark was a top priority.

If a crack was too wide to step across, we searched for a solid snowbridge, and wove a route around the pit if a bridge wasn't available. Such lateral route deviations often added significant travel distance, so bridges were preferred. Some spans were strong enough to support a dump truck. Others were eggshell fragile, crumbling with a whoosh at the slightest vibrations of nearby feet.

Then there were the bridges that *might* break as you crossed. The first man was the tester.

The crevasse bridge to haunt my dreams was skinny as a porch step, four feet thick in the middle, impossibly arched over a twenty-foot wide crack. I led across, doddering my skis an inch at a time while probing for weakness with an inverted ski pole. Cardo and Pimmy were behind me, matching my pace, managing the rope attached to my waist.

"Keep the rope tight in case this thing breaks," I said. "I'm stopping for a minute."

While on a snowbridge, your agenda is to get off the thing, not linger like you're touring a museum.

"What are you doing?" Pimmy shouted. "Keep moving."

"Give me a minute. This thing is ultimate."

"I don't care how ultimate, get across."

Careful not to shift my skis to the side and fall off the bridge, I ignored Pimmy's nagging, stood frozen in the exact middle of the flossy span, and contemplated the underworld. Skylight lit the first twenty feet down. After that, a blue-ice dimness morphed into a pit of frozen black air. I knew there were men down there who'd died during climbs. Their constituent particles would someday reach the glacier toe, spill into the McKinley River, and flow to their final rest as silt on the floor of the Bering Sea. I willed myself serene and confronted the mountain below instead of the one above.

WE'D NOW ENDURED SEVENTEEN days as human pack animals, with no more fun than inventing bulk-food recipes and disobeying the principles of NOLS expedition behavior. Arguments flared. One blow-up raged regarding who was raiding the chocolate stash—the Mr. Goodbars were ever popular. Another heated meeting ensued after discovering too much weight had been left at a lower camp, and that we couldn't carry all of it in the single portage Whisnant's schedule dictated.

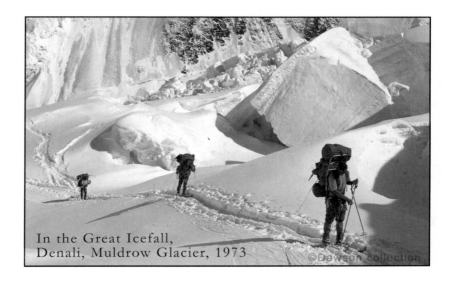

In the Great Icefall, Denali, Muldrow Glacier, 1973
©Dawson collection

"Every load I carry is more than my share, you know that," Caffrey snapped. "Someone took advantage, thinking I'd grab everything he left."

We'd all seen Caffrey lug amazing loads, including one time he stacked three thirty-pound food boxes on top of a five-gallon gas can—120 pounds-plus. The problem stopped after the meeting. Nobody wanted to tangle with Caffrey, nor be shamed as lazy.

Adding to my unvoiced frustration, I'd realized that, for me, skiing down mountains was as crucial as climbing them. Yet here we were, *on skis*, on this storied, snow-covered monolith, and the only real turns-for-fun downhill skiing I'd done was a matter of yards.

Instead, when we headed back down the glacier for another portage lap, our downhill "skiing" facsimile worked like this: The lead man glided slowly, damping his speed by snowplowing his skis in a V-wedge or making small turns in the established track (to avoid unknown crevasses). Those behind the leader let their planks run—not too fast—while reeling rope slack in their hands and releasing the slack as the leader sped up. Excellent in theory. But glacier slopes are manufactured by nature, not by ski-area grooming machines. All too often, the rope snapped taut at inopportune moments and jerked you like a hooked trout. After the resulting fall, the rope dragged its human catch in whichever random direction the conspiracy of snow and momentum dictated—likely vectored toward the maw of a crevasse.

And yet, some of us were mountain skiers as much as mountain climbers. So now and then, we grabbed a handful of real turns. On one such day, myself, Pimmy, and Cardo were hauling a portage over an exceedingly broken section of the glacier, the Hill of Cracks, when I spied a velvet-smooth expanse of snow, crack-free. Though the slope's appearance only meant that the ubiquitous crevasses lay hidden under snow-shells, in my turn-deprived state this was the smooth skin of a bedmate awaiting a back rub. I pointed out the slope to my mates: "Hey, let's make some turns after we drop our loads." Nobody objected.

Upon our return, we began skiing the heavenly pitch as glacier-safety choir boys lined up horizontally on the slope, spaced apart on the rope, with no dangerous slack between us.

Our sinless existence lasted three turns. Pimmy belted out a *whoop!* Instead of keeping his distance and managing the rope, he was arcing powder turns twenty feet to my right, the cord between us drifting on the slope above in a useless fifty-foot loop. Another whoop, this time to my left—Cardo with a beard-splitting grin pumping rhythmic arcs four yards away, the rope again slack between us.

Skiing, really skiing, the Hill of Cracks was one of the riskiest things I've ever done in the mountains. If a crevasse had taken one of us, the slack rope would have dropped the first victim fifty feet, jerked taut, and pulled the other two skiers into the abyss like a mugger stealing a necklace. Yet I have no shame. My heart still swells when I think of my two friends, how they loved to ski, and the gift of those moments.

As we approached three weeks of eyes-to-toes slogging, tensions festered, and character traits surfaced. Kendall overanalyzed everything from oatmeal to rope knots. Cardo would agree with the consensus, and then do the exact opposite—if he even agreed to anything. In some ways, Cardo reminded me of my father: bearded, passive, rolling through life—the opposite of me, the self-absorbed climbing fanatic.

"Let's send an advance party a few days ahead," I argued. "To mark the route. Then everyone else can finish the load carries."

Who should lead the advance party? Me, no question.

A round of shaking heads nixed that. There would be no shirking our task as human mules; we'd take equal turns at route setting.

Caffrey took it in without saying much—without smiling much either. Once, as I watched him lash a big load on his pack, he anger-handled the food boxes and fuel cans, pulling the straps so tight they looked to cut the baggage in half. But at least he showed his feelings. Quiet, enigmatic Ward, however, was getting on my nerves. I knew nothing of his climbing background and wondered what he'd do if things got rough.

As we leapfrogged our camps up the Muldrow, Caffrey and Ward set their tent apart from the main cluster, avoiding team meals and social interaction. During route-finding discussions, Caffrey seemed to go against things more to be a contrarian than for any logical reason. Ward passively followed his friend. I had wanted, if not expected, our nine men to function as a surrogate family. Something like the clan I'd been part of for a moment in Aspen—until my father and mother succumbed to the false promises of hippiedom. This split in our ranks was a similar mess.

I should have reached out to Caffrey and Ward. But I never thought of it—an embarrassing reveal of who I was—in contrast to the NOLS philosophy I professed to embrace: expedition behavior and kindhearted diplomacy.

Perhaps Caffrey's problem was nothing more than social burnout. Who wouldn't feel at least some angst when forced to interact with the same eight yammering nabobs day-in and day-out? Did he just want a moment, a day of peace? Ward, the same? I felt that way myself. And to make things more tense, we were running out of food.

We'd consumed fifty pounds of rations during an unplanned three-day addition to our approach march and continued burning calories like human bonfires. A typical breakfast was a four-quart pot of sweetened oatmeal shared between two guys. We went to bed with carbo-swollen bellies or risked bonking during the next day's slog.

Weeks prior, our brown cardboard ration boxes had stacked shoulder-high; now, the pile came up to my thighs.

Food cache, Denali approach, each box 30 pounds   ©Dawson collection

Whisnant called a meeting. Brushing newly fallen snow off our wax-treated ration boxes, he told us, "We barely have enough food to get us in position for a summit attempt, spend two nights, and get back. If a storm strands us, we'll starve. I wish we'd brought the radio."

Park Service rules required us to carry a two-way radio. In Anchorage, we'd learned the blasted thing would cost around a thousand dollars and weigh upwards of eight pounds. The discussion had gone one direction: "What would we use it for, to tell the Park Service who's dead?"

Cardo stared at the food cache and did the math in his head. "We can go half rations. A pound of food a day per man, instead of two."

Caffrey frowned. He could not help being the calorie-consuming hulk of our team. Cardo's idea must have sounded ridiculous to him. It did to me—even though my bird-like physique was as calorie-efficient as a man can get. Over the past weeks, I'd punched three new holes to shorten my leather belt.

I remembered Petzoldt's teachings—calories were as crucial to his philosophy as boots and backpacks: *Half-rations could pull us down the rat hole of lethargy and denial.* Pushing Petzold's wisdom aside, I kicked at the new snow. "Keep going. We'll do Karstens Ridge and make a camp at Denali Pass. Climb on half-rations to make it work."

"Let's see how long it takes to do Karstens Ridge," Whisnant countered. "Maybe we'll quit after that."

19 | THEN CAME THE WIND, 1973

DENALI HAS TWO ICY summits, about two miles apart: the North, 19,470 feet, and the main, 20,310 feet. Located between the summits is 18,200-foot Denali Pass and the beginnings of the Harper Glacier. Although small compared to Alaskan mega-glaciers, at around a mile wide and four miles long, the Harper plays an important role. Rather than terminating at a melt-toe and feeding a waterway (as do many, if not most, glaciers), the Harper ends where it cracks to pieces—some the size of small towns—and dumps over the Harper Icefall, a quarter-mile-wide, 2,500-foot precipice of broken blue ice and vertical stone at the head of a mile-wide gorge, where lays the Muldrow Glacier. The Icefall's constant avalanches nourish the Muldrow into existence—and form an impassable barrier for climbers.

The climbing route bypasses the Harper Icefall by following several miles of Karstens Ridge, a skinny arete to climbers' left of the Harper. Because of wind, snowfall totals—even earthquakes—there is no standard way to gain Karstens from the Muldrow. Each expedition picks its best estimation of a route based on length, angle, and the amount of rock-hard blue ice rather than easily climbed snow.

Cardo, Pimmy, and I took one of the recon days. As we skinned nearer to the Harper Icefall, hundreds of automobile-sized ice boulders studded the glacier surface around us, like hoodoo rocks jutting from desert sand. We agreed that most of these had fallen from the Harper and then been transported downstream by the conveyor glacier, giving the illusion we were in a hazard zone. Even so, we suspected that larger icefall avalanches could reach our position. Such would be certain demise.

We spotted a snow-covered, reasonably angled route up to Karstens—day's work done. Yet for some unvoiced reason, probably the primal desire to explore, we continued up the Muldrow, closer to the icefall—moths to a flame. We stopped for a talk and snack. The still air was just below freezing, spooky warm for 11,400 feet, even in May. As we shared trail mix and dried fruit, the noise of ice calving off the Harper echoed from the gorge walls. Most of the sounds were no more ominous than a dump truck dropping gravel. But every so often came thundering reports, like dynamite blasts on a highway project.

"This place is freaky," I mumbled behind the bandanna tied over my sunburned lips. "Be ready to run."

Pimmy leaned on his ski poles as if gathering a beginner ski class. "It doesn't go big very often, maybe every couple of hours. And we're not that close. Besides, you know you can't outrun an avalanche."

"Yeah, but which minute of which hour?" I said.

"This might be over with," Cardo muttered. "We don't have enough food. We could turn the expedition now. Bag this whole thing."

Between us, uneasy silence floated in the cloying air.

I shuffled my skis and remembered the past weeks when sheer willpower had moved our crushing loads overland to the Muldrow—when the distant hulk of Denali had pulled us through our pain as a nirvanic beacon. Even two days ago, I'd as soon have chopped my left leg off as mention the word "retreat." Now, I wasn't so sure. I'd come here to find the essence of mountaineering and make a clean break from dysfunctional romance and the mess of my family: my lost father, my stressed-out mother, and Keith. Now Denali seemed just as freaky.

THE NEXT DAY, OUR food problem was solved.

"Lane and I found a food dump," Kendall gushed as they skied into camp after a Muldrow portage. "A Japanese team must've abandoned it. We found rice, noodles, and pills in blister cards. I took some. Feeling pretty good."

Within the hour, we gathered our shovels, tied into our ropes, and Kendall guided us to the "Japanese cache." Clued by the sun-rotted nylon fabric and paper scraps protruding from the glacier, we dug like Alaskan gold miners. The ramen and salty dried seaweed cooked up fine. And thanking Kendall for his test run, we gobbled the mysterious red and yellow pills, figuring they must be vitamins—why else would climbers have packed them?

With our food supply expanded by about a week, we'd left the Muldrow Glacier, leapfrogged through two camps on Karstens Ridge, and constructed a snow camp at 17,500 feet on the Harper Glacier. We were now perched on Denali's upper flank, well above the highest altitude any of us had experienced during other climbs. That afternoon, we watched a cauliflower thunderstorm boil beyond the Alaska Range foothills—we were at eye level with the top of the clouds because of our elevation and the earth's curvature.

Later, when the sun lowered, millions of reflections winked from the gray-brown tundra sprawling to the far horizon—lakes and ponds of varying sizes and shapes. The effect was that of a planet-sized, mirror-studded disco ball. It was the most extraordinary landscape I had ever seen.

John Whisnant,
Karstens Ridge,
Denali, 1973

©Dawson collection

Our position was good for memories and photos, but it also exposed us to the full brunt of the weather. As we languished in camp during our second day on the upper Harper, smearing waxy Sno-Seal waterproofing on our boots, mare's tail cirrus clouds drifted overhead like folded curtains.

I pointed at the sky. "You know what those mean. Storm coming. I can feel the pressure behind my eyes."

"Those clouds look like what you see in the Wind Rivers before a blow," Whisnant said. "We're near where those seven guys died in that 1967 storm. They found one guy frozen, sitting where his tent was before the wind nuked it—still holding a tentpole! We'd better build our wind walls higher."

We got to work, shoveling and sawing blocks of windpack from the glacier, stacking them atop the waist-high wall already encircling our clustered tents. We quit when the wall reached our shoulders. Enough? Our tents were better than those of the 1967 unfortunates. How much better, we didn't know.

Two hours later, the first wind of the storm hit. It wasn't much, a gentle thirty-miles-per-hour gust that barely cooled our cheeks. But we knew danger rode the wind, and we crawled into our tents like so many frightened cattle. Sure enough, soon came the wolf.

Our snow walls helped, but a ninety-mile-per-hour wind that can fork around the summit of Denali has little trouble curling over a five-foot-high fence. The worst blasts announced their arrival with a building, demonic roar. With seconds to spare, we knelt with our sleeping bags cinched around our waists, grabbed the aluminum tent poles to prevent them from folding like milkshake straws, and fought for our lives.

Maybe it was the fear of being blown to Anchorage, but for whatever reason, I came down with a stomach bug during the storm. Our tents had storm doors in one end, simply a drawstring-closed nylon sphincter tube the size of a man. When the gale slowed from tornado velocity, I'd poke my head out the tube, tighten the drawstring around my neck, and spew into the wind. During one such session, Kendall was outside on his hands and knees, fully face-masked and goggled, re-tying a tent guyline. "You looked like a sick drunk hanging his head out a car window," he told me later. "Luckily, the wind wasn't blowing in my direction."

Thirty hours after the storm began, the clouds scuttled out, and the wind quit like someone had switched off a fan. Still whacked, I lay in our tent and soaked in the music of an expedition: clanking cookware, laughs, snapping ski bindings. I forced myself to dress and lurched out the tent door. "Pimmy, let me tie in with you guys and ski a few steps. See how I feel."

"Sure, Lou, good to check if you're better. You had us worried."

I scrubbed my face with snow, took several deep breaths, clipped the rope to my harness, clicked into my skis, and waddled a few steps. At stride number three, my back straightened, my breathing slowed, and my skis became part of my feet. Denali, the regal snow dome perched above the Harper, had reached inside me and twisted my spirit like a sponge. At least for the moment, I was as fresh and fit as the day we'd started.

ALASKA IS KNOWN FOR its inhospitable terrain, but Denali Pass takes the prize. The nearest tree is fifteen miles and 14,000 vertical feet away. The thin air provides half the oxygen of sea level and can kill you in various unpleasant ways. Rescue in 1973 was borderline impossible. And topping all, the pass's topography squeezes and speeds up the wind. Airflow a few thousand feet below might clock sixty miles per hour; funneled between the south and north summits of Denali, that same breeze can exceed a hundred.

During our expedition planning, we'd decided to camp on the pass instead of lower down on the Harper Glacier. We figured this was a better position for a summit attempt, and we liked the idea of being off the glacier, away from the ever-present crevasses.

Yet tenting here was insanity. In the winds of Denali Pass, the best tent could soon become a kite with human passengers—assuming it did not disintegrate first. Snow caves were our sole option. Good theory. Another matter in practice.

As we excavated, the soft snowpack soon gave way to punky, air-filled ice we chipped with our ice axes, handful by handful. Every so often, we chopped through fist-width tubes the wind had bored within the icepack. Our gasoline stoves needed a modicum of ventilation, but the excessive airflow from these tubes was a concern. Most snow caves are relatively warm, hovering just under thirty-two degrees (snow is an excellent insulator). Instead, our huddle would be a crawl-in freezer.

Caffrey and Ward camped in one cave while the remaining seven of us lodged in another. Ours was far from palatial, yet adequate: nine feet in diameter and high enough to stand in with my head bent forward, with a crawlway entrance.

I spread my sleeping bag on an ice shelf resembling the built-in bunk of a concrete prison cell. My six companions crashed on the floor in a tangle of clothing and sleeping bags.

As payment for my perch, I nursed the cookstove: melting snow, making pasta, and serving tea. To escape the stove exhaust, I periodically pressed my face into a wind tube next to my perch, taking deep lungfuls of pure, chilled air pushed in by the Denali winds. When the wind calmed, the cavern warmed and filled with carbon monoxide, cooking steam, and the miasma of unshowered men.

Our first morning in the cave, I crawled outside to empty my pee bottle. A light wind pushed small gossamer clouds through the inky-blue sky. *Summit weather?*

Back inside, I kneeled next to the man-pile. "Guys, the weather is ultimate. We can climb today, get it done, and get out of here."

Whisnant rolled toward me and pulled his balaclava up off his altitude-puffy face. "We need a rest day. Everybody's fried after digging the caves. And more acclimation is smart."

"Yeah, I guess," I said, climbing back to my ice pallet, now melted and refrozen slick like a skating rink. I didn't have the energy for debate, and Whisnant was probably right.

THE NEXT MORNING, AFTER cave night two, the mountain was cloaked in warm, chunky fog—if you call ten degrees warm. No shadows. A light breeze had smoothed the snow over the previous day's footprints. We were in the "egg," a whiteout. Yet the day was climbable, and we knew the route to be no more difficult than a crampon-booted walk (as agreed, we'd leave our skis). The weather was the danger. If a storm hit, all bets were off. Nobody mentioned the radio we'd refused; a weather forecast would have been helpful.

Twenty minutes into the slog, I retched a slug of acidic fluid. It spattered pale brown on the snow in front of my boots. After that, I felt better.

CLOUDS AND SPITTING SNOW muffled the summit. There were no views. Still, I sensed the beyond—the subtle thinning of the air, the void falling away, my eyes six feet above the biggest mountain in the world. I shook a few nearby hands.

Kendall kicked a boot into the soft snow. "We could have been the first to ski this thing. It would be easy."

I agreed. The cold had penetrated my parka and three underlayers. Puke still stung halfway up my throat. A quick ski down had all sorts of appeal. Not to be.

Jim Burton removed his mittens, tugged the gold band off his ring finger, and hurled it into Denali's miles-deep southern abyss. His decision: toss the struggling marriage. I took this as a somber moment, a time to remember how marriages fail, how my parents had failed.

In two hours, we were inside our snow caverns, joking and laughing over steaming mugs of cocoa. After a night's sleep, we'd shoot down the Harper and Muldrow glaciers like we were leaping over moguls and dodging tourists on Aspen Mountain.

ICE CAVE, DAY THREE—SUMMIT yesterday. For some unknown reason, our cave interior was colder than ever, around ten degrees, forcing us to keep our sleeping bags pulled to our shoulders or necks. Pimentel crawled out to take a crap. Ten minutes later, he returned, voicing guttural moans that sounded like "help me." His hands were cold-clawed, his pants and underwear down around his knees, packed with snow from the wind of a full-bore storm. The monster had returned. Could we wait it out?

Ice cave, day four. I cracked open my copy of *War and Peace*, picked for its expeditionary length, 1,300 pages. The printed words might as well have been Sanskrit. Carbon monoxide or altitude? Most likely both. Great literature was supposed to save you, not measure your demise.

I fed the snowmelt pot with ice I chopped from the cave wall. Thirty-below-zero air moaned from the wind tubes, sometimes accompanied by a puff of spindrift. Chores completed, I zipped my sleeping bag around my neck, stared at the black-sooted ceiling three feet above my head, and thought of my mother's homemade bread.

Such mental wanderings led to nowhere but a sadness deeper than the pit where Burton had discarded his golden promise. *Climbing 'till I died* was getting a little too real.

ICE CAVE, DAY SIX. Emptying our pee bottles and bowels were the only motivators. To avoid frostbite or worse we scraped our cat holes inside the cave's access tunnel, now grown to fifteen feet long through the drifted snow. While digging, I turned up frozen turds.

I recalled one of Petzoldt's oft-repeated fables: "By day four, urinating in their sleeping bags. By day five, dead."

When I placed both hands around a thigh, my thumbs and index fingers connected. Atrophy.

Ice cave, day eight. Morning. Whisnant sat up, clutching his sleeping bag under his arms and over his chest. His black wool balaclava was pulled down, his mouth and eyes showing through their respective openings, a terrified, furry-faced animal. "How much food do we have?" he said. "Fuel?"

"I checked our stash yesterday," Burton said. "There's enough for a day, maybe stretch it to two. After that, we'll just lay here and go to sleep."

Tim Lane groaned like someone was pulling out his fingernails. He'd become the skinniest of our lot and the most affected by the altitude. Our other one-syllable responses were just as expressive.

Whisnant unzipped his sleeping bag and kneeled. His hat brushed the cave's ceiling; it had sagged under the weight of new snow. "We need to leave. My journal says we've been on this mountain for thirty-seven damned days. We might die trying to get down the Harper. But we have to go."

"There's a little less wind," Kendall said. "It might be doable."

The vote was unanimous. Cardo crawled outside and ducked into Caffrey and Ward's cave, asking if they were game. They were more than ready.

After an hour of frantic packing, we crawled from the cave's entrance tunnel, faces concealed behind facemasks and goggles, and fought to stand upright in the gale. Kendall, our designated navigator, glanced at his compass and wordlessly stepped onto the Harper Glacier. We all knew the stakes: If we messed up the compass work, if our sense of direction failed, we'd wander like mindless zombies, and unlike them, we'd die.

It was late morning. The whiteout swirled, a mix of clouds and blowing snow. At its worst, it was like someone had wrapped a white, translucent bed sheet around our heads. The storm had collected the new snow into drifts that ranged from knee-high to chest-high. Tied to our ropes in fifty-foot intervals, we'd ski or walk a few feet of easy, windpacked snow, then run up against a fence-like heap. Kendall would stomp his way through, leaving a narrow, soft trench that barely helped those coming behind. At one point, I glanced back to find Whisnant, his skis strapped on his backpack, sunk up to his stomach, paddling the snow like a dog in a swimming pool.

Hours later, we were still searching for the handful of marker wands we'd placed on the route before the storm. Kendall stopped often, head down, compass in hand. It was too cold and windy to use a map. He was going by memory. I felt like we were wandering but said nothing.

Sometimes fortune favors courage—and astute use of the compass. Four hours down from Denali Pass, a patch of deep-blue sky ripped open above us. A hundred yards ahead, a solitary marker wand protruded six inches from a mound of snow. From there, it was just a matter of additional compass work and spotting a few more surviving wands to find our stashed tents, food, and the descent route. I couldn't believe our luck.

After a night and part of the next day in our tents, our dwindling food supply dictated reality. We'd march until we either collapsed from exhaustion or made it down Karstens Ridge to the Muldrow. So, under the low-hanging sun of late afternoon, we loaded everything from the stash into our packs and continued.

When the evening cold snap hit, around thirty below, we were still at altitude on the Harper, about 15,000 feet. As we descended, Lane began staggering, talking nonsense. Kendall deciphered his altitude-fuzzed ramblings to mean his feet were numb—the first stage of crippling frostbite. There was only one solution. As the rest of us continued ahead, the pair sat in the snow for an hour without shelter, Lane's bare feet pressed against the skin in Kendall's armpits.

We regrouped at Browne Tower, a rocky area demarcating the transition from the Harper to Karstens. Below, we expected to find a wind-stripped Karstens Ridge, easily downclimbed. Instead, the storm had deposited a swale of fresh snow, about six feet deep, just several feet wide in places. To our right, 4,000 feet of air dropped to a glacier for which I had no name. To our left was the Harper Icefall. And once we were farther down the ridge, steep slopes of ice and snow dropped to the Muldrow—one of these was our descent route—perhaps marked with a few pieces of equipment we'd left two weeks earlier. It was Capitol Peak's Knife Ridge writ large.

Skiing the ridge crest was not even a thought. Instead, the lead man held his lashed-together skis and poles crosswise on the snow in front, using them for support as he stomped out a waist-deep trench. The rest of us followed, knowing this was the crux of the entire climb, knowing one misstep would be the end. Three hours and two hellish miles later, we descended a snow-loaded avalanche slope to the Muldrow, set camp, and collapsed. We'd been moving for ten hours.

Tim Lane,
Denali, 1973
©Dawson collection

THE NEXT DAY, SEVERAL of us were sitting on snow blocks in front of Whisnant and Burton's tent. Caffrey came over and told us that Ward, who was in their tent, was convinced an avalanche would soon wipe all nine of us off the face of the glacier. "Unless we move camp right now," Caffrey said, "the two of us will pack up and leave."

I wasn't clear on the dynamic between the two friends, who was the leader, and who followed. Whatever the case, Caffrey was asking us to split the expedition, to violate a foundational safety precept.

Whisnant launched into a lengthy discussion, which devolved into pleading for the pair not to leave. When this had no effect, he wrote up a separation agreement, figuring it would communicate the gravity of splitting the expedition, and thus keep us together. Instead, Caffrey and Ward signed the agreement, packed their gear, and set off down the Muldrow Glacier.

I couldn't believe it. Admittedly, the crevasses were easier to identify and skirt after a month of springtime had melted or at least shrunk the snowpack overlaying the ice. But you still stood a good chance of falling into a crack on a glacier such as the Muldrow. And with just two guys on a rope, self-rescue was a world more difficult, often improbable.

Later, I surmised that Ward might have been mentally off-kilter. But I was never convinced. Was he nothing more than grumpy? To identify the mountain's scariest hazard, maybe he needed a mirror. Maybe that was all any of us needed. Were Caffrey and Ward the sane ones? Perhaps I was the lunatic for wanting to tackle this frozen hell.

DAY FORTY. WE ATE the last of our food when we reached the lower Muldrow Glacier. Six hours later, with near zero body fat as a reserve, I'd already gone ketogenic. The hallucinated rainbows and lawn sprinklers were as real as my hand in front of my face.

Pimmy broke out a fingernail-size vial of cocaine. "Bolivian tin miners use this for hunger. They mine like crazy."

A few sniffs, and I was marching down the glacier like a sprinter off the starting blocks. My jog lasted ten glorious minutes, until the last microgram of glycogen was vacuumed from my liver like sawdust under a shop vac.

Somehow we kept moving, down the ice, over McGonagall Pass, and then the twenty-mile reverse slog through the muskeg mounds and willows of our overland approach.

While wading the McKinley River, the flow knocked Cardo on his ass and pushed him downstream in a sitting position, water up to his chest, inches from drowning. Too weak to stand up under the weight of his backpack, he voiced pitiful, incoherent bleats, looking at Pimmy and me to save him. Yet we were weak as toddlers, unable to do anything but watch. As he drifted, he pressed his hands against the river bed and hopped his butt sideways until he could crawl to shore. Tough guy.

River crossed, we paused and looked south at the shining mountain. My feet throbbed from the near-freezing glacial water. I was faint with hunger. Mosquitoes swarmed like a living blizzard. Pimmy slapped a thousand of the bloodsuckers at once on his thigh, raised his headnet, and licked them from the palm of his hand. I laughed with the rolling river, laughed with Pimmy and Cardo—and then wobbled through the last two miles of wetland and spruce forest.

At Wonder Lake, a tourist family anointed us with a sack of Oreo cookies.

"Yeah, we climbed it."

As for Caffrey and Ward, the Park rangers said they'd checked in and survived. I never saw them again. And neither did any of our other expedition members.

FOR MANY YEARS AFTER returning from Denali, I lived my focus: cliffs of stone, snow-swathed mountains. Romantic relationships were secondary, if that. Consequently, I learned how to move over ice and rock as few people could. In this I found transcendence of a sort: creative athleticism. And yet, was I doomed to repeat the same adrenal mania over and over, like a looping movie? Denali was alive. Was I?

BOOK III
VERTICAL YEARS

Author on Independence Pass, 1974

©Michael Kennedy

20 | MONSTER TOWER, 1973

AT FORTY-ONE, HARVEY CARTER'S body was anything but youthful. A lifetime of strenuous climbing and manual labor had scoured the cartilage from his joints and clogged his fingers with arthritic tissue until they resembled sausages. Moreover, a decade of ski patrolling had taken its toll: avalanche mitigation, guiding rescue sleds down the gnarled gullies and horse-sized moguls of Aspen's signature ski hill. When the jump off "Harvey's Rock" didn't end well, his spinal disks screamed, "enough!"

To ease the pain, the Little Nell bar was thirty yards from the ski lift base, down a flight of worn-gray concrete steps.

While Harvey's motivations in befriending younger Aspen climbers were much about congeniality and mentorship, his was an obvious agenda: enlist a cadre of "rope guns" he could deploy on climbs to compensate for his physical decline. Thus adding more lines to his list of first ascents, plastered over desert climbing like a twenty-page executive résumé.

In summer 1973, Michael Kennedy and I climbed Curving Vine, a two-day ascent on the sheer Diamond face of Colorado's 14,259-foot Longs Peak. Harvey noticed—his protégés were ready for the big time.

"Get a week off work. Bring all your ropes," the master growled. "A climb in the Fisher Towers. I can't tell you the exact plan until we get there ... Jerks might steal the first ascent."

Michael and I had seen, but never climbed, the fantastical, jumbled turrets of the Fisher Towers near the Colorado River east of Moab, Utah. The dramatic group of formations—said to be the largest such array in the western deserts of the United States—brought an M. C. Escher drawing to mind. Eroded flutes decorated most vertical surfaces, like a mad architect's castle ramparts. The coloration changed with the sun: midday ocher pastels, fluorescent oxide-reds at sunset. One tower, Ancient Art, zig-zagged upward in hinky angles as if supported by magic. And the king, the blade-capped Titan—at 900 feet, it was the tallest free-standing, natural rock tower in the United States.

It all came at a price.

When mesmerized would-be ascensionists quit their gaping and placed a hand to the Fishers, they were as likely to find a thick layer of desiccated mud as to touch the Cutler sandstone beneath. Cone bugs that feasted on bat blood and that of any other available mammals infested the Fishers' cracks and bivouac ledges. You needed ski goggles to prevent temporary blindness from wind-borne sand. The temperature could push 100 degrees, then drop to near freezing at night. Climbers vowed never to return. Yet they did.

THIS TRIP'S ROPE GUNS were my Denali companions, Kendall Williams and Cardo Merrill, along with Kennedy and tree-trunk-legged, tousle-haired Aspen skier Michael "Pokie" Pokress.

Over the years, Harvey had organized many such expeditionary forces. He was credited (along with his enlistees) with a dozen first ascents on various towers of the Fishers—including Sundevil Chimney, by far the hardest of the Titan's two routes. Cardo had been fodder on that appropriately named gem. He'd told me they'd worked in daily shifts. Each climber gave their all for ten hours of grit, grime, and grunt, gained a rope length of 150 feet, then drove to Moab for rehydration on 3.2-percent Utah beer before rejoining the fray. Or, they drove back to Aspen and stood in the shower until the hot water ran out. The route thus progressed, albeit as a battle of attrition.

As expected, Harvey kept his war plan secret until we reached the rutted desert sand of the Fisher Towers parking lot, far from telephones and bar stools. But his plan was obvious. As the five of us climbed from his van, our heads craned upward like begging dogs. Just a mile away, the Titan Tower stood against the sky like a Manhattan skyscraper, its west face glowing the color of clotted blood in the afternoon sun. I tried to grok a route through the blank sections, overhangs, and curtains of dried mud. I got nothing. It seemed the wall loomed from an alternate universe, a place where the sport of climbing was yet to be invented.

The Titan, Utah, Sun Devil Chimney, west face in shadow to left

©Dawson collection

Harvey's gruff voice broke the stark desert silence.

"Used to call it Monster Tower. Still is. And that face is the biggest line, probably the hardest. I've got a route figured out. It's about 900 feet. There's a few ledges for sleeping, but the face is vertical, so for every ledge, there's an overhang. Pack for at least three nights on the wall. We'll fix ropes on the entire route, so we can easily move up and down—if it takes longer than three days."

We spent the afternoon sorting gear, filling water jugs, and shlepping huge packs through the red-rock arroyos of the two-mile approach hike. That night, we slept rough beneath the route's first pitch: a shoulder-width chimney lined with dried mud that powdered off at the touch.

Morning, Harvey instigated the sufferfest. As he hacked bucket-sized holds into the mud chimney's walls, a cone of sandy dross grew knee-high on the ground below. The rope curved upward from Pokie's belay to Harvey's waist, unfettered by protective anchors. Should he come off, he'd take a forty-foot-plus screamer into his dirt pile. *Soft enough to survive? We might find out.*

But the Harvoid clung like a spider, flailing his hammer against the desiccated mud, throwing so many F-bombs my water bottle boiled. We had our lunches out by the time he exited the chimney to a weedy ledge the size of a small bedroom. After establishing anchors, Harvey threw down a rope that we climbed with mechanical rope grippers known as Jumar Ascenders, or jumars for short. Such would be our process for the rest of the climb; the leader progressed the route, and everyone else followed by jumaring the anchored fixed rope.

Cardo took the next pitch, then Harvey put me on the lead. I draped my torso in blue and orange gear slings, strapped on my piton hammer, and set to it.

Par for the Fishers, fist-thick dried sludge covered most of the rock. I swung my hammer like a pickaxe, carving craters through the dirt where I guessed there might be a crack, and if not a crack, solid enough rock for hammer-drilling a hole and installing an expansion bolt (a construction fastener used for concrete or stone). Climbing ethics held that fewer bolts equaled a better, more notable climb, yet first-ascensionists used them when necessary.

Manual hammer drilling, in the context of desert sandstone, involves pressing a drill bit against the rock and slowly rotating it while slamming it with a hammer. While doing so, you stand in nylon foot slings supported by your previous gear placement. You reach as high as possible and hammer until your arms give out and drop to your sides. After a rest, you hammer again and again while fragmented mud and stone dust rain through your shirt collar and lodge under your climbing harness, where they scour your skin like sandpaper.

Soon, I'd had enough.

To avoid more drilling and impress my mentor, I pounded a knotted sling into a muddy crack and hung from it.

"What the hell?!" Harvey bellowed. "You just trashed my sling!"

I pounded in a few pitons. Thirty feet higher, I drilled three bolt holes in a row.

"That's the way to go," Harvey shouted. "Don't mess around. Just hammer that drill!"

A fingernail-width seam split an otherwise blank section. Could this silence Harvey's nagging? I had a special piton on my gear sling: a rurp, a flat piece of steel the size of two postage stamps, strung through two holes with a loop of shoelace-diameter cord. The name riffed on the tongue-in-cheek acronym for Realized Ultimate Reality Piton. I doubted Harvey had ever used a rurp.

Two hammer blows sunk the rurp to the hilt. I shifted my weight. It popped out, bopped me on the forehead, and I was airborne. With stretch and slack, the rope caught me fifteen feet lower, where I hung free from the rock like a Christmas tree ornament.

"What the heck are you trying to use that dumb thing for?" Harvey barked.

Was this really climbing? Yosemite was looking like heaven, maybe a woman back in camp, the scent of California bay trees, my long blond hair flowing in the wind rather than matted into sweat-and sand-glued dreadlocks.

Assorted acrobatics got me back on the climb. I pounded a four-inch piton into the rurp seam. It sank as easily as the tent stakes I'd driven during family camping trips back in Texas. Five hours later, I pulled onto a ledge and fried the last of my arm strength drilling oversized holes for a pair of three-inch-long belay bolts.

Kennedy took the next pitch. The rock ahead was a weird bile-green, bluish color, punky. Crystalline salts crusted the surface and dusted off when brushed by a rope or foot. A chemical tang lingered after I rubbed my tongue against my front teeth.

During a previous desert trip, Moab Rock Shop proprietor-prospector Lin Ottinger had offered to loan me a Geiger counter.

"You might find something on the cliffs," said the weather-wrinkled rock hound as he held out a chunk of dusty blue-green stone, spit on it, and rubbed his thumb over it like he was polishing a watch crystal. "Uranium ore is this weird-colored stuff. We could partner up, make some money."

Thinking about Ottinger's words, I wondered if Kennedy was shortening his lifespan each time he blew powdered chemicals out of a bolt hole and into his face. Maybe we should have packed the radiation tester.

WE PASSED THAT NIGHT on a ledge about 400 feet up the wall, and rallied as the rising sun ignited the Ecclesiastical towers seven miles to our west. Unlike the Fishers, the Ecclesiasticals were known for pleasant climbing on their clean, maroon-colored Wingate Sandstone. No mud. I wished I were there.

Harvey claimed the next lead. As he draped gear slings over his shoulders, his appearance struck me. He was the archetypical desert-rat climber; his ruddy facial skin and ratty, stained clothing blended perfectly with the desert's rust-colored oxide soil and multi-hued rocks. His tools, too: the nylon waist harness abraded to a fuzzy dirt-and-sweat-infused strap, like an ancient saddle cinch; the piton hammer, its head worn to a prune-sized nub. There was something mystical, as if this man were the climbing equivalent of Carlos Castaneda's desert shaman, Don Juan Matus. I half expected Harvey to turn toward me, widen his eyes, and say, "Does this way have heart?"

The band of pebble-studded conglomerate rock above—no mud—appeared crackless, blank, with no piton placements. Yet this was Harvey, the climber with a sixth sense for desert stone. He skimmed his battered hands over the rock like he was reading braille, finding fingernail-width cracks next to the stones and pebbles embedded in the sandstone. He'd insert the tip of a piton in these imperfections, then tap it with his hammer—*ting ting ting*. Sometimes the piton fell out. But when the steel found a way, he wailed on it like a blacksmith, sinking the spike until the head and eye mashed into the rock like a wad of Play-Doh.

As the sandstone shaman pounded away, a constant rain of effluent poured on our heads. Cardo, with his previous experience, had come prepared. He sported a black-felt chapeau—once a cowboy hat—the brim now slouched over his ears, the crown peaked like a Halloween costume witch's hat, ideal headwear for a rain of either the liquid or sand variety. Me? I was hatless and resorted to combing my fingers through my neck-length hair, trying with little success to rake out the grit.

Harvey was not a speedy climber, but his pace on this pitch dropped below my most pessimistic standard. About every fifteen minutes, his rope moved upward in a spurt of mere inches, punctuated by strangled calls for tension and annoyed requests for slack. At this pace, attentive belaying wasn't necessary. Instead, we girth-hitched the rope to an anchor within arm's reach.

When Harvey called for slack, we released the knot under a rain of slurs. When a shout for tension echoed, we pulled on a hanging loop of rope like an eighteen-wheeler tooting his air horn—all the while keeping eyes on our reading material. My chosen book was Lobsang Rampa's *The Third Eye*. I liked the part depicting the insertion of a wood splinter into the protagonist's forehead, to invoke clairvoyance.

THE BIVOUAC LEDGE SERVED for two nights. It was similar in size to a standard-width, twenty-foot-long hallway—comfortable for sleeping, if not sublime. Soon after nightfall, the moon slid behind the Ecclesiasticals in a composition of natural perfection: the Priest Tower, with his hooded head tilted to the Nun Tower in front of him; Convent Mesa to the right, 3,000 feet long, silhouetted like a battleship running dark. Bats swooped, often inches from our faces, harvesting insects lured by our stink. A gentle breeze dried our sweat-soaked T-shirts. We slept as if floating on a calm sea, our only annoyance the fetor wafting from our privy at the far end of the ledge.

As I'd realized while Harvey bulled his way up the climb's first pitch, this was nothing like what I'd pictured as the climbing life. Yet I loved the work, loved the intellectual struggle—route-finding, gear. The danger, too, was intoxicating. Sleeping next to a shit hole, however, I could do without.

As Kendall tackled the next day's leading, Harvey insisted we needed "more supplies" and left for Moab. He showed up the following morning at the base of the wall without a backpack. "We need to quit the climb for now," he yelled from the ground. "Leave fixed ropes to our highpoint. Gotta go back to Aspen, do some business."

We'd pushed the route to within a few hundred feet of the summit. But the man had spoken.

HARVEY AND I RETURNED three days later. The others had bagged out of sandstone nirvana with such excuses as the newly popular, "Have to work."

We jummared our fixed lines, then spent the day on what became the best pitches of the route: speedy free-climbing up cracks with hardly a hint of dirt. The day waned. We slid down our ropes to our camp ledge.

Morning. Clean cracks behind us, dried-mud time again. To start, I stood on Harvey's shoulders and drove my longest piton into the mud clogging the back of a wide crack. Sand dribbled from the shaft as I applied body weight. While trying not to lean back and yank out the piton, I stepped high in the sling, hacked a deep pocket in a futile attempt to find actual rock, and then drove another stake. Each placement held my weight. None were strong enough to hold a fall. I could hardly believe it: *after devoting myself to the clean granite of Yosemite, I was climbing vertical dirt?*

After just two 150-foot pitches, darkness was coming fast. Thinking the summit to be a day's climbing away, we had left our overnight gear and food on the bivouac ledge below. Because of the complexity and sideways-leaning geometry of the day's pitches, rappelling to the ledge would be impossible without headlamps.

"We'll bivvy without gear," Harvey said as he grunted and cursed his way through rigging a half-hanging, half-standing stance fifteen feet above me. "Desert tradition."

I stood in a three-foot-diameter, sand-floored alcove, dressed in all the clothing I had: a T-shirt and threadbare cotton pants. Harvey tossed me half a smashed Snickers bar. The temperature dropped into the forties. A stiff wind kicked up. I began shivering. With the body fat of a carrot, roped to a cliff, unable to move more than a few feet, hypothermia could suck out my life in two hours. Under the last light of dusk, I found myself again using my stubby piton hammer as a pickaxe, this time while attempting to bury myself in the still-warm sand on the floor of my bedchamber. I quit when I excavated a wriggling green centipede the length of my index finger. *Desert tradition?*

The shivering worsened. *The rope, thick and dry—insulation?* With nothing to lose, I wrapped my legs in tightly nested coils, then my torso, and finally my arms and head.

First light. I'd survived the night in my nylon-and-sand sarcophagus, bandaged like Nefertiti awaiting the afterlife.

The remaining climb took two hours via clean cracks in the Moenkopi sandstone caprock. When we shook hands on top, the shivery night still showed in Harvey's tight jaw and watery eyes. I wasn't hooting for joy either, having slept all of ten minutes.

Yeah, it's the highest tower around. Okay, let's go home.

On the last of our twelve descent rappels, I leaned back in my tangled nylon slings and closed my sand-scratched eyes. I was hungry. The night chill still clung to my skin. The insect bites on my calves itched like I'd slept in a doghouse. The grit-flayed skin under my waist harness smoldered like a third-degree sunburn. My formerly white pants were stained a blotchy oxide red. I breathed my stench. And yet, a delayed summit euphoria welled through my stinky, beat-up body. Inspired by the master, I'd gone all out on a first ascent of a major climb.

I wanted more.

21 | THE WORD IS WHEN, 1974

HARDLY A SUMMER WEEK passed when I didn't climb with Michael Kennedy. And if we weren't climbing, we were talking about it—all while our crew enjoyed the resort-town life: parties at every turn, and for the singles (most of us), available, athletic women who could double as fashion models—some did.

Yet beyond the cliffs of sun and the girls of summer, a separate reality loomed: ice climbs and winter ascents of 14,000-foot peaks. *Alpinism.* The word sounded like a religion. Maybe it was.

And the religion had its saints, the hardcore climbers depicted in the climbing literature we devoured like teenage boys passing around a centerfold: magazines and gear catalogs illustrated with photos of icicle-bearded men—mittened paws death-gripping their tools of ascent, mouths frozen in the half-grin-half-grimace of victory. By their words and images, we knew these icons had kissed the sky.

So, as the winters came, Michael and I fashioned ourselves after our heroes. As we cooked up ideas for things cold and perilous, the only question was, "When?"

IN EARLY DECEMBER 1973, we were scarfing late-morning blueberry pancakes at The Village Pantry, my favorite Aspen breakfast place. Late, because starting at six a.m., in the dim light of a yet-risen sun, we had climbed the Grotto Wall Traverse, a four-pitch rock route on the Independence Pass crags a short drive from town. In summer, we scampered up the Traverse just to feel the flow, hardly needing ropes. Not today.

When we'd parked at the Grotto Wall this morning, the temperature was five below zero. Instead of cutoff jeans and dainty, smooth-soled climbing shoes, we'd sported our full winter kit: winter-thick waffle-soled boots, layered jackets, and gloves worthy of an Apollo moon mission. During the climb, I'd almost fallen in a few spots and had frost-nipped a fingertip.

Why the torture? We'd read that our heroes trained by tackling comfortable summer climbs during what they modestly called "full conditions."

Between mouthfuls of butter-sogged pancakes and scalding coffee, talk turned to Capitol Peak winter climbs. Two years prior, in winter, Fritz Stammberger had pioneered the first ascent of Capitol's north face wall, thus making the second winter ascent of the peak—by a steep, technical route.

"We should do a winter climb on the north face," Michael said.

I forked a pancake chunk and stirred it through a puddle of syrup. "There's a first ascent to the right of Stammberger's, about 2,000 vertical feet. Rock and snow, maybe a little ice. Pimmy and I climbed part of that line last summer. Rockfall cut our rope. In winter, maybe ice will glue the rubble down."

"When?" Michael said.

FRITZ STAMMBERGER WAS A tall, wavy-haired German expat with a Schwarzenegger build and male-model face. Along with the aura he'd gained from a Himalayan expedition during which two of his companions died, he was known around Aspen for his aggressive alpinism and physical training regimen. He was often sighted skiing *up* our local ski areas while lugging a stone-filled backpack, and walking around town with snowballs clenched in his bare hands—prep for gloveless winter rock climbing.

While Stammberger bordered on being a caricature of the Teutonic brute, he was not a top-grade rock climber.

"He can hardly do a five-nine," I scoffed over beers with Kennedy.

This scoff was a blatant attempt to dispel my envy, as I couldn't help but notice Stammberger's extreme ski descents and bold winter climbs. Not only had he ticked Capitol and other fourteener winter-climbing firsts, but in June 1971, he'd skied the north face of North Maroon Peak, another steep, cliffy fourteener near Aspen. His line down Maroon was world-class, equivalent in difficulty to contemporary descents in the Alps.

One summer day, I encountered Stammberger at the Aspen post office. "You should try the Cryogenics route," I stealth-bragged. Cryogenics was a steep 5.10-graded rock climb with a finger-crack crux, an Aspen test piece. I'd led it a few days prior. Fritz wasn't capable of the route's difficulty.

Stammberger smirked and ran his gaze over my wiry, six-percent-body-fat physique. "Lou, you are too much the spider."

I forced a chuckle and tried to feel superior. Yet my glory moment fell flat. Stammberger was Aspen's Übermensch of alpinism—and we both knew it.

While I would never admit it to Stammberger, I practiced his snowball routine. From what I could tell, it only toughened the mind. Fine.

MICHAEL AND I SKIED the nine-mile approach to Capitol Peak on a warm, blustery January day in 1974, sweating under sixty-pound backpacks stuffed with the accouterments of full-spectrum winter mountaineering: ice axes, ropes, pitons and piton hammers, cookstove. We set our tent next to Capitol Lake, on the mountain's west side, rather than the usual east-side winter basecamp at Moon Lake.

The following morning, intermittent graupel squalls pelted our nylon tent roof like someone was tossing pea gravel. Michael unzipped the door, and we looked outside. A half mile across the frozen lake and way up, Capitol's summit dissolved in thick gray clouds. What we could see of the rocky north face looked black, huge, mysterious, and cold as outer space.

"What do you think?" Michael asked as he stirred the breakfast oatmeal. "Graupel means the weather could change. Should we go up there? Take a look?"

"Take a look"—that worthy phrase I'd first heard from my father—was now climber's code for giving something a go, a mutual denial communication that allowed either partner to beg off without losing face. Should the adventure go sour, once safely perched on a bar stool you could shrug and say: "Yeah, we were just taking a look."

"Well, since we're *just taking a look*," I said, "let's leave our sleeping bags here. But bring the stove and a cookpot, in case the full conditions are a bit fuller."

After stomping through knee-deep snow for a few hours, we began the actual climb: a wall of stony rubble, cemented together by the frozen moisture of winter—typical Elk Mountains. I took the first lead, brushing snow off handholds and fiddling gear into icy cracks.

Fifty feet up the pitch, I jammed myself inside a shallow declivity, back against one side, feet against the other. I hammered a steel piton into a crack at the extent of my reach. Tink tink tink, just like Harvey Carter. The long knife-shaped spike sank a quarter inch at a time—lovely—until, *thud*, the hammer slipped and delivered a full-force blow to the middle knuckle of my left index finger. I dropped my hammer on its leash, grabbed a handhold with my right hand, and groaned in agony.

"I think I broke my finger!" I shouted as I flexed the suffering digit inside my glove—it exploded with the unique pain of damaged bone. "Watch the rope," I said. "I might quit—or fall."

Gritting my teeth, I managed to reacquire a hold with the four functional fingers of my smashed hand. I reclaimed my hammer, finished driving the piton, snapped in a carabiner, and clipped the rope. *Would the rock holding the piton resist the load of a fall, or at least bear my body weight should Michael need to lower me?*

The pain of my smashed digit went from grade ten to seven, probably because my hands were freezing.

"I don't think it's safe for me to lower from this piton," I spoke loud over the fifty feet between us. "I'll keep going. I can deal with the finger."

"Okay, try to get more gear in."

The climbing eased, not so steep, with larger handholds and footholds. But the rock was looser. Twenty feet above the piton, I looped a nylon sling over a forearm-length spiked rock and used the sling for a step. Needing the sling for the route above, I reached down to retrieve it, tugged, and the rock fell out, bouncing off the mountainside ten feet from Michael. It would have killed him.

I scrambled up easier ground another hundred feet, out of Michael's sight. His snow-muffled shout rose from below, "You're almost out of rope."

To safely belay Michael as he seconded the pitch, I needed anchors. Yet the only available features were chunks of rock protruding from frozen mud. After my experience with the falling spike, I wasn't trusting any of that. There was one option: the mud itself. I sledged my remaining piton into the solidified goo, shoved my ice axe into a patch of snow, tied myself in, and yelled, "On belay!"

The tradition in such situations is for the belayer to bellow something like: "Don't fall or we'll both come off!" Yet, rather than confusing things with illegible shouts, I figured: *Michael's strong. He knows this is sketchy. He won't fall.* But I kept the rope tight, and my feet jammed against a couple of rocks, so I would not—in theory—be plucked from the mountain should he slip.

The clouds thickened. The misted sun touched the ridge to the west. A light wind blew. Michael reached my belay stance, glanced at the bogus anchors, and said nothing as he grabbed our gear sling and began the next pitch. He looked like a pro, carefully placing his feet and using his ice axe as a third hand. The sun slipped away. Despite not having sleeping bags or a tent, we never mentioned retreat.

Capitol Peak, Elk Mountains, Colorado

Knife Ridge

Slingshot Direct

©Peter Kelley

As NIGHT FELL, WE reached a bedroom-sized saddle 200 feet below the summit. We had no flashlights or headlamps—we'd wait for morning. Under the shifting light of a cloud-filtered moon, we kicked out a shallow depression in the snow, fired up our stove, and drank a few cups of hot water. After the stove sputtered through its last droplets of fuel, we lay down and spooned. Light snow dusted us.

The clouds thinned and lifted. Skiffs of breeze-blown snow sifted over and around our nest. I lay on my side, front to Michael, back to the sky. Tendrils of cold crawled from my neck down the skin of my back as if a prankster were dropping ice cubes through my collar.

The lights of a coal mine flickered fifteen miles to the west. I squeezed closer to Michael and pictured the miners underground, sweating through their T-shirts. I pictured Stammberger and envied his bulk. He was right; I was too much the spider.

Daybreak, the clouds dropped, blocking all but a hint of warmth as a lazy sun worked its way from behind the mountain above us.

Our layers of wool and synthetic fleece had functioned well as overnight wear. Neither of us were hypothermic. My wool shirt was key, a custom job I'd designed, sewn by my mother. It had a Velcro-fastened Nehru collar, and the extra-long sleeves covered my wrists when I reached upward during a climb. I thought of my mother's fresh-baked honey soaked bread as Michael passed me the last of our trail mix, half a handful.

Despite our layered clothing, without a proper breakfast we'd soon visit shiverland, and then worse. We needed to move—to escape up and over the summit, return to camp.

The last technical lead was mine, a dark granite wall webbed with stringy white rime-ice.

My smashed finger burned when flexed but functioned well enough to keep me climbing. The precarious, loose rock was the challenge.

The wall's every ledge and shelf hosted a slew of stones. Lacking the winter gluing effect we'd hoped for, all could fall at the touch of a glove or tap of a boot toe: pebbles, fist-sized rocks, the occasional watermelon boulder.

Michael was below me on our tiny bivouac saddle. He had no shelter from the missiles I might trigger, and they'd fall too fast to dodge. Anything larger than a pebble could kill him. And with no means of requesting rescue, even a moderate injury was a death sentence.

Under the summer sun, I'd pranced over this dicey junk pile in my nimble climbing shoes. Now, I couldn't feel the footholds through my double-layer winter boots. Thick clothing immobilized my arms and legs. And the cold was alive and mean. It stung my throat as I breathed, reached inside my gloves to bite my fingertips, and painted my eyebrows crusty white.

I climbed like a cat, each step calculated, each piece of gear placed so the rope flowed without dislodging even a pebble. At the crux, I wedged a jam nut in the only choice, a crumbling crack, hitched a sling to the nut, and stood with my left foot in the sling.

The nut grated and shifted position.

My last reliable protection was twenty feet below. Should the nut pop, I'd fall at least forty feet, bouncing off ledges, grinding over the rough rock like a log in a woodchipper—certain injury, not to mention the stones I'd dislodge on my buddy.

A gust of wind shot a sheaf of spindrift snow into my face. My sunglasses were buried in my backpack; my goggles were in our tent back at camp. A spurt of adrenaline narrowed my squint-eyed vision to just the nut and the patch of rock in front of me.

I needed to move up and exit the sling, always an awkward process—like stepping from a ladder onto a house roof. I curled my uninjured right hand over a hold the size of an inverted teacup, but my wool-lined leather glove mushed under my fingertips, obviating any helpful purchase. I pulled the glove off with my teeth. It tasted of wet sock and orange peel. I grabbed the icy hold with my bare hand and then moved up. With each panting exhalation, drool seeped through my clenched teeth and dripped over the glove. Another move gained me a no-hands rest on a ledge, where I put my glove back on.

My Stammberger snowball training had proved beneficial after all.

"Nice lead," Michael said when he arrived at my belay. "I can't believe you didn't knock any stones down. That thing was a minefield."

A few minutes later, we'd scrambled the final yards to the top. After the obligatory handshake, I pulled our last dregs of food from the kangaroo pocket on my parka front—six dried figs in a plastic bag.

Michael dredged up enough energy to estimate his camera's manual exposure. He shot several of me, said, "Here, take the camera. It's all set." The ensuing images speak: two men barely past their teens, woolen hats pulled low over brows, icy beards, deep eyes. Neither of us managed the toothy half-grin of our heroes. But then, we were not their equals.

Michael Kennedy,
Capitol Peak summit, 1974

WHILE INTERVIEWING US ABOUT our Capitol climb, a journalist asked how we'd dealt psychologically with the ever-present dangers.

"We knew diddly about avalanches—which was good," I deadpanned. "Otherwise, we'd have died of fright."

Such flippancy—laughing at danger—came easy to me in those days.

Yet behind the beers and banter, Capitol was for us a huge deal.

On what we eventually dubbed the Slingshot Direct, Michael and I had made a first ascent of an alpine wall—in the deep of winter. This was alpinism in all its glorious power, amplified by the technical climbing, the forgoing of food and sleep, the consequently altered reality, the first ascent. A focus, a reduction of life to the rock and snow of a mountain, a battle, a melding. I can't say it was an exaltation; it was too grim for that. Maybe the exaltation came later.

Michael had found his purpose. With his organized mind and the physical training of our hardcore mountaineering lifestyle, he went on to a storied career in alpine climbing. And as his years of the big peaks rolled, he referred to our Capitol climb as "Liberating, special … It was the first."

Unlike Michael, and despite the power of the Slingshot, I was not enamored of complex, logistically intensive alpine climbing.

I'd try a few expeditionary adventures over the coming years. Yet my passion was speedy—often one-day—stabs into the wild. Challenges where my dance, my rock&ice athleticism (and eventual skiing skills) were paramount. And throughout it all, every hour of every day, the warm folds of Yosemite Valley worked their seduction.

Still, Capitol was seminal in my career. That final pitch would always be the finest of my life. It had combined every element of mountaineering: technical skills, toughness, and mind control. And beyond all that, I'd practiced my craft in such a way as to preserve lives, mine, and my rope brother's.

In our ways, both Michael and I had kissed the sky.

22 | FRIENDS OF JARDINE, 1974

FOR MOST AMERICAN CLIMBERS—AND many, if not most, from the far corners of the globe—there is no more iconic cliff than Yosemite's El Capitan. During the typical California Sierra day, the "big stone" shimmers pale-tan and glow-white, magical, under the range of light's incandescent sun—3,000 towering feet of granite, solid, yet riven by countless climbable cracks. The first time I saw it, the first time any climber sees it—you stand frozen, awed by the immensity, the swooping symmetry of the glacier-carved granite; "the very heart of the earth, speaking to us ..." as photographer Ansel Adams wrote.

Yosemite Valley,
El Capitan to left
©ReplayAll-Dreamstime

Throughout alpinism's modern era, climbers have sought El Capitan's equivalent cliff: sky-piercing majesty, a short walk from a road, T-shirt weather during spring and fall (other than afternoon thunderstorms and the occasional rainy cold front), world-class rescue team almost within shouting distance, nearby improved campground designated for climbers. And for any cash-challenged seeker of granite, a cafeteria where tourist children abandoned their plates of egg scraps and bacon shards. You didn't need a wallet for a hearty breakfast, just faster hands than the busboy. Swapping spit with strangers seemed inconsequential; climbing-bum philosophy held that free food was health food—and germaphobic wimps could bring their own fork in a pocket.

El Capitan's equivalent does not exist.

AND THEN THERE'S THE first time you climb El Cap. Rich Jack and I had got ours in October 1973, just after I'd finished the Titan tower with Harvey. We picked a storied route for our virginal excursion, Dihedral Wall, said to be the most "natural" line on the cliff because it follows a series of obvious cracks, many of them part of the route's eponymous features. In these giant open-book inside corners, you could sometimes make a few free-climbing moves to save time on the piton pounding. All good, but our primary motivation was avoiding other climbers on the more popular routes.

By now, Rich and I were a speedy, well-oiled machine. We often found ourselves passing teams who'd started ahead of us on longer climbs. Passing was a hassle: tangled cordage, grumpy slowpokes—best avoided.

Funny thing was, I wanted the Dihedral Wall to be extraordinary, a ceremonious entry into another dimension of the rope-and-carabiner universe. Maybe I'd see God or at least one of his assistants? But the climb was somewhat routine: just a taller cliff, where instead of two nights, we spent four—and where the rock was rock, not hardened mud like the Fishers.

Yet there were moments: gifting a jug of water to a party in need, a hanging bivouac, cozy in our nylon fabric hammocks strung high on the wall, looking down 2,000 feet to the ground and across the valley over the Merced River to the bulky light-gray Cathedral Rock spires, where dozens more routes waited. And the isolation, humbled in the immensity of stone and sky, every action consequential, rapid, decisive, mortal.

Again, that transcendence of alpinism, a hint of the Creator.

RAY JARDINE WAS IN the Valley that fall of '73 as well. Since Rich and I had passed his graduation test the year before and now proved our chops via the Dihedral, Ray invited us to join him for a handful of more demanding routes. Some I led, some I followed; all gained nods of approval from the bearded, bespectacled guru.

So far, the time I'd spent with Ray had been full-on mentorship. He'd shared the basics, taught me how to tape my hands, the climber equivalent of teaching me how to tie my shoes. And after that, he'd shared the gold: Yosemite crack tricks, training tips, rope management. Because of his help, I was close to his equal as a climber. And in some ways, I probably was.

Winter came. With it came the Slingshot first ascent on Capital Peak, ice climbing, more reps on the pullup bar I'd installed in my bedroom doorway.

SPRING 1974. MY CAREER in outdoor education hadn't worked out. It paid less than dishwashing and was often just as tedious. Carpentry was money, especially in Aspen, a resort town with a steady influx of wealthy customers. But pounding nails instead of pitons was far from a calling.

Extending what I'd begun with NOLS, I still had a half-baked vision of becoming a professional climber but little idea of how that worked. At the least, I needed to climb at top levels; make a name for myself, get sponsored, and gain a stable of high-dollar guiding clients. There was motivation in that. Yet far more than ego or career, I loved the raw athletics of climbing and the addictive high of accomplishment. Hence, when I wasn't pulling countless climbs on the crags, I was on the practice boulders and pounding out endurance runs.

When Ray Jardine telephoned me in late March, I was as primed, fit, and willing as possible. On the right day, I could manage two consecutive one-arm pullups.

"How about working on a list project with me, climb most of the named five-ten pitches in the Valley?" Ray said. "There's around thirty."

Hit the coolest routes in Yosemite with one of the best rock climbers around? The familiar surge buzzed behind my sternum.

"I'm totally into that," I replied.

"There's something else, Lou—a secret project. I'm inventing a type of hardware that'll change climbing forever. I need help with testing. And bring a headlamp wired to a big lantern battery you can hang from your shoulder harness."

"What's the headlamp for?"

"I'll let you know after we see how fast we do those hard pitches."

I quit my construction job, and emptied the food from my kitchen cabinets into a cardboard box I jammed between the ropes on the rear floor of my battered, pale-green 1968 Volkswagen Beetle. The beater bug had come cheap because it had a gaping hole for a roof—the owner's daughter had rolled it, destroying the factory sunroof and crunching the surrounding metal structure. I'd bolted a sheet of plexiglass over the top, removed all the seats but the driver's (to make room for sleeping), changed the spark plugs, and called it good. Applying the brakes took two pumps of the pedal. I'd fix that later.

When I rolled into Ray's campsite two days later, he and his wife, Sandi, were making dinner. Along with their cook stove and food boxes, the usual climber's gear dump graced the brown wooden picnic table: a chain of carabiners, sweat-stained shoes open and airing. Next to a coil of fuzzy, work-worn rope, a blue cotton towel was sprawled over an uneven mound the size of a grocery bag.

In moments, I'd learn that Ray, an aerospace engineer, had innovated a revolutionary piece of climbing gear. Until now, hammering pitons or placing jam nuts (also called "stoppers" or "chocks") into cracks had been the standard means of protecting rock climbs. Pitons were out of fashion, damaging to the rock, and strenuous to install. Nuts were variously sized chunks of aluminum you wedged into a wider part of the crack above a constriction, then clipped to your rope with a sling and carabiner. They worked well if the crack had plenty of constrictions and wasn't flared. Otherwise, you could end up taking long, often dangerous leads above your last protection. Enter Ray's invention: he'd designed a spring-loaded camming device (SLCD) that fit almost any part of a crack—faster and easier than hammering pitons or fiddling with stopper nuts.

Ray swore me to secrecy—"people copy my ideas"—and pulled the shroud off his babies. Instant thrall. As he called them, the dozen prototype

"Friends" were constructed from silvery hand-machined aluminum. Each device comprised four circular cam lobes, mounted sideways, like flower petals, at the end of a five-inch aluminum handle the thickness of a toothbrush. There were six of the larger "#3" Friends, sized for hand-width cracks, with lobes about the size of a beer bottle bottom. The six smaller "#2" Friends were sized for finger-width cracks.

As Ray explained, you prepared a Friend for placement by pulling the trigger bar as if gripping an oversized hypodermic syringe, which in turn retracted the cam lobes. You then inserted the Friend into a suitably sized crack and released the trigger, freeing the spring-loaded cams to rotate outward and anchor themselves against the sides of the crack.

Ray picked up a Friend in one rock-scabbed paw, wrapped his index and middle fingers over the trigger, pulled the lobes in, and released them with a snap.

"When a climber hangs or falls, the curved lobes press outward with amazing force. They hold by friction—the rock can be smooth as a baby's butt. They took huge test loads on the dynamometer, and I tried them in real cracks by tying a big rock to a rope and kicking it off a cliff. They held even better than I expected."

Throughout Ray's talk, I'd been almost speechless, stunned, while my intuition shouted: *this is the holy grail of climbing gear.*

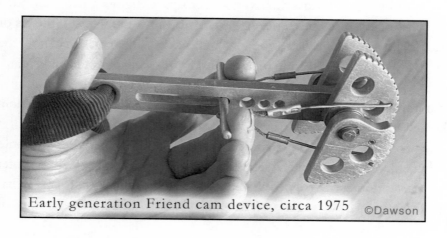

Early generation Friend cam device, circa 1975   ©Dawson

RAY SAID HE'D LED a few easy climbs with the devices but only partially trusted his prototypes. He'd always put in regular gear to back them up, and while he'd tested them in the cracks at the base of a few Yosemite climbing routes, he'd never fully protected a higher-grade Yosemite climb with them.

Ray's hesitation in testing the Friends on himself came as no surprise. After belaying him dozens of times, I knew he was a smooth, strong climber—yet wasn't the kind to run out his leads and risk lengthy falls. His style was sensible and safe—but his was not the go-for-it psychology needed for testing climbing gear. Accordingly, as Ray alluded, the final goal remained: using Friends instead of conventional gear for the first time on 5.9 and 5.10 Yosemite climbs. Doing so would be the breakthrough for Ray's innovation.

Inaugurating the Friends would require faith—and a dose of stupidity. Ray had chosen the right man for the job.

On April 22, 1974, Ray and I stood at the base of Midterm, a slippery, 130-foot, hand-and-finger-width crack climb ending with an offwidth. Rated 5.10, it was on our ticklist. Ray dropped his backpack to the ground and yanked out his rack of proto-Friends.

"A lot of that crack is the right size for trying these. Take the first pitch, see if you can use them." He grinned. "You'll be the first to do a Yosemite Valley lead with them."

I grabbed a Friend, hooked my fingers over the retraction trigger, and worked the cams in and out like I was vaccinating a horse.

"Sure, man, I'll give them a go," I said, without a single brain cell registering that the only thing between me and death would be an unproven gadget I'd first laid eyes on less than a day ago.

The climb began with a finger-width crack. When I reached a likely spot for a Friend placement, I positioned myself so I could free one hand. I unclipped one of the smaller Friends from my shoulder sling and forced my fingers over the trigger bar while bracing the shaft against my palm. It felt ready to pop out of my hand, so I bit the attachment sling in my teeth. Dropping it would not make Ray happy—these pre-production units were worth thousands of dollars in labor and design time.

Still holding the sling in my teeth, I dipped my head forward, plugged the device into the crack, and released the trigger. The four lobes sprung open and nestled against the crack sides.

Unlike our usual protection, the Friend hung suspended in the crack with no bulges or constrictions blocking it from pulling out. It looked weird and scary. I curled my fingers through the attachment carabiner, shook it, then jerked it in the direction I'd fall if I came off. It pivoted inside the crack but did not move a millimeter downward.

"I got one in!" I yelled. "Should I place more gear to back it up?"

"I would," Ray replied.

That was him. This was me. I clipped the rope to the science-fiction thing, did not install backup gear, and climbed past it. As I moved up the climb, I plugged in most of the Friends—still without backing them up. At the belay ledge, I clipped into the semi-permanent anchor slings left by other climbers, set a Friend for backup, and yelled, "On belay, climb!"

When Ray reached my belay ledge, he behaved as climbers do and studied my anchor system—the only thing between us and the ground had he fallen while following the pitch.

"Good lead, Lou. But next time, place Friends so they're axially loaded. They're not as strong with the handle sticking out perpendicular to the fall load. You had a couple placed like that on your lead. And let's fix this one here at the belay."

Whoops. Human trials indeed.

A few days later, I took a fall on a Friend. It worked. I caught Ray smiling. We continued using the Friends, carrying them to climbs while hidden under our jackets or draped with a spare T-shirt.

A FEW PITCHES ON our list were high on El Capitan: The Stovelegs, a series of perfectly sized hand and fist cracks named for climbing's most famous MacGyver moment, when the 1958 first ascensionists used iron woodstove legs as pitons to fit the slot's wider dimensions. The day we climbed the 'Legs, we made it about halfway up the storied monolith before we rappelled off at lunchtime. Instead of stove legs hanging from our gear rack, we had jam nuts and Ray's Friends, and we couldn't believe how fast we'd climbed.

23 | DAY OF THE NIAD, 1974

BACK AT RAY'S UPPER Pines campsite—away from prying eyes—we slid onto the picnic table seats. "So, Ray, what's next?" I asked as I peeled athletic tape from my hands. Despite a sweaty day of Yosemite crack climbing, it didn't come off easy if properly applied.

"Lou, you're a solid climbing partner," Ray said. "Want to team up with me and Kris Walker, try to be the first to climb El Capitan in a day, Nose route? You and I will swap leads. Walker will jumar our ropes and clean the gear. No haul bag, just day packs."

I sucked in a breath. Ray's idea was way more visionary than anything I'd suspected.

A one-day ascent of a typically multiday route was less exalted than the first ascent, but it sometimes came close in repute. And the Nose, arguably the world's most famous rock climb? Most Nose climbers spent two or more nights. It had never been done within one 24-hour period. The first Nose in a Day (NIAD) would make climbing history; catnip for my ego, but I had other motivations. Speed climbing El Cap was the Mona Lisa of mountain athleticism. The creative inside me wanted a part in the brushwork.

I had briefly met Walker at Forrest Mountaineering in Boulder, where he worked and had a financial interest. He had a reputation as an aid climber who didn't lead more strenuous free climbs, instead devoting himself to the intricacies of ropes, gear, and stone. He'd previously completed two solo big-wall first-ascents on the 900-vertical-foot Diamond face of Colorado fourteener Longs Peak: a challenge equal to Yosemite's cliffs, only with alpine weather and about half the oxygen of sea level.

I'd failed on the Diamond as many times as I'd succeeded—always with a partner. I could not imagine soloing the thing, lashed to the sheer granite wall for days on end. Weakened by altitude. Anticipating the inevitable afternoon lightning, and when it began, counting the seconds between each flash and thunderclap. Five seconds, one mile away; then four seconds, then two, until you stop counting, consider the electrically attractive steel pitons slung from your shoulders, and start praying. Walker was a man apart.

OUR PREPARATIONS FOR THE Nose were adventurous in their brevity, if not ludicrous. Walker and I had never climbed the entire route. Ray had climbed it once, several years prior, and our recent experience on the Stovelegs was sure to help. But the upper pitches of the climb—for us, the relative unknown—involved complicated direct-aid climbing, exemplified by a maneuver known as the King Swing. This technically demanding time-sapping pendulum traverse could best anyone so presumptuous as to try for speed.

As for skills, by now, I'd measured myself against many climbers on many routes and knew I was above average in speed. Ray and Walker were players as well. Even so, to think we were fast enough to scorch a time record on the most renowned wall climb in the world—provided the weather cooperated and we didn't lose the route—was more than a little hubristic. There were better, faster climbers. Some were practically residents of Yosemite, squatting at the nearby Park Service climbers' campground. Why these climbers had not already ticked a one-day Nose ascent, I didn't know. Perhaps the complacency of familiarity? Whatever. Ray had the vision. Thanks to him, we'd give it our best.

THE DAY BEFORE THE climb, Kris Walker skidded into Ray's campsite in his silver Porsche 914. "Made it in fourteen hours," he said from the driver-side window. "Never got pulled over."

Walker's roguish hair and boyish twenty-two-year-old face reminded me of John Denver.

"Man," I said, "how fast did you drive that thing?"

"About one-twenty a few times, downhill with a tailwind."

Normal drive time from Boulder to the Valley was at least twenty hours, often stretched with an overnight. *Walker had cannonballed it in fourteen and without being pulled over? If this guy climbed as fast as he drove, our success was ensured.*

"Weather and partners are the variables," Walker said as we counted carabiners and ran our ropes through our hands, checking for the soft spots that indicated damage. "I can clean the route as fast as you guys climb. We've got a fifty-fifty chance at nose-in-a-day but a one hundred percent chance of a great climbing adventure."

"We'll jumar someone's fixed ropes to Sickle Ledge," Ray said. "It's around three-hundred-fifty feet up to there."

Hold on, I thought, shouldn't we climb the first pitches if we're going for a record?

I said nothing about the ropes, nor did Walker. Ray called the shots, and his plan was reasonable considering climbing's ever-mutable ethics. Using a few hundred feet of fixed rope to begin the Nose was common, if not the norm—we'd jummared such lines a few weeks ago to access the Stoveleg Cracks. Unless our total time crowded close to the twenty-four-hour mark, was the time saved by the ropes a moot point? And did any of this really matter? In the end, whatever our style, adventure would be had—on the most exalted rock climb in the world.

AT FOUR A.M., UNDER a dim crescent moon, our headlamp beams bounced over El Capitan's pale-gray granite like the flashlight tag I used to play in Texas with my brothers. From the dark above, the fixed rope dangled as if supported by magic. I thumbed open the gates of my two Jumars, clipped them to the cord, and made my first vertical steps of the day. The sun-damaged nylon creaked under my weight while a temperate breeze carried the scent of the ponderosa pines fast shrinking below. Any concerns about our style dissolved. As far as I knew, no sane human had ever attempted a complete climb of El Capitan with little more than a jug of water and a baggie of trail mix. We were adventurers, explorers in the best sense of what Harvey Carter had taught me.

Late morning, we were well past the Stovelegs. Ray's prototype Friends had saved us a minute here, five there. Yet beyond gadgetry, our muscle-powered machine ate elevation like an Indy car clocking laps. True to his promise, Walker cleaned our gear and jummared with uncanny speed. Ray, whom I'd experienced many times as a cautious, reserved climber, moved more efficiently than I'd ever seen. And I had never been so motivated, so blended with the mountain. I said little, just climbed until my fingers bled.

Halfway up the wall, our blur of rope and hardware resolved atop Boot Flake, a vertical slab the size of a high-school basketball court, roughly shaped like a high-cuffed boot, adhered to the cliff with no visible means of support. It was common for climbers to wonder when the Boot might kick and then peel off—such wondering was best done while still on the ground, not while you were standing on top of the thing.

Topping the Boot meant it was time to fly: switch crack systems via the King Swing. I clipped my rope through the anchor carabiner, said, "Lower!" and Ray dropped me a lonesome seventy feet. Stretched by my weight, the single strand of 11 mm rope connecting my waist harness to Ray appeared skinny as knitting yarn, weak, easily cut by an errant quartz crystal or falling rock. I looked down. The 2,000-foot void was calming in comparison.

Suspended from the rope like a harnessed window washer, I galloped sideways across the cliff, seeking velocity, legs perpendicular to the wall, scrabbling like a cat-chased mouse at the weightless apogee of each swing. Hitting upwards of twenty-five miles per hour at the bottom of the arc, I skipped and pranced, a floating ballet, thinking *faster, faster*—finally latching my fingers over the goal, a large handhold close below the next belay stance.

The King Swing took us to the mystery lands, the dark side of the moon. Now, the stone led the way: soaring inside corners, cracks, the sun-faded nylon slings abandoned during some long-forgotten epic, the occasional bolt in its drilled hole, rusty, protruding, bent—suspect yet used.

At three p.m., we reached Camp 4, a series of small, broken ledges 2,400 feet above the ground, some no larger than a chair seat, others around the size of a child's bunk bed. As Ray and I organized gear, Walker dragged himself onto our ledge. He clipped the anchors, stood tall, and tugged up his dangling pack. "We're doing it. I'm feeling great," he speed-talked while swigging water from a duct-taped plastic bleach bottle. "We need to average forty-eight minutes a pitch. We're hitting that, sometimes better! How many more pitches from here?"

I pulled a crumpled, hand-drawn diagram of the route from my pocket. "Looks like ten, depending on where we set up belays. Ultimate! We might have it!"

AS I BEGAN THE pitch off Camp 4, I leaned back in my slings and checked the sky. While the morning had dawned as a deep-blue pool, a few puffy clouds had worked their way in as we climbed. Such clouds are not innocent decorations in a mountain range such as the Sierra—they morph quickly. And that they had, now murky and dark-edged, blocking the sun.

Feeling the threat, I ramped my speed, breathing hard, often hanging by one hand from a sling while I reached high to place gear or clip a fixed piton. Twenty minutes, thirty, I was closing on the next belay stance when a peal of thunder echoed through the Valley, rumbling from wall to wall like distant artillery.

Another detonation, closer, then came a burst of shotgun hail. Three minutes later, it was raining so thick I choked on it. Wearing only a water-logged cotton T-shirt, I yanked my tissue-thin rain jacket from my daypack and shivered like a soaked puppy as I dangled from a single rusted steel piton.

Seeking shelter from the angry sky, I pressed my forehead to the wall. Fear tightened my chest. We couldn't climb through what was virtually a water-fall. And if the chilly rain continued into the night, we'd go hypothermic; someone might die—maybe we'd all die.

The deluge pounded for two hours. Afterward, my fire still burned; Ray's not so much. So as the sun disappeared behind the Valley walls, he put me on the lead for the grunting workout along a horizontal crack where an overhang the size of a small carport, the Great Roof, attaches to the cliff, then the easily climbed cracks to the couch-sized ledges of Camp 5.

As night fell, I was still juiced, thinking our chances were good. In the globe of my headlamp beam, I continued past Camp 5, up the next pitch, to a belay stance on a small, man-sized ledge called the Glowering Spot. Eight pitches remained from here to the top. My adrenaline-biased mental calculations said we'd ace those pitches at a maximum of fifty minutes each—about six hours of night climbing. *Could the twenty-four-hour mark still be ours?*

final bolt ladder

Camp VI

Glowering Spot

Camp V - bivvy

The Great Roof

afternoon storm

Camp IV

Boot Flake
King Swing

El Cap Tower

Stoveleg Crack

Sickle Ledge

fixed ropes

2900

Empire State Building, 1250'

El Capitan, Nose Route
NIAD attempt, 1974

start

©Steph Abegg

I looked up the cliff as far as my headlamp illuminated, about twenty feet. A frayed sling hung from a crack. Did it mark the route, or someone's wandering mistake? If we strayed off-route, we could end up stranded, ledgeless, hanging by our waist harnesses like leashed and abandoned dogs, cold and hungry in the dark verticality.

Below us, a half mile of elevation away, car headlights scribed their tracks on the valley floor, drivers oblivious to the cliff and the climbers above. A light breeze blew, further cooling the damp rock. The soggy, unmoving rope sagged from my anchors like a drooping willow branch.

"Come on up, Ray!" I yelled. "It might rain again. We need to go!"

Instead of hearing the click of Ray's Jumars and feeling his weight tension the rope, his answer came unexpected: "It's too wet, too risky. We're tired from the storm. We'll bivouac here. Finish tomorrow."

I leaned back, twisted to the side, and looked down. I couldn't see Ray or Walker in the darkness, just their headlamp beams darting about.

"No ... Noooo, we can do this!" I yelled. "I'll lead all eight pitches. It's not far, easy climbing now."

"No, Lou!" Ray shouted. "I'm calling it."

If my frustration had been electricity, it would have shot through the rope and zapped Ray. Yet the filibuster rules on a roped climbing team—as do experience and age. Ray was likely correct to have called it. Wet ropes are nearly as heavy as steel cable. We were tired. The damp rock was slick, eliminating the use of hand and footholds to assist our direct-aid moves. One slight mistake in the darkness, untying the wrong knot, pulling out a piece of gear too soon, could end us about thirteen seconds later—when we became one with the scree at the base of the cliff.

Walker said nothing. Later, he told me he was okay with Ray's decision, while not adamant one way or the other. He was confident in his rope skills; all he had to do was follow Ray and me.

I groaned, adjusted the anchor sling connecting my waist to the wall, and prepared for yet another shiver bivvy. How many had it been? Gothic, Capitol Peak, The Titan, more. Most any unplanned night in the wild means just one thing: you screwed up. *Had we?* I nibbled my last palmful of walnut and raisin crumbs and made myself small as the night stroked my bones.

THE DAMP AND COLD of the bivvy flogged the spunk out of us. As dawn broke, we moved like shackled convicts. I offered to lead, and Ray gave me the nod. Seven pitches later, I halted below the last pitch of serious climbing, a 50-foot series of expansion bolts protruding from an otherwise blank section of rock.

"I'll do this one," Ray said, as he jummared to my stance.

And so it ended. As consolation, the actual climbing had taken us twenty hours. We'd proved the NIAD was possible—even without the time saved by the fixed ropes. Moreover, I figured that our total time of about twenty-nine hours on the wall cut previous times by a significant margin.

As for pushing on through the night? While Ray's caution was the path of wisdom, I always regretted not giving that final effort a go.

Before the climb, Walker had guessed we had a fifty-fifty chance for success. We failed. Yet, as he'd also surmised, the climb had been one hundred percent a grand adventure—in that sense a success. Of all the mountain days of my life, it was one of the worst, and it was also one of the best.

(L to R) Ray Jardine, Sandi Jardine, Lou Dawson, Kris Walker, after attempting Nose route in a day, 1974

©Jardine collection

24 | TRIPS WITH PETERSON, 1974

TWO HOURS AFTER FINISHING the deproach hike off El Capitan, I jumped into Walker's glorified Volkswagen and we drove back to Colorado. (I'd lent my car to someone who'd needed to return home early.) We swapped naps and steering duties. I broke ninety a few times on the bumpy straights of Nevada but didn't have the guts for more. When Walker took his turn, redlined the Porsche's engine, and hit a hundred, I wasn't sleeping—not until the engine vapor-locked and forced us to take a roadside doze while the fuel lines cooled.

Back in Aspen, I scored a carpentry gig and wallowed in the warm mud of my one-person pity party, until the cliffs called.

Kennedy was around. Weekdays, he'd pick me up after work, and we'd savor an evening of roped climbing or bouldering on Independence Pass. Rich Jack, Cardo, and the rest of our crew joined now and then.

On a warm summer day, Michael Pokress and I challenged Fritz Stammberger's speed record on 14,025-foot Pyramid Peak. At one point, I looked behind to see Pokie power jogging straight up a gravely scree slope. He lost all upward momentum yet continued pumping his world-class legs, his feet skidding, stirring up a cloud of dust like a street sweeper. We made it in 2:07, missing Fritz's time by minutes, but set a record for the peak's westside route.

IN LATE AUGUST, DON Peterson visited town to enjoy our local cliffs and a woman named Merriam. In the years since I'd met Don, we'd become climbing partners and friends. We'd roped up during NOLS courses, climbed in the Tetons during time off, and paired up for a few pitches in Yosemite. Three years prior, late summer 1971, I'd joined him for my inaugural alpine ice climb, a first ascent up a dizzying ice sheet on a tall Wind River peak named Mount Warren. In camp the day before the climb, I strapped on my crampons and practice-spiked up a fir tree like an arborist on a pruning job. At the time, that was the extent of my high-angle ice-climbing experience.

Since those early climbs, my adoration of Don as a world-class climber had grown to real-life respect. Besides his physical strength, he was smart, with a biology degree and a penchant for philosophy. And, as I'd learned at NOLS, Don had indeed climbed with Royal Robbins, master of rock. That pairing should have been a rousing success. Instead, it was fraught. And not because of Don.

In June 1969, Don and Robbins had made a new route on the sheer 2,000-foot face of Yosemite's Half Dome. Their bold line was beautiful, direct, on what some called the steepest wall in Yosemite. It was also an eight-day torture; cracks too wide for the pair's gear and blank rock where the sole means of ascent was hammer-drilling hundreds of expansion bolt holes. Robbins named the route Tis-sa-ack, after a Native American legend.

Robbins's subsequent magazine article head-hopped between multiple protagonists' inner thoughts, creating a tale of gnarled tension between him and Don. I thought this to be a literary-cool construct—what better story than human conflict?—until I realized Robbins wasn't a mind reader, and much of the piece was thus fictional. The gist characterized Don as a temperamental upstart. And many readers, if not most, didn't get the literary device. They took Robbins' scribbles as if the article had multiple authors. As a result, Don was famous overnight—as the carper of the royal Royal.

Despite the negative image Robbins had painted of Don, after spending time with him, I'd found his puckish humor, friendly demeanor, and impressive climbing skills showed any supposed character flaws were indeed fabrications. The first time I brought up the Tis-sa-ack literary debacle, Don paused momentarily, pinched his brow into his trademark intellectual frown, and said, "He's an ass," with an ironic intonation best answered with a laugh. I couldn't help but agree.

A FEW DAYS AFTER Don arrived in Aspen, we climbed Mad Arab, an awkward, poorly protected route on Independence Pass that Kennedy and I had put up a few weeks prior. While coiling our ropes, we gloated over how well we'd climbed—the 5.10 crux had felt like a 5.8.

"We're both in great condition," Don said. "Let's hit the Valley this fall. There's one pitch you'd be perfect for: Left Side Hourglass. Some say it was the Valley's first five-eleven climb. And it's dangerous."

Despite his allusions to mortality, Don's proposal was irresistible. We'd bonded while climbing in Yosemite during the preceding spring (just before the NIAD attempt) and worked together nicely. He was a strategist, balancing my tendency to take life one moment at a time.

It would be a few years before I learned the downsides of impulsivity—and sensed how like my father I was in that regard. For now, as a 22-year-old, I relished my in-the-moment craziness—and appreciated partners such as Don, who balanced it out.

"Let's do it," I said as I snapped carabiners onto the gear sling draped from my neck. "But my Beetle won't make it. The engine knocks, and I stop it with the parking brake lever. Either it'll die, or we will."

"Not a problem, Lou. Merriam has a brand-new Beetle. She said to borrow it any time."

That was some impressive girlfriend mojo on Don's part.

The next day, we jammed our backpacks and ropes in the tiny front cargo trunk of Merriam's Saturn-yellow Bug, dipsticked the oil, and headed west. An "odd couple" relationship soon manifested.

At twenty-five, Don was only three years older than me, yet he defaulted to the role of seasoned elder. This tag was valid. He was more than just a strong, well-rounded mountaineer. In contrast to the many climbers who proudly called themselves "dirtbags," Don was an academic who wore collar-popped golf shirts and traveled with a carefully packed sports jacket.

As for me, "dirtbag" was accurate. I was a feral high-school dropout who owned three pairs of pants, sometimes didn't wear underwear, and had never climbed with any guy named Royal.

In sync with his golf shirts, Don drove Talladega style, pressing the accelerator against the floorboard as he snapped the stick shift with precision flicks of his climber-thick wrist. So long as he brought the Volks' back to his girl—without the help of a tow truck—all was well.

In contrast to Don, I drove Merriam's shiny Bug like I piloted my consistently unreliable vehicles: with a lazy touch on the transmission, no haste on the throttle, and appreciation of a functional brake pedal.

My style impeded Don's Talladega dreams. While driving mellow on long stretches of yardstick-straight Nevada highway, I received lengthy lectures on what RPM was appropriate for what gear and how much to exceed the posted speed limit: "Precisely four miles an hour over, Lou—that way you won't go over five."

Fed up with Don's vehicular academics, I went passive-aggressive, held our speed to precisely four marks *below* the limit, sat back with a smirk, and mumbled about saving gas.

By way of revenge, Don taught me table manners.

We ordered chicken soup at a truck stop. As we sat at the counter between a couple of ball-capped truck drivers, my etiquette coach held forth: "When eating soup, bring your spoon out, away from you, then up and back to your mouth. Like this ..."

"Wow, I never knew that, Don. Excellent! It'll keep stains off the only sweater I own."

APART FROM OUR BROTHERLY banter, I admired many things about Don. His love of training topped the list. Show him a pullup bar, and he'd suggest a contest. Lengthy runs were typical. So it was, when we camped along Highway 128 near Moab, Utah, and began several days of sport among the red and gray sandstone cliffs towering above the Colorado River.

One morning, Don went for a jog, returned to camp, and grabbed the car keys. "I'm driving back up the road for a bath ... Saw an excellent dipping spot in a creek."

I settled in with a book. Shady cottonwood tree, camp chair, autumn in the Utah desert: better than driving around, hunting for a bathing spot.

An hour later, the yellow Bug pulled in. Don slid from the driver's seat, stood up, and flung the door shut with a thunk that echoed from the cliffs across the road.

"I'm minding my own business, taking a swim, cleaning off," he said, voice seething with indignation. "A bunch of cowboys show up with rifles and accuse me of being a pervert. Said they're calling the sheriff!"

He grabbed the book he'd been reading, a volume of Plato, and carried a camp chair down to a sandy lounging spot on the river's shore.

A few hours passed. Near the moment I thought the weirdness had lifted, a Grand County sheriff's deputy pulled his brown, push-bar-equipped Jeep Cherokee behind the Bug. He spoke on his radio momentarily, exited his car, and got in my face.

"You the perv exposing himself?"

A surge of paranoia rose in my gut—I was back in high school, Sheriff Whitmire looking to bust my friends and me. Clearly, the deputy had identified us by our sunflower Bug. It was likely the only one within a hundred miles—and in the hinterlands of 1974 Utah, such a thing was probably considered a perversion in of itself.

The correct reaction would have been to admit nothing. Yet fear had its way.

"Wasn't me," I blurted. "It was the guy down there by the river."

The deputy arrested Don and hauled him off to Moab, but not before Don, as he ducked into the cruiser's rear seat, said, "Follow us in. Bring my street clothing. Don't forget my sports jacket."

I grabbed Don's apparel and followed, uncertain what else to do.

After enduring my friend's etiquette lessons, I was getting a laugh. But this wasn't funny. *Don might do jail time, and I'd ratted him out!*

At the sheriff's office, a deputy told me Don had chosen a swim spot visible from a ranch owned by Mormon patriarch Tommy White. "One of his young daughters comes running home, says, 'There's a naked man in the creek!' We'll hold him tonight and see what the prosecutor says tomorrow."

The following morning, when I pulled up to the cop shop, Don was sitting outside—wearing his sports jacket. He said he had easily convinced the prosecutor he wasn't a deviant, "just a guy taking a bath."

As far as I knew, Don's jacket had rescued him from a grind through Utah's justice system.

THE NEXT DAY, WE drove into Reno, Nevada, and parked near the university. Shrugging on his sports jacket, Don announced, "Let's have lunch near the school. I know a professor here."

Don was probably sick of me—and Utah lawmen—and wanted to sample an academic vibe along with a coed or two. I stood nearby as he stopped at a wall-mounted pay phone to call his friend.

As Don chatted, three police cars, lights flashing, vectored him like he'd robbed a bank.

"Hang up the phone, mister. Hands up."

"May I finish this call?" Don replied.

The officers stood tall and placed their hands on their guns.

"No, you can't finish the call. Against the wall!"

As Don leaned against the wall like a movie criminal, two plainclothes detectives showed up and spoke with the uniforms.

"His jacket looks like the guy's, with those patches on the elbows. But the rape suspect from last night is fatter with blond hair. Release this man."

If he'd needed it, Don could have sprung the alibi of the century: "No way it's me. I was in jail for indecent exposure."

I'd been considering a sports jacket of my own. Now, I had second thoughts. Were such vestments as likely to get you in trouble as get you out?

As for me being the guy who dimed him out during "the great bath incident," Don could have taken it the wrong way. Yet my Judas moment won his heart. When retelling the story, he relished quoting my words:

"It wasn't me! He's down there by the river—reading Plato."

Don added the Plato part. Or maybe I said it. Either way was okay.

DESPITE OUR MISADVENTURES, ONCE we reached Yosemite, Don and I had meshed as climbing partners. We were peaking athletically, and Ray Jardine had taken a break from climbing and lent me his prototype Friends—the only twelve or so in existence, as far as I knew. I was delighted, not to mention proud, with Jardine's validation of my climbing talent.

Ah, the arrogance of youth. As much as any skill I possessed, I remained a lab rat. Now, Don was as well.

Along with questioning the safety of beta gear, I was concerned about the Friends being something akin to cheating. As it turned out, any worries in that regard were unfounded. Innovative climbing gear was common, and early adopters were always seeking an edge. Moreover, while the Friends were fun and sometimes an advantage, several of our testers soon broke, and the lack of sizes limited their value. In particular, I was glad the larger versions awaited manufacturing, thus keeping my off-width crack leads on par with other "Friendless" climbers.

Author on Outer Limits, Yosemite, testing prototype Friends cams, 1974

©Don Peterson

FRIENDS OR NO FRIENDS, we soon found ourselves on The Vendetta, 5.10-b, four pitches of Yosemite cracks. Interestingly, perhaps ironically, Vendetta was one of Royal Robbins's many first-free ascents, this one made in 1968. Don cruised the first pitch, a physical hand-crack leading to an easy chimney. After that, an off-width crack, my specialty. As we'd done on Independence Pass, we sailed up the entire route like a practice climb. Which in a way, it was, because after that we hit hard.

I liked the names of our climbs, and their provenance—the pitches where modern crack climbing had begun: The soaring cracks of New Dimensions, the Valley's first 5.11; Outer Limits; the rough rock of aptly named Meat Grinder. And on the modern side, we made a first-free ascent of a climb Jardine had named Wild Thing (the only significant first I accomplished in the Valley, later erased by a rock slide—such irony).

For me, Hourglass Left Side was the highlight of our partnership. When hardman Peter Hann made the Hourglass first ascent in fall 1972, his feat was heralded as the first unrehearsed 5.11 pitch in the Valley. This referred to the then-new maximum difficulty rating, bumped up from the prior max of 5.10-d, and Hann having never before touched the route.

When Don and I went after The Hourglass two years after Hann's first-free ascent, the seldom-attempted climb was still worthy. The crux was an undercling. You grabbed the underside edge of a horizontal hanging flake, hung your butt perpendicular to the cliff, and pressed your feet against the rock in front of you. The action resembled bicep curls combined with horizontal squats.

Added challenges particular to the Hourglass: purchase for your feet on smooth, nearly hold-less rock, and the flake-crack leaning up and left, meaning you had to move both horizontally and vertically.

As for the danger, beyond two pieces of permanently installed gear, placing conventional protection was demanding, if not impossible, and the crack was too wide for our proto-Friends. A swinging leader fall from the poorly protected section of the climb would smash you into a jagged rock that Hann called a "chopper." Unlike other 5.11s, where you could take a leader fall without impacting anything, a slip here could break you, or worse.

With Don's encouragement and deft belay, I dipped my hands into my chalk bag, took advantage of my bird-like body weight, and pulled on the undercling like Yosemite granite was all there was in the universe. There was no angst, no hesitation, no fear. I worked my hands up and left in a shuffling motion. My feet found the micro-holds as if by telepathy. The dangerous part ended where the crack went from horizontal to vertical. I slotted a hand in a solid jam, installed a piece of protection gear, and that was it.

With Hourglass Left and other 5.11s scribbled in my climbing journal, I could have forgotten the high mountains, taken up a life as a semi-professional rock jock—or more likely as a penniless sports bum—plying my trade on sunny crags from California to Spain. Yet, in the complete menu of mountaineering, Yosemite granite was a mere appetizer. It was time again for the full plate: the highlands, the cold, the ice.

SOON AFTER OUR YOSEMITE campaign, Don contacted me with a plan as far from warm granite as Neptune is from the Sun: Grand Central Couloir on Mount Kitchener, in the Canadian Rockies, in winter. This 3,500-vertical-foot ice and snow line was an unclimbed Canadian plum—unclimbed because rockfall and avalanches pounded it with fearsome regularity. In answer to that, Don figured we should attempt Kitchener in deep-winter conditions, when rockfall was minimal, and avalanches calving off the summit ice cliffs were (in theory) uncommon. Somehow, we failed to remember that winter brings snow, and snow brings avalanches.

Don still lacked a reliable automobile—he'd broken up with Merriam and her yellow Bug. I was doing no better in the female department, but I'd upgraded from my brakeless Volkswagen to a dirty-white Ford Econoline van purchased from my climbing buddy Steve Shea. A muscular fellow with thoughtful, deep-set eyes, Shea was always among the first of our Aspen-area climbers to up the levels, be it on rock or ice, or at the slideshow party afterward. I'd been on the same rope with him hundreds of times. Thus, I had no reason to doubt his words as we closed the sale: "It's a beater, but everything works."

"Beater" was right. The van's interior walls were stripped to bare metal. It stank of dirty socks and armpits. The seats bled chunks of yellow, solar-rotted foam. The plywood bed swayed like a carnival ride until I nailed a diagonal brace across the rickety legs. But, if "everything worked," the price was right: equivalent to a few dozen cheese enchilada plates at La Cocina, the mid-priced Aspen restaurant frequented by our climber crowd.

I should have kept my Volks' and enjoyed the enchiladas.

WE LEFT ASPEN ON a sunny morning in November 1974, with several days and 1,500 miles between us and Jasper, Alberta. Six hours in, on a lonely Wyoming highway, ten below zero, ground blizzard swirling over the road like a rock-concert fog machine, the Econoline's cab heater failed, totally.

Don Peterson and the van, to Canada, 1974   ©Peterson

The radio—"everything works!"—told us an arctic air mass had settled over the northern U.S. and Canada. Long-distance driving in such conditions was foolish, even with a fully functional 1970s automobile. And mountain climbing? Doing so during "normal" November temperatures in the high Canadian Rocky Mountains was ridiculous enough. Instead, we were headed into thirty-below-zero territory, to climb a north-facing gully where the sun of winter never shined.

We acted our age—young and not so bright—and continued north, hunched under shoulder-draped sleeping bags while wearing every piece of mountaineering garb we owned. Duct-taping the windows shut did little to help. So, as Don drove, I lit our gasoline mountaineering stove and set it on the floor mat under his legs. He leaned his face over the exhaust plume, inhaled through his nose like he was smelling roses, and said with a half-grin, "If I get woozy, grab the wheel."

The driving portended the climbing. When we finally arrived, we discovered the winter-blasted Kitchener couloir was far from a viable climbing route. Instead, it was little more than an avalanche chute, funneling every particle of falling ice and snow into a hundred-foot-wide gash.

We tried it anyway, of course.

At the end of our first day in the couloir, we bivouacked inside a shallow, blue-ice crack that opened perpendicular to the slope, with a somewhat level floor. We configured our tent so that its roof slanted in line with the couloir's slope and plane. In theory, the inevitable avalanches would scoot over us as we bunked. Sure enough, a series of smaller avalanches were soon hissing over the nylon like wind-sifted sand.

We'd finished dinner, cinched up our sleeping bags, and just nodded off when the big one hit, bellowing like a semi-truck as it attempted to rip us from the mountain. The ice under us shook; the tent flapped like a flag in a tornado, but it held. After that, we spooned into the deepest corner of the tent and waited for daylight like homeless men on the bitter streets of winter.

Come morning, we figured the previous night's slides had purged the route and made it safe enough for a mad dash to the top. So we pushed higher, tandem-solo, no rope. Five hundred feet past our bivvy, the familiar booming sound again echoed from above.

Don shouted, "Avalanche!"

We ran, seeking shelter at the edges of the couloir, dancing on our crampon front-points like we were auditioning for the Bolshoi.

We reached safety in time for the torrent to pass, downclimbed what little of the route we'd accomplished—and sped for home, properly spanked by the Canadian Rocky Mountains.

25 | TOOTH DECAY, 1975

I WAS TWENTY-THREE—LONG PAST stabbing pencil lead into my fingers out of boredom. But one thing hadn't changed: I still sought danger and physical pain as the antidote to tedium. Yet the ballet of stone wasn't giving me the zing of the formative years. Where the dance had once stung deep and sweated me with fear, there was now an irksome mundanity. Were bigger mountains the solution? Expeditions?

Since the Denali snow cave adventure, I'd become skeptical of lengthy, committing trips. But repressing such skepticism was easy in the face of boredom. And nothing is boring about Alaska.

In the early 1970s, a gigantic Alaskan precipice generated buzz among the climbing community as something on the fringe, dreamlike, a last great problem of the era. Fifteen miles southeast of Denali, the cat-fur-gray, snow-patched east face of the Moose's Tooth swooped skyward 4,500 vertical feet from glacier to summit—1,500 feet taller than El Capitan. It was one of the world's finest unclimbed big-walls—judged by its looks, while ignoring the difference between remote, storm-blasted Alaskan alpine climbing and sunbaked Yosemite frolics.

In 1973, eminent climber and founder of Patagonia Inc., Yvon Chouinard, had tried for the route's first ascent with his A-team. Reportedly, "deteriorating cracks" had turned them back.

Chouinard's attempt grabbed the attention of four of our Colorado crew: Michael Kennedy, Cardo Merrill, Cardo's ski patroller friend Sully Sullivan, and me. We were all veterans of Yosemite's biggest walls, but more, we'd mastered the crumbly rubble of Colorado's Elk Mountains and the solidified mud of Utah's desert spires. Could we not handle punky Alaskan rock better than Yosemite celebrity climbers spoiled by their exquisite Sierra granite? Claiming a first on the Tooth seemed possible, even likely.

June rain misted the windshield of bush pilot Cliff Hudson's ski-equipped Cessna as he wallowed to a stop on the slushy snow of Buckskin Glacier, a quarter mile from fog-shrouded Moose's Tooth. We climbed out and watched Hudson kick our gear from the side door like chucking garbage at a landfill. The engine roared as he spun the plane on its tail wheel, puddle-jumped a few crevasses on his takeoff roll, and disappeared through a break in the clouds no wider than his wingspan. In a matter of seconds, as if nodding to the primacy of the Alaskan bush pilot, the clouds snapped shut and darkened, leaving us unable to fly out even if we'd radioed Hudson and begged.

As Alaska-scale atmospherics barfed a thick slurry of rain and slushy snow, we loitered in our tents for a week, trading damp paperback books while our circadian rhythms rotted under the midnight sun. When a hand-sized patch of sky finally appeared, we crawled from our hovels to see the entire wall for the first time in days. Rafts of fog the color of aspen bark clung to the cliff face, tongues of snow blew from the summit. This was not sunshine, just less storm. We longed for the sun. I even prayed for it. One should think before praying.

Tantalized by that brief snap of blue, we climbed through three rainy days. We left fixed ropes to our highpoint and rappelled to our tents every evening. After each monotonous dinner, I'd stare at the translucent orange tent roof until the two-hour Alaskan "night" began, and nod off with my cheek and ear pressed against the slimy nylon gear sack I used for a pillow.

When morning came, and with it the rain and the indecision, I longed for a girlfriend, and though I never spoke of it, my mother. I felt nothing but homesick as I trudged over the glacier snow to the wall like a man dragging his sorry ass to a soul-killing factory job.

On our fourth climbing day, the weather warmed, and the clouds broke. Answered prayer. We quit our ground-based game and winched our overnight gear up the route.

A thousand feet up the climb, about one-fifth of the way, we drilled a group of four expansion bolts—four because the rock was some kind of punky amalgam that made us want for a bigger drill and longer bolts. Exhausted, we deployed our bivouac hammocks and tried for a few hours sleep in the Alaskan night light. From there, we aimed to leapfrog up the face via a series of such bivouacs.

The next morning, Michael hung from the bolts seventy feet to my left, belaying me as I pressed the route. Cardo and Sully were below, hauling the last of our gear. I'd shed my malaise and was keen to explore where no person had ever climbed. I stood in slings attached to finger-sized steel hooks known as "cliff hangers" that gripped tiny rock features, similar to a cat claw on a teacup rim. My hooking technique was a point of pride—a mix of courage and finesse.

I paused on a solid hook placement, stood tall, relaxed, and looked over and down at Michael. Everything was as it should have been: bolts tied with an organized network of webbing, haul bags hanging like oversized fruit, sleeping hammocks deployed. *This rock isn't all bad ... what can stop us now?* Just then, a series of hollow thumps came from above, like walls flopping down during construction demolition. I looked up. A billowing cloud of white filled the sky.

"Avalanche!" I yelled, pressing my helmet brim to the rock and willing myself insect small. Not that cowering would do much good. Hooks held little more than body weight. Should even a minimal amount of snow smack me, the force would pluck me from the rock like a weed, and I'd take a long, bone-crunching fall to my last protection. And if the avalanche were more than a piddle, it would rip me from the face, shred my rope, and fling me to the glacier below.

A few wads of snow pattered my helmet and shoulders, but the slide's bulk passed to my left as blurred white streaks mixed with chunks of falling ice that buzzed like bullets.

It was over in seconds, leaving only the sound of meltwater sheeting over the rock. Below, Cardo and Sully sheltered under a steep section of the climb. As for Michael, a horse-sized pile of slush had built up on our hanging equipment and his back, bowing him in a facsimile of religious supplication. He raised his helmeted head, shook his shoulders, and began pawing snow off himself and our gear. I was amazed he was alive.

I extended my arms and straightened my back, forcing my body from its fetal curl. "Anything hit you?" I yelled. "You hurt?"

Michael looked at me with laser focus. "I'm okay," he said. "But the weight of the snow pulled three anchor bolts partway out. I don't think they'll hammer back in—crap rock. And it's getting warm."

He raised an arm and pointed at the wall above us.

"There's tons of snow stuck up there, ice too. The sun is peeling it off!"

My rationalization engine went into overdrive. *Didn't that slide clean all the hanging snow? Isn't it like lightning? The chances of hitting twice in the same place, nil?*

I shouted the most ludicrous question of my life: "Should we keep going?"

"No way, man, that thing almost ripped us off the face!" yelled Michael.

"Lou!" came Sully's shout from below. "We can't climb through avalanches. Let's rappel off this thing, radio Hudson, get the hell out of here!"

At that moment, a human-sized wad of slushy snow vomited from above and thudded into the slanted wall ten feet to my left. It sounded like a falling climber impacting the ground, or so I imagined.

I got religion.

We scurried down the wall like rats racing before a flood.

I HATED OUR MOOSE'S Tooth debacle: the wasted money, gray-sky sodden weather, isolation from lovers and family, my lethargy—and yes, the lousy rock. Clearly, expeditionary alpinism wasn't my game.

Back in Colorado, I continued shifting my focus closer to home, enjoying Aspen and the mountains with a more impulsive style. Rock by day, friends to party with, a woman who invited me to her backwoods cabin "whenever you feel like it."

I journaled an enormous string of Colorado rock climbs that summer, over sixty days on everything from short-hard pitches to a first ascent on the Longs Peak Diamond. But though I reveled at first, I was soon treating those fine days like a widget counter on the nine-to-five plan. I woke up every morning not even thinking of climbing and did dopey things like forgetting my climbing shoes.

One day, I remembered it had been a month since I emptied my pack. I plucked it from the nail where it hung on my wall, flipped it, and shook the contents to the floor. A plastic bag containing a greenish moldy bagel rested on the resulting gear heap.

An autumn trip to Yosemite assuaged the burnout—with two highlights. First, another El Cap route, with a twist: a wealthy eighteen-year-old adventure seeker, Gary Ramo, had hired my climber friend Larry Bruce to guide him up the West Face of The Captain, and Larry hired me to help.

Larry was a tall man with unruly ginger-blond locks and facial hair to match. One of his eyes bulged unnaturally, resulting from a bottle thrown by a passing motorist while he was cycling. The oft-tearing orb gave him a slightly crazed appearance, belied by his kindly nature. He lived in Aspen, and we'd been partnering on climbs for over a year.

Ramo wasn't capable of leading any pitches, so we taught him how to jumar and informed him he'd do so for the entire climb. While he didn't seem to mind his relegation to climbing just the ropes, Larry and I weren't entirely comfortable with our client jumaring every inch of the cliff. It was weird climbing a storied big-wall without climbing it. Yet the money was fat—an entire climbing season's groceries, replacement gear, and beers—so we rolled with it.

The second morning, as we packed our haul bag after a hammock bivouac, Larry checked in with Ramo.

"You okay with not leading any climbing, just jugging the ropes? You bored?"

"I dropped acid," Ramo replied. "Still tripping—not bored at all!"

Larry looked at me from the corner of his eye, the zany one, then rechecked our boy's knots.

FIVE DAYS LATER, I was again on The Captain, partnered with Michael. Our goal: the Salathé Wall, reputed as the best rock climb in Yosemite—and maybe the world—because of the beautiful crack climbing and perfect rock extending over most of its 3,000-foot length. It was a natural line, a route made for climbing.

With Michael's blessing, I yanked a surge of motivation from my burnout and led the more challenging parts of the Freeblast section of the route, a chain of ten free-climbing pitches, several rated 5.11. We swapped leads on the upper, direct-aid climbing. It was a fine three days with my brother of the rope.

I was still peaking as an athlete—climbs filled more pages in my journal. Yet talent is one thing, enthusiasm another. I was embarrassed to admit it even to myself, but climbing continued to feel like widget counting. During solo bouldering sessions, I napped in the shade as if I'd returned to the forests behind Aspen High School.

Luckily, when it came to mountaineering, there were plenty more over-stimulating endeavors.

Author, ice, 1974   ©Kennedy

26 | ICE, 1975-1977

WHEN WINTER PULLS THE heat from Colorado, hundreds of waterfalls freeze in place, producing ice climbs of infinite variety: narrow pillars, wide flows, often vertical, some overhung. As the 1970s rolled, I pursued those frozen lands with the same vigor I applied to rock. And after a few years of trial and error, I had it wired. Technical skill had a part in this, but so did the bottomless reserve of stupidity I rationalized as courage. This led to ropeless soloing a half dozen ice routes, an existential endeavor if there ever was one—not in my father's self-actualized sense of the word, but in the sense of ceasing to exist. As one friend put it, laughing, I now qualified as a "goddamn maniac."

IN THE EARLY DAYS of alpinism, "ice climbing" most often meant ascending lower-angled slopes of compacted snow while using an ice axe as if it were a cane or for chopping steps if the route was solid ice. When I'd climbed the Mount Warren ice sheet in the Wind Rivers with Don Peterson in 1971, we'd wielded a conventional ice axe in one hand and in the other, a makeshift ice dagger cobbled from an ice piton wrapped with electrical tape to form a handle.

As climbers of the 1970s discovered the joys of vertical, crystalized water, they found the traditional tools were a joke: awkward, often useless. But just as evolving attitudes and gear (such as Jardine's cams) were bringing a quantum shift in rock climbing, so too did ice climbing progress. The reinvented ice axe sported a shorter shaft and a curved or drooped pick. On the steeps, you swung one in each hand, like a pair of war hatchets, planted the downward-slanted picks in the ice, and used the shafts as portable handholds. On thin ice—as thin as two stacked nickels—you could hook just the pick-tips and so progress. The new designs even worked on bare rock, where you clawed the picks on tiny ledges or jammed them in cracks. Redesigned ice-screw pitons were easier to place and remove. And, strapped to your boots, the modernized "twelve-point" crampon had the traditional downward oriented spikes underfoot, with an additional pair of horizontal spikes protruding forward from the boot toe, allowing you to kick into the ice and ascend face-in without chopping steps.

Around 1973, Aspen based engineer-climber Peter Hutter designed and retailed an early droop-pick ice climbing tool, the Roosterhead. While other designers were producing such tools (the MacInnes-Peck Terrordactyl for one), Hutter's Roosterhead was in several ways superior. The weight and a vibration-damping aluminum shaft helped it pierce ice with a solid thunk. The steel of the pick was strong and resistant to bending. An extra, for-ward-facing triangular spike under the grip, the "rooster foot," protected your knuckles from the ice. Hutter set me up with a pair of Roosters—no charge. It seemed my reputation as a bold climber had a side benefit.

With a Roo' in each fist and twelve-pointers on my boots, so long as the day was cold and the ice was present—thick or thin, vertical to overhang-ing—it was mine.

Peter Hutter's Roosterhead ice tool, 1974   ©Dawson

IN WINTER '72, I caught my first sight of the Ames Ice Hose. I was driving Highway 145 behind Telluride Ski Resort, heading for Ophir, a small cabin village, to visit a friend. When the 400-foot frozen waterfall came into view a half mile across the valley, my eyes bugged like a landed fish. The bluish ribbon sprouted from a thin, twenty-foot-wide pillar at the base of a rugged, snow-patched cliff. After nearly disappearing in a human-sized fissure, it expanded to a bluish-white stripe, fifty feet wide at most. After that, a broader, glowing-white sheet of fluted ice ended just under the canyon rim.

Most of the Ames ice was at least vertical, while plenty of it appeared to overhang a few degrees. The narrow spots, the hose, would require a combination of rock- and ice-climbing skills, a form known as "mixed." As far as I knew, nothing in Colorado came close to what the Ames route promised.

I wasn't ready for an ice climb of such magnitude. That did not keep the Ames first ascent from my dreams.

JANUARY, 1976. WE HAD the new tools and fresh attitude—and the Ice Hose still awaited a first ascent. The mission fell to me, Michael Kennedy, and Steve Shea.

Since he'd sold me the heater-challenged van that Peterson and I had driven to Canada, Shea had become Aspen's closest approximation of a European-style multidiscipline mountaineer. He climbed ice and rock at top levels and skied the steeps.

(Fritz Stammberger had vied for that position but had never upped his rock-climbing skills. Still, he'd kept his uber-cred and aced all us young Aspen bucks when he married Playboy centerfold Janice Pennington. Sadly, Fritz was gone now. He'd disappeared in 1975 while solo climbing in Pakistan.)

As these were the days before refined weather reporting, we drove through an unexpected storm from Aspen to a friend's cabin we'd borrowed in Ophir. The sky that night pumped wet snow like the Pacific Ocean was hanging overhead. If we'd been ski mountaineering, avalanche paranoia would have chased us home.

Yet this was ice climbing, a short distance from a cabin and paved road. Why worry?

The following morning, we noticed a few hefty avalanche paths above us as we skied the approach trail, but paid them little regard.

The first pitch was Michael's. Fifteen feet up, while scrabbling on ice no thicker than cardboard, he fell and planted headfirst in the soft alluvial snow at the bottom of the climb, his boots waving in the air like oversized wind-blown weeds. Shea and I helped him to his feet, and, true to his nature, he was back on the climb in minutes.

Pitch two, Shea's, was a shallow, ice-choked chimney—the hose. He said little, breathing like a marathon runner as he pressed one cramponed boot against dry rock and repeatedly kicked the other into the ice until he risked shattering anything useful. At one point, as he pulled himself past the overhanging crux, he finally spoke: "This fucking thing is hard!" Translated, it might have been the hardest ice pitch he'd ever done.

The two pitches ate most of the day. Above Michael and Shea's stopping point, a pillar of interwoven wrist-thick icicles—chandelier ice—led to the broader sheet-like formation, some 200 feet high. The pair rappelled and left fixed ropes for our return.

I'd not climbed an inch, instead spending six hours at the base of the route, hopping from foot to foot like a mad jigger to keep my toes from freezing—while longing for the custom-made puffy parka I'd left back at the cabin. I called the jacket my "walking sleeping bag" because it made me look like a cocoon with legs; more than once, I'd slept in it outside in the winter.

My chance would come the next day on the climb's mysterious upper pitches, when I'd swing my ice tools again and enjoy the exalted privilege of being a goddamn maniac. And this time I'd bring my coat.

During our ski out, a field of blocky avalanche ejecta covered the trail, fallen from the slopes we'd noticed on our approach.

"Weird," I said as we clambered through the maze of suitcase-sized snow chunks. "If you guys had climbed faster, we'd have been here sooner, maybe died."

"Yeah, and it's still snowing," Shea replied. "We'd better watch it tomorrow, ski through here one at a time. I wish we'd finished today. We don't have any dinner or breakfast food."

Back at the cabin, Shea and Michael drove out for groceries, but the storm had closed the road to Telluride and its grocery store. The only store they could find was a gas station with a candy shelf. Shea purchased their entire inventory of peanut M&Ms.

That evening, we relished a sumptuous repast of two pouches of M&Ms each. Still short on calories, I grabbed a half-full jar of strawberry jam from the kitchen. "Dated two years ago," I said as I removed the cap and sniffed. "Nothing black floating on the surface." We dipped two spoonfuls each. In five minutes, my stomach felt like I'd swallowed an angry rat, alive, and my hands trembled like I had advanced Parkinson's. It took me three hours to fall asleep.

AFTER A SUGARY BREAKFAST, we gathered our gear and headed into the dumping storm. Though I didn't mention it, this time I packed my big jacket.

When we reached the climb, we found our wet ropes had frozen stiff, making the use of Jumars tedious and fearsome. When least expected, they'd slip down, usually just a few inches, but there was no way of knowing if inches would become feet, then yards, then ...

To safety our Jumars, we tied stopper knots on the cord dangling below us, or attached a loop to our harness. Theoretically, the knots would jam the slipping ascender, or the harness loop would catch us before we cratered and died. In normal (read summer) conditions, the process was easy—today, not so much.

When I needed a safety knot, I held the rope to my mouth, blew on it, and whipped it against the ice to soften it—all with little effect. I was tempted to channel my inner Jack London survivalist and thaw the ice-sheened cord by urinating on it. Shea and Kennedy would not have appreciated that, so I kept my hand away from my fly and managed a few safety knots, though not enough for total confidence. As my distance above the knots grew from feet to yards, I continued on faith, stopping every few feet to shake, jerk, and otherwise convince my ascenders not to slip backward. My companions did no better. It took us five hours to climb 300 feet of rope.

By hour five, the sun had long retreated behind the ridge above. Our ropes had softened during the past few hours but were quickly refreezing. All we'd done so far was jumar. We needed to make new ground. I left my suspiciously bulging backpack with Michael and Shea and tackled the ice sheet. It climbed at a grade more manageable than yesterday's leads—easier than we'd suspected. That's not saying much. The pitch was vertical water-ice replete with several sections that felt overhanging, though that might have been the sugar diet.

Michael took the next section, the last pitch of the ice climb proper, ending about a rope length under the canyon rim. From below, it looked easy: straightforward hooking and hacking with his hand tools. Wrong. The ice was too thin for reliable screw placements. Michael's single piece of half-decent lead gear was a nylon sling tied around a wrist-thin tree branch. Magical protection, something along the lines of magical thinking.

Night descended as we gathered atop Michael's lead. The Ames Ice Hose was a done deal, a top first ascent of our careers. It was time to rappel off the thing and head home. But there were no handshakes, no backslaps. When I held a loop of rope, it levitated horizontally like frozen, wind-blown laundry on a winter clothesline. Rappelling such cord would be hellish, if not fatal. Instead, we needed to gain the canyon rim, build a fire, thaw and dry our ropes, and rappel or hike the following day.

Again on the lead, I did what I did best: a manic charge, this time on a near-vertical pitch of snow hummocks interspersed with slabs of frozen moss. In the dark. No protection.

On the canyon rim above the climb, we foraged blind through the night, tripping over deadfall while gathering firewood. Ever the NOLSie, I dug out my waterproof matches and kindled a blaze. We stacked pine-bough beds on the six feet of snow between us and the ground. Nearby tree branches served as hangers for careful rope drying. Nylon melts all too easily.

In the campfire's glow, I grabbed my bulky backpack (we'd rope-hauled it and another sack of gear up the climb). Grinning at Shea through the smoke, I opened the top flap and yanked out my blimp-sized jacket.

"Dawson, what the hell, that's what we were hauling?" Shea grumped, half laughing.

"I'm skinnier than you are—need it so I won't freeze into a block of ice, like I almost did yesterday, thanks to your endless lead."

Michael threw another log on the fire, and we divided the last of our M&M'S. The single item missing from our camporee was my father's favorite Dinty Moore canned stew: the sweet, cholesterol-soaked carrot slices, the meat that required the faith of a child to believe it was beef.

Despite the deep snow, we found enough firewood by breaking dead branches from trees. And while I was the best dressed, everyone had adequate clothing. One doesn't sleep much in such situations, but I heard a few snores.

ICE CLIMBING FRESHENED MY commitment to the vertical, but even this feral sport paled in the face of my wandering spirit. Out of habit, I visited Yosemite that spring with my brother Craig, an excellent climber, and aced almost forty of the more arduous routes, among them Twilight Zone, Chopper Flake, Folly Right Side, and a one-day speed ascent of Half Dome's "standard" Northwest Face big-wall. (The latter with Ajax Greene, another of Yosemite's devoted minions of rock).

The journal pages marched on. Like the previous fall with Peterson, I was at an athletic peak. Yet it felt like I was climbing the same pitch, on the same rock, over and over again. What was next?

Next was obvious. Having been on planks since my teens, I was an okay skier; I could slog with the best and had survived Denali. Yet I'd never learned to ski in the genuine sense of the word: wring out my boards, master the mountain.

Any man who called himself an alpinist skied better than okay, and likely skied the steeps as well. How to become that skier? I knew just one path: the abandon I applied to rock and ice. "Ski to die!" it was called by bar-stool pontificators with plaster-casted legs and bandage-bedecked foreheads. A trite phrase meant to evoke a laugh. But I came to hate it. Not because of its absurdity—no skier seeks death—but because I became a genuine ski-to-die poster boy.

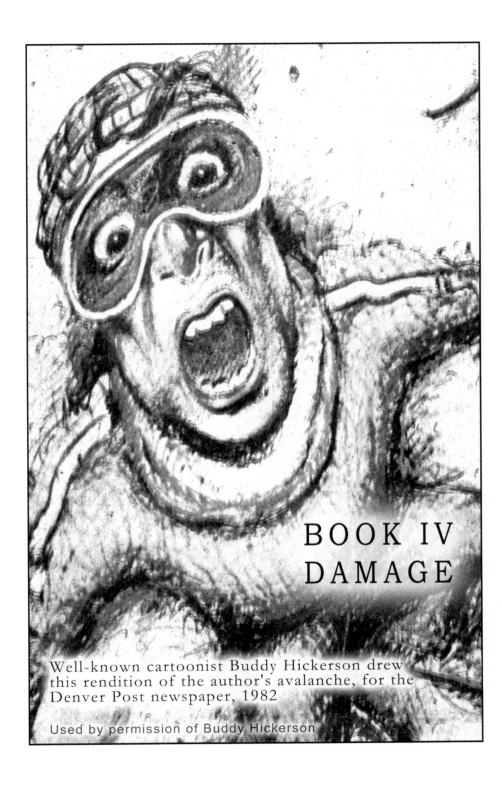

BOOK IV
DAMAGE

Well-known cartoonist Buddy Hickerson drew
this rendition of the author's avalanche, for the
Denver Post newspaper, 1982

Used by permission of Buddy Hickerson

27 | SKI TO DIE, 1976-1978

FLASHBACK: NEW YEAR'S EVE, 1973. As I step inside the Durant Mine barn, the Jimi Hendrix guitar licks squalling from a pair of dishwasher-sized speakers sound loud enough to set my hair on fire. A mix of tobacco and pot smoke swirls over bare lightbulbs. The floor shudders beneath a hundred shimmying, arm-flailing, stoned-out dancers. I turn sideways and dodge through the crowd. A few yards in, there's something squishy under my front foot; I'm about to step on the back of an over-served reveler sprawled facedown on the matted carpet—I change course. When I reach the room's rear, a shiny-eyed headbanded longhair holds out a Corona and something stronger, something white. "Want some?" he offers with a wink.

I don't refuse. After all, I'm home.

Durant Mine Barn, 1973   ©Alan Becker

In 1969, a ragtag assembly of Aspen creatives sought affordable space for photography classes. Just east of the base of Aspen Mountain, a five-minute walk from the ski lifts, the abandoned Durant Mine mechanical shop and storage barn—a cavernous, two-story, 3,600-square-foot relic of the past—was situated ten yards from its namesake mine tunnel. A lease was signed—open-ended because a demolition crew could show up any day. The founders then set to transforming the rat-infested dungeon into their version of hippie artisan utopia.

Because the town approved the project for day use only, the illegal barn-dominium apartments were stealth-built, exterior windows and such installed during weekends—while the building inspector was fishing, golfing, or whatever building inspectors did on their days off. Budgets were tight; most materials were scrounged. The mishmash of rusted tin and splintery plywood resembled the ramshackle shacks of a barrio, yet possessed an undeniable artistry.

Indoors, the salvaged barn wood and exposed framing reminded me of our family home back in Crazy Acres. Tattered vinyl couches and junkyard carpet remnants appointed the downstairs common area. The nearby mine's drainage provided tasty, non-chlorinated water, tapped via fifty feet of black-plastic irrigation pipe. The residents claimed they'd had the water tested for toxins—*passed!* Even so, while enjoying a cool glass of the crystal fluid, one still wondered: any two-headed babies out there?

Most of the founding creatives had moved on a year or two after the beginnings, leaving what came to be called "The Barn" to its destiny: budget beds for young ski bums, steps from the ski lifts.

WHEN WE RETURNED FROM Denali that summer of 1973, Kendall Williams was boarding at The Barn, as was Michael "Pokie" Pokress. They suggested I sublease. "Graeme Means and the other guys think it's okay," Pokie said. "They know you from your climbing, thought you'd be a cool housemate."

My first room was a converted storage loft, accessed via a ladder-like stairway made from an antique prospecting sluice, leading to a sixteen-inch-wide plank bridge with a wobbly two-by-four handrail twenty feet above the common area below. Trip and you'd crater next to the wood-burning stove. I joked with my fellow "barnoids" that a lady wasn't worthy if she failed to walk or crawl the plank. The same went for the resident.

When the owner of my subleased room returned, the Barn boys approved my bunking in the water heater closet. There I slept next to the blue-yellow light of the gas burner, like a cowboy snuggled to his campfire—though, judging from the moist-sweet aroma of natural gas combustion, I was far from the starlit prairie. After four atmospheric months, I migrated from my monoxide palace to a "normal" barndominium. I borrowed a chainsaw and installed an operable window. My health improved. And ski school commenced.

KENDALL, POKIE, AND A rat pack of other top skiers dominated Aspen's world-famous ski hill. Working as waiters, realtors, or any job that enabled flexible daylight hours, each winter they exceeded the hundred-day goal of most any serious slider. While riding the chairlifts, you could identify these guys from a thousand yards, especially Kendall: fast and smooth, cutting fat arcs in a style ahead of the time. And Pokie, he skied with raw physicality; his ruthless turns were known to snap the strongest fiberglass laminated skis.

The mandate was unsaid yet irrevocable. I would chase the rat packers down the slopes until I learned to keep up. The first few months, I crashed every run. As I gathered my scattered gear, my senseis showed no mercy and skied ahead. More than once, I limped into the Barn long after they'd racked their planks, my hat somewhere on the hill, wet hair decorated with ice crystals, cracked goggles crooked from my neck like a bowtie after a fistfight. As I stumbled to the ski storage room, my torturers grinned and nodded as they sipped beer next to the hot wood stove.

I worked as a nightshift dishwasher to free my days and learned to ski. Glory days. Yet, what of the heart?

While majoring in skibum-ology, I had not forgone the amorous side of the lifestyle. The easygoing relationships varied: a schoolteacher, ski instructors so fine in their blue Anba of Austria parkas, and others. Days and nights of wine and roses for all involved. Yet, while my lifestyle might not have looked like it, I was never all-in with casual affairs, never comfortable with '60s style "love." Deep in my heart, a faint yet persistent voice told me there there had to be something more.

Michael Pokress,
North Face of North Maroon Peak,
Elk Mountains, Colorado, 1976   ©Kendall Williams

Michael Kennedy invited me for dinner one summer evening at the Aspen home he and his girlfriend rented. Their pretty, hazel-eyed housemate caught my attention.

In contrast to typical mountain-town denim and nylon, Eva Breton favored pastel capris and pink shirts. She was giggly, borderline childish. While I enjoyed her playfulness, I soon learned it hid plenty of smarts—she was fluent in Italian and a skilled survivor of Aspen's service jobs and scarce housing.

Eva didn't climb. Aside from occasional cross-country ski outings, she skied only at the resorts. I had long ago quit obsessing on the mountain-sports resumés of my romantic prospects. Those things still mattered, but emotional and physical compatibility trumped all—we had both.

Here was the relationship that mixed an unsaid version of long-term commitment with casual intimacy. I was never sure it was love. Did that mean it was not? We hooked up with others during our time together and had long periods apart—at one point, Eva spent a year in Italy teaching English.

Our relationship was perpetual motion. What more could a young buck ask for?

Yet for me, and I sensed for Eva, a current of inadequacy flowed beneath—*there is something more, something better*. During our rare discussions of the future, she always asked what I wanted. "I don't know," I'd mumble, thinking *this is not it*.

"Can't you even tell me what you want? Can't we spend more time together, be a real couple?" she'd respond, brushing back her blond hair with one hand, squeezing my forearm with the other, tears glistening in her eyes.

More often than not, I barked something back, and the shouting began. When it went from bad to worse, as it often did, the fights devolved into near-physical violence sparked by the frustration of unmet expectations. The clock of life was ticking, and we could not see the time.

What will life be should I never marry? Grow old alone?

I smothered my doubts under a blanket of danger: soloing ice climbs without a rope, touching avalanche slopes, skiing at breakneck speeds. Worse, after living a primarily substance-free life for around five years after high school, like the frog who doesn't notice himself brought to a boil in slow-heated water, I'd segued out of my quest for fitness, sobriety, and spirituality. Instead, I had become a mountain-town cliché, existing for nothing else than the adrenaline, the drugs, the ego trip of first ascents, the narcissistic glee of extreme athletics.

MARCH 1977. SIXTEEN INCHES of powder snow fell overnight, leaving a Colorado morning so clean and robust it shot sky-blue tractor beams through The Barn's rusty tin roof. As I sat beside the wood stove and slapped my ski boot buckles closed, the spice-candle scent of molten wax drifted from the ski room. I knew this day was one in a hundred, as did my cohorts, Kendall and gravel-voiced Graeme Means.

Graeme was, in some ways, the most conventional of our cadre; he worked as an architect. But normality ceased just past the tip of his drawing pencil. The tales were many, most of them true, recited with an impish grin and lit eyes. Such as his times hiking in a kilt—Graeme enjoyed celebrating his Celtic heritage—and fending off women interested in what lurked beneath.

I looked forward to hearing more of Graeme's racy tales, perhaps while riding the ski lifts.

Our skis were waxed, pockets held a candy bar or two, sunscreen smeared on our noses, the kitchen sink was stacked with breakfast dishes someone might wash tomorrow. One thing remained.

"Hey," one of our cohorts said as he held out a hand displaying two Chicklet-sized, reddish paper squares. Owsley blotter acid, first-rate stuff, made especially for the Grateful Dead band and their pajama-panted fans. "Let's cut these in half and go for it."

I grinned as I fetched the scissors.

Today would not be my first psychedelic skiing adventure. I preferred such indulgences—while ignoring the possible consequences of rocketing down a mountain under a throbbing fuchsia sky on skis that felt twenty feet long.

Thoughts were few, action was all. We spun the dial to eleven, blasting powder-covered moguls, dodging slow-motion tourists, and reveling in adrenal toxicity while charging nonstop runs from top to bottom.

Had I reached another level? Master of snow, on par with my idols or perhaps even the gods? Yet again, I was nothing more than a chemical legend in my own mind.

A HALF HOUR BEFORE the lifts closed, we stopped for tea at the Sundeck summit restaurant—a last-run tradition—where we joined ski club coach Murray Cunningham and architect Harry Teague.

After sharing a few cosmic revelations, Kendall took a last slug of Lipton and plucked his hat from the apparel we'd piled on the table. "I've got a ride arranged so we can ski Keno Gully—be back in Aspen for dinner at La Cocina. There's avalanche danger, but we can avoid it—ski the trees and the sides of the run."

The Aspen Mountain in-bounds ski slopes sit on the northern end of seven-mile-long Richmond Ridge. Numerous backcountry ski runs drop from the resort boundary down the western side of the ridge, ending at the Castle Creek road a few miles from town. Since the resort's early days, backcountry skiing these runs had been a beloved—albeit dangerous—local tradition.

I was coming down from my acid trip enough to stop drooling on my neck gaiter and say something coherent: "Okay, I'm ready."

We departed the restaurant four hours before nightfall with no back-country gear: no snow shovels, no extra clothing, no first aid kit, and in 1977, no cell phones. We did have our pocket litter; the roach clips and wallets would go unused, but the cigarette lighters would come in handy.

As I CLOCKED HIGH-SPEED curves down Keno, I flowed in the acid moment, patterning Kendall and Pokie: work the terrain, let the skis find their way.

Then it imploded. Vegetation closed up my line. A patch of breakable snow-crust tripped me. A thatch of aspen saplings tangled my left ski. The binding failed to release. I heard as much as I felt the wet *pop* as the bones of my lower left leg gave way.

The ski remained trapped. Momentum spiraled me to the left. I ended up sitting in the soft snow with my skis still attached; my left foot twisted 180 degrees backward, big toe pointed at my butt. As I struggled for position, my butt sank inch by inch, causing the ruptured bones at my boot top to ruck up my ski pants in a sickening parody of a broken 2x4.

It looked like my leg was twisting off.

"Help me!" I screamed. "Broke my leg!"

Kendall and Graeme slid to a halt a few feet from my ski tips. As I tried to straighten my leg and ease the searing pain, Kendall pushed a thicket of branches aside, unlatched my ski bindings, and gently twisted my foot back to its natural orientation. He'd worked as a ski patroller—this wasn't the first spiral fracture he'd seen.

"No blood," Kendall said. "Not compounded, but almost. I can feel the busted bone ends just under your skin."

As Graeme held my foot, Kendall broke a pair of gnarled branches from a nearby aspen tree, pulled off his belt, and fashioned a makeshift splint.

"We need to get you out of the avalanche path," he said. "We'll have to carry you ... Only a couple hundred feet, but it's gonna hurt."

Kendall and Graeme held my shoulders while Harry and Murray linked their arms under my legs. Together, the four men carried me across the snow-filled gully like a wounded soldier in a firefight. Someone postholed deep into the snow every few steps and tripped, sending jolts of ungodly pain through my leg, which despite the splint was nothing more than a loose bundle of bone splinters. At each stumble, I screamed in agony before pleading, "Stop! Put me down, just leave me here!"

Finally, we reached the safe zone, where I lay on my back on a couch-like pallet sculpted from the snow. Thus immobilized, the pain ratcheted down from ten to eight. *Peachy. Now what?*

Graeme: "Things could be worse, an avalanche, somebody dead. Not sure what we should do now, though. You can't move, right?"

I groaned, frustrated. I could crawl a few yards at most before pain and exhaustion put me down.

We were a thousand feet above the valley floor. Steep, avalanche-prone gullies, brush, and deep, sugary snow made a quick do-it-yourself evacuation impossible. Darkness was an hour away.

"No, I totally can't move." Pause. "Need a rescue."

"Someone needs to go right now," Kendall said. "Tell the sheriff what's going on, tell some ski patrollers, tell Harvey Carter. That'll trigger an official rescue. But it might not happen until morning."

Right—with no camping gear, not even a shovel, let's sit around the campfire singing the Grateful Dead-enhanced version of "Kumbaya." All while my circulation-compromised tissue went morbid, leading to amputation. If I didn't die of hypothermia or a fat embolism first.

"We need friends to help get me out of here tonight," I said. "Whoever goes down, get on the phone and call everybody we know."

"I'll do it," Murray said, clicking into his skis and shrugging off his jacket to leave with us.

A few dozen friends—without rescue gear or experience—were not going to hustle my wracked body down the mountain. Why were we thinking such wacky stuff?

Our acidic inebriation didn't help with rationality, but that was just part of it. In the late 1970s, there was a lack of trust between our younger backcountry crowd (climbers, skiers) and authorities such as the sheriff and mountain rescue team. They were devoted to the cause, but their response to accidents was painfully slow. So, while Murray did notify the authorities, they played a minor role in my rescue. Instead, however improbable, our network came through.

It went something like this: Having made his phone calls and dropped in on a bar frequented by patrollers—including Carter—Murray was driving through town on his way back. He spotted Durant barn resident and rat-pack skier Gerry Sullivan walking home with an armload of groceries. Gerry was locally famous for his two-plank skills and uncanny ability to outfit himself solely from ski shop discards and thrift shop bargains. What he could do on a pair of Rossignol skis pulled from a dumpster was nothing short of amazing.

Murray stopped and rolled down his window. "Hey, Lou broke his leg in Keno. We need all the help we can get to get him out. First things first, somebody needs to break trail up the mountain. It's gonna be hard."

"I can do that," Gerry said. He threw his groceries into the back seat, hopped in, and drank half a jar of honey, knowing he'd need the calories. Fifteen minutes later, he was bulling his way up Keno Gulch through the willow thickets and sugary, quicksand snow, wearing the bulbous foam Moon Boots he wore as street shoes, jacket tied around his waist.

He arrived soaked to the skin with sweat and melted snow. Luckily, we had a fire going, or there might have been two victims needing rescue, him with hypothermia caused by his soggy clothing.

DARKNESS FELL. DESPITE GERRY's broken trail, climbing to the accident scene was exhausting, and the entire route followed a known avalanche path. And yet, activated by the telephone chain Murray had begun, face after face appeared in the firelight: "Lou ... Hang in there ... What can I do?"

Despite the people massed below and the crowd growing around our campfire, nothing happened—there was no feasible way to move me down the hill. The mood shifted to despair.

Suddenly, shouts filtered from above us. A light beam glinted off the white bark of tightly packed aspen trees. Someone was descending from the ski resort, with a rescue sled? Doubtful. Steering a seventy-pound Cascade ski patrol sled down the steeps in the dark of night—threading through trees that were a shoulder-width apart while avoiding avalanche slopes—seemed impossible.

When Harvey Carter skidded to a stop by our campfire, standing between the curved six-foot handlebars of a red patrol toboggan, I thought for a moment I was hallucinating. Then reality hit, and a hint of concern penetrated my amazement. *Why was Harvey here? Did he not know who he was rescuing?*

The previous summer, Harvey had smacked his meaty fist into his open hand and threatened to beat the hell out of me for stealing the first-free ascent of a rock-climbing route he'd claimed. Fearing for my jaw, I'd avoided him to the extent of skipping climbs when I saw his car parked nearby.

Now helpless, on my back, a wounded animal, I looked up at my recent nemesis and erstwhile mentor.

"Well, Harvey, shall we continue the feud?"

Harvey replied in his gruff voice, loud—the same old curmudgeon, yet with a tinge of concern, even kindness: "Nah, let's forget it."

I had not heard that hint of fathering since he'd coached me through my

214 LOUIS W. DAWSON

near-death experience in the Yosemite squeeze "chimbley."

THE TERRAIN WAS HARSH; some would say impossible for a loaded sled: dense brush with drops that Harvey launched like he was stunting for *Ski Patrol: The Movie*. Willow branches rasped the sled's fiberglass sides and scrubbed over my blanket-covered face. Dozens of friends and their friends had stationed themselves along the evacuation route to help with the sled. Harvey's brusque commands were the soundtrack: "Grab that rope, Graeme ... Let go here ... Pull the sled over to the right, Marty ..."

DOCTOR RODNEY KIRK OPENED my leg and screwed the assorted bone shards together as best he could. After a week in the hospital, I was gobbling a dozen calcium pills daily and crutching around like I'd aged fifty years. At five weeks, Kirk put me in a walking cast. "Walk on it, Lou, to stimulate the healing, but don't overdo it."

I overdid it, of course. After a month at a friend's bungalow where I could roam without stairs, I moved back to the Barn. Within days, I was working as a carpenter while still casted, drinking too much alcohol, and toughing out the healing like I toughed out my climbs.

Bone tissue doesn't care how macho you are.

"It's a delayed union," Doctor Kirk said at my twelve-week appointment, as if describing an undercooked bowl of ramen.

This wasn't ramen. And I had no health insurance.

I was soon unemployed, on crutches month after month. My lost life haunted me—the ice-climbing tools I'd not gripped, the skis I'd not ridden. I spent most of every day in bed in my Barn room, watching an antique black-and-white television with a coat hanger for an antenna.

Food stamps and a county disability program kept me from starvation. I befriended a painkiller named Darvon. The Barn denizens forgave my rent. My mother and father didn't have the financial resources to help. Perhaps my grandfather did, but I was too ashamed—or prideful?—even to ask.

Somehow, I motivated myself to borrow a typewriter from Michael

Kennedy and write an article about the accident. *Powder* magazine co-founder and editor David Moe visited Aspen that summer on business. He knew me by reputation. That previous winter, they'd published an ice-climbing article illustrated with Michael's photos, some depicting our adventures together. When I mentioned writing something, Moe encouraged me to send it in.

Powder published "Out of Bounds and Out of Luck" in their November 1977 issue. I was embarrassed by the amateur prose, as well as not having mentioned my substance-addled idiocy. Readers told me they liked the article. I figured they were being polite.

Yet one aspect of the *Powder* story echoed genuine and sweet: Harvey Carter, our feuding forgotten, looking down in altruistic compassion upon his damaged protégé and hauling him off the mountain, like Superman plucking some poor soul from the clutches of disaster.

WINTER CAME. I CONTINUED my nosedive into the pit: despair, zero motivation, self-medicating with cocaine, strong coffee, and everything in between.

In desperation for normalcy, I hitchhiked from Aspen to Sun Valley, Idaho, to see a girl. A ride dropped me off at two a.m. outside Pocatello, at a crossroads next to a darkened gas station. With nothing more than a thin jacket against the Siberian cold, I stood on my crutches and shivered until a fat, gray-haired man picked me up and hit on me.

After three days in Idaho, I borrowed money and bought a plane ticket home.

Back in Aspen, my network of supportive friends was a phone call away: Eva, Michael Kennedy, Harvey Carter, others. I ignored them and took up with a rambunctious nurse I'd met in the hospital. We had fun. Some of it I remember.

Ski to die.

THROUGHOUT ALL THIS, RICH Jack and I had remained close friends. Our big-wall climbs were long in the past—El Capitan, Longs Peak, Black Canyon. But the bond of shared adventure remained. By nature, Rich had always been a caregiver. He worked as an EMT now, while pursuing a career in nursing. His wife, Sandra, a nurse, had previously worked with an orthopedic surgeon in Seattle, Dr. William Boettcher.

Rich and Sandra sensed the darkness closing over my life, their friend limping around like a polio victim—and too often inebriated.

Sandra insisted Boettcher was the solution.

"He's amazing, such a good surgeon, and a good man," she said with a hint of mothering. "I think he can get you fixed—otherwise, you'll be disabled for life, maybe lose your leg."

By March 1978, I'd lived disabled for a year. I flew to Seattle and lodged at Sandy's parents' home. Boettcher took me under care as a financial indigent and rodded my left tibia with a stainless steel spike extending from knee to ankle. Within a few days, I was partially weight-bearing and improving fast. To celebrate my "I'm healed!" moment, I went clean and sober, prizing peaceful meals with Sandra's retired parents, sailing Puget Sound with her sister in a twelve-foot wooden Herreshoff Haven. With the help of these fine people, I'd snapped the reset switch.

All too soon, I'd learn the reset switch had a powerful return spring.

BACK IN ASPEN AFTER two months in Seattle, I tossed my crutches. Michael Kennedy got me a handyman job at the *Aspen Times* building, where he produced *Climbing* magazine. I enjoyed working with my hands again, making a paycheck, and being around Michael's success. And I began seeing Eva Breton again. I laughed at her stories of the free-ranging pet monkeys her parents kept in North Carolina, how the mischievous little buggers snagged food off dinner plates. "Are they house trained?" I asked.

"Are you?" she replied.

In answer to such queries, I sensed no future in skiing, climbing, or domesticity—because I felt almost nothing. My leg walked okay but was a half-inch shorter, and the fracture site was too sensitive for a ski boot. Depression lingered.

Without the counter influence of athleticism or my straight-laced Seattle friends, I picked up the partying again. And after I pounded a cocaine dealer's door at four in the morning—with predictable results—I knew I was still in trouble.

My friends had pulled me partway from the pit, but I needed something stronger than friendship. Rehab was appropriate, but the thought never occurred to me. And I was a clever user, adept at hiding just how far into the abyss I'd fallen.

While organizing my room, I surfaced a year-old letter from my mother in Crested Butte.

"My darling boy," she had written. "You know you have my total support in whatever you do. I am always with you in spirit."

Patricia Dawson was forty-eight years old, still living in the cabin she and Keith had enlarged in 1973. They'd stayed together for four years after that and split just before I'd broken my leg. Despite the weirdness of the early days, Keith and I had always been friendly. Yet there was a darkness when he was part of the household: his temper and the uncertainty of his role as a father figure to my younger brothers.

Things were easier now: the two older brothers were in the area but on their own, Tom was living elsewhere as well, and Keith was gone. Just my single mother in one of the West's coolest mountain towns, thriving in her drafty house with its world-class interior decorating.

Despite my bitterness regarding my parents' 1960s meltdown, my mother's letter stirred a warmth. Early summer 1978, I made the call. She sensed the need.

"Darling, come live with me for a while. You can help around the house: chop firewood, do some carpentry. You'll heal with the help of my cooking. Tapley and Craig will dig having you on this side of the mountains."

I wasn't sure my mother knew any "healing" would involve much more than my leg. I should not have doubted.

WITH THE ROD'S RIGID support, my bones were close to fully knitted, but my Aspen party-boy behavior pointed to one thing: it was time for a lifestyle reset. I loaded my ride with my carpentry tools, climbing gear, and two shopping bags of clothing, drove the four hours from Aspen to Crested Butte, and moved into my mother's low-ceilinged attic bedroom. The window overlooked Coal Creek. I left it open every night and slept to the music of the water and the yeasty fragrance of fresh-baked bread.

Hippie Patricia had made it to the good side of the sixties. Now, with her drug consumption no more potent than an evening glass or two of cabernet and the occasional joint, her true self flourished. Her paintings—flowers, soft renditions of snowy alpine landscapes—sold well out of local galleries. She worked as the mayor's executive assistant, managed the Center for the Arts, and enjoyed respect as a town elder. In the later times of her Crested Butte residency—thirty-plus years—more than one prominent local would call her a "creative force."

That's not to say my mother had entirely transmuted from her earth-mother hippie phase. Since day one in the 'Butte, she'd heated her cabin with nothing but wood, and cooked on a chrome-trimmed Great Majestic wood-burning cookstove. She swore the 350-pound iron behemoth made better bread than a gas or electric version. My taste buds agreed, though a more noticeable effect was how swinging a six-pound firewood-splitting maul kept her as thin as the models in *Vogue* magazine, to which she'd subscribed since her years in Texas.

Unlike my mother, my father was far from thriving. Near as I could tell, he still floated in a chemical doldrum while small-time drug dealing and dabbling in silversmithing: buttons made from buffalo nickels. I acted the dutiful son; during a visit, I'd brought my tools and built him a barnwood and glass display cabinet for his wares. Yet, considering my own behavioral proclivities, it was better I stayed out of his sphere.

AS FOR MY MOTHER, I'd expected a good bit of her influence, but her maternal power surprised me, as well as her skiing. She'd become smooth and confident on the slopes, and wrote of skiing with me, of "keeping up." While watching her thrive, I recalled her dark days and mine—the days we'd both left behind. With that, her effortless love, warm smiles, and accepting eyes, the healing was deep. And if my feelings were true, it was permanent. And my shorter leg? An extra insole solved the problem.

28 | OUTWARD BOUND, 1978-1979

IN CRESTED BUTTE, I picked up a few handyman gigs, helped my mother with chores, and began a return to carpentry and small-time contracting. The reset was working. The partying was not self-abusive—just fun times as a resort town twenty-something, hanging with my brother Tapley, occupying a bar stool on occasion.

Rock and ice climbing had lost much of their appeal. Yet the hills still called. Inspired by my mistakes, I'd formulated a life mantra: "Play by the mountain's rules instead of my own." A lofty goal—maybe a cliché. But I practiced my edict. When I rock climbed with my brother Craig in nearby Taylor Canyon, I was more thoughtful, with less compulsive mania. And I figured that come winter, there'd be no more ski-to-die—though I yearned for my planks.

COLORADO OUTWARD BOUND SCHOOL'S (COBS) personnel manager, Steve Andrews, telephoned in May 1978. He'd gotten my number from a mutual climber friend.

"We figure top mountaineers make successful instructors," he said. "You know safety and technical climbing ... You're a good mentor for the students. Join our instructor course. We hire out of that."

Andrews was right about the technical side—but a mentor and safe instructor? Granted, I had a hefty dose of life experience. Yet my drug-stunted emotional age was probably around seventeen—a far cry from my chronological age of twenty-seven. As for safety, my past few years had a few things to say about that. I'd cleaned up my act and embraced a mantra, but could I live up to my ideals and Andrews'?

Doubts aside, I was flattered by the call. Was there something to this? Despite previously rejecting work as a mountain guide and NOLS instructor, my heart told me that working outdoors, sharing the alpine wilderness with others must be better than making sawdust for a paycheck, in the company of grumpy carpenters as likely to hurl a hammer as they were to express a measurement as something unmentionable in polite company.

ANDREWS CONTRACTED ME TO work three summer Outward Bound courses out of Lake City, in the heart of southern Colorado's San Juan Mountains, three weeks each. As did NOLS, Outward Bound broke their courses into groups of around twelve students, with each "patrol" accompanied by an instructor and assistant. A course included around five patrols. The course director was always a former instructor with a fancy for management and the associated pay raise. When I showed up at the base camp house, my leg virtually healed, fit and cut from running and climbing, Director Ted Kerasote greeted me with a compliment:

"A climber like you will be great for the school."

I wondered ... But I wasn't going to argue the point.

Ted was a compact, muscular fellow and a published author with a pile of magazine bylines. As had the publication of my *Powder Magazine* article, my leg-healing rebirth into outdoor education tickled my author aspirations. So, I brought my manual typewriter to base camp. *Maybe Ted would critique my course reports?*

Baby steps. My first writing project was a staple-bound, copy-machine cookbook for standard Outward Bound food rations. Ted corrected my spelling—which took some work. I named the biscuit recipe "Lori's Buns" in honor of a female instructor I enjoyed hiking behind.

MY FIRST COBS COURSE (we pronounced it "cobs," as in corn cobs) as an instructor combined a hefty dose of rough backpacking with a handful of fourteener summits. Any technical climbing was little more than hiking with ropes. The students were thrilled with the entire package—some deemed it "life-changing." While I was delighted to be their facilitator, the low-end guiding bored me to the point of brain damage. I wasn't sure I could take two more courses of the same.

After we'd sent my first-course students home, I joined Ted for a beer on the front deck of our Lake City base-camp house. We'd stripped off our shirts under the alpine sun—an even tan was a COBS instructor essential. The scent of linseed oil stain cooking off the wall behind us reminded me of my mother's oil paints.

"Taking the students backpacking and doing fixed-rope peak climbs is okay," I whined. "But it's boring, not Outward Bound worthy. Can we spice it up?"

Ted stretched his bare legs in the sun and considered my comment. (I'd never seen him in long pants.)

"You could do some canyoneering. Descend Difficulty Creek and hike out via Cow Creek. Might be a first," he said. "You'll need a bunch of rope work to get your students through there, so take two days—the rough part is about three miles. Arrange with our logistics guy to pick you up at the Cow Creek trailhead. Write detailed course reports for future instructors."

I was all over this—a first, exploring. I was astonished the school would allow me to lead my patrol down cliffy, unknown Difficulty Creek, where flash floods could take us out, waterfall-draped cliffs might exceed our longest rope, and rescue was improbable. I had my guide skills from NOLS and my technical climbing chops—but I was far from a canyoneering expert. *No problem,* I thought, *better the adventure; this is Outward Bound, not a soap sales convention.*

My assistant and I gathered the students around our campfire and hatched the scheme.

"We're doing something different for the next few days, canyoneering down Difficulty Creek. We could be the first."

Seventeen-year-old Judy raised her hand. "What's canyoneering?"

BEFORE OUR INAUGURAL DROP into Difficulty, we camped on a timbered shelf above the canyon, yards from the first cliffs. The night sky was clear, no moon, the wilderness star dome I never tired of. I grabbed my sleeping bag and pad, ambled a few yards from our campfire, and bedded with my face to the sky. Judy and another student spread their bags next to mine. We lay there calling out shooting stars, talking of life: how it got so complicated, how our days in the wilderness were so easy, how to bring some of this goodness back home. The faint drone of Difficulty Creek filtered from below, like traffic on a distant highway, while the night breeze sighed through nearby spruce branches.

OUR TWO DAYS DESCENDING Difficulty Creek canyon went something like this: If the terrain was steep, with fall potential yet hikeable, I installed climbing gear or tied slings around trees and lashed everyone to the side of the canyon. I then forged ahead and rigged the route. Dressed in nothing but my cutoff jean shorts and running shoes, coiled ropes on my shoulders, I speed-scrambled like a mountain goat across the cliffs and scarps. After installing somewhat horizontal fixed ropes—often using all the 450 feet of cord we had—I dashed back to the students, loving my mini-solo, delighting in the intellectual challenge of creating the route, craving the water's throaty roar, and the sting of alpine sun on my shoulders. One by one, my charges clipped into the rope with a sliding carabiner and hand-lined their way along the canyon wall.

At NOLS, we'd been big on "Tyrolean traverses," aerial tramways built with our climbing ropes, tensioned with makeshift pulley systems, designed to move wilderness travelers and their heavy backpacks over savage rivers. Falling back on such skills, I built two Tyroleans over Difficulty Creek. One was mandatory, switching riversides to circumvent a waterfall and cliff; the other I built for fun.

Life was sweet, dangling over waterfalls while inhaling mountain-pure creek spume with hints of trout and granite—then depending on teamwork to move everyone across the tensioned Tyrolean tram rope. It all looked riskier than it was—by intent, perceived risk enhanced the student experience. As for real-world danger, such as broken ropes, it was there, but I knew how to mitigate it.

THE EDENIC LIFESTYLE SEDUCED me: compliant, appreciative kids to lead, goals to achieve, and a low-paying yet reliable job I was proud of. The mentor part was working as well. During each course, we sent the students out for periods of solo contemplation with paper and envelopes to write letters to themselves.

"Seal the letters, self-address, and hand them in. I'll mail them to you after the course," I told them.

After I mailed the letters, I'd receive multiple replies, thanking me for directing them to "write to myself" and often including statements such as, "You taught me more than mountaineering skills ... You taught me to be myself and put out 100 percent even if it hurt."

Had my trials—busted leg and troubled times—taught me something I could share?

During campfire talks, I'd often repeated one of Ted's favorite sayings: "Strive for excellence, and the necessary and sufficient shall become second nature."

In light of Ted's words, I realized my students had taken Outward Bound to heart. They had strived and found reward. And despite my chaotic, failure-prone life, I'd had something to do with the outcomes.

I SIGNED UP FOR an Outward Bound autumn course and three winter courses, all based out of Leadville, Colorado. With my ski mountaineering skills, how could that be tougher than cantering through the San Juans while working on my tan? The question was soon answered.

Leadville teeters on a windy shelf at some 10,200 feet elevation, just under timberline, next to and sometimes on top of the mineral wealth that inspired its 1800s boomtown name. It is the highest incorporated city in the United States.

The Outward Bound base camp was seven miles southwest of town and 500 feet lower—more protected yet still exposed to Colorado's high-altitude brutality. While wintering in the area, you lived in a constant barrage of anemic vehicle batteries, icy roads, and air so dry that minor respiratory bugs often put people in the hospital. It was enough to drive a person to drinking and rebellious behavior based on the time-honored philosophy: "If things are this bad, why should I care?" Accordingly, the town's taverns had done a hopping business since tobacco-spitting prospectors plopped sacks of gold dust on the bar and said, "I'll take one of everything, including her."

TIM LANE WAS WORKING OB winter courses. In the five years since our Denali climb, he'd become a thick-bearded Buddharupa of the hills—one of those quiet guys you know understands the words of the wind. Between courses, he pursued a career in avalanche forecasting while backcountry skiing every chance he got.

Lane and his friend Jerry Roberts, an OB instructor with a puckish demeanor that validated his black Rasputin beard, taught me the art of surviving Leadville winters. Such skills involved enthusiastic drinking at the aforementioned taverns, immense servings of backcountry skiing, and all the irreverent humor the pair could cook up.

At their best, the two crazies constructed a pair of Velcro-covered gloves, then chased a flock of sheep around a roadside pasture to create a zany photograph depicting the classic cowboy bestiality joke.

"Did you guys actually consummate the melding of human and ewe?" I asked.

Roberts grinned and said, "Ask Tim."

All I got was Lane's trademark eye twinkle.

Then there was the time we raided the unlocked base-camp food storage to provision one of our backcountry skiing expeditions. A ten-pound brick of lard-veined industrial bacon did the job.

I'm not sure why we thought our banditry would escape notice. Maybe we didn't care what happened so long as we got our daily dose of pork-powered powder.

Course Director Denny Hogan and the logistics staff called us into a meeting upon our return. Nobody was smiling.

"Did you guys loot the food room?" Hogan said. "You're making me go bald."

It wasn't just our thievery destroying Hogan's follicles. He'd been at the Halloween party when Roberts had whipped it out and pissed on a guy costumed as a urinal. And though he couldn't prove it, Hogan had a pretty good idea that Lane was the scofflaw who'd crashed the company van into a snowy pine forest, then hiked home to avoid a DUI.

"Yeah, we thought the food was extra."

"Don't let it happen again."

While engaging in frat-boy shenanigans wasn't precisely "playing by the mountain's rules," something inside me made such things seem okay. Perhaps the influence of my father, the nonconformist outlaw? I didn't obsess, but it was there.

We made up for our failings through teaching—the only reason Hogan didn't fire us. We shared our knowledge with generosity and intention—though imparting fundamental ski skills to our students was a fraught endeavor.

There were always a few total novices and never-evers whose learning needed the repetition of lift skiing. And the gear didn't help.

The school loaned every student a pair of rail-stiff, heavy-as-sin Olin alpine skis mounted with Ramer ski-touring bindings. Unless maintained and precisely adjusted, the "Reamers" (as we called the bindings in jest) were known leg breakers—verified by my Keno Gully accident. To remedy this, COBS installed the Ramers without the rear boot-heel latch-down unit used to shift the binding from walk mode to ski mode. The resulting free-heel setup was less injurious during a fall but required exceptional skill and balance to "ski" in the modern sense.

Outward Bound's philosophy on assigning students to their twelve-person patrol was to "churn," meaning you drew names out of a hat, thus mixing everything from cultural background to gender, to athletic ability. This approach was said to stimulate personal growth through the challenges of group dynamics.

As a result, students in a winter or early spring patrol varied from solid skiers to never-evers. The better skiers handled the Olins surprisingly well, but it didn't matter. The churned patrol followed the lowest denominator skier, and was thus condemned to mind-numbing low-angle traverses, linked with awkward kick turns that resembled a ballet plié, only with six-foot two-by-fours lashed to their feet. Leading such a group downhill was as exciting as counting pebbles. My assistant and I would make two turns, stop and supervise for five minutes, repeat, and repeat.

I valued the concept of the churn. But there's a time for educational philosophy—and a time for skiing.

My next course was contracted for May, when the alpine snowpack enters a springtime melt-freeze cycle that makes for less avalanche danger and easier skiing on a crystalline surface known as "corn snow." *With the right group of students ...*

I met with Hogan over a jumbo pan of scrambled eggs I'd whipped up in the base camp dining hall.

"I can't stomach another patrol with mixed skiing abilities," I said. "Next course, how about we select the ten best student skiers, utilize the spring snowpack, and teach them *real* ski mountaineering, with Tim Lane as my assistant?"

Hogan gave my plan the nod. I figured he pitied my plight.

It went well. While the free-heel Ramer-mounted skis didn't support the most advanced descents, we enjoyed plenty of legitimate skiing, including partial descents of a few peaks. This could have been enough—happy students being our primary goal. Yet my plan for the ultimate ski mountaineering course had another component, something I had not mentioned to Hogan.

A FEW DAYS BEFORE the course had begun, I was having beers with Lane and stocky, fit OB instructor Bruce Adams. He was known for his ski alpinism and climbing chops.

"I'm gonna try skiing thirty peaks in thirty days. Thirteeners and fourteeners." I boasted. "You guys want to help?"

Lane looked at me like I was nuts. "How can you do that when teaching an Outward Bound course? Humans need sleep and time for swallowing wine."

Adams half-grinned and replied, "When do we start?"

I laid out my plan: Ski as many peaks as possible while leading my next course, then a peak or two a day near Leadville, 'till I reached thirty.

"Bruce, join me for as many as you can. Lane, you too if you've had enough wine."

An orgy of glisse ensued, as did an atmospheric blessing. For most of thirty days, bluebird skies and cool mornings were the Colorado norm, ideal conditions for springtime ski descents. A week into my customized ski mountaineering course, we climbed a peak nearly every morning. I'd lead the ascent and then ski down (while leaving the downhill guiding to Tim, bless his heart). Later, while the students napped, I snuck from camp and stealth-skied another summit. Some days, I banged out three peaks.

When I skied Mount Elbert (Colorado's highest), Lane and I marched our twelve students up a broad, snow-filled couloir on the peak's northwest flank. Without skills or gear for steep skiing, they left their skis stabbed into the snow below the summit. I packed my planks to the top and skied down while Lane herded our cats. Late that afternoon, I topped Frasco and Casco peaks, two high thirteeners near our camp.

As planned, Adams and I teamed up after the course. On our first day, we dropped the first descent of the north face of fourteener La Plata Peak. The next day, we skied the steep, expansive west side of 13,942-foot French Mountain. Crystalline three-inch sun fins covered the forty-five-degree pitch. Each turn broke bushels of fins from the slope. They followed us down in a tinkling wash that flowed over our skis and around our ankles when we stopped—an avalanche of sorts, but pretty.

At the thirty-day mark, the deed was done: thirty ski descents, thirty peaks. I had found new potential: extended days of cardio effort, the ability to ski anything in Colorado that snow stuck to, and the mental game of sticking with an extended project. It was one of my life's best, most enjoyable ski mountaineering endeavors.

Spring passed, then summer in Crested Butte, carpentry, and the revival of my rock climbing on the sandstone walls of Zion National Park and Utah's Titan ("Monster") Tower, where a friend and I made an early repeat of Sun Devil Chimney. The multi-day wall was as hard and hot as it sounds. During the descent's twelve rappels, blowing sand scratched my corneas so badly I was nearly blind by the time we grounded. My partner led me by hand as I stumbled along the exit trail.

Winter came. With it came a Crested Butte season ski pass, a job in a cabinet shop, and countless backcountry days in the surrounding West Elk Mountains.

Mountain life. More to come: the good, and the not so good.

29 | IF YOU FALL, 1980

THROUGHOUT THE DECADES SINCE we'd first met as teenagers, Chris Landry and I had led parallel lives as Aspen-based alpinists. I'd forgiven him for blowing me off when I asked him to teach me climbing. Or perhaps I'd retaliated by out-climbing him. But there was one arena of alpinism where Landry would always rule. Having grown up on his planks and raced during school, his gift was skiing. It was thus only natural when, in the late 1970s, he combined his climbing and skiing into the arcane discipline of extreme skiing—loosely defined as descending heretofore "unskiable" climbing lines.

Chris Landry, 1978

©Kennedy

As the apex event of his career, in May 1978, Landry stunned Aspen locals and soon the national ski mountaineering community with the first ski descent of the east face of 14,025-foot Pyramid Peak, the fourteener near Aspen where I'd ventured with the Ashcrofters fourteen years earlier.

Approaching sixty-degrees steep, outcropped with 300-foot cliffs, prone to avalanches, the "Landry Line" was a fearsome climbing route, let alone a ski descent.

Landry continued to pursue his passion for the steeps. In 1981, *Sports Illustrated* magazine featured his story in a lengthy, mostly authentic article about extreme skiing. Titled "It's Got Its Ups and Downs," the piece led with a pull quote: "The definition of extreme skiing is pretty simple—if you fall, you die."

While Landry had never said those exact words, the "If you fall ..." aphorism gained a life of its own, and you may still hear it wherever ski alpinists gather—said in jest, sometimes whispered in fear.

I would never be the natural-born skier Chris Landry was. Yet starting late, in my teens, was a net positive. I didn't take my two-plank skills for granted. Instead, as with my climbing, I worked my butt off to master the sport. And, underpinned by my barnoid mentors and self-taught by my thirty-peaks-in-thirty-days project, with no overt intention to do so, I'd become a capable extreme skier. Inspired by Landry, my Ophir ice-climbing partner Steve Shea, and the extremists of the Alps, I now sought my potential in magical places, where, in fairness to my betters, I'll state it this way: to live was not to fall.

South (left) and North Maroon peaks, the Maroon Bells

In the Elk Mountains, ten miles southwest of Aspen, rise two ridge-connected fourteeners, South and North Maroon peaks, known collectively as the Maroon Bells. Their ocher coloration and bell-like shape form a unique natural artistry—they are said to be second to the Matterhorn as the most photographed peaks in the world. In fact, the "Bells" are so compelling, someone once promoting the state of Utah mistakenly used them as the branding image on a matchbook, much to the amused howls of Coloradans.

The Bells were not technically nor athletically challenging climbs—hundreds of people topped them every summer, and I'd scaled them dozens of times. It wasn't inaccurate to call them a "somewhat steep hike." Yet their loose, maroon-colored sedimentary rock and ubiquitous cliffs made them treacherous. An innocent slip could result in an ugly accident almost anywhere on the climbing routes. And because ropes dislodged rubble onto climbers below, most climbed without the safety of a cord.

Yet, despite its hazards, the fragile rock had a benefit. When coated with snow—which reduced rockfall frequency—the Bells' uneven erosion created an infinity of skiable features: deep-walled thready couloirs, sneaky traverses around the cliffs. All steep and technical. True extreme skiing.

In 1976, Pokie Pokress, Kendall Williams, and another individual had made the first descent of a steep, east-facing snow gully on South Maroon Peak. Since then, the "Y Couloir" had become a local ritual, and a forty-five-degree bunny slope for skiers of Landry's caliber. What better place to progress my skills?

My DAY FOR SOUTH Maroon Peak began when my mental alarm jerked me awake at three a.m., after five hours' sleep. I lay on my back and checked the stars outside the unzipped tent door. *Clear night that'll cool and firm up the snowpack, fine day to come.* With that minor detail out of the way, I closed my eyes, pulled my sleeping bag tight around my neck, and dozed off. Ten minutes later, I woke with a start, sat up, and jolted from my nest before dreams again won the moment. I made tea, snapped my boot buckles, and was off.

After climbing the lower flanks of South Maroon—moderately angled snow, a few scrambles over rock outcrops—I wandered up a deep, low-angled, rock-walled cleft feature known as the Garbage Chute. As I stomped my crampons into the night-hardened snow flooring the chute, water gurgled somewhere under my feet. Following the previous afternoon's snow-destroying, avalanche-triggering sunshine, a subnivean creek was draining the mountain. It warned me not to dawdle.

Exiting the Garbage Chute, dawn glowed behind my back, painting the snow a pastel orange. I switched off my headlamp, crossed a low-angled snow bowl, and began climbing the steeps of the Y.

The refrozen springtime snow was perfect, sheened with ice that my crampons punched with ease yet held without breaking out and slipping. I climbed fast toward the summit ridge, invoking my full cardio power: plant ice axe, move one foot, kick crampon spikes in, shift other foot, kick, pull axe, and plant it again. It was a dance, and I loved it. The world distilled to rhythmic breaths, the mountain in front of me, the faint watermelon musk of spring snow mixed with the scent of my sweat.

Sunrise flowed over the Elk Mountains as I reached the six-foot-wide, twenty-foot-long summit. Here, my timing presented a dilemma. If I began my descent immediately, the slick-frozen, crampon-friendly snow in the couloir would be dangerous to ski, if not impossible. If I waited an hour, no longer, the sun would soften it to a buttery, edge-friendly consistency. Yet, my only exit from the summit was a few hundred feet of steep, icy, west-facing shaded snow. If I waited for the sun to soften this pitch—at least two hours from now—the couloir would, by then, have thawed to a slushy avalanche trap.

When I thought it through, the choice was easy. I'd control my fate on the west-facing ice rather than chance an avalanche in the couloir.

I sat on the summit for just under an hour, warm in the sun, drinking water and nibbling on a sesame bagel. The west face of Pyramid Peak dominated the eastern view, wrinkled with dozens of snow-filled couloirs—several appeared to yield ski routes from near the summit. I chuckled to myself. *I'm looking at mountainsides for ski descents the way I used to study them for climbing routes. Didn't see that coming during my days with Jardine and Peterson.*

Time to drop. I snapped into my bindings and breathed deep. Performing the skier version of tiptoeing, I sidestepped ten feet down from the summit to where the angle eased a few degrees. While standing on my uphill ski, I tilted and scraped my downhill ski against the white ice, testing for edge hold. It gripped. I sprang a few hop turns to the base of the summit cap, shot across a still-frozen, teeth-rattling traverse, and followed the summit ridge to the couloir entrance.

During my hour wait, the sun had broiled the couloir to perfection: dense snow sheeted with two inches of solar-softened crystals. Each pure, arcing turn was as gentle and easy as those on a green run at a ski resort—albeit with somewhat more tilt. Within a half hour, I was done, skis A-framed on my pack, hiking toward camp through snow-patched rocky devastation from winter's gigantic avalanches.

Feeling not a hint of fatigue, I stopped, turned, and looked up at the snow and reddish rock of South Maroon. Affection for the mountain and a surge of pride swelled inside me. This adventure was another level, on a mountain known for fatalities. On the touchy pitch off the summit, I had skied where to fall was certain death, and I lived.

The climb, then the ski—there was a completeness to it. Now, more than ever, I understood why Landry was so compelled. Because I was as well.

And, "if you fall?" My mountain friends and I would soon learn that question encompassed much more than skiing or climbing.

Back in Crested Butte, I still had a rent-free bed at my mother's house and enough money for more days away from work. I spent my mornings skiing the last of Colorado's spring snow, followed by long naps on her sun-drenched western deck, with Coal Creek as a soundtrack. It was mountain-town bliss—until life in paradise once again crashed.

JUNE 18, 1980, CRESTED Butte. While gassing up my Subaru (I'd upgraded from Volkswagens), I encountered Pimmy Pimentel and Michael Pokress. They wore their Aspen street garb: button-downs and clean jeans—a step above Crested Butte casual.

Pimmy bro-punched me in the stomach.

"I'm glad you're healed and climbing again. I'm flying these folks over to Aspen for business. See you at your mom's for dinner."

"Cool," I replied. "Good to see you guys."

It was just another day in our alpine playground.

After our Denali climb, Pimmy had taken up flying, moved to Crested Butte, and continued his friendship with my mother and brothers. He was generous with his blue, twin-engine Cessna 310, asking only for fuel money contributions when he flew his friends around. The previous winter, he'd dropped me in Jackson, Wyoming, for an avalanche-safety training.

A few hours after seeing the boys at the gas station, I was sunning on my mother's deck, shirt off, asleep, when loud weeping broke my dreams.

"It's Pimmy," my mother wailed between sobs. "Plane crash."

Two private airplanes, one originating in Crested Butte and the other in Aspen, had taken a low route over the intervening Elk Mountains (doing so saved time and fuel). At a relative velocity of some 400 miles per hour, they collided near the summit of East Maroon Pass. Everyone died: twelve, including Pokie, his pregnant wife Ellen, and Pimmy.

In speechless shock, I sat in the alpine sun and stared at a haystack wave in spring-swollen Coal Creek. It built two feet high, collapsed to nothing, and then built again, over and over. As I let loose a sob, Tapley slumped beside me, his face pulled tight in a mask of grief. Just as Pimmy was like a brother to my mother, so he was to Tap.

"Oh man, what should we do? What should we do?"

"We should go up there," I said, addled by grief, not thinking clearly. "Anything's better than sitting around here. If I don't move, I'm going to throw up."

I grabbed my ski mountaineering gear and met Tap outside. He kick-started his single-seater motorbike and scrunched forward until his knees were under the handlebars. The patch of seat behind him was the size of a postcard. It would have to do. I locked my arms around his waist, and with my skis A-framed above my head, we motorcycled twelve miles of dirt road and jeep trail to snowline. From there, we hiked a mile of sloppy afternoon snow to timberline, where the wreckage was scattered over an open, snowy area near the summit of East Maroon Pass.

The rescue volunteers had posted a guard who wouldn't let us near, so we took up an eerie vigil in a grove of shoulder-high timberline conifers 300 feet up the hill from the crash site. A few clouds drifted across the sky, a cool breeze blew. We watched as a helicopter lifted a torn passenger compartment. Several corpses were still belted to their seats, one missing an arm, others worse. As the afternoon shadows lengthened, the helicopter returned and retrieved the guard. The wind gave way to an eerie calm. We left our hideout and stepped over torn scraps of aircraft aluminum and human bone to view a crushed object resembling the results of an automobile compactor. It was the engine wrapped with a few scraps of red cowling.

Right then, right there, was a need for remembrance.

Greater tributes were for later. Today, we would ski. We hiked to the top of a snow slope overlooking the crash site. As the snow cooled and firmed under the setting sun, I clicked into my ski bindings. Tapley had no skis, so he clutched the top of my backpack and stomped his motorcycle boots onto my ski tails. Our first attempt failed when his feet slipped. He climbed back on. This time, he stuck, clinging to my backpack like a pilot fish.

"Here's one for you, Pimmy!" we shouted over one turn. "For you, Pokie," on another. "For everybody!" we sang as my skis cast a comb of glistening snow into the air behind us.

Robert "Pimmy" Pimentel, 1978

30 | A WINTER SEA, 1979-1982

FLASHBACK: A GRAY FEBRUARY day in 1979. Outward Bound course director Randy Udall and I were cooking our lunches in the industrial kitchen at the OB base camp near Leadville. I watched as he dumped an entire stick of butter into his bubbling pot of macaroni, followed by a quarter pound of cheddar cheese. Repulsive, yet fascinating.

This guy's bile ducts were world-class, and who doesn't love butter? Yet there had to be more than genetics or a culinary tick behind the gastronomy.

Randy was a friendly, fair-complexioned bear of a man. Though he came from a prolific political family (father Morris was an Arizona congressman, and Uncle Stewart had been interior secretary), as far as I knew he shunned politics. Instead, he was a winter mountaineering fanatic, sporting frayed fleece jackets and skiing hatless through snowstorms while his hair froze to a crusty bonnet.

As I scarfed spoon after spoon of Randy's delicacy, I shared my latest ski mountaineering plan: Climb and descend Mount Massive, a 14,421-foot fourteener within striking distance of our Outward Bound basecamp.

"There's a doable ski descent route, a broad pitch on the west side. Too much avalanche risk for a solo. Want to come along, dig me out if I 'lanch? We can ski the approach this afternoon."

Randy scraped the macaroni dregs from the cookpot—the good stuff—and loaded his plate.

"Sure," he said. "Let's bivvy at timberline. I'll climb on foot while you ski it. The ridges and some of the scree flanks are wind-blasted bare."

That night, we camped in a grove of waist-high altitude-stunted conifers on the southerly flanks of Massive. No tent. Snow moon above, no need for flashlights or headlamps. We pulled our sleeping bag drawstrings tight under our armpits and sat with our backs propped against tree stumps protruding from the snowpack. We brewed Lipton tea. I did three spoons of brown sugar. Randy did four. He took a noisy sip, pulled a stick of butter from his food bag, peeled back the paper wrapper, and bit a chunk from the yellow log like it was a gourmet camembert.

More dietary weirdness. Maybe he'll explain.

We wrapped our hands around the warm mugs as we talked of skiing the great alpine lands—up, down, across. With the emphasis on *across,* because I was hanging with a prince of ski traverses.

SKI MOUNTAINEERING HAS TWO branches. While the sport most often involves climbing up (on skis or foot) and skiing down, the ski traverse is a point-A-to-point-B journey. Peaks and other terrain undulations might be involved, but the primary goal of a traverse is a predetermined endpoint. Overland ski traverses take this to the extreme, such as ski treks to the North and South Poles that involve no summits, just phenomenal distances.

Among his many amazing traverses, Randy had crossed Baffin Island for five weeks in 1976, tracked by polar bears who, Randy was fond of sharing, "made pawprints the size of pie plates." A year later, he and John "Izzo" Isaacs, a former NOLS instructor, had ski-traversed the Wind River Range end to end, ninety miles. This was stuff for the history books, and it cut straight to my seeking heart.

Randy pumped up the stove and kindled another brew. The moonlit snow glowed white as daylight. Sleeping was for later, as we shared our waking dreams.

"The Baffin trip inspired me to travel more like an Inuit," Randy said, barking his trademark laugh deep in his barrel chest. "They eat tons of fat. Lesson learned. A stick of butter works better than candy. Calories forever. Amps up your metabolism. And keeps you warm at night."

I held my hand out in surrender. "Pass the butter."

After an unusually warm night's sleep, we climbed Massive's vast western scree slopes in a gathering winter storm. The entire way, visible to the side, was a continuous stripe of skiable snow—telling me it was worth it. As I slid from the summit, my planks clattered through a field of sastrugi, randomly shaped humps of wind-eroded icy snow that varied in size from airline baggage to overturned cooking pots. Randy hooted encouragement from the hiking trail.

"You could have starred in a Ginsu knife commercial—slice and dice," Randy joked as we packed up our gear at camp. "Glad you didn't fall. You'd have slid into the rocks, ripped yourself up."

SKI DESCENTS AND OCCASIONAL rock and ice climbs were my thing now. But I had no overarching goals. Casual carpentry jobs and commitment-free relationships were the extent of my ambition. Randy's talk of ski trekking tickled my core. Was planning and executing a lengthy traverse the rudder for my drifting boat? Was pursuing such things a lifestyle I'd enjoy? Something with constant movement, rather than the deep-freeze caves of Denali or the sodden tents of the Buckskin Glacier? Time to find out.

Back home in Crested Butte, I pulled a brown cardboard box of maps from under my bed. My father's 1950s mountaineering book, Edmund Hillary and George Lowe's *East of Everest,* was tucked between charts of Peru, Wyoming, Alaska, and Colorado. I picked it up and flipped through the pages. Sweet memories of my adventure-seeking dad flooded back to me—and it hinted at such things as ski traverses. The book was a sign.

Eight USGS quadrangle maps covered the high Elk Mountains, all with titles that stirred a cloudburst of memories: Capitol Peak, Maroon Bells, Gothic. I taped the quads edge-to-edge and spread the bed-sheet-sized chart across the floor. In minutes, I'd conceived a fifty-mile ski route that, more or less, followed the winding spine of the range.

Several fourteeners marked the way. The king was 14,099-foot Snowmass Mountain, which during winter boasted an enormous, snow-filled, east-facing bowl perched above mile-long Snowmass Lake. It was the most skier-logical peak of the fifty-four fourteeners, yet because it was so remote, it was only skied once or twice every spring (if that), never in winter. And to my knowledge, no one had ever skied from the tip-top of its small summit pyramid. Could this be more than a ski traverse?

WHILE I ENJOYED SOLO adventures, this trip required partners. Breaking a trail in deep snow, without help, could kill a man from exhaustion, and traveling in a group was safer regarding avalanches—someone to dig you out. So, during the winter of 1979–1980, I shilled the route to my alpinist friends like I was selling cars. Most everyone, in Crested Butte and Aspen alike, gave me a skeptical stare and logical reasons for not touching the idea:

"Too much time."

"Too dangerous."

"Too weird."

But one guy bit.

John Quinn was a building contractor with a middleweight fighter's build, rough facial complexion, and take-no-bull attitude contrasted by a puckish sense of humor. Several years earlier—before I'd broken my leg—we had met by chance on a ski lift, paired via the singles line. Minutes after we loaded the chair, he pulled out a thick peanut butter and jelly sandwich.

"Looks tasty," I said as I yanked a box of crackers from my backpack, ripped the top off, and stuffed my mouth. In our shared reality, so long as the lifts spun, real skiers rode them without stopping for lunch. We struck up a friendship. While in Aspen, I carpentered on Quinn's projects—he was an excellent builder—and we partnered for ski days, both resort and backcountry.

IN MARCH 1980, QUINN and I attempted our planned Elk Mountains ski traverse. We broke trail for twelve days through knee-deep powder and completed most of the dream line.

Only the dream was not so dreamy. Constant storms and the consequent need to follow avalanche-safe routes nixed any possibility of fun downhill skiing. And, should such runs have presented themselves, we were so spent from the trail breaking, we'd not have noticed. It seemed endless, marching for hours, burning calories like a trash incinerator, packing and scouring a knee-deep trench that only the guy behind you would ever use or appreciate. The wind and apocalyptic snowfall often filled our track within hours, blocking an easy retreat.

At the end of each day, in full-blown slog-induced dizzy exhaustion, we joined in singing a fractured version of "Cielito Lindo," the mariachi classic: "*Ay ay ay ay, yo soy ... Slogerro.*" Our weirdo serenade pushed us the last few miles to camp, where the *sloggerros* consumed another 2,000 calories of whatever grub surfaced from the mess in our feed bags, shivered for seven hours, woke, and did it again.

We had done a radical thing. Yet I'd wanted the views, wanted to slice fields of fluffy Rocky Mountain powder, fly down at least one major mountain instead of imagining where the mountain hid behind the storm. I had no sense of completion, no vibe of accomplishment.

Still, I was sure the Elk Mountains traverse could be everything I desired—albeit with suitable weather and partners. It became the focus of my mountaineering aspirations and, for lack of something better, the focus of my life.

With Ted Kerasote (right), Elk Mountains traverse, 1981. ©Dawson Collection

A YEAR LATER, THE SECOND TRAVERSE garnered more interest. Quinn was again up for it. My former Outward Bound boss, Ted Kerasote, joined and invited his friend Frank Coffey, a personable ski patrolman from Crested Butte. Two of my Aspen buddies brought it up to six: Peter Kelley, a realtor who did most of his business on the ski lifts, and curly-blond Harvard graduate ski instructor Richard Compton, whom I'd met at the Ashcrofters thirteen years before. I wasn't sure why the snow torture of our first try at the traverse hadn't registered on these guys' mountain radar—especially Richard, with his brainy pedigree. After all, they'd heard the tales of Quinn and I slogging our asses off with nothing but a handful of teaser turns to show for it. Whatever, my new prospects were suckered—*more men for the work!*

Five days in, the mood soured. Par for late-winter Elks weather, a storm had hit us on day one and never quit. From then on, we'd plodded from dawn to dusk through choking snowfall, shelled head-to-toe in nylon, breaking trail like blindered plow horses.

Exacerbating the pain party, inspired by Randy Udall's minimalism and biased by my introversion, I'd convinced everyone to try tentless camping. We slept solo, on top of the snowpack, inside tube-shaped bivvy sacks just large enough to cover our sleeping bags. Sheathed within our textile burrows, we survived each night in six isolated worlds of condensation and sock musk.

So long as the weather wasn't too vicious and you didn't spill your pee bottle, our sleeping system worked. It eliminated the weight of tents and conserved the caloric expenditure of snow-cave excavation.

But a big part of winter mountaineering is the congeniality and relative comfort of a tent or snow cave. To understand, consider the task of donning ski boots after peeling yourself out of a bivvy sack, standing in your socks on a jacket spread over soft snow. This after a night alone, with no opportunity to discuss the next day's plans with your mountain brothers.

As Ted soon pointed out, we'd become six individuals surviving solo rather than as a team.

Besides the solo sleeping, I'd convinced everyone we should cook speedy meals without shelter—caloric consumption prioritized over taste and conviviality. Food was fuel. Fix it fast, consume it cold if necessary. I had ignored the primacy of appetizing rations.

During one ridiculous repast, we paused for dinner on the side of a mountain amid a storm at 13,000 feet. As darkness fell, we shoveled out a meager windbreak. It had near zero effect. The forty-mile-per-hour gusts dumped snow into our bowls of chewy, over-salted rice faster than we could spoon the swill into our mouths. My companions were not happy. Richard told me later that he'd vomited when he'd stepped away to urinate.

My rationing theme was a problem as well. I'd based our diet on Udall's high-fat concept—yet I'd decided that butter was wimpy. Real men ate real fat. So, once or twice a day, we cooked three strips of bacon each, then fried English muffins in the resulting puddle of grease.

While our "grease burgers" were not the most appetizing victual known to man—and downright disgusting when the suet congealed under a dusting of snow—they did the job. Except for Ted. Before starting the trip, he'd been on a low-fat diet. A few bites of our oleaginous muffins sucked his gallbladder dry of fat-digesting bile, and he doubled over with cramps.

"Lou, this is the most hideous creation I've ever put in my mouth. The food you planned is making me ill. Can you make me a muffin, kind sir, and hold the lard?"

I cooked a dry muffin on a pot lid.

"Perfect," Ted said as he smeared it with strawberry jam and gobbled it down like a doggie treat.

At Snowmass Lake, Ted and Coffey outvoted my hard-core sleeping methods and shoveled themselves a palatial snow cave. The rest of us deployed our bivvy sacks under a spruce tree. Dumb move. We were now within the Gothic Triangle, a fifty-square-mile area known by meteorologists to have triple or more the Elk Mountains' average snowfall.

When I awoke the following morning, inside the dark of my bivvy sack, I could bend my legs at most three inches, and my arms were straight-jacketed to my sides. I panicked for a moment—buried!—then calmed down, pushed my arms up, and opened the zipper over my face. A shrug and a wriggle freed my torso. I sat up and looked around. Over two feet of snow had fallen overnight, transforming my pallet into a child-sized bathtub.

Just then, a gust of wind blew a wad of snow from the branches above. It landed next to my head with a thump. Buried alive in an open bivvy? Could happen. I had to admit that a snow cave was the solution—to be constructed later after seeing what the day brought.

I again made breakfast alfresco, hunched over my roaring gasoline stove, hood up, goggles on. A half inch of snow accumulated on my shoulders, melting and wetting through my so-called waterproof shell and fleece layers, ending as an evil tickle on my skin. Snow soon smothered my food bag, pots, and pans. It was like cooking while immersed in a freezing swimming pool.

Above us, Snowmass Mountain lurked behind the murk, waiting to see if we'd ignore the avalanche hazard.

I'd hyped Snowmass all week: "The big bowl, man, steep enough for turns but not too steep—a mile of knee-deep powder. You only get it that way in winter. And if we drop the little summit bump, it'll be a first."

Ted and Coffey emerged from their cave, rested and nourished. The remaining four of us resembled half-drowned dogs, ready to dig a snow cave of our own and nap all day. Yet pow-lust is a powerful thing.

"Let's head for the peak," I declared. "Might as well do something to warm up. If the clouds break, we'll be in position to nail it."

"That's ridiculous," Coffey said. "Avalanchy as hell."

I bent forward, sheltering the soggy paper map under my chest, and set a compass bearing so we could travel blind.

"Let's ski the mile across the lake, *take a look*," I said, modeling my father.

We could see perhaps ten feet in front of our ski tips. Beyond that, the white void began and, as far as we knew, ended at the North Pole.

After following the compass needle to the lake's approximate midpoint, we conceded the futility of climbing an invisible mountain under a falling sky. But we were not giving up.

We sat on our backpacks and waited for the miraculous clearing spell we *knew* would soon rend the clouds. I studied the toes of my black plastic ski boots. Pellets of graupel snow pattered my jacket hood. Five minutes, thirty minutes, an hour. *Would this ever end?*

Just as the mood bottomed, someone made one of those waggish observations you get when things make it hard to laugh: "I'm thinking mink-fur bras, like Sandra has back in Aspen."

All six of us howled, stoned on mental exhaustion and grease burgers, visualizing various females modeling their wares, or maybe one of our compadres as the Snowmass Lake drag queen.

I keyed in on the merriment.

"Let's salvage the day! Remember those gullies on the slope by our camp, dropping to the lake? If it's going to dump forever, let's get some use out of these heavy-duty ski setups we've been hauling around."

WE YO-YOED LAP AFTER LAP on the lakeside slopes. Sometimes, when a skier came down, the only thing visible was a black ski-pole basket protruding from a swirling white cloud, from which hoots of joy emerged.

Mountain reality soon quashed our merriment.

In our powder frenzy, we'd spread out on the uphill track, existing in personal spheres of hard-breathing climbs and transcendent turns. Only after completing lap three did we find Coffey and Ted standing next to the holes they'd shoveled while extricating themselves from partial burial in an avalanche. Had they been fully buried, they'd have suffocated before we noticed their absence. Ted's voice trembled like he'd survived a high-speed automobile crash.

"Close call. I'm over this."

We pulled our hoods tight, bowed our heads to the blizzard sky, and glided back to camp in monkish silence. We bivvy-sack holdouts surrendered and dug another snow cave. That evening, as I bent over the gasoline stove in a cloud of vaporized pork fat, I could not forget how my leadership had almost caused the demise of two friends. *If we were this much on edge, with judgment so flawed, could worse yet come?*

The Gothic Triangle continued its work. Cowed by the uncanny snowfall and spiking avalanche danger, we cut bait and skied twelve miles downvalley to Snowmass Resort. When we shot a team portrait on the town's outdoor mall, I held a heaping handful of snow toward the lens while thousands of dime-fat flakes rained like the ash of Pompei, softening the camera's record of our faces as though parts of us remained in the mountains above.

IN FEBRUARY 1982, SOON after my thirtieth birthday, Quinn, Kelley, Udall's superhuman traverse partner John "Izzo" Isaacs, and I again embarked on the traverse. This third time—the charm?—we packed better food and slept in snow caves if there was any chance of a storm.

At Snowmass Lake, we woke to a bluebird morning despite the Gothic Triangle's threat of snowpocalypse. Four hours later, I stood alone on the snowy summit of Snowmass Mountain while my partners waited in the bowl below.

I clipped into my planks and slid twenty feet to the easterly face, the sole ski route from the summit. While the pitch dropped just a few hundred feet, it pushed fifty-five degrees. I worried about falling but not about avalanches. When slopes this steep hold snow, it usually peels off below your skis in manageable chunks and cascades.

My crew watched my mini-avalanches puff small clouds of snow, then pile to a stop where the angle lessened. Alpine entertainment.

As we slid down to camp, a slate-gray cloud bank curled over the mountain like a gigantic hand. Then it snowed, as usual.

THREE DAYS AFTER SNOWMASS Lake, we dropped our backpacks next to Conundrum Hot Springs and slid into the blessed warmth. A faintly sulfurous mist swirled from the water, obscuring my companions' faces and seeming to muffle their words. I leaned back against the rocks rimming the pool and rubbed my bare feet together, free after ten days of confinement.

I'd been visiting Conundrum for fifteen years: that first adventure when I'd lost my winter innocence—so many other trips. It had become a place of legends: my own and more. I thought back on my favorite.

"Ever hear of the guy who skied up here naked in the middle of winter, no gear, spent the night in the springs, and skied back?"

"Come on, Lou, you're full of it."

"Really, it was around 1971, back in the hippie days. Kent Addison, that yogi dude with a turban. I skied with him afterward. He said he brought some dates and dried pears in a fanny pack, nothing else. He wasn't kidding. The guy cross-country skied nude whenever he felt like it, freaked out people up in Hunter Creek. He'd come striding along, ventilating like a blacksmith bellows, swinging in the breeze."

"He sure won the lightweight gear prize," Kelley quipped.

We laughed as we stuffed our water bottles with snow and floated them like bath toys, to melt drinking water. As I had so many times before, I pondered the view twenty miles downvalley to Red Mountain, the elevated residential area on the north side of Aspen. It occurred to me that someone there with a telescope could probably see us skiing the slopes above the spring, tiny specks moving on a field of white.

THE NEXT MORNING, DARK gray clouds raced over the summits above us, filtering the sun into a dim, heatless orb. A low-pitched *thrummm* permeated everything, the winds of a low-pressure storm system. Quinn and Kelley called it quits and skied the valley route out. For Izzo and me, the choice was a given: climb and ski the last leg of our idealized route, up and over the Elks' highest mountain, 14,279-foot Castle Peak.

Gaining Castle's west ridge, the wind came in full fury, making face masks and goggles mandatory. As I stumbled along, Izzo scrambled up the scree some distance ahead, skis strapped upright on the sides of his pack like dual antennas. He held his arms spread wide, death-gripping his poles for stability. The nappy clouds and wind-lofted snow screened his figure to a wraith. A wind blast brought me to my knees. I pushed up with my ski poles and continued my wobbling strides—to be knocked down again five minutes later. *Ascend, or flee?*

In silent agreement, we continued through the cauldron, up and, eventually, down.

Down to what?

While skate-skiing the last mile of snow-covered road to civilization, I searched inside for the bliss of accomplishment—but all I found was melancholia. I'd obsessed on the Elks Traverse for four years and trekked it thrice. After weeks of ascetic slogging, I had found the truth of these mountains: a brilliant land of adventure, where, through our strength, my mates and I survived an environment so alien, so anti-life, it could have been another planet. Yet none of this was the expected antacid for my soul.

A decade had passed since the peak of the Aspen weirdness: when Winkler had overdosed in the bedroom next to mine, when my parents had wandered apart. Was it time to settle down, quit spinning the run-wheel once and for all, and commit to a life partner? *Maybe I'll open up to that.*

Intentions are one thing, actions another.

31 | AVALANCHE RAGDOLL, 1982

BOB LIMACHER WAS A *skier by passion and a home builder by profession. He lived on Red Mountain, high above Aspen, with expansive views of the Elk Mountains. Limacher enjoyed studying the peaks through his Bushnell Space Master spotting scope—especially in winter. At thirty-power, he had a bird's-eye view of skiers on distant slopes.*

Just after sunrise on a blue-sky February morning, Limacher zeroed his eyepiece on Highland Bowl, a 2,000-vertical-foot, three-quarter-mile-wide concave face of pristine backcountry snow dropping from 12,392-foot Highland Peak, four miles as the crow flies southwest of Aspen. The mountain where, as a boy, I'd made my first solo climb.

Over the previous decade, "The Bowl" had become the town's forbidden fruit of a ski run, hanging from the sky, taunting any skier who cared to look—and we always looked. Steep. Powder-filled by storms and wind until it resembled a brimming bucket of flour. But although it was part of the Aspen Highlands ski area permit acreage and a short hike from the top of the ski lifts, Highland Bowl had been closed from day one to all but the ski patrol and their chosen few.

As one so chosen, Limacher had skied Highland Bowl the previous day. It was one of the best powder runs of his life. With the help of fine-tuned optical glass, he could relive the joy.

Rosy morning rake-light defined every contour: buttery wind swales, the jagged edges of broken cornices, chains of cuticle-shaped ski tracks. Limacher swept the scope up his tracks, following them toward the treeless summit. He smiled, remembering the flow of powder snow over his thighs, washing past his face when a turn dug extra deep, coating his goggles.

When the summit came into view through the scope, he was startled to see two individuals nearing the top. The ski lifts were two hours from opening. "You won't believe this," Limacher said to his wife. "There's two people on Highland Peak with skis on their packs, like they plan to ski Highland Bowl. Amazing they're up there this early."

Limacher tweaked the scope focus and concentrated on the scene. These had to be outlaw skiers sneaking into the Bowl, intending to leave only tracks before the ski patrol could arrive to shoo them off—or have them arrested for trespassing.

....

THE SKIERS LIMACHER WATCHED were me and Izzo Isaacs, my Elks ski traverse partner. We had attended a party at Peter Kelley's house the previous evening, where we'd heard someone bragging about his friend having skied the Bowl that day.

"Patrol ran one of their rare heli trips," the informant had announced. "Bob Limacher was a guest. They skied three runs in the North Trees. *Three.* He said it was the best powder of their lives."

I was livid—a mechanized affront to my sacred outback. In my world, all worthy backcountry skiing was human-powered.

I turned from the perfectly proportioned ski instructor I was wooing. Mountain over woman, as always.

"Skiing the bowl that way is BS," I proclaimed to the room, taking a hearty swig from my bottle of Corona. "That North Trees line isn't the actual Bowl. The real line is B1, the steepest line straight off the summit. And a helicopter?

With my ego running free, I nodded to Izzo and lowered my voice.

"Man, let's sneak up Highland early tomorrow morning and show them how it's done."

Play by the mountain's rules? Motivated by pride, I was way past obeying my edict.

Poaching Highland Bowl was not an uncommon activity for Aspen's more aggressive, backcountry-oriented skiers of the late 1970s through the 1990s (the Bowl opened as part of the Aspen Highlands ski area around 1999). To avoid being caught and fined, poachers often climbed the ski resort before sunrise, skied the Bowl, then exited through backcountry terrain below the Bowl, down to Castle Creek Road, where they'd hop into a pre-stashed car or hitchhike back to town.

EARLY THE NEXT MORNING, Izzo and I met in moonless darkness at the base of Aspen Highlands. The place was deserted—ski patrollers home in bed, lift chairs hanging in silence from their fat steel cables. Dawn was still an hour ahead. A biting breeze swept down from the slopes above. I pulled my fleece neck gaiter up over my mouth and cheeks.

"What line should we ski?" I asked as we strode across the parking lot, our headlamps glinting on the snow.

"Dunno," Izzo said. "Let's wait 'till we're on the summit, evaluate the avalanche danger, then decide."

"Sounds smart," I said while thinking the opposite: *One goal, one line, B1.*

The rising sun warmed my face as we skinned along the summit ridge. The Maroon Bells appeared an arm's reach away; beyond sprawled the ridges and valleys of the Elks Traverse, prompting memories of my struggles and adventures with treasured companions. I wanted to stop, shrug off my backpack, and stare at those mountains for ten minutes. But there was none of that. Instead, we hurried up the final ridge to the Highland Peak summit.

Haste was essential. If the ski patrol suspected any bowl poaching or saw tracks, they'd call a sheriff's deputy, who would park on Castle Creek Road at the Bowl egress. More than one skier had pocketed a ticket for trespassing. If we finished extra early as planned, the officer would still be at Little Cliff's bakery, enjoying his coffee and a chunk of monkey bread.

We selected a spot a few feet leeward from the summit and dug a snowpit to evaluate avalanche danger. Usually, this entails an examination of the snowpack layers. A higher avalanche risk exists if the layers come apart too easily when pried with a shovel blade or pressed with a hand. This time, our dig was nearly useless; we hit the ground two feet down with no meaningful layers to evaluate. Still, the shallow pit revealed one thing: the prevailing winds had stripped tons of snow from the mountain's westerly reach, and dumped it below us on B1.

Izzo stowed his shovel in his backpack and cinched the lid.

"I don't know—there's some wind loading. What do you think?"

With my gloved hand, I made a sweeping gesture at the surrounding mountains. "No avalanches on other slopes with the same aspect as B1—that shows it's probably safe."

Izzo sensed my drive.

"I'll stay close to the side, make a few turns, and pause on those wind-stripped rocks below the entrance," he said. "We should ski one at a time. Your beacon on?"

"Yeah," I said. "If the snow feels okay, I'll knock out the whole run in one push. Watch me from the rocks, so you're safe if it slides."

....

THIS SHOULD BE GOOD, *Bob Limacher thought as he got comfortable in the chair behind his scope. He watched the first skier make seven turns, then stop on a patch of bare ground on the side of the pitch, as if he were setting up for photography. Then the second skier descended, his turns paralleling the first skier's tracks. Suddenly, he stopped in the middle of the slope. Odd, Limacher wondered, why hesitate on the run of a lifetime?*

At that moment, a dark crack shot through the snow above the second skier, and the slope instantly morphed from a peaceful field of white to a flowing mass. Seconds later, the skier disappeared in a colossal slab avalanche that blasted downhill under a towering cloud of white powder. Limacher moved his scope with the avalanche. He spotted the trapped skier again—a flash of red and black—as the slide went airborne over a steep transition. Then, in the time it takes for a breath, the catastrophe disappeared behind a ridge in the foreground, leaving behind a cloud of glinting snow crystals.

"God—I just watched someone get caught in an avalanche!" Limacher exclaimed to his wife as he picked up the phone to call 911. He figured he had witnessed someone's death.

....

AS I LAUNCHED FROM THE SUMMIT of Highland Peak, my skis flexed under my feet as powder snow washed to my knees and pressed against my thighs. One turn, two, three—hundreds more waited below. This was the run I had wanted forever—each rhythmic arc the stuff of skiers' dreams—and as sweet dreams often do, it ended too soon.

After a few flowy turns, my ski tails punched into a hollow snow layer. I skidded to a stop, inverted a ski pole, and probed the snowpack. The pole sank like something was pulling it from my hands, the same unstable layer I'd felt with my skis.

I was standing in the middle of an avalanche slope, primed to go big. If it ripped, I'd take what ski mountaineers call "the ride," and it might be my last.

A hundred feet across the slope and somewhat above me, Izzo stood against the sky and watched.

Suddenly, a three-inch-wide crack—an avalanche fracture—snapped open in front of my ski tips and made a gunshot sound as it shot up and across the slope. My gut knotted.

I locked my eyes on Izzo, like a drowning man grasping for a rescue rope inches beyond his fingertips. A split second pause, then the snow broke apart around me, rushed downhill, and knocked me off my feet.

As the avalanche took me down, I clawed my ski pole grips into the icy bed-surface exposed by the slide. If I could stop myself, or at least slow down, the beast might leave me behind, clinging to the mountainside with a catchy story to share over beers back in Aspen.

But my desperate attempt at salvation achieved nothing more than carving two meager grooves under my fists; I was already moving too fast. Seconds later, the tumbling snow flipped me headfirst down the mountain, twisted off my skis, and became the vortex of my savage plunge to hell.

Violence reigned as I fell ever faster. I tumbled—ragdolling with no arm or leg control.

My left femur exploded, sending a surge of vibration throughout my body as if I were a tuning fork. I hadn't impacted a rock or a tree. Instead, crosscurrents of snow had pulverized one of the strongest bones in the human skeleton like a twig in a tornado.

The avalanche spit me over a terrain lip. I flew, engulfed in the powder cloud. My broken leg, attached to my body with just a few shreds of skin and muscle, flapped like a whip. As the quiet, airborne snow gave a moment's respite from the cascade's low-pitched bellow, I gasped for breath and inhaled the torrent: an earthy scent reminiscent of the damp ground sometimes encountered while digging snow caves during my ski expeditions.

In a second, maybe less, the snow thickened and darkened as I dropped from my flight into the monster's gut. I sucked in another shuddering breath.

The atomized snow clogged my nose and mouth.

Impact. A flash of light. My stomach roiled as the slide crushed to a halt. My bladder loosened. I spit snow from my mouth and gulped for air.

Author's avalanche, Highland Peak, 1982

©Dawson collection

Somehow, just four inches of snow covered my head and face. I freed one arm and brushed the snow from my eyes with my bare hand—the avalanche had ripped off my gloves. I was on my back, pinned from the neck down, under several feet of debris.

I struggled to move, to extricate myself. But when I pushed with my legs, vomit welled in my throat as my left thigh and right buttock burned with white-hot pain. I stopped fighting, and watched the tiny figure of Izzo, still near the top of B1. Skis strapped to his pack, he slowly downclimbed the steep, slick surface exposed by the slide, stopping often to check his avalanche transceiver for a signal.

I was far below, out of transceiver range, nearly invisible, surrounded by large chunks of snow with only my head and one arm unburied. As Izzo neared the bottom of the slide path, he spotted me about the time his transceiver beeped. He stumble-ran through the blocky avalanche debris, threw down his backpack, and brushed the caked snow from my neck and shoulders.

"Oh, man, Lou. How bad is it?"

I was fading, eyes closed to slits. I struggled to speak.

"Maybe broke my femur—something wrong with my butt, too ... Need a rescue." I mumbled through cold-tightened lips.

Izzo's first-aid training kicked in: check for bleeding, treat for shock, prevent hypothermia. Melting snow matted my now hatless hair, sucking heat from my body faster than my shocked metabolism could replace it. He brushed my head with his hands, doffed his knit ski cap, and pulled it over my ears.

If anyone could dig fast, it was Izzo, the stone-mason mountain man. But his strength didn't help free my legs—it took him fifteen minutes to nibble with his shovel and finish with his hands, then fingers, so as not to move my tortured skeleton more than necessary. After checking for blood—none—he packed snow around the femur break to act as a splint and tucked his extra jacket over my torso.

A shattered femur is life-threatening—half of victims die. Fast rescue was the priority. The avalanche had also ripped the right trochanter bone from my pelvis. While less severe an injury than the femur, the trochanter is where the big gluteus muscle attaches—the beef that gives skiers their sculpted rear ends. I'd have been close to helpless with just the femur break. Add the trochanter injury, and moving just a few inches was agony.

"I'm gonna leave now to get help, but that'll take a while," Izzo said. "I'll have to climb out of the Bowl to the ski area. That'll be quicker than skiing into the valley, maybe not getting a ride into town."

"Head up there on foot ... Not skis ...," I stuttered. "That south-facing stuff, more solid, safer. Maybe there's a phone at the top of the lift ... Ski patrol ... Maybe getting ready for work."

"I don't think they'll be there yet, Lou," Izzo said. "Still too early. I'll need to ski down the runs, find someone or a phone at the bottom."

Izzo raced up the sunlit bowl faster than I had ever seen him climb. Sometimes, he sank to his knees, lurching forward to stomp out of the resulting boot holes while reaching with his arms and swimming ahead.

Oh man, he's doing it. But will it be fast enough?

I had no way of knowing it, but when Izzo made his last steps over the rim of the Bowl and onto the ski slopes, he encountered a group of ski patrollers already staging a rescue. Bob Limacher's phone call had connected.

WHILE IZZO COMPLETED HIS climb and encountered the unexpected help, I lay there in the starkness with no more insulation than a jacket and a hat, femur fracture bleeding internally, core temperature crashing. A human popsicle with the handle stick broken off. The nearby conifers closed in like a curtain. The sky dropped to my face. Minutes ticked, an hour. A mix of grief and shame washed through me.

How could I do this to myself, to the people I loved?

I shivered hard and gave myself over to it. Soon, a peaceful warmth blanketed me. A presence emanated from the forest, from the blue-dark sky above, from the tangled snow crystals I lay upon. It was a presence neither gentle nor harsh nor judging, listening in silence to my thoughts, my breaths.

I closed my eyes and faded into the oblivion of acceptance.

Strong fingers pinched my cheek.

"Lou, Lou! Stay with us! Wake up!"

A ski patroller in a blue jacket with white crosses kneeled close.

"Yeah, yeah, man," I garbled through frozen lips.

"Let's get you to the hospital."

THE EMERGENCY ROOM WAS a flurry of movement. Through a half-conscious fog, I felt a warm hand holding mine and heard the sound of my ski boot buckles snapping open. A nurse draped a heavy re-warming blanket over me and pushed the edges under my torso. Later, the ER doctor told me they'd measured my body temperature at 94 degrees—the soon-lethal phase of hypothermia. After tumbling down Highland Bowl for no more than seventeen seconds, I'd spent four icy hours on the mountain.

My first hospital night played out like the proverbial soap-opera medical scene: beeping machines, nurse visits, and a traction cable anchored to a hole the doctor had drilled through my leg just below my knee, without anesthesia, as I watched. Eva Breton and my mother hovered at the edge of my awareness. I muttered about angels.

I remained in the hospital for almost two weeks, recovering from the overall trauma, wheelchair-bound after two surgeries. Eva was there constantly, swapping cold packs, emptying my pee bottle when I couldn't make it to the bathroom, harassing the nurses when they were late with pain meds.

Kristina visited, unexpected. We hadn't exchanged a word nor seen each other in nine years. Her face crumbled and her eyes watered as she stooped for a hug. I looked away in shame, loathing the weight of my mess: the boy who danced over mountains, broken, following her mother and Meta with my foolish ride on the storm. After a few minutes of awkward conversation, she walked out the door, never looking back. Her strained body language said it all. She'd had enough of avalanches.

A constant string of friends dipped in. There was joy and there was laughter. Joy, because my chances of being in a hospital bed instead of a casket were about one in a hundred, and Bob Limacher had skewed the odds. Laughter at my predicament, festooned with tubes and cords, the proverbial hospital robe with its breezy rear opening. And when I laughed, I didn't bellow it out as before—there was a tightness, a submission. Something was trimming the edges of my pride.

A new-age friend arranged a psychic reading.

"You've been blessed with powers," the seer said as she bobbed a quartz crystal over my prone body. "But you now must divert more of that power for others—share the mountain beauty, share the joy, respect your body. Stop seeking only pleasure."

A fraud could have guessed most of that stuff after talking to my friends. But it was true. So I vowed a journey of change, revisiting the goals I'd formed after my broken leg and rescue three years earlier. That time, I'd been high and stupid. This time, it was pure stupid.

Play by the mountains' rules.

Noble intentions are one thing, life another. In a fit of painkiller-fueled optimism, I figured marrying Eva was my new beginning. My mother provided the engagement ring—a family heirloom she said was "just waiting in my jewelry box to get used." With her and my longtime skiing and climbing buddy Kendall Williams looking on, I asked Eva, "Will you?" and slipped the ring on her finger. She said "yes" and wept. I smiled in medicated ecstasy.

We cracked a bottle of bubbly there in the hospital room and shared it with a nurse. It tasted fake.

BOOK V
HEALING

©Dawson

32 | POSITIVE POWER, 1982-1984

"GOD IS LOVE," MY mother was fond of saying, before she stopped speaking of God.

As a kid back in Texas, I'd completed the confirmation class at our Methodist church. While the nuances of Christian theology were far beyond a fidgeting 12-year-old, I grasped the basic gospel: a forgiving, loving God who worked through his son (or was his son, in some weird way). With the enhancement of a ghost roaming around performing "works," the whole thing was like something out of my dad's sci-fi books. Yet unlike lizard aliens and starships, I believed the gospel because I saw no reason not to.

By the time we'd moved to Aspen, neither the words "church" nor "prayer" were in our family lexicon. Yet I'd kept my confirmation Bible, a skinny New Testament, in a dark red slipcase with a silken marker ribbon. I'd flip through it between yoga sessions and attempts at meditation, thinking that running my eyes over the words somehow made me more spiritual. Not much came of that. But knowing God through creation was a biblical concept I did take to heart.

As I flowed up the cliffs and down the mountains, I sensed a power in their majesty, a force beyond material—the love my mother had spoken of. But I didn't quite get it. I'd figured that as much as I loved the mountains, they'd love me back, softly. That they also loved as tough as their ice and stone was a fact I'd intellectually acknowledged but never took to heart. Now I understood. Highland Bowl had delivered a full dose of tough, so said the sound of my snapping leg bones.

Was there something softer, gentler in the equation?

Uncle Frank and Aunt Sue visited a few days before my hospital check-out. At 65, Frank had aged well. His hair was longer yet still above his ears, his face tanned not from boating but from altitude. The couple had sold their

Dallas boat dealership and lived part-time in Crested Butte. As retirees, Frank enjoyed a second childhood on the ski mountain, and Sue reigned over the sprawling second home they'd nicknamed the "Turkey Nest."

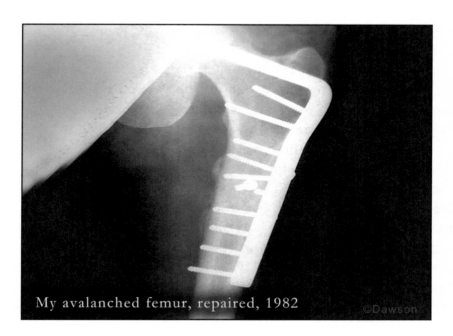

My avalanched femur, repaired, 1982   ©Dawson

Aunt Sue was quiet, practical, and what I thought of as Southern. I remembered stuffing my mouth with white-bread jelly sandwiches she mass-produced during Texas play days with my cousins. Clearly, her steady hand had underpinned the heyday of Frank Pillsbury Marine Sports.

During my time in Crested Butte, Frank had become an adult friend. Moreover, I'd come to revere him as a mentor in his commitment to family and what it meant to be a man. He had made a solid living, cared for his brood, and left youthful heroics behind while remaining active and physically fit.

Yet Frank wasn't perfect. In conversations, he'd alluded to the internal conflicts not uncommon to those who opt for marriage and children. I sensed Frank had thought about leaving it all for the independent life, perhaps as a hunting guide, fishing boat captain, or ski instructor. But despite any doubts and temptations, he'd embraced the life of family and self-sacrifice. Courage isn't just about hanging from cliffs.

There was another thing: Frank and Sue were evangelical Christians. In the hospital, as we chatted about the ski season, I dreaded the witnessing I knew was coming. No born-again worth their Bible could resist such an opportunity.

Sue pulled a book from her purse and passed it to Frank.

Here it comes. They're dropping a Bible on me.

"Thought you'd like this," Frank said, handing me a well-used blue hard-cover. The spine was torn halfway off; a vertical crease broke the front cover cardboard. "It's about positive thinking, healing, making your life work. It helped me change ... I had some issues with my temper."

Surprised it wasn't a Bible, I glanced at the title: *The Power of Positive Thinking.* We said our goodbyes. With nothing better on tap than daytime television, I opened the book and was soon devouring every chapter. Norman Vincent Peale's quaint, dated writing style was off-putting (it was first printed in 1952, the year I was born). But Peale's words about thought and prayer were so moving I teared up. It was as if I suddenly saw my life in a new light, with new possibilities. Chapter five, "How to Create Your Own Happiness," was my guidebook to the future. In classic self-help style, along with collected anecdotes proving his point, Peale offered dozens of mantras such as this:

> To become a happy person, have a clean soul, eyes that see romance in the commonplace, a child's heart, and spiritual simplicity.

By my interpretation, Peale had distilled a successful life into four key elements. Seeing romance in the commonplace was easy; even a fresh set of truck tires got me going—and there was always the memory of Wind River trout. Child's heart? How I loved to play on rock, ice, and snow. And spiritual simplicity? Wasn't that about avoiding endless philosophizing? I had that covered too: wasn't hanging from cliffs or skiing down mountains the best way to dance with the absurd?

A clean soul, though—that one puzzled me. Did it mean forgiveness instead of bitterness? Self-confidence? Love?

Out of the hospital, balancing on crutches with Peale helping me find a measure of inner peace, I obsessed over the ethos of risk sports—their role in human happiness. I churned the silly "ski to die" trope through my brain like I was preparing to spit it out. *Tons of fun—until someone bled.*

I should have thought more about my father, his outlaw tendencies that I'd emulated—and where that had gotten both of us. Instead, I trophy-pasted my Highland Bowl trespassing citation into my scrapbook. The court judge had levied a fine and restitution. A friend paid the bill, no strings attached. While the crime didn't bother me, accepting the handout did. It reminded me of my father leeching off Grandpa. At least I didn't have a wife to suffer through such indignities. But I did have a fiancée.

A month after the avalanche, I moved in with Eva. Three days later, we were fighting as much as loving. The idea of marriage was ridiculous. Eva refused to remove the ring. I grabbed her wrist and pulled it from her finger as tears dripped from her chin. I could blame the opiates for being a brute, but that would have been a lie.

When it came to mountains, it was easy to have a clean soul. As for my human interactions, there was room for improvement.

Frank and Sue suggested I heal at their Dallas home and installed me in their guest cottage next to the swimming pool. The hinted condition: that I join them in worship every Sunday morning at nine o'clock.

I was embarrassed to mention church during phone calls with my Colorado friends, much less one of those "born-again jobs," but I liked it. I dug the contemporary music, the metaphysics. I dug the take on Christ as the anarchist guru with a 2,000-year tenure. One sermon covered healing—physical and beyond—and the power of prayer. Another touched on forgiveness of self and others, as liberation. This was nothing like the Jesus-freaky judgmental weirdness I'd been indoctrinated to expect.

What did I have to lose? I followed Christ's instructions, bowed my head every night before bed, and pled for healing of flesh and spirit. The earth didn't shake. Yet there was something, a shimmering in my reality, an odd flavor of peace and promise of change. I kept praying. And there were other transformations.

Since dropping out of high school, a nightmare had haunted my sleep: me as a full-size adult, wedged into a six-year-old's school desk, surrounded by children, scared mute. Enough. My situation was ideal—time, city—for obtaining my high school equivalency certificate. I attended a preparation class with a dozen chain-smoking felons and received my diploma from the Texas Education Agency on June 15, 1982.

The nightmare stopped. Acting on an idea that had churned through my head since the Elk Mountains traverses, I borrowed Sue's IBM Selectric typewriter and outlined my first ski-touring guidebook. At the same time, I forced myself to learn touch-typing and worked on my atrocious spelling.

In Aspen two months later, the doctor smiled as he pinned my X-rays on the light board.

"I haven't seen many bones heal this fast," he said. "You can go to ninety percent full activity, then normal by winter."

Hallelujah! On Thanksgiving day, cheery ski instructor Ned Ryerson and my old friend Richard Compton joined me for my reentry celebration. We hauled our sleeping bags and a precooked turkey dinner to the top of Colorado's highest peak, Mount Elbert. After digging a chest-high snow cave in the summit cornice, we chowed down and boozed up with Udall-inspired hot-buttered rum. We then attempted to sleep off our cholesterol cocktails at 14,440 feet.

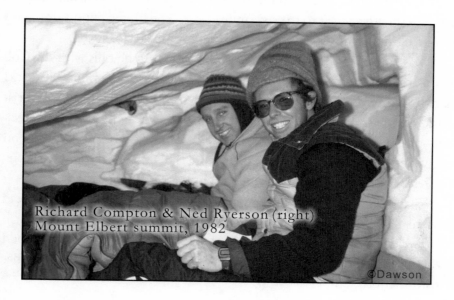

Richard Compton & Ned Ryerson (right)
Mount Elbert summit, 1982

©Dawson

The next morning, we needed every liter of Ned's cheer and Richard's quiet strength. The headaches had us speaking in one-syllable words, most of which began with the letter F. Richard's lips were tinted cyanotic blue. I fell over, dizzy, while clicking into my skis. That no one died of altitude sickness was a certifiable miracle.

There was no threat of avalanches, but was my posturing as less of a risk taker less than honest?

AFTER ELBERT, LIKE A fresh divorcé in a dating panic, I began dipping into backcountry terrain, solo, during high-risk avalanche days. The first turns were bliss, back in the saddle and all. And yet, at the close of such days, I didn't feel the familiar old endorphinic glow—only shame. What kind of person spits in the face of the gods? Realizing this, I did a complete one-eighty as to my avalanche caution. So much so that I sometimes contended that a reasonable route choice was dangerous, and took an alternate line with lower-quality skiing. Some of my friends hinted I was paranoid. Possibly. Yet I'd faced the white void and preferred the alternative.

The clincher? A gear company published a poster with a photo of Highland Bowl taken just hours after my avalanche. It advertised an avalanche rescue beacon. Rather than my ego-inflamed figure arcing through a turn while spraying snow on the camera lens, the poster depicted my pitiful ski track leading into the slide fracture. I thumbtacked the poster to my bedroom wall as a reminder.

LATE IN 1982, I bought a vintage 1952, eight-by-thirty-foot mobile home in the Woody Creek Trailer Park, fifteen minutes downvalley from Aspen. The interior smelled like wet newspapers with a hint of something worse. Mildew stained the ceiling where the roof leaked. The seller claimed the owner before him was an avalanche casualty, which creeped me out. But for the first time in my adult life, I had a secure living situation, a "house" of my own near the mountains. A step forward.

Yet what of love? Did I want to finish my life as a mountain monk, never married, childless, substituting serial adventures for a household and stability, a thousand Kodachrome film memories spilling from my closet, cats eating my toes after I passed on, alone?

Some guys seemed okay with that (excluding the cat teeth). But the thought of it terrified me.

My father's lifestyle didn't help with the fears.

My brother Craig phoned.

"Dad is in Delta County jail. He got busted for growing pot."

I stared at the dirty yellow walls of my trailer and laughed to conceal the pain.

"For how long?" I asked.

"He's doing ten days. Told me he didn't have any money for the fine."

Out of thousands of people growing and selling marijuana in Colorado, they'd arrested my recalcitrant father. And might there be some of him in me? The answer was definitely yes.

I could not face talking to the man.

THE FLIP CAME DURING winter 1983–84. I hacked together a storage shed in my little trailer-park yard, organized my tools, and enjoyed as much high-pay carpentry work as my mind and body could handle. It was Aspen—somebody with money was always building something. Days off were for skiing, trailer improvements, and, come spring, lots of mountain biking.

I was back to what I called the "mountain-town float"—the physically healthy version, anyway. Yet some parts were not so floaty. I was thirty-two, with mountain monkhood a scary possibility.

Some of my friends had already slipped a ring on the finger of their mountain girl, Michael Kennedy for one. Seeing my old climbing buddy's matrimonial success, I had to believe my future bride was out there somewhere—the operative word being "where." As for "bride," if someone had asked me what that meant, I had hardly a clue, though I was willing to learn.

33 | PEN PALS, 1984-1987

ON A SUNNY MARCH day in 1984, I unlocked my post office box and retrieved a mysterious white envelope. The return address caught my eye, hand-penned in perfect cursive: "Lisa Spieler, San Francisco."

> A year ago, I walked into a friend's house and saw a picture of a smiling man climbing an icy cliff. Since then, I've been interested but a bit hesitant. But I have fifteen minutes left on my lunch hour ... I'll be 25 in March, and I have brown eyes and brown hair. I graduated college last June and moved to San Francisco for work. Living in the city is a challenge. I'd prefer to be in the country, and I often ache when I can't skip the office for a bike ride. However, San Fran is so full of character (and characters) that I can't help but enjoy it. Write and tell me about yourself and those beautiful mountains.

"A mountain man is waiting for you in Colorado," Lisa's friend Kellan had teased more than once when the pair lamented their search for male companionship. She'd gesture toward a photo Christmas card mounted on her refrigerator. "Check Lou out. I got to know him and his mom when I lived in Crested Butte with his cousin. I dare you to write him."

I wouldn't have thought Kellan's kitchen art was the ideal introduction for a beach-warm SoCal girl. I was hanging by my hands from two Rooster-head ice tools stuck in a frozen waterfall. Then again, opposites attract.

In those days before Match.com and email, Lisa and I soon became pen pals, with a five-month lead-up to our first date.

Lisa wrote about her work at a bank and her beloved ocean and bicycle. I replied with words of my beloved mountains and my passion for bicycling (the latter was honest yet mercenary). I was soon thinking about more than putting pen to paper, to the point of wondering if and how this beach-baked Cali-girl and I could make a life together, especially if one of us—Lisa, if I was honest with myself—had to leave our natural habitat.

Her letters helped quell my doubts: "I was born on a farm during a snowstorm in Wisconsin."

A snowstorm had to count for something, right?

Christmas card, early 1980s

©Jon Waterman

It was a bold move for Lisa to get on an airplane to meet me. I would not have had the courage. While we'd exchanged snapshots a few months previously, I wondered if I'd recognize her in real life. No problem. The tanned, shapely brunette was easy to spot in the line of passengers walking across the Aspen airport's summer tarmac. Athletic. The prettiest woman in the entire crowd of upscale resort folk. And when she got close, a brilliant smile and her eyes, large brown stunners.

"Hi Lisa, these are for you," I mumbled as I handed her the first bouquet I had ever bought, white and yellow daisies. A friend had suggested that red roses were too aggressive. He was wrong. The moment overwhelmed me. All I could see were those eyes. My mouth was so dry I couldn't swallow. And I sported a grin that would make a lottery winner proud.

I'd spent the previous afternoon detailing my truck. In that regard, the roses would also have been the better choice; they'd have done a superior job of masking the nose-wrinkling scent of the two bottles of Armor All detailing fluid I'd flooded over every available surface.

I was falling in love—or maybe I already had. And based on Lisa's letters—the ones I'd checked my mailbox for each day without fail for five months—I figured she had similar feelings. Accordingly, the all-important question: *How might our long-distance relationship resolve?* I was still a mountaineer with summits on my mind. So I'd readied a line for the drive home from the airport.

"No matter where this goes, I'm not leaving the mountains," I said. "They're too much my life, as a climber and all."

Lisa smiled. "I like new adventures. Let's see what happens."

I wanted to rush things, but knew that wasn't the way. Instead, I kept my hands off and organized a few easy mountain-bike rides. And, as what I'll admit was a test, I took her on a hike that required wading a frigid, thigh-deep cascade. She aced it, which ticked my mental scorecard, but it wasn't the end-all. I was aware of my friends—and myself—having picked trophy partners based on a checklist of athletic accomplishments. I'd seen those relationships fail time after time. I focused on avoiding that pitfall by basing a relationship on a potential mate's inner qualities: kindness, compassion, positivity. I knew Lisa had all that, by her words, smile, and the spirit behind her eyes.

Still, I was only human and couldn't help but think of the eternal question: *Can she ski?*

Lisa had skied during family vacations. So, I wasn't concerned about her skills, at least on moderate terrain. Beyond that, I had no plans to push her; I wasn't the maniac of my avalanche days. Still, could she shift from beach life to mountains? Learn to love backcountry ski touring? Would a beach girl's union with a mountain man work? Some adventure-prone DNA was required, and a willingness to go outside the box. I needn't have worried.

Lisa was of Swiss heritage on her mother's side. She'd spent a few idyllic summers in Europe, hiking in the Alps with her uncle. And there was more: In 1907, Switzerland's first tourism-oriented funicular was installed on a mountain near her ancestral village of Chur. Lisa's maternal grandfather,

Simon Jenatsch, was a human-powered recreation purist. A railway accessing a mountain summit? Heresy!

"Grandpa Simon sabotaged the base station," Lisa told me. "They stuffed a one-way ticket to America in his pocket and said, 'Don't come back.'"

Edward Abbey roll over. An eco-warrior in the Spieler family tree!

Simon Jenatsch, circa 1909

On the final night of Lisa's visit, we spread our sleeping bags on the rough-sawn deckboards of a tumbledown backcountry cabin near the top of the Aspen Mountain ski area. The air was still and warm for the altitude. We lay on our backs, side by side, heads and shoulders out of our bags.

"This is the most peaceful place I've ever been," she said. "It seems like the stars are everywhere."

I reached out my hand. Hers was there.

I'd spent a thousand nights under the backcountry sky, and it never failed in its glory—never failed to bring forth something unique. Tonight, with gin-clear alpine air free of city-light pollution, the stars appeared as if layered. First were those so bright they seemed to float ten feet above us, then the fainter, farther ones until there was nothing more than the infinite blackness that made you small in a good way. We didn't need words; I knew this moment only came once in a lifetime. Lisa's gentle breaths and the warmth of our intertwined hands told me she felt the same. I thought about rolling toward her, the soft curves, the kisses fast morphing from gentle to eager. But I lay still and soaked in the moment. I'd never felt this much love for anyone or anything.

We fell asleep, still holding hands. That was enough.

The next morning, we packed early and drove down the mountain. We drew two large coffees from the big chrome urn at Little Cliff's bakery. Lisa had a powdered donut; I gobbled two apple turnovers—Cliff's were the best, half their weight in sugar.

At the departure gate, we hugged and stood close.

"Can I visit you in a few weeks?" I asked.

"Absolutely. Meet me in Santa Barbara, and I'll take you for a moonlit swim in the sea. We'll stay at my parents' house."

A moonlight swim sounded like precisely the thing—provided a beach blanket was involved. So, I wrapped up my carpentry job, stored my tools, and bought a plane ticket. As for the parents' house part of the plan ...

From correspondence with Lisa, I'd known her parents were wonderful—kind and stable. Her father was a builder, just like mine had been in his early days, and her mother helped manage the business while making a home.

Long-married Lillian and Hans Spieler were the antithesis of the hippie, free-wheeling, long-separated Patricia and Charles Dawson. I dreaded having to explain my family dynamic.

How could I describe my father if they asked what he "did?" Talk about jail? And I'd have to mention they'd been divorced forever.

But I rallied.

Hans and Lillian were smiling when we walked through the door of the Spielers' ranch-style home, though you could see the questions in their eyes. When I shook hands with Lisa's father, his grip was that of a carpenter, rough and strong. "So yet," he said. "We meet der Bergführer." His accent matched Schwarzenegger's to a T.

Not wishing to overstate things, I just called myself a carpenter who climbed mountains. And when the subject of family came up, my dad was a "photographer," mother an "artist."

My possible parents-to-be? As my visit extended over a week, Lillian Spieler was as loving to me as though I were one of her sons. And Hans: having immigrated from Germany after World War II (he'd worked on a farm during the war) with no English and no money, he was now one of the most reputed building contractors in Santa Barbara County. Eight years younger than my dad, he was balding, clean-shaven, quiet, dry-witted.

Hardcore Hans, I thought, and that was a compliment.

No parents are perfect, but some more than others. I'd found the Dawson counterbalance in Hans and Lillian—and their daughter. Here was a healthy melding: my creative family and Lisa's hard-working people.

The night of my arrival, Lisa made good on her promise. The surf was knee-high, the water just warm enough, and she didn't forget the blanket.

A FEW MONTHS LATER, Lisa returned to Colorado with two bulging suitcases and a pair of white Nordica ski boots. They were not the boots I'd have chosen. That didn't matter. Her father had bought the boots because his daughter was moving to Colorado. They were symbolic: a sweet dowry, yet a little scary. I'd never lived with a woman for longer than a few months.

Through autumn, we biked endless miles, and explored the Elk Mountains as the aspen leaves turned golden and snow dusted the fourteeners.

My completed renovation of the trailer bathroom was a highlight. Lisa appreciated having a solid floor instead of a plank spanning bare joists over the stygian crawlspace. I'd neglected to mention the black widow spiders I'd encountered while renewing the plumbing below the toilet.

Come winter, I ramped up the ski touring while keeping to mild terrain to help Lisa grow a love of the sport. There were hiccups. One blunder began while researching backcountry ski huts near Aspen for a guidebook I was writing. Hand-sized triangular blue diamonds nailed to trees marked the standard routes—follow the dots. I wanted more for my readers: alternates, shortcuts, opportunities for self-reliance.

While studying the maps, I noticed a ridge and mountain face connecting two huts. As a shortcut, it trimmed three miles off the marked route. But more, it had a few downhill pitches steep enough for ski turns.

The map hadn't shown the new-growth aspen suckers crowded so close even the squirrels feared them.

Night fell as we forced our skis and twisted our knees around and through hundreds of skinny whips that bent double when we grabbed them for balance. At one point, all I could see of Lisa was her headlight flashing in the jungle behind me. Unlike times in my youth when I might have impatiently raced ahead, I waited.

"You okay?" I asked when she caught up. "Just *survival* ski—don't try making turns like on the ski hill. Just kick-turn and follow my tracks."

"Your friends warned me about bushwacking, getting 'Dawsonized,'" she laughed. "Now I'm a member of the club."

"Well, at least avalanches can't happen in vegetation this thick."

When we finally reached the hut, our black gloves and pants smeared with white aspen-bark powder, Lisa ran her fingers through her hair and said, "Is there a special brush for twigs?"

From then on, when the subject of Lisa's skiing ability came up in social settings, she'd say something like, "I'm a survival skier. I can get down almost anything without falling. And I have my personal guide."

While my friends understood Lisa's meaning, more than one wag couldn't resist a tease: "That means you survived Lou Dawson?"

YES, LISA WAS THE one. For the first time in my life, rather than vague fantasies, I could envision a lifetime of commitment. What I'd formerly voiced as the "M-word" rolled off my tongue as it should—*marriage.*

Yet I remained afraid of matrimony, of the commitment. *Was this the answered prayer I maybe didn't want answered?* The hamster wheel of my nomadic alpinist lifestyle still spun under my feet; I needed to jump off and stand on solid ground. Was it possible to meet a woman through the mail and make a life with her? The answer lay in action, not rumination. So I took the long lead on the climb, the best route to the summit, and went for it.

Wanting to show I wasn't terminally wild, rather than proposing on a mountaintop or the ski hill, I wooed Lisa by candlelight in a quaint Aspen restaurant. Over the tiramisu, I offered the ring (a new one, to be clear).

Ten months later, on September 7, 1985, I watched my promised bride walk down the aisle of Aspen's red-quarry-stone Methodist church on her father's arm, draped like a supermodel in her ivory satin gown, beaming the biggest smile I've ever seen dazzle her face. When we kissed, I didn't want to stop.

We held the reception at a nearby guest ranch where the bar stools had horse saddles for seats. Along with a couple hundred friends and family, we boogied our tails off to my brother Craig's rock band, imported from Cal-

ifornia. Tapley was our official videographer. My mother whirled through
the crowd, doing her best Isadora Duncan, and somehow avoided the fully dressed pool jump most of us other celebrants engaged in. My father
meandered with a dazed expression on his face and left early. Lisa's family
embraced her new circle; Hans and Lillian smiling, laughing, joining in the
dancing.

As I clinked beer bottles with my male friends, more than one of them
grinned, chuckled, and said something like, "Amazed you did it, man," followed by the eternal ski-town relationship query: "But, can she ski?"

With Lisa,
Mount Hood

©David Swersky

WE KICKED OFF OUR marriage with a road trip out West, exploring the
Utah desert on bicycles, ending with two temperate October weeks in Santa
Barbara. Then there was the second honeymoon, a few years later, when we
enjoyed a Dawsonized week of ski touring on Oregon's Mount Hood. We
booked the historic Timberline Lodge, perched on the side of the mountain
in all its big-timber and stone Cascadian glory. Our cozy room, decorated
with antique wooden skis, shared a wall with the clattering, equally antique
elevator. It was loud but nothing compared to our creaky old bed.

Every morning before sunrise, we left the lodge and skied on volcanic Mount Hood, its summit rimmed with ice-white gargoyles formed from moisture drifting off the nearby Pacific. I set Lisa up with sharpened crampons and a new Black Diamond ice axe.

We climbed twice to the summit. I skied down; she downclimbed to where we'd left her skis at the base of the steeps. During our first climb, I showed her how to descend high-angle snow while facing inward to the mountain, an awkward yet effective skill.

"You'd better learn to do this right," I said while lightly grasping my ice axe and standing sideways on the steep slope—my macho mountain guide pose. "I'm supposed to stay alive so I can father your child, but you need to be around for that to happen."

Her laugh echoed total agreement.

Afternoons, we skied to the lodge for pool lounging and five-star grub in the Cascade Dining Room. The dessert cart was a hit. The waiter was psychic or a fellow ski mountaineer; his servings of black forest cake were double slices, topped by what looked like a quart of whipped cream.

In Aspen, I made excellent money as a carpenter. Lisa worked as an accountant with a fantastic boss. Despite the challenges of full-time jobs, the newlywed glow did not fade. We spent nearly every summer weekend camping out of my truck, cooking on the tailgate and spreading our sleeping bags under endless stars. Long before it was a thing, we biked the dusty mining trails of Moab in view of the sandstone towers I had climbed, and raced mountain bikes in some of the first such events.

ONE SUMMER, WE PACKED rain jackets, toothbrushes, and a credit card into our fanny packs, hopped on our mountain bikes, and rode for five days through southern Colorado, taking every dirt road and backcountry pass we could find. On our last day, we were backed up behind a thousand sheep while riding into Silverton. The herder gestured us through. An icy drizzle fell as we bumped our front wheels against the muddy-white creatures.

When we finally reached town, shivering and coated with dollops of slimy sheep-dung flung from our knobby tires, out came the credit card. Lisa ran a hot bath in the old Teller House hotel's full-length white ceramic clawfoot tub, and together we soaked away the day—after a lively attempt to slosh most of the water onto the floor.

Weeks later, Lisa was still raving about that bath. I didn't need to be reminded; few memories are so fine.

With the sheep, Silverton, 1985   ©Dawson

Out of Aspen, we hiked the alpine and napped in fields of purple lupine and yellow goldeneye. Come winter, we ski-toured to backcountry cabins, where we lay in each other's arms as the orange glow from the woodstove warmed our skin.

And yet, there were steeps and peaks still to ski, stories to make and tell. Could I combine my new life with my old obsession?

34 | FOURTEENER SKIER, 1987

LEAVE IT TO OLD friends to shake things up. Twenty months past my nuptials, John Quinn telephoned.

"I need a break from school, from MBA intensity. Let's get back to it, ski fourteeners for a week," he said, his tone weary but hopeful.

"When?" I answered.

John Quinn, Mt. Lincoln, 1987

Most of Colorado's 54 fourteeners had been skied at least once. Yet, with a few exceptions, they were not known as compelling ski goals. There was near zero knowledge of the best descent routes. There were no skiing guidebooks, YouTube tutorials, or social media tips. And a handful of summits, Capitol Peak for one, had never been skied. My inner Rudi stirred, he of *Banner in the Sky*. In the mystery lay the magic.

ON A BRIGHT DAY in late April, Quinn pulled up to the Dawson trailer-house in his green Jeep Wagoneer: bench seats as sleeping bunks, a heater that worked, four-wheel-drive—the ideal rig for a Colorado road trip. I threw in my ski gear, sleeping bag, a box of topo maps, one pair of spare socks, and three briefs (things had changed since the climbing bum days). We didn't bring any camp cooking gear—too much time and irritation. Instead, we'd choke down our breakfasts on the move, carry pocket snacks, and find restaurants for dinner. Mexican, if we had our way.

We started the party with Grays and Torreys peaks, two ridge-connected, bulky fourteeners near Interstate 70 out of Denver. In the darkness of a moonless night, we parked at the trailhead and stretched out on the Jeep seats, the slight backward tilt of mine keeping me from rolling onto the floor.

When our wristwatch alarms shrilled at 4:30 a.m., frozen condensation coated the windows like the walls of a walk-in freezer. We oozed from our sleeping bags, kicked the iced doors open, and hopped like sack racers as we pulled on our cold-stiff ski boots. We munched granola bars for breakfast as we stumbled along the rocky trail to the snowline. Sunrise greeted us at the Torreys summit.

To check both peaks off our list, we traversed the connecting ridge to the summit of Grays, skied a few thousand feet down an open gulch, and then crampon-hiked back to the summit of Torreys. From there, we opened it up almost 4,000 vertical feet above Quinn's Jeep, on a vast, moderate-angle line known as "The Big Ol' Stripe of Snow." Enjoying gravity-fueled high-speed carves, we banked like fighter jets, arc to arc, flying in formation, sometimes wing to wing.

We were soon swilling margaritas at the first *restaurante* we found.

"That was an amazing run," I said, scooping tortilla chips through picante sauce—the first of three baskets—with enchilada plates on the way. "But if we're skiing fourteeners, let's go for some steeper stuff."

"You studied the map all the way from Torreys," Quinn said. "See anything worthy?"

"Sure, Quandary Peak. Looks like you could drive a snowcat up the thing. Boring. But the map shows a bunch of steeps off the sides."

We drove to a Quandary viewpoint late that afternoon, and I opened Borneman and Lampert's *A Climbing Guide to Colorado's Fourteeners*. This sole 'teener guidebook of the 1980s was heavy on history and other cultural content, spiced with a few climbing routes for each peak. It was a compulsory read. But within its 255 pages, the only mention of skiing was Stammberger's "daring ski descent of the North Maroon Bell."

Yet there was hope. The book mentioned "glissading," butt-sliding down snow slopes for a quick descent. From my years of mountaineering, I knew glissading to be an exciting way to die, as when you strike an ice patch and rocket into a rock field or over a cliff. I also knew it worked best on steeper terrain. Perfect.

Quinn searched for a parking spot as I read out loud from the Quandary description:

"From the summit, a perfect couloir descends the south face. It will deposit one squarely at the Monte Cristo dam after five minutes and one of the *best glissades* in the state."

I laughed. "Anything that's a so-called best glissade must be an awesome ski descent—that thing is at least 3,000 vertical feet. Let's run up there tomorrow and nail it. Hope there's no glissaders in the way!"

It was one of our best runs ever. The couloir brimmed with compacted, avalanche-safe springtime snow while a hand-thick skiff of powder buttered the surface. It was steeper than Grays and Torreys, narrower.

Such terrain features often relax too soon. The Quandary line stayed in character until we shucked our skis on the shore of the small reservoir on Monte Cristo Creek and hiked for ten minutes down the dirt road back to the Wagoneer. Later that day, I began calling the line "The Cristo Couloir" in a public nod to its geography and a private nod to faith.

Over the coming days, I studied Borneman like a medical textbook and pored over my maps until my eyes twirled. We thus made divinations about which peaks might yield *the line*. I enjoyed figuring out how to ski mountains almost as much as skiing them. Typical guidebook writer?

Day three, we hit Mounts Lincoln and Bross, two enormous yet easy peaks connected by a broad, one-and-a-half-mile ridge. We skied a couloir off Lincoln and climbed back to Bross, where we won the prize. Laughing at the ease of it all, we sailed down the stupendous Moose Creek gulch and gully system—a vertical half-mile snowy confection my skis could have carved even without their driver.

AFTER A SNOW-COOLED BREW at Quinn's Jeep, we drove a half hour south to the village of Fairplay. As a pre-dinner dessert, we decimated the historic Fairplay Hotel's famous pizza-sized sweet rolls, garnished with a Udall-worthy half-stick of butter. Carbs restored, over the next two days we picked off Mount Bierstadt, named for the painter, and Pikes Peak, where the poem was written that became the song "America the Beautiful."

Southern sojourn completed, we returned to Leadville, the culinary center of 'teener skiing. The old mining town boasted one of my favorite dining establishments. In full view of fourteeners Mount Elbert and Mount Massive, next to slag heaps left by the smelters of the silver boom, The Grill restaurant had been serving miner-sized plates of beans, rice, chicken, and tortillas for as long as anyone could remember. During my Outward Bound winter, I'd spent more evenings there than I deserved—for good reasons. The dining area was warmer than our snow caves, and there was something special about the cracked red-vinyl seats and the velvet paintings. It was a welcome contrast to Aspen, where the authentically hip establishments of my youth had continued their fall to soulless glitz.

We took a booth. The bottomless basket of tortilla chips topped off the glycogen and replenished the sodium. Saucy chicken enchiladas rounded out the experience.

That night's bench-seat bivouac was on the shoulder of State Highway 91, a mile from 14,155-foot Mount Democrat. After driving through the area over the years, Democrat's northwest face had stuck in my mind. I'd imagined a ski route woven through dozens of cliffs.

We woke at four a.m. to find the windshield coated with three inches of snow. Quinn fired the engine and switched on the wipers. There was nothing but darkness through the glass, not a hint of moonglow, no stars. Cancel.

Back in Leadville, cozy in the Rose Café, we nursed mugs of burnt coffee as I consulted the Borneman-Lampert guidebook. A nearby option surfaced: 14,043-foot Mount Sherman, where, according to the authors, a plane had once crash-landed on the peak's sprawling upper reaches—with survivors. The consummate mountain for a storm day? Perhaps, but we were clueless as to automobile access from Leadville. The book had nothing. Turning to the next best option, we queried our middle-aged, ruddy-faced waitress.

"You know how to drive from here to Mount Sherman?"

She harvested an armload of plates and wavered next to our table.

"Isn't that somewhere near Buena Vista, honey?"

She was off forty miles, so we dropped in on Leadville's single sporting goods store. Three pairs of vintage Rossignol rental skis leaned against the wall behind the gun counter. The overweight, gray-haired proprietor stabbed the map with a nicotine-browned fingertip.

"Yeah, that's the road up to the mountains. I know guys who hunt up there. Try driving east, up the hill above town."

After wandering through a subdivision, we found the road and parked at timberline near an operating mine. A whiteout muzzled the windshield. With a Robert Ludlum novel propped over my bacon-stuffed belly, the Jeep's heat vents were my new best friends. Or so they were until Sherman's sideways gravitational pull penetrated our caloric torpor.

"Might as well ski up there, *take a look*," Quinn said.

"Yeah, I think you're right."

We followed my compass needle into the storm. About every ten minutes, the clouds peeled and exposed the route. From a snowy saddle, a wind-scoured ridge led us to the top.

I tossed my pack next to the stacked-rock summit cairn and pulled out a water bottle.

"We can't ski this ridge; it's grass and rocks. We'll have to hike down."

At that moment, the wind scattered the clouds, and a vast snow-filled bowl materialized below us, connected to the summit by a swatch of white. It had to be the same bowl where the plane had crashed—most of it too low-angled for much avalanche danger. We skied to just above timberline and exited by climbing over the saddle we'd crossed during the ascent.

Faith had borne fruit, a lesson I could always use.

After another Grill-provisioned carb session, I resisted getting a motel room—thin wallet. But Quinn prevailed as the voice of reason. We needed showers like we'd been working construction on a summer day in Dallas. And sleeping on beds instead of sticky plastic Jeep seats was darn appealing.

We left Leadville at our usual pre-dawn start time and returned to attempt Mount Democrat's northwest face. This little gem was the most complex and dangerous skiing we'd tried. At a maximum of 45 degrees, it wasn't excessively steep, but several connecting gullies were inches wider than the length of our skis, and numerous traverses crossed just a few feet above cliffs, where a slip meant death.

Quinn maneuvered through the cruxes with ease, blending, it seemed, with little concern. I felt the same. This was the perfect graduation from Torreys' reaches and Sherman's bowl—not because of the danger, but because the intricate nature of the route was something we'd touched on throughout our years of skiing, yet never handled with such mastery.

As I glided behind Quinn down the mile-long valley back to his Jeep, I thought about steeps—why they're special. Halfway between the vertical and the horizontal, a line bisects the world. On one side, gravity rules. On the other side, forty-five degrees and beyond, when you spring off the snow during a turn, for a moment, you fly, weightless. Beyond the challenge, beyond the athleticism, steep skiing was about wings.

BACK HOME, QUINN JOINED Lisa and me for *cervezas* on the front steps of our trailer. Our ten-by-twenty-foot patch of grass was greening up, needing a mow. Summer was near. After counting on my fingers and determining that I'd skied seventeen Colorado fourteeners, the conversation turned to the beer-o-clock norm for all mountaineers: future adventures.

"You should ski all fifty-four fourteeners," Quinn said. "Cool project. You'd be the first. I'll bet every peak has an okay route from the summit or near enough. Way better than summer hiking on trashy rock piles."

He was exaggerating about the trash. But the point stuck.

During our trip, I had pondered skiing all fifty-four peaks—and journaled it as "dreaming." But sometimes dreams became real: the Yosemite hard pitches with Jardine, my thirty peaks in thirty days, marrying Lisa after years of thinking a life partner was, at best, improbable.

That evening, I scribbled a checklist and tacked it to the wall above my desk. Thirty-seven to go.

Mountain bean-counting is common: *He's climbed Everest seven times!* But obsessing on a checkbox, rather than the climb in front of you, gets people killed. Does playing by the mountain's rules include keeping a scorecard? Could I be a bean counter with a brain? While spooned against my bride that night, I lay awake.

Over the recent years, I'd come to believe my higher power spoke to me in various ways (though I often chose to ignore it). Sometimes, words bubbled up in my mind—the mystical side of the divine. Other times, the lessons came through people's words. And, all too often, the big guy spanked me through the consequences of my actions: "that blatant voice, ignored at your peril," as I'd heard sermonized. The Highland Bowl avalanche had been my first conscious experience of such words. And, more than anything, I'd learned there was always an answer when I asked.

So I prayed: *Was I still too much Rudi the mountain boy? Was I on the verge of my old foibles, peaks over people, mountain adultery? Should I go after the fourteeners?*

A peaceful, mind-stilling *Yes* came to me, with the answer as much in the peace as the *Yes*. I was fit, with the latest gear and a mature attitude. I'd spent most of my life mastering ski mountaineering. This goal was absurd on the grand scale of humanity—yet it was my calling. *Do it right, with lessons learned.*

Lisa and I were childless. We had dependable jobs and savings in the bank. My first ski-touring guidebook, *Colorado High Routes*, was on the shelves. Lisa knew I wasn't the idiot who'd danced with death in Highland Bowl. When I told her about my big new plan, she wrapped me in her arms.

"Our bed's cold when you're away. But when you come back from the mountains, your eyes shine a brighter blue. I love that."

I had my permissions, and *the project* began.

Three days after my conversation with Quinn, I went for the cliff-banded

north face of North Maroon Peak. Übermensch Fritz Stammberger had
made history here with his 1971 first ski descent. If my quest had a spiritual
center, this was it.

While skiing the steeps of the Maroons was no laughing matter, a significant part of the challenge lay in the nine-mile access road. During springtime,
when the ski routes came into condition, the road dried off yet remained
gated, thus making for a tedious, uncomfortable approach. There were numerous solutions for this problem, none ideal: walk the hard asphalt, ride
a bicycle, or cut the chain and drive the road after installing your own lock
(and risk a fine). Best in my opinion: a smallish motorcycle you could muscle
around the side of the gate.

So it was that one o'clock a.m. found me puttering along our valley's
main highway (which led to the closed road) on a small trailbike borrowed
from our next-door neighbor. Max speed was thirty-five miles per hour, and
my skis stuck up from my backpack like flag masts. I worried about a cop
stopping me out of cop-ish curiosity to discover I had neither the registration
for the motorcycle nor the license to drive it. Yet other than a hypothermic
chill from the morning air, all went well; I leaned the moto against a tree at
Maroon Lake and had at it.

As I broke through timberline on North Maroon, early morning alpenglow tinted the snow a watermelon pink. I strapped on my crampons and
began climbing Stammberger's line. The frozen night-crust made for easy
step-kicking. Then the sun rose over Pyramid Peak, the crust softened to
nothing, and I sank to my thighs in soupy, avalanche-prone snow.

I was in the exact area where ski mountaineer Theo Meiners had fallen,
tumbled over a cliff, and survived. Quinn liked to joke about Theo's near
demise, calling his accident "Meiners' Memorial Ski Jump." I didn't care to
make the second-ever jump—avalanche-assisted—survival unlikely.

The face held another route more protected from the sun: a steep gully,
fifteen feet wide in places, first skied in 1978 by my El Capitan guiding buddy
Larry Bruce. A ten-minute traverse took me to its shadowed confines, where
I found icy, avalanche-safe snow.

Would this variation net me a ski descent from the summit?

I topped Larry's couloir and climbed southwest, searching for continuous skiing. Step by step, I grew ever more excited as snow connected the entire

way. The summit register's lightning-fused steel cables were an interesting touch. I checked the sky.

No thunderclouds. Excellent.

After a swig of water, I clipped into my skis, dropped, and linked up the snow I'd just climbed. The couloir remained shaded, frozen, rough as gravel. No-fall terrain yet avalanche-safe. Number eighteen.

Spring ended with seven more peaks. Two yielded the steeps: Mount Sneffels, Snake Couloir, and Wilson Peak, East Face. The others were easy, lower angled, replete with forgiving snow. And, when I momentarily forgot my preference (nice word for addiction?) for the extreme, they were fun.

Quandary Peak, Cristo Couloir

WITH SKI SEASON DONE, Lisa and I were cozy in #A4 Woody Creek Trailer Park. I'd set up an office in our tiny spare bedroom and had a fourteener guidebook under contract. I liked showing my wife I had work as a writer. But we both knew I needed to keep my carpentry career, so I'd lined up several building jobs. And inspired by my frequent forays into our spider-infested crawl space, we'd decided to finish renovating. I was on cruise control. Sort of.

Half of the fifty-four fourteeners had felt my skis. Capitol Peak, the most technical of them all, loomed as the witchy tower. Next spring, perhaps?

35 | PEAK EXTREME, 1988-1990

OVER THE YEARS, WINTER ascents of Capitol Peak had become routine. By now, I'd ticked it a half dozen times, once solo and once with my brother Craig. Kennedy had blasted it in a single February day, car-to-car, a harbinger of what would become a string of alpine climbing firsts, culminating in 1985 with his first ascent of the northeast face of Nepal's Ama Dablam.

Living amid such alpine culture, attempting Capitol's first ski descent was mandatory—and perhaps I possessed the key. I remembered the Knife Ridge in winter and the small cornice that often eased the way. *Would the cornice be thicker after springtime's sticky snowfalls? Would it be wider? Could I ski across the Knife?*

March, 1988. I'd stuttered through four fourteener descents since the calendar had clocked over to the new year. All were vicious, windy, cold as an asteroid in the shade. A February scrape down the thin snow of Mount Antero was the worst. The summit boulder field looked to be covered with creamy white powder—it was ten inches deep over the saber-toothed rocks. When I took my planks in for repair, my ski technician laughed, said, "What did you do, ski down a rock pile?"

"As a matter of fact, yes," I answered.

When the snows of March finally hit, Lisa joined me for a ten hour day on 14,162-foot Tabeguache Peak, where we ski-climbed through a grove of ancient bristlecone pines as the sun fell through the western sky. I caught the summit, then spent too much time photographing the methuselahs. We skied back to our truck in the dark. By now, my wife was used to such adventures. Three weeks later, I went for Capitol. Lisa stayed home for that little excursion—headlamp skiing through the pines was one thing, the stone ramparts of Colorado's toughest fourteener were quite another.

Lisa, 1988
on Tabeguache Peak

Izzo Isaacs, Elks Traverse participant and my Highland Bowl avalanche companion, joined as my Capitol Peak support partner. We agreed he'd stash his skis below the steeper terrain, then climb and descend on crampons while handling the climbing rope we'd use to protect ourselves (in theory) from being avalanched off the peak like bugs scoured off a windshield. We'd begin early, while the snow remained crusted from the night's chill, avalanche-safe. Yet once the sun hit, the snow would loosen and destabilize. That's when we might need the rope.

IZZO LOOKED ON AS I skied from the knee-high stack of rocks marking Capitol's summit, rounded the summit cone, and dropped through a small, fifty-degree cleft. This path placed me on the mountain's eastern flank, the avalanche terrain I'd avoided during my winter climbs, where a fall would launch me over the peak's east-facing precipice—a thousand feet of clean fourteener air down to Pierre Lakes. I'd backpacked there in the summer. Pretty water, lots of trout. Today wasn't the day for fishing.

As my adrenals hissed like an espresso machine, I whispered a prayer and traversed 400 yards just a few hundred feet above the cliffs.

As I prepared to step onto Knife Ridge, my memory of reaching this point with Kennedy after our north-face ascent fifteen years earlier surfaced: *We were wrung out. But compared to the roped pitches of our Slingshot Direct route on Capitol's north-face wall, navigating a small cornice and scooting along the Knife on our butts had felt like strolling a sidewalk.*

This time, the traverse looked easier still. The expected cornice was there, thick and strong, starting with a comfortable section nearly as wide as the length of my skis, narrowing to a few feet at the end where the sharp ridge made way to easy ground.

Moving slowly, belayed by Izzo in case the cornice broke, I shuffled across the ridge in eight minutes. The infamous Knife, never known as a ski route, was no more difficult than drifting through a ski-lift line—if I ignored the yawning abyss to either side. When I rejoined Izzo I couldn't help smiling, thinking: *crossing that thing has to be the most unique skiing I've ever done.*

As I CHASED THE remaining fourteeners, public awareness of ski mountaineering was going through a sea change. That previous winter, in late 1988, director Greg Stump had released his independent ski film *Blizzard of Aahhh's*—a manic masterpiece that presented adventure skiing as a heady (pun intended) mix of mountaineering, partying, and cliff jumping. It was everything the next generation craved: loosely plotted yet bounteous eye candy, hot skiing, yahoo fun, ideal fodder for the TV screens hanging above ski-town bars.

Halfway through my first viewing, I was certain *Blizzard* was the most influential ski flick of the late twentieth century. Yet all was not perfect. The flick spoke of its content as "extreme skiing," when most of the action scenes were more akin to skilled acrobatics, hence exploiting the term "extreme" and perplexing those of us (admittedly few) who sought the true radical—those of us who went by Landry's mantra: "If you fall, you die."

Slogans were one thing, money another. It was obvious the *Blizzard* talent—Mike Hattrup, Glen Plake, and Scot Schmidt—were, to some extent, professional skiers. Although this was a low-budget, independent film, I figured they might have received at least a pittance of monetary compensation while enjoying free lift tickets and probably all the skis, boots, bindings, and flashy attire that ski-industry marketing shills could attach to their speedy visages. Or maybe the director just bought them espresso and sandwiches. Either way was better than zero.

I had missed any sort of "pro" gig when I wound down my rock climbing career and broke my leg the first time. And I'd always figured that eschewing commercialism made me pure—not to mention that self-promotion felt like having my introverted eyes gouged out. Yet travel money and free gear had appeal. The fifth (or was it the sixth?) time I watched *Blizzard*, I got to thinking: *If I forced a bit of hagiographic chest pounding, might a handful of swag come the way of the fourteener extreme skier?*

I embarked on a meager PR campaign: sent out a couple of press releases, got a smidge of media coverage in regional Colorado publications—and eventually a mention in *Powder* magazine. The free fluorescent-yellow jacket and two ball caps were appreciated. But you can't eat nylon, and it won't fill a gasoline tank. In jest, a tad bitter, I shaved a stripe through the center of my hair, front to back—to riff on Plake's famous mohawk. Only Lisa understood the haircut—after I explained.

Whining aside, I did enjoy *Blizzard*: the implied friendships, the skilled athletes, the not-so-innocent joy, and, most of all, the validation of what I preferred to call "adventure skiing." North America's ski culture had changed. My fourteener quest was legit, or at least somewhat understood by the mainstream. So, despite all the driving, the expense, the aching joints, the storms, and the avalanches, with Lisa's support I stuck with the vision. By May 1988, my list of skied fourteeners had grown to thirty-three.

WETTERHORN PEAK, BY SOME rankings the 49th-highest Colorado mountain, is small by fourteener standards. Nearby Uncompahgre Peak—the sixth highest—promenades as a regal, flat-topped landmark you can see from many spots in southwest Colorado. Wetterhorn isn't as easy to pick from the skyline, and its east face rises a meager thousand feet above its basin footing. It's a pretty rise, though. During snow seasons, a triangular face of white shines from the distance—as obvious a ski route as ever existed.

For my go at Wetterhorn, I teamed up with Bob Perlmutter. As it should be with great alpine companions, Bob and I had first met in the mountains eleven years prior on the flanks of 12,965-foot Mount Sopris.

Rising more than a vertical mile from its base, with twin summits connected by a stunning drop-curved mile-long ridge, Sopris is the first mountain to greet travelers entering the Roaring Fork Valley (the local of our residence) from Interstate 70. There's a pullout for the inevitable photo-takers. But it's not uncommon to see a landscape-stunned driver parked on the highway's narrow shoulder, hanging out their window, shooting photos until fear of decapitation overcomes the artistic instinct.

Mount Sopris, Crystal Chute   ©Dawson

FLASHBACK, LATE SPRING 1979. The snowline in the Aspen-area mountains was melting ever higher. I'd spent the past winter with Outward Bound and recently completed my thirty-peaks-in-thirty-days project. Summer called. But resistance was futile when Kendall Williams and Richard Compton proposed skiing the Crystal Chute, a stunning 3,000-vertical-foot couloir gracing the west bastion of Sopris.

We made good time step-kicking on night-hardened snow. Despite the easy climbing, I mulled the story of a fellow who'd fallen down the entire chute wearing shorts and a T-shirt. It was said he'd left ribbons of flayed skin on the abrasive springtime snow crust and spent time in the burn ward—something about skin grafts. I gripped my ice axe a little tighter.

As the morning brightened, two strangers closed the distance below us. When they caught up, I noticed the leader, a short, wiry fellow, wore a pair of woolen NOLS knicker-pants, replete with a Thelma signature butt-patch. His skis were A-framed on his pack. But where were his ski boots? I was climbing in mine, Kendall's and Richard's dangled from their backpacks.

Happy to meet another NOLSie, I introduced myself.

"You guys climbed fast. You planning on skiing in your hiking boots?"

The NOLSie jammed his ice axe in the snow and rocked back on his heels, resting his leg muscles like a pro.

"Hey, I'm Bob Perlmutter. I've been skiing other peaks with this rig: Mount Hayden, Castle. Want me to kick some steps?"

"Sure," I said while thinking that once Bob was on skis—in hiking boots—we might witness another customer for the burn ward.

The moment Bob took the lead, his strong, rhythmic pace told me he was a product of Petzoldt.

"Nice job on the steps," I said when we reached the top.

After a convivial summit snack, I smirked as Bob fastened his hiking boots into his ski bindings, shouldered his backpack, and poled off. Seconds later, my smirk dissolved to jaw-drop amazement as Bob crouched over his skis and chained two dozen flawless turns, each throwing a rooster tail of snow like a power boat.

Bob Perlmutter,
Mount Sopris, Crystal Chute, 1979
©Dawson

NINE YEARS AFTER THE Crystal Chute, I stood with Bob Perlmutter on Wetterhorn Peak—number thirty-eight of my fourteeners ski project. Since meeting on Mount Sopris, we'd teamed up for scores of descents, stoked with the synergy of a fine alpine partnership.

I turned from checking my finicky Silvretta 404 ski bindings, and took in the sunrise-garnished view. Puffy clouds boiled above and to the south of Uncompahgre Peak, blocking the sun's heat, which we'd counted on to soften the icy face. On most days, our timing would have been perfect: clip into our skis, fly. Instead, the petrified snow laughed in our faces as the clouds swirled.

The wise move in such situations is to nap and await the softening. But once you've dozed, snacked, shared lies, and emptied your tea thermos, gravity pulls at your legs like a living thing. And today, the thickening, ever-closer clouds asked for action. If we skied after the clouds blanketed the face, we'd be inside a whiteout—in the egg—where we'd lose our depth perception. If vertigo overcame us, attempting to ski the icy steeps could be suicidal.

Should we strap our skis to our packs and downclimb the route?

I dropped first, willing the clouds to hold off long enough for the descent. After two turns over a fifty-degree swale, I slid to a stop and pulled my camera from the nylon bag belted to my chest.

I watched Bob through the lens as I clicked. His days of skiing in hiking shoes were long past. Instead, his plastic ski touring boots transmitted every nuance from mind to feet. With each jump turn, his skis floated a foot or so above the snow as he swung them around—though his were not exaggerated leaps. This was instead an elegant unweighting, a glider lofting an air current.

Bob's skis chattered as he hockey-stopped ten feet to my right.

"Here come the clouds," he said, as tendrils of mist flowed over us like a horror movie.

In thirty seconds, I could see only my ski tips and a soft-focus Bob wavering behind the gauze. The air smelled moist, maritime. Snowflakes stuck to my goggle lenses and melted into water droplets.

"I can hardly see anything," I loud-talked into the murk, "but I think the snow is grippy enough to ski. Still, if we fall, we're going for the ride."

"Nobody's falling," Bob said. "Let's take it easy ... Try a few turns."

Bob at his best. Whenever my confidence ebbed, he filled the gap.

The snow surface ahead blended with the cloud like a photographer's seamless backdrop. Eyes open or closed, not much difference. The key here was to ski slowly, so my body wouldn't outrun my compromised senses.

I planted both ski poles for balance and sensory input, then pushed against my downhill ski, released the edge, and allowed it to slide for a split second. While platforming off this tiny amount of momentum, I sprang upward, splayed my uphill ski so it would pre-edge once I brought it around, and completed the turn with a choppy sideways slide. I'd been learning this specialized turn on other steeps but never executed it with such confidence.

I caught a foggy glimpse of Bob making the same moves while using his bicycle-strong quads and compact stature to glean a little more pop from his turns. At the bottom of the steeps, we glided under the cloud bank into the bowl below the face. We stopped and tapped ski poles—the skier equivalent of a fist bump.

There were no howls of victory. It all felt rather common.

It was weeks later I found the significance. Eyes closed, I relived staring blindly into the fog, while my skis scratched the icy snow like fingernails. The mountain had shown me the way.

THAT SUMMER OF 1988, my father married Lee, the woman he'd been with for around a decade. Lisa and I attended the wedding atop the sage-covered Colorado mesa, where the couple had remodeled a mobile home. Their creative configuration reminded me of my father's previous dwellings. Lots of windows and plants. Wanting for repairs yet functional. I thought it sad that he'd built beautiful houses and lived in a trailer. But so did Lisa and I.

I'd never thought about having a stepmother. Lee was pleasant and chatty with me and my brothers; I'd expected things to be harder, more awkward. Even so, I couldn't help thinking of my mother and wishing she and my dad had worked things out. More, Lee's age was off-putting; she was thirteen years younger than my father, closer to my age than his. Yet, as I watched them interact, she seemed good for him, bringing out his best. Had she the secret to handling this creative, kind, yet dysfunctional man? In any case, Charles had a new family—I assumed he'd stabilized financially with Grandpa's continued help and Lee's influence. I thought of him often and called infrequently. He said it was "weird" I didn't visit more. I wanted to be honest and tell him why, that it was too uncomfortable. Instead, I just said I was busy, while knowing I could be a better son.

SOMETIMES, SKIING FOURTEENERS WAS just plain funny.

Jon Waterman was a rugged alpinist with brown, knife-cut hair and lungs the size of a camp cooler. In 1978, we'd spent a month paired as Outward Bound instructors, chasing lost students and maxing our heart rates while racing each other up alpine passes. A decade later, he was a well-known author and wilderness traveler. I respected that; I liked rubbing shoulders with success. But it was personal too. Of all my friends, Jon was the one who most sensed my change in attitude after my two accidents. In the foreword for a fourteener guidebook I'd later author, he would write:

> People thought Lou was still cheeky as ever. But his closest friends knew he had become somewhat of a "fox of the fourteeners," determined to avoid accidents, to learn everything possible ...

IN SPRING 1989, I CONSCRIPTED Jon for a stab at Mount Wilson, a somewhat obscure fourteener in the San Juan Mountains of south-central Colorado. Wilson had two ski routes I knew of, but they weren't visible from surrounding roads. Solution: *Just climb the thing and flow.*

We left Aspen late and parked under a star-filled sky, strapped our sleeping bags on our daypacks, and bashed our way by headlamp through crowded evergreens in what we guessed was the general direction of the peak. My A-framed skis snagged so often on overhead branches that I resorted to carrying them in my arms like a rifle. Around ten, we bedded on a cushy squirrel midden under a fir tree. Though not discussed, we knew we should have spread our sleeping pads next to our car, risen early, and climbed the peak in one simple push.

When my watch alarm shrilled at two a.m., I rolled over in my sleeping bag and said, "You mind pulling the stove out of my pack and starting the brew?"

As seasoned alpinists, Jon and I were okay with four hours of sleep—so long as there was coffee, hot and strong.

"Sure," Jon muttered as he rustled through my backpack.

I expected the click of a Bic, the comforting hiss of flaming gas. Instead, the rummaging rodent noises increased. As did the verbiage:

"Where is the frigging stove fuel, Lou?"

I sat up in my sleeping bag, moaned, "Crap, I left it back in the car."

Disaster. Nothing hot, no joe, four hours' sleep, *no caffeine.*

In desperation, I grabbed the plastic bag of arabica, ripped the ziplock, pressed it over my face like a feed bag, and huffed the earthy aroma. *Ah, yes.* I grinned at Jon, grabbed a pinch, and stuffed it behind my lower lip like I was loading chew.

"Hey, that's tasty. Maybe I'll get a boost?"

"Hand that over," Jon said as he snatched the bag from my hands.

We were soon gagging on ground coffee, laughing like loons, and snapping flash photos of our char-coated tongues. The caffeine buzz was way harsher than our usual three-cup dose. And Mount Wilson soon fell to our whims, my last fourteener of the season.

COME FALL OF 1989, Lisa announced she was pregnant. Inspired by a certain diminutive black dress, we'd had fun making that happen. And once it did, our relationship held joy and purpose beyond anything I'd imagined. It was primal, tribal, breeding, covered by my love for a woman with child—a love that blew me away with its power to dominate the hierarchy of needs.

As for other needs, it was time to make a nest more permanent than a cramped trailer on a rental plot. Three days after Lisa told me she was pregnant, we found a small, decrepit, demolition-ready bungalow nearby. The price was right: a little cash—eased by a loan from Lisa's parents—and a lot of work.

After gutting the place, we hired a house mover to lift and hold the structure while I built a foundation. I spent eight months of ten-hour days strapped with my tool belt, taking the project from framing to turnkey (and no doubt seeking to honor my in-laws' help).

As a goof, I swore to my bride I wouldn't cut my hair or shave until we moved in. My hair soon went rockstar—only without a perm—and as the months rolled my scraggy, untrimmed beard approached ZZ Top proportions. When I worked outside, the neighborhood kids crossed to the other side of the street as they walked by. I hung up my skis for the duration—otherwise, the temptation would have been too much.

Home restoration, 1989

©Dawson

In spring 1990, I finally got my face cleaned, my ears lowered, and my rusty skis out of storage—and we moved into our new abode. The timing was good; Lisa was swollen to twice her normal size, healthy and happy, ready for motherhood.

"Two-oh-five!" she'd exclaim with a laugh as the scale creaked.

I was enjoying every gram, with particular attention to the double-Ds.

Spring also brought the enticement of resuming the fourteener project—although the window was closing on Lisa's June due date. After a few discussions, I zeroed in on two easy, safe peaks—Ellingwood and Blanca—next to each other, a one-dayer. Granted, the drive made it two days, or more. And "easy" can mean a lot of things.

I laid out the logistics.

"If you're feeling okay and don't need me here for a few days, I can make it back well before your due date."

"That will work," Lisa replied with her bright, trademark smile. "Sounds like those peaks are straightforward, and you'll have your emergency radio."

I'd taken to carrying an amateur radio handset programmed with the frequencies for a repeater system covering most of Colorado. It worked well from high ground, less so in valleys where the terrain blocked line-of-sight transmissions. Still, it was better than nothing, and it gave Lisa peace of mind when I was out by myself.

I got to packing my gear. And thinking: *My father's fade from parenting. Not me. I'd cancel my fun tickets in a microsecond if I were needed at home—now or after the birth. Still, was skiing peaks a few days before becoming a father an irresponsible undertaking? My typical routine?*

THE COLORADO ROCKY MOUNTAINS' longest sub-range, the Sangre de Cristo, extends some 200 miles south from the town of Salida to the New Mexico border. An alpine crest defines much of the Sangre, rarely exceeding ten miles in width, lofting to nine fourteeners. Of the fifty-four, these 'teeners are arguably the most difficult to ski. Not because they're steep or hard to access—though all but one or two are that—but because the entire span of the Sangre is most often as dry as Arizona asphalt.

In the pre-internet days, determining Sangre snow cover was as much a mystery as the lost Spanish treasure hidden in the valleys below. Over the past years of my 'teener project, I'd suffered the white-knuckle, deer-dodging six-hour drive almost two dozen times. During most of those sojourns, I found my chosen peaks to be scree-covered monoliths the color of pencil lead—rather than the white citadels of my dreams—and returned home with nothing to show for it except a handful of gasoline receipts. In my estimation, summiting Mount Everest had better odds.

This time, Ellingwood and Blanca rose from the scraggy-brown desert as incongruous castles of white. Just two more peaks—then go home to be a father? That was the plan.

MY DAY HAD BEGUN at midnight with a three-hour walk up a gravelly four-wheel-drive road to snowline. From there, the ascent was a fun crampon up the steeps of Ellingwood, then a ski down the southerly face where I weaved in and out of three couloirs to connect the snow. After that, I climbed easy ground to the summit of Blanca and launched again, this time down a broad open slope covered with peanut-sized corn-snow crystals. The turns on that reach had required nothing but hints from my knees.

In the basin below both peaks, I sat on a boulder, opened my journal on my thigh, and popped a Brach's Coffee Nip into my mouth. As the cold of the night-chilled granite stung through the seat of my pants, the sun climbed above Blanca. A light brown coyote roamed 200 yards upwind, hunting mice. My cuticle-shaped ski tracks glowed on the face above, and the mountain reached inside my chest. A tent, food, more days couched in the arms of the wild—was there ever enough? But I'd had my days, my months—more than most men could ask of several lifetimes. I pictured Lisa. When I'd left home, she was a week from her due date, clearly with nothing more important than becoming a mother.

Coyote continued his oblivious wander. I rolled the word "father" off my tongue. My hands trembled as I scribbled three words in my journal: "I miss Lisa."

During the quadriceps-frying hike down to my car, mind in military-grade sleep deficit and my caloric reserves burned to cinders, I sobbed like a child. The drives, the expense, the danger—I'd figured skiing the fourteeners would be challenging, but not this hard. Three mountains to go. I'd reached my apex as a mountain athlete years ago. *What was I trying to prove? Was I back in the cage, spinning the hamster wheel, blinded by smoke from the burning bearings?*

Six days later, on a bluebird morning, I was sprawled on our bed like a lazy king, reading Tom Clancy's latest. Lisa was squeezed into our narrow walk-in closet, seeking a dress that fit what I best termed her "maternal stature," when she uttered the three-word launch code of motherhood: "My water broke."

BOOK VI
FATHERS

With Louie and Lisa, Mount Baker, Washington, 2011

36 | THE KID & THE LIST, 1990-1991

THE MOMENT MY WIFE'S proclamation reached my ears, my throat closed, and adrenaline pushed fuzzy darkness into the corners of my eyes. I croaked out an astonished "Wow!"

Lisa emerged from the closet with a dress in her hand and tossed it on the bed. "Where's the go-bag?"

I flopped from our bed and stood, daddy-in-the-headlights.

"What?"

"The blue duffel with our stuff for the hospital. You wanted to stash a book in there in case things take a while."

"Oh yeah, here under the bed. But we need the car keys. Where the heck are the keys?"

Lisa looked at me like I was crazy.

"Hanging by the door, where they always are. Did you get gas?" Suddenly, her face turned white, and her hands moved to her swollen belly. "Ow, my first contraction!"

Our battered Honda Civic fired on the first crank, and off we raced to bring forth a new life.

In the hospital room, I brushed Lisa's sweat-soaked hair from her forehead and clenched her hand. At each contraction, she squeezed my knuckles so hard they crackled.

She belted out a throaty scream.

The tiny head of our son broached the world—and then the rest of him.

When I could think, I prayed, marveled at what women do, and contemplated how flesh and spirit are so intertwined.

We named our son Louis III in honor of my paternal grandfather and called him "Louie." He was born a tiny, high-altitude baby, four pounds, ten ounces. Shortly after birth, his skin and eyes took on a weird, yellowish tinge.

"A common thing," the doctor said. "Newborn jaundice. He'll be fine."

The condition required Louie to spend a few hours a day for a couple of days in a bassinet equipped with blue overhead light bulbs. My head almost burst when I saw our neonate sprawled under the blazing lights, his pencil-thin legs protruding from a loose white diaper resembling Mahatma Gandhi's loincloth, a fabric eye protector banded around his bird-sized head.

"Common thing?"

It helped that Lisa's visiting mother wasn't troubled by the lightbox. There was good reason for that. The other part of Lisa's snowstorm origin story was that Lillian had birthed her in the family farmhouse on her grand-mother's bed. My mother-in-law probably figured that if this was a hospital, why worry?

Louie, Lisa, Santa Barbara, 1991   ©Dawson

IN SPRING 1991, with Louie healthy and almost one, Lisa and I sat down at our dining room table and had the talk. "This is still my calling," I said. "I need to touch the mountains, write the books, and, if nothing else, finish skiing the fourteeners. Three to go, two hard. After that, we'll see."

Lisa looked at me with luminous eyes and nodded like I was announcing a trip to the library. It helped that our little man was nestled on her full bosom, lunching, both mother and child in oxytocin ecstasy—and a little voice, saying, *"Let him go. The DNA donor has achieved his mission."*

Was all this nothing more than biology?

While saying goodbye for the first mountain of my final triad, Crestone Needle (as extreme as it sounds), I snagged one of our infant's tiny, yellow, leather-soled baby socks. I wadded it into my first-aid pouch between the ibuprofen and band-aids.

It wasn't all biology.

By May, I'd worked Crestone Needle and dropped what I figured was Little Bear Peak's first ski descent. One fourteener remained: Kit Carson Peak, the monarch of the northern Sangre de Cristo Mountains. As the 14,165-foot highpoint on a bulky two-mile-long ridge, Carson looms more than a vertical mile from its surrounding foothills and ranchlands, black and gray, rocky, always more cliffs than snow. If Carson had been unskied, I might have quit or delayed my project until the following year. The thought of doing it was almost too much—the deer-dodging, six-hour drive from Aspen, the uncertainty, the time away from Lisa and Louie.

Yet Kit Carson had been skied in 1987, by brothers Howie and Mike Fitz and their friend Bob Pfeiffer. I'd gotten to know these guys as fellow four-teener skiers, and they'd shared their beta. By their account, Kit Carson had a somewhat hidden south-side route; a snow-filled rift they'd dubbed "Cole's Couloir." They claimed Cole's caught plentiful snow from prevailing winds and that, unlike other Sangre ski routes that came and went like ghosts, this one was usually there when a skier needed it.

I dredged up a slug of motivation and phoned Glenn Randall. Since I'd met him in 1982, while he was writing a book that included stories of our Aspen crew's climbs, Glenn had become an accomplished alpinist and fine photographer. Unlike the blank stares I often received regarding my fourteeners project, he understood my quest as a valid endeavor of alpinism. Glenn had been photographing my recent descents and aimed to document the culmination. While solid on his planks, he was not a skier of the steeps, so he'd leave his skis lower on the mountain and burn film while on crampons.

We trailhead parked at one a.m. and began the trudge—and, for me, the pain. After thirty-nine years, I felt each peak, mile, and vertical inch in my muscles, joints, and bones. The ankle of my twice-broken left leg had given up first. Now, without a wisp of cartilage, the bone-on-bone joint was attempting to glue itself immobile with arthritic tissue. It burned like a solar flare if I did anything more aggressive than push a shopping cart. When we stopped to shed our jackets, I gulped dark-orange pills like Halloween goodies and prayed I'd last.

Cole's Couloir was about twenty feet wide. A rock rib defined the right side, with a steeper wall on the left. Instead of following the fall line as most couloirs do, it slashed diagonally across the peak's steep south face like the switchbacked leg of a hiking trail. The gully was thick with snow. But the summit above appeared Sangre-bare, unskiable.

The urge to retreat was overwhelming.

Was this another desiccated failure? So many now ...

Yet I'd learned you should always complete the climb when skiing the Sangre, as you never knew where you might find snow. Faith was vital. So, with a nod to the lot of the mountaineer, I shouldered my pack and began kicking steps up Cole's. Turned out it was fun; I even forgot the summit and skiing for a few minutes and sank into the rhythm of crampons and axe.

Midway up Cole's, the summit ski route revealed itself: a small triangular face, white with snow, connected to the snow we stood on. "Continuously skiable!" I shouted, then sprinted the remaining 300 feet. Faith had won.

As I stepped onto the summit of Kit Carson—the last of my fourteeners—I dropped to my knees and tilted my head to the sky. Glenn planted his ice axe a few yards below me. He pulled out his camera. I wept as I stood and raised my ice axe in the clichéd pose of alpine victory. Cheesy? Nope, it fit the moment to perfection.

After the photos, I propped my backpack behind me and sat perched on the sharp summit like I was lounging in a recliner.

I swept my eyes across the Sangre de Cristo peaks, rising so close they appeared touchable: Crestone Needle, Crestone Peak, then to the west, the San Luis Valley's vast quilt of ranches, roads, and brown desert.

Closing my eyes, I thought of Lisa back home—her support, the child we'd made. And I pictured my skiing heroes: Fritz Stammberger, showing the way, and Chris Landry, surpassing the impossible.

My father drifted into my mind, the younger version, the adventure version: his delight in the hills, books, camping, and helping me climb my first mountain. What if my father were here with crampons and skis? As I slid down Cole's Couloir, he was.

Childcare, 1993

©Glenn Randall

37 | TALES OF THE 10th, 1943-2001

IF THERE'S SUCH A thing as good timing for a midlife crisis, Kit Carson Peak should have triggered the proverbial event. I was thirty-nine with a completed bucket list, settling into family life as much as I could settle, fond of responding to greetings with cynical barbs such as "let the decline begin." There was also a growing fondness for beer.

And yet, despite my laying out the welcome mat, the half-a-life virus held off for three years after Carson.

Finishing the last details of our house restoration provided months of distraction. After that, rearing a toddler kept me looking outside myself—nothing is more humbling than diaper changes and the associated way a boy child gives new meaning to the word "fountain." Creative compulsions helped as well: guidebook writing, photography, magazine articles. Lisa was kind and loving as always.

Despite it all, late in 1994 at age forty-two, I collapsed into midlife as if I'd fallen into a man-sized mud hole.

The prompts were many. While I lived as a stay-at-home dad, scribbling for pennies, Lisa suffered a commute that took an hour or more each way on a highway nicknamed "Killer 82." As I watched her sacrifice, balancing motherhood and work, I thought too often of my mother and how unhappy she had been working in Dallas while raising children. As a supposedly enlightened man—with zero experience—I'd laughed at the concept of the happy homemaker wife behind the white picket fence. I now knew something along those lines could be legit. Lisa agreed. We had the fence—I'd built it myself—but that was just a start.

Adding to the midlife fray, my body was in what an automobile mechanic might call "accelerated wear due to off-road use." After several ineffective surgical debridements—polite language for carving bone from a living person—my left ankle was three steps from a meltdown, and my knees sounded like frying bacon when I rose from a chair. Typical stuff for an aging athlete. But it never feels typical.

Chief among my many foibles: Lisa and I had purchased a primer-gray 1948 flatfender Jeep a few years prior—the same model the *Aspen Times* had described as the Dawson blight-house's "alluring yard art."

At first, our project car was innocent fun. We wrenched the ancient flatty into a semblance of restoration, sprayed it rattle-can yellow, installed seat belts, and named it Rumble Bee.

Most summer weekends, we loaded up the 'Bee with a picnic cooler, a handful of spare fuel filters and a gallon of water for the steaming radiator, and wheeled the old dog for many a family adventure on our nearby 4x4 trails. I was channeling my father, this time in a good way.

The good part didn't last. Mix an old Jeep with a male-midlife brain, stir with a half-inch socket wrench, and duck.

I subscribed to *Four Wheeler* magazine, where no tire is tall enough nor U-joint strong enough. Thus girded by literary inspiration, midlife survival was just a matter of withdrawal to my fully tooled man-cave garage. There I guzzled gallons of watery beer while bolt-by-bolt constructing a jeepish rock-crawler as a substitute for the blond and Corvette. All to the tune of credit-card-melting lyrics such as, "Yes, dear, I need the new welder—to fix that kitchen cabinet hinge."

When things got difficult, I could tell Lisa was concerned. Yet she instinctively knew that the old me was inside there, somewhere, and that a plate of chocolate chip cookies, delivered with a smile, was far superior to anything our family doctor might prescribe.

Beyond yellow Jeeps and other detours, more than any other midlife toxin—and despite my emotional healing atop Kit Carson Peak—my father's history remained. Almost every day, I thought of his military debacle and subsequent tumble through the 1960s maelstrom. Not only did I remain ashamed of his mistakes, but I worried the dark parts of his character were time bombs buried inside me, their fuses hissing: the depression I'd tasted the first time I'd broken a leg, the substance abuse.

During the dog days of summer—without the snows of winter as a distraction—I sat on our front porch swing (the one Lisa and I had built from an old ski lift chair), ate vanilla ice cream, and cracked my Bible. Combined with my sugar high, the gospel lightened the gloom.

Still, I spent most of my book time overthinking Christian philosophy and running rabbit trails, such as checking the word "snow" in my study guide. Most of the thirty or so biblical snow references did little for me, though Isaiah 1:18 leaped from the page; the prophet spoke of forgiveness—sins becoming "white as snow."

Forgiveness. It didn't take a genius to receive the message; it wasn't the first time I'd heard it. The idea appeared in nearly every self-help book I cared to read, including Peale's *Positive Thinking*. "Forgive seventy times seven," Peale wrote, alluding to biblical teachings. "That means 490 times." *Not that tough a count if you stick with it,* I thought. As for snow, it melted down to drinkable water; the double metaphor was no more esoteric than that. *Forgiveness and snow. It was a start.*

Come winter, there were bright spots in the gloom—namely, the world-class skiing outside our front door. From Louie's first glissando through our snowy backyard to family laps on the ski areas, powder days, and backcountry hut trips, skiing was our mission. Those laughing days in the Colorado sunshine were such a joy—falcons on the hunt, glistening snow under our steel and plastic wings. If "skiing is life," as was said, here was proof.

A few years into it, the malaise began a schizoid bounce. Some days felt normal—even exceptional—especially the family ski days and road trips. But nearly every day had its challenges. Between frequent bouts of indecision and apathy, I'd latch onto small things that grounded me: nostalgic glances at my climbing journal, guidebook writing, John Grisham's addictive beach novel, *The Rainmaker*, a slate-gray, glacier-polished pebble I'd pocketed during a Canadian road trip with Lisa and kept on my office window shelf.

The worst of it—and what led to the best of it: I could not stop reflecting on my father's life, and somehow, after ruminating to the point of emotional exhaustion, I saw my path. I needed to move, to begin those 490 steps, see the good in the man, see his story from his eyes. So, rather than letting the fragments of his military history fester inside me like shrapnel, starting around 1996, I began a journey of understanding.

My father was in his early seventies, still living with Lee in their mesa-top mobile home. He seemed settled, happier. *Would he be more willing to dish about his army stint?* Not to be. The most I got during a phone call and a few brief visits was, "I'm a pacifist." Yet the pieces of his story were out there: the bits he'd shared over the years, the written history.

Private Charles Craig Dawson, 1943

©Dawson

From my readings, I learned that, in late 1942, the men of what would become the 10th Mountain Division began populating the Camp Hale mountain warfare training center, thirty-two miles as the crow flies northeast across the high Continental Divide from Aspen. By November 1944, they were in combat in Italy.

Hale was far from the romanticized encampment often implied in modern media. In reality, it was savage, uncomfortable; a temporary dystopian metropolis of more than a thousand buildings and upwards of 11,000 people—virtually all men—shoehorned into a narrow alpine valley. The recruits, many of them sickened by the 9,200-foot altitude and constant smog of throat-burning coal smoke, nicknamed the place "Camp Hell." They snarked that any soldier who quit mountain training and transferred to combat was a lily-livered coward.

Still, the Hale experience (along with training in other locales) made for effective combat preparation, as well as a fabled postwar seeding of mountain recreation. When the soldiers returned from World War II as heroes—having won significant Italian high ground—thousands of them involved themselves in the nascent American ski industry, as well as in mountaineering and outdoor education. Many settled in Colorado.

NINETEEN-YEAR-OLD PRIVATE CHARLES DAWSON transferred to Camp Hale in August 1943.

"It went below zero during our winter training camps," he had recalled during a campfire conversation a few years after we moved to Aspen. "When I woke up, a sheet of ice was over my sleeping bag's face opening. I broke it with my fist. An officer thought I was strong because of my size, so he made me carry a solid-steel M1 mortar baseplate. I was tall, but that meant nothing. Combined with my full Army backpack, that forty-five-pound hunk of steel had me carrying over a hundred pounds."

Those were the only "Camp Hell" details my father imparted until a stoned-out evening a few years later, when I got a snip of the AWOL story:

"I was with another Hale guy. We figured to get to Mexico. We made it as far as New Mexico and holed up in an unoccupied ranch house, eating their food. The sheriff found us. It was 'come out with your hands up!' like in the movies."

My father never shared why—but my take wasn't far off. I later acquired his Army service records. They held what I'd long suspected, a tale far darker than the campfire yarns: After two winter months at Hale, Achilles tendonitis, sprained knees, ankles—"attributed to skiing." Spring 1944: "Absentee wanted ..." A month later: "remanded to await trial," hospitalized due to "psychopathic state." Then: "General court-martial ... Fort Leavenworth ... Five years hard labor." He received a dishonorable discharge in November 1945 after 566 days behind bars.

As for what prompted his release, it remained the enigma my mother had alluded to during my younger days. But that didn't matter so much as his subsequent familial neglect during the 1960s and the inescapable fact that my father was a quitter.

As I put the pieces together, I grew ever more perplexed that my father had pulled up roots in Texas and moved to Aspen, where 10th Mountain veterans by the hundreds had settled after the war. *Was his choice to live among these guys a quest for redemption? Or was this nothing more than a troubled soul who, in those early Aspen years, sought the healing of mountain sublimity: jeeping, hiking, the family picnics with his four sons—sitting cross-legged on the red-and-white picnic quilt my mother spread beneath the aspen trees' dancing shade? And when such things did not heal the man's spirit, were the chemical sixties no more than self-medication?*

LIVING IN THE ASPEN area didn't help with my paternal angst. Every week, if not every day, I encountered a 10th Mountain Division war hero. There was Bil Dunaway, *Aspen Times* newspaper publisher and *Climbing* magazine cofounder. There was Stuart Mace, a craggy-faced mountain man who operated a sled-dog business in the same valley where we'd built our first Aspen house. Even Chris Landry's father was a vet.

When I met these individuals and their families, I wanted to hold my head high and say, "I'm a vet's son, too." Yet I felt no pride, and alluding to my father's sins seemed self-indulgent—even exploitative. So I kept the secret.

In 1982, a group of ski-touring enthusiasts founded the 10th Mountain Division Hut Association and began building backcountry cabins near Aspen (intended for nightly rentals to ski tourers and other non-motorized recreators). To embrace my roots and perhaps atone for my father, through 1987-88, I wrote the system's first guidebook, then produced the Association's newsletter for a decade. All worthy stuff for my budding career as a ski writer—yet personally rough. Dozens of 10th Mountain Division veterans were involved with their eponymous hut system. Everywhere I turned, yet another reminder of my internal conflicts seemed to materialize.

I finally had the facts: 10th Mountain history and my father's involvement. But getting the facts straight is just an entry point to forgiveness.

IN 1988, I SCHEDULED a newsletter interview with Fritz Benedict, a storied Aspenite, 10th veteran, and hut system founder. When I showed up at the entrance to his office, he was standing in a cloud of dust, sweeping his driveway. Such humble effort was typical of seventy-three-year-old Fritz—a successful architect and now a renowned Aspen town elder.

He gestured toward the door.

"Let's get a drink of water and chat. We'll talk huts, and I have something for you."

Benedict's swept-back silver hair and strong-boned face reminded me of my father. As usual, I hoped he did not remember Private Charles Dawson.

We had a fascinating talk about cabin architecture and Benedict's daring experience commandeering a boat in Italy during the war. As we wound up the chat, he pointed to a creased newspaper lying on his desk blotter.

"This is the *Camp Hale Ski-Zette* newspaper, March 1944," Fritz said, gathering the paper and handing it to me. "Take it home for your writing. Read the article about the Leadville-Aspen ski trek. I wasn't on the trip, but always knew about it. Thirty-three Hale guys skied fifty miles midwinter over the Continental Divide, through where we're building huts."

I'd heard vague legends of 10th Mountain soldier studs marching fifty miles across the mountains, seeking women, booze, and a few turns on the ski hill above Aspen. The stories said they'd finished the trek at the Hotel Jerome Bar on Main Street. There, they leaned their skis next to the door and partied as hard as they skied, stoked by a caloric cocktail they invented: a bourbon-laced vanilla milkshake known as the Aspen Crud.

Hyperbole?

Back home, as I read the article and inferred the route from my experience in the area—it was my backyard—I knew these thirty-three men from Camp Hale had made mountaineering history. I fantasized about skiing their route, drinking an Aspen Crud at the finish, and writing a magazine article with a history angle. Then I forgot about it.

In 2000, a dozen years after meeting with Fritz, I was pawing through the dented steel filing cabinet supporting the right side of my desk, hunting for writing ideas. The *Ski-Zette* article materialized in my hand. Two minutes after rereading the piece, a surge in my chest told me I had a job to do: re-create and document the soldiers' trek and, through that process, somehow empathize with my father—despite his not being there. I wasn't sure how the empathy part would happen, but I had an inkling. It would be more on the emotional level than intellectual.

Was this the final step of my midlife pity party? Mix a teaspoon of snow with a gallon of 10th Mountain Division, stir in some Isaiah-inspired forgiveness, and toast it all with an Aspen Crud?

The idea was starry-eyed wonderful, with one problem: I knew almost nothing of the route details of what I dubbed the "Trooper Traverse." Yet I felt an intense need to retrace it dot by dot, to invoke a time-traveling emotional osmosis. I wanted to do more than make informed guesses about the soldiers' experience. Somehow, I'd be there with them.

The *Ski-Zette* report was brief and vague. It indicated the trip had taken four days. The men had headed west from Leadville, conquered every ridge and avalanche-prone couloir of the Continental Divide, and finished on the Jerome's bar stools. I needed more.

I emailed the Denver Public Library 10th Mountain Division Resource Center. Bingo. They possessed the archives of several deceased Trooper Traverse skiers, including a Lieutenant Richard Rocker.

On a smoggy summer day, I showed up in Denver and donned the obligatory white cotton gloves. Rocker's papers smelled of mildew and a hint of ink, and they had the vibe—a time-warping thread tied to Camp Hale—as if the intervening fifty-six years were a week. I soon struck the mother lode: an extensive, neatly typed trip report, and farther into the stack, a mind-blowing sheet of Kodachrome color slides—an unusual medium for the early 1940s.

One priceless image depicted the crew nearing their first highpoint. A few hundred yards above them, perhaps twenty feet tall, a massive granite boulder perched on the mountainside as if God had dropped it from the heavens. This boulder was a key signpost—but I still needed more details.

Ralph Ball, a 10th veteran, lived five blocks from our home. He was a slim, fit fellow in his eighties, known for bicycling about town, chatting up neighbors on his way to the post office. Lisa and I had met him during a 10th Mountain Huts event. I had no clue he'd been on the Traverse until I dug into my research and noticed his name on the roster. My neighbor? Talk about serendipity! With Ralph's help, I established additional details, including the exact starting point.

Throughout my research, I felt the presence of something more than just my ambitions. It was as if an unseen force was bringing the resources, the intersections. Often sweet, sometimes bittersweet—as when I missed an interview because of a recent death—the process didn't stop.

Troopers climbing to Darling Pass, signpost boulder is circled, 1944
Richard Rocker photo, Denver Public Library

The 10th Mountain Huts had recently constructed Uncle Bud's Hut, named for Traverse participant Bud Winter. From the ensuing hut dedications and such, I learned that Bud had enlisted straight out of high school. At nineteen, he was among the youngest on the Trooper Traverse and, from what I gathered, among the most gung-ho of the lot.

"What a trip!" he'd written in a letter home. "I have acquired the name 'Rugged Winters.' I guess I was in a little better condition and tired some of the other fellows out when I was trailbreaking ... All went well ... It was beautiful and something I will never forget."

Rugged Winters shipped to combat in Europe soon after the Traverse. And there he rests, under a small white cross, eight miles south of Florence, Italy.

My heart synced with Rugged. I saw him as symbolic of my father—the raw innocence, the quest for adventure, the uncertain outcomes.

As to the route, I now had much of it mapped. So I contacted ski journalist Brian Litz, who pitched an article to *Skiing* magazine. They bit. He'd shoot photos, I'd write. Additionally, a few years prior, I'd started a website, *WildSnow.com*, where I was building an internet publishing project. I figured the Trooper Traverse would, eventually, serve as dynamite website content. (A few years later, around 2004, *WildSnow* burgeoned in popularity as blogging became a thing.)

I TEAMED UP WITH my Trooper Traverse partners on a warm day in May 2001 near the Leadville Outward Bound base camp. Stocky, blond-haired Brian Litz was the archetypal adventure companion: positive encourager, backcountry skilled—and willing to haul camera gear. His friend Chris Clark was a clean-shaven, muscular fellow, eager for the journey, known as a powerful skier. Though my lousy ankle was now partially fused and less painful, I was the weak link, the oldest, embroiled in middle-aged uncertainty.

Author, map work, Trooper Traverse 2001

The first night, we camped in the forest near the Naugahyde Palace cabin, where Lane, Roberts, and I had absconded with the contraband bacon back in my Outward Bound days.

During breakfast, night-chilled alpine air spilled from the highlands above us—I wore my gloves as I spooned granola. When the sun rose from the 13,000-foot ridge to our west, we rousted fast, eager, and skied the snow-covered road a few more miles to the weathered mine buildings next to the Naug'.

"I remember the mine buildings," Ralph Ball had told me. "One was pretty big, tin roof, wood slabs on the sides."

Everything matched Ralph's description. But what ahead? Clark called a halt and unfolded the squiggly lined USGS topo map. I pointed to the obvious pass into the next drainage, where the contour lines arced together.

"Outward Bound calls this one Darling Pass," I said. "The *Ski-Zette* says the soldiers crossed 'Champion-Deer Mountains Pass.' That could be any of several routes. But the Darling Pass option makes sense. Deer Mountain is right next to it. You guys think it's the way?"

Brian pushed his dangling camera to the side and studied the map. "If that's not it, we'd have to bag the trip—we don't have an extra day for wandering. Looks like the best option ... Let's hump it up there."

A half-hour upland, I laughed. Just below a saddle, between two rocky summits, there it was: Richard Rocker's "Trooper Boulder," as distinctive as a freeway on-ramp sign. I closed my eyes and whispered a quick *thanks*.

At that moment, my father came to mind. I wondered what Rugged Winters would have thought of him all those years ago. Nothing good? And now, so many decades later? Through the lens of time, perhaps Rugged would have understood and told me that were it not for an impulsive mistake, my outdoorsy, adventure-seeking father might have been here in 1944, skiing over the mountains to Aspen. For my part, a baby step of understanding, yet a step.

Our mission was clear: follow Rugged and his mates to the Jerome Bar.

THINK LIKE A MOUNTAINEER; chances are, you'll find the way of other mountaineers—even if they journeyed your path almost sixty years ago. Like day two, three flowed with my research notes. By early afternoon on another sunny day, I was confident we'd skied the soldiers' route over the Continental Divide to the final topographic barricade, the Williams Mountains.

While of average height by Colorado standards (the highest peak topping out at about 13,382 feet), the topography of the Williams resembles that of the high and rugged European Alps: couloirs, granite, cliffs everywhere. Deducing the soldiers' route up this side of the range was an easy call. A single line of lesser resistance led to a notch in a ridge between two cliffy peaks.

We figured the other side might offer an easy option as well. Wrong. When we reached the notch, we stood atop a forty-degree steep couloir plunging a thousand vertical feet into the Hunter Creek valley. It was a modern line as a ski route—not something skiers would have desired (or even considered) in the 1940s.

"You think we messed up?" I asked as I peeled the climbing skins from my ski bottoms. "This seems like too much for guys in 1944. But I don't see any other way off here."

"It'll be dark in a few hours," Clark replied. "We have to do it. Maybe we'll pick up the soldiers' route down there, somewhere."

Williams Mountains, Trooper Couloir   ©Brian Litz

Skiing the couloir wasn't difficult with our lightweight packs and third-millennium skis. *But had the troopers descended this on their seven-foot-long planks, eight pounds each, rigid as steel railroad tracks? With seventy-five-pound backpacks?*

I'd skied such gear: Conundrum on my father's skis, and the NOLS-issued army-surplus boots and boards during the Grand Teton winter climb attempt. There was no way I could ski this line on equipment like that. I figured we'd strayed off-route.

Later, while reviewing the archives, I determined the soldiers had descended the same couloir.

"We looked down a steep, rock-studded gully that disappeared from view in snow and growing darkness," Richard Rocker had written. "Better to risk it than stay where we were."

Double humbled, I dubbed their line the "Trooper Couloir." Rugged and his mates were indeed the snow gods of legend told.

Trooper Couloir behind us, we found a patch of dry ground, gathered winter-damp aspen wood, and built a smoky campfire. Clark boiled water and warmed our last freeze-dried chicken dinner. With a full belly and a cup of Red Zinger tea, I curled on my sleeping pad, warm in the peace of days well spent.

Brian stirred the fire. A gout of flame pushed away the darkness.

"What's it like being a dad and a husband, Lou?"

I sighed and scooted my damp, sock-covered feet closer to the heat.

"I'll be honest. It's been tough having a kid in my late thirties. It just takes it out of you, and there's no off-switch. And now, a half-fused ankle. I'll never ski like when I was twenty or thirty, and don't ask me about climbing. But man, that stuff means nothing after following the soldiers these past days. Like Bud Winter, they faced being blown up or shot. Who am I to complain?"

Later, cozy in my sleeping bag, thoughts raced: *Time to quit my midlife whining? This trip is a blessing, following the soldiers' footsteps. A revival of my mountain joy, a start to understanding my dad. But can I bring these feelings back into my life with Lisa and Louie—or better yet, have such experiences with them?*

During my year with Outward Bound, "transference" was an oft-discussed issue. If the student experience was akin to a summer camp with roped amusements, we instructors were nothing more than playground monitors. Conversely, if our students went home with renewed self-confidence, buoyed by the high of backcountry recreation, we'd done a better job.

But it got more subtle than that. I'd circle my charges around our last evening campfire and ask them, "What is adventure?" The discussion soon drifted from physical adventure to emotional and even spiritual. The ultimate goal? Leverage their newfound confidence to inspire more adventures, whether in the forest, the city, or the spirit. And do so with the joy they'd found in the wild.

I felt poised for the transfer. I'd return home with my hill song—Bud Winter's exuberant take—renewed for my adventure as a family man.

THE NEXT MORNING, LIGHT rain spit from a muddy sky. We skied into Aspen, met up with Lisa and Louie, and leaned our skis next to the door of the Hotel Jerome Bar.

"You guys know how to make an Aspen Crud?" I asked the bartender.

"Sure do."

"Well, we just skied over the mountains from Leadville, like the 1944 mountain troop soldiers who invented that drink. We're producing a magazine article. Comp us a few?"

"Congratulations! Have all you want," the bartender said as he grabbed a bottle of Rebel Yell off the back bar and fired up his blender.

We raised our glasses.

"This one's for you, Rugged Winters," I shouted, as in my mind's ear, I reprised the snow troopers' marching song:

"Ninety pounds of rucksack / a pound of grub or two / he'll schuss the mountains like his daddy used to do."

That nailed it. Our re-creation of the Trooper Traverse was a rebirth for me. In an odd, reverse way, we had honored the soldiers and my father along with them. While he'd not been there, skiing over the Divide in February of 1944, I sensed the adventuresome teen who'd been unable to resist the call of the mountain troops. *Might I have done the same?*

Skiing Magazine published our Traverse article. The editor's surname was Miracle.

38 | BORN AGAIN NOLSIE, 2001

ON A SUMMERY EVENING a week after the Trooper Traverse, I stole into eleven-year-old Louie's bedroom to hound him about his screen time. He was on the top tier of his bunk bed, laptop glow illuminating his face like bad makeup. Standing in the dark, I pondered how to handle this. I was a role model on the work side, making my living with the 'net, writing, and building websites. Yet all this was in my home office fifteen feet from Louie's bedroom, clocking mega screen time—a good bit of it worthless web surfing.

While suppressing my hypocrisy, I prepared to blurt out something like, "Shut that thing off and hand it over."

Louie beat me to it. He set his computer aside, hung his head over the bunkrail, and asked, "Dad, can we do a long hike and camp in a new place every night?"

The boy's query stunned me speechless. What in the web-world had he been browsing? Or had I spouted more idealized tales about my NOLS and Outward Bound days than I cared to admit? I hoped he'd sensed the hill joy I'd brought home from the Trooper Traverse—and the church-youth outdoors program I codirected was a help. But any goodness those things sourced was fast disappearing under the dregs of my midlife poisons. In truth, at forty-nine, I wasn't much more of an adventure dad than my disjoined father had been at my age. But my son spoke into my life, bouncing me off my flabby daddy-butt like I'd sat on a campfire.

"Maybe we could do that, but let me think about it," I muttered as I backed out the bedroom door and retreated the six steps to my office. It was significant, brilliant that Louie was the instigator—but I was more bewildered than elated. My fingers rested on my keyboard, paralyzed. Louie's question rattled through my mind: *Where to go, what to do, could we afford it, could my body hold up to a summer backpacking trip?*

LOUIS W. DAWSON

Then reality hit.

Cripes, I just skied the Trooper Traverse with a heavy load of overnight gear. Petzoldt taught NOLS in his sixties. I should be ashamed, letting my kid hunker in his room, when we could rove the mountains together—hooking trout, battling weather, climbing peaks, swimming in mountain lakes so pure you could bottle the water and sell it. I can do this!

Feeling a surge of joy, I shoved my keyboard aside, spun my office chair to the bookshelf behind me, and grabbed my dog-eared, red-and-green *Field Book: Wind River Range*. I'd kept this classic guidebook within reach for thirty years. Now I knew why; it was time to obey the altar call of the Winds.

"Come in here," I shouted to Louie. When he peeked through the office door, I held up the book and flipped it open to the "Tips for Anglers" section. "This is mostly a climbing guide. I'm not sure how much climbing we'll do, but we'll backpack and fish. It'll be amazing."

Louie briefly examined the classic pen-and-ink fishing illustrations, said, "Cool," and then flew out the doorway into our great room, shouting, "Mom! Mom! Dad says we're going backpacking—for a week!"

I KNEW THAT NOTHING fancier than backpacking through pristine wilderness would make this a superior trip, yet I wanted trout to be part of it. So I called my former Outward Bound compatriot Randy Udall. He'd since become a Wind Rivers fish fanatic.

"Where should I take Lisa and Louie?" I asked, "Not too hard a hike, guaranteed catch?"

Randy laughed the deep bark he always did when the conversation turned to escape from offices and other despicable junk.

"I'm not sharing any secret spots. But a smart call is the northern Winds. Try the drainages out of St. Lawrence Basin. Lots of lakes, most thick with trout."

"How do we make sure we catch something?"

A hint of religious zeal entered Randy's voice.

"Use a casting bobber, fill it half full of water for weight, tie it to a spinning reel, and add a fly casting leader with a black ant or a moth. Hurl that sucker out there. Do it right, you can go 200 feet!"

I hit our nearby discount outdoors store and bought Eagle Claw rods that converted between spin and fly casting via a clever, reversible handle. They were the same brand and model we'd used at 1970s NOLS.

It's 2001, and I'm shopping for the same gear—no better confirmation of my NOLSie revival plan.

We assembled our Randy-rigs and headed for the quiet street next to our house. Louie swung his rod like he was swatting a tennis highball—*zzzz-zzzziiing*—his cast sailed down the road and through a stop-sign intersection. Not quite the Udall 200, but he was three times Louie's size. I got similar results. We grinned in unison. There was something about hurling an object—a primal urge to project power and unearth the hunter buried deep in every human psyche.

WE PACKED A COMBINED ration plan: NOLS bulk-style peanuts, brown sugar, oatmeal, macaroni, cheese, a few envelopes of tuna, and two freeze-dried chicken dinners for those times we didn't feel the call of culinary creativity. The cornmeal/flour fish breading mix, dosed with pepper and salt, was optimistic. And most important was trail mix, the hiker's hourly fuel ration.

"Let's make the gorp," I smiled at Louie. "Grab that two-pounder of peanut M&M's, dump it in the mixing bowl."

The sound of hard chocolate candies ringing against stainless steel brought the memories: Trail mix for Denali, day-hike snacks, Rich Jack and I mixing a batch for the Dihedral Wall. Rich always wanted more candy.

"Leave out the raisins," he'd say. "Chop up some Tootsie Rolls."

Next came a handful of walnut pieces, and, as a crowning flourish, I added Dave Farny's secret sauce, learned long ago at the Ashcrofters: a sprinkling of ground coffee. The mouthwatering aroma of nuts and chocolate rose as Lisa and Louie stirred the gorp with their bare hands, folding the colorful candies into the mix like kneading bread dough.

It came time for the final taste test, a handful each. I knew Louie would love the sugary parts of our homebrew trail mix, but wondered about the coffee enhancement. An acquired taste? When I swatted the boy's hand away from a second serving, I had my answer.

WE APPORTIONED AND WEIGHED the food according to the meal plan I'd sketched, and piled it in a heap on our kitchen island.

Lisa squinted at the meager stack of plastic bags, "You sure that's enough?"

"It's a little less than the normal two pounds per person per day, but we'll eat plenty of fish," I answered.

"The last time you caught fish in the mountains," Lisa reminded me, "was when we backpacked into that lake for our first wedding anniversary. What, seventeen years ago?"

One-Two-Three Lake,
first wedding anniversary, 1986   ©Dawson

During that legendary adventure, my new bride had joined me for an overnight backpack to One-Two-Three Lake, a treeless high-alpine tarn, east of Aspen. When we dropped our packs on the sandy lakeshore, I produced a hidden bottle of bubbly.

"We'll have this with the fish I catch for dinner."

My bluster had broken the third law of fishing: *never promise*. But I went on faith, tied on a moth fly, and cast long. Bam, a thirteen-inch, pink-high-lighted cutthroat came to Papa. As we sipped champagne straight from the bottle, I explained how an angler friend had nicknamed the lake for how many casts it took to catch three fish.

"Believe me, Sweetie, fishing in the Winds will be easy. It'll be just like One-Two-Three Lake."

There it was, another fishing promise.

AT THE FEET OF the Wind River Mountains, parked at the deserted St. Lawrence trailhead, I woke with my head hanging out our Chevy Suburban's rear-door opening. (Lisa and I had slept on the truck's floor.) The sky was cloudless, pale blue, lightly hazed from distant wildfires. Sparrows chirped and flitted. A light breeze brought the scent of sage, spiced with a hint of cowpie. As the new-day sun heated my face, I thought of nothing more than cooking our breakfast oatmeal.

Lisa rolled over and kissed me. Without a word, I reached my arm over our sleeping bag, pulled her close, closed my eyes, and floated in the moment.

When the morning's first mosquito hummed past my ear, I eased from our nest and barefooted over the crinkly dry August grass to Louie's tent. At his age, he'd sleep until noon.

I shook his tent like a hurricane and said in my loudest dad voice, "Hey, let's hike."

The young squire was packing in thirty seconds.

Our first camp was outside the core of the range, next to a trickling, two-foot-wide creek—not much of a fishing spot. But I kept my mouth shut and helped Louie rig his rod with the conventional leader and fly—no need for the Udall hurler. As Lisa and I cooked dinner, we watched our child on the water, casting with focused energy. He returned empty-handed but smiling.

"Didn't catch anything. But I had fun. There was a little one—couldn't sneak up on it."

The next morning, under a clear sky, we ripped open a granola bag and boiled water. Louie gulped three cups of hot cocoa. Lisa had tea. As we cinched up, my ankle hurt with that pain only damaged bone can make, but my mind was Zen-clear. This was my place.

I hiked ahead solo. A gentle breeze murmured through alpine fir trees and limber pines, blowing tar scent from sun-heated sap. Mosquitoes swarmed, but not so thick as to require headnets. A pebble-sized horse fly buzzed me. Its singular purpose was to land on my bare skin, sink its blade-like mouthparts, and sip my essence. The miniature monsters rarely got to the sipping part because the bite stung like a hornet and ended with a hand slap. Today, the fly was sluggish, barely surviving the cold August nights. It landed on my bare arm and sat there like it couldn't decide on the menu. A firm swat and it tumbled to the ground, lay stunned for a moment, and flew off. Tough buggers.

Where the trail crossed bare, glacier-carved granite, I felt the ghost of the ice—blue and cold, once having risen a thousand feet above my head, its inconceivable pressure chewing the stone under my boots. We'd taught at NOLS that the glaciers had flowed this low as late as a thousand years ago. I wanted them back.

A yellow-bellied marmot chirped. I replied, voicing high-pitched *eek, eek* sounds the puppy-sized rodents had always answered back when my vocal cords were tight. The critter granted me two skeptical replies before it figured out the scam, turned tail, and ducked under a rock.

We reached Enos Lake at lunchtime—five hours for what would have been a two-hour hike in my youth. But who's counting? Warm, intermittent wind chased away the mosquitoes. A few yards across a grassy margin, the rippling lake water was near level with the trail—Carnegie Hall for a Udall fly presentation.

"Let's rig and catch lunch," I said, thinking, *this better happen; Louie striking out yesterday was not lasting fun.*

Just then, a glugging splash hooked my fisherman soul. Tasty beasts indeed thrived here—one had snagged a snack. Carrying only my rod, I strolled to the shore and hurled my casting bobber like throwing an Olympic javelin. It plopped down exactly where the amphibious feedings had occurred. Slam, my rod bent double. Line spun from my reel. The buzzing drag brake sounded like a bee hive. I snubbed the line with my index finger as I dialed up the drag with my left hand and yelled, "Got one!" It was fatter and longer than any trout I'd ever landed. Soon Louie joined the fun, and then Lisa. Both made catches.

There on the lakeshore, we lit our camp stove, breaded our quarry, and fried it in olive oil. The tender flesh fell off the bone with just the gentle pluck of a pocketknife.

Lisa grinned. "If I ever wondered about fish, I'm wondering no more."

With my belly full of pink filet worthy of a five-star restaurant, I shut down our noisy gasoline camp stove and lounged next to Lisa with my pack as a backrest. A light breeze pushed ripples against the lakeshore stones, where they made tiny lapping sounds just on the edge of hearing. My brown wool pants were cozy warm against my skin. I opened a ziplock of gorp, picked out the M&M's like I was plucking blueberries, and popped them into my mouth one at a time.

Louie was back at it, yards away, whipping his rod in whistling arcs that hurled his bobber so far I was afraid he'd snag the grass on the opposite shore. Every fifth cast brought in another trout he then released off his barbless hook.

Rarely is life so glorious.

We meandered a half mile farther to Tigee Lake and found a sandy, flat campsite tucked behind several granite boulders near the lake, protected by squatty conifer bonsais molded by timberline wind and snow. Wolverine Peak's rocky steeps rose from across the water, graced by a shining pocket-glacier—the corporeal remnant of my icy ghost. Two dark-gray, pyramid-shaped spires jutted from Wolverine's west ridge: Thunderbolt and Lightning Rod. I daydreamed myself years younger, here with Kennedy and a pile of climbing gear.

LATE AFTERNOON WAS HOT, muggy, and buggy. We danced around our campfire in free-form choreography, seeking enough smoke to repel the mosquitoes but not so much to choke ourselves.

"It's getting cold at night—the buggers know this might be their last day alive. They're getting greedy," I said. "Let's take a dip. It'll feel great to wash, and we'll be invisible to the bugs for a few minutes."

Lisa threw another handful of sticks on the fire. She pointed to Wolverine Peak. "Glacier water? I did the dishes down at the lake, my hands are still numb."

I nodded. "It's cold. But that's what makes the magic."

THERE COMES A TIME for every alpine enthusiast to lose their cold water innocence. I'd lost mine thirty-four years ago, at the Ashcrofters.

On the third morning of my stay, our cabin of six was deep in our adolescent sleeping comas. Our instructor, Jim Ward, swung the door open and shouted us awake like a drill sergeant: "Sneakers on! No socks, just your underwear. Run and dip!"

We gathered on the grass outside our cabin, arms wrapped over our bald chests to ward off the morning chill. Our white cotton briefs fluoresced like luminescent watch dials in the predawn light.

Ward began a slow jog and shouted, "Come on, stay behind me."

After working up a sweat, we stopped on Castle Creek's splash-wetted bank. The flow was loose and loud, fallen from the melting snowfields above. It smelled like rain. As Ward waded in, the water frothed and furrowed around his shins.

"I want you boys in here pronto," he bellowed as he kneeled, swung his arms forward, and snapped three full-immersion push-ups.

Some kids tiptoed into the water like it was sulfuric acid. Others stood on the bank, shellshocked, until Ward yelled them in. I figured I might as well get it over with, marched in with a proud, high-knee stride, risked one sputtering push-up—and fled for shore yowling like a tomcat. Then the glow hit, and it was good.

The alpine plunge had become a ritual ever since that first morning on Castle Creek. It was more than just an adrenaline spike; it was a way for me to bond with the land, the environment, and the universe. After mere seconds of icy water flowing over my skin, I emerged cleansed.

FIRST INTO TIGEE LAKE, I grimaced from the chill-pain, yelled, "I'm going for it," pitched forward into the water, and levered the requisite three pushups. Dissolved sunscreen stung my eyes as I stood, shouted "*Awooo!*" and took four strides to shore. As I air-dried, my skin tingled like I was rolling on pine needles.

Lisa waded in and dropped to her neck, making sounds somewhere between joy and pain with a feminine timbre I enjoyed hearing echo across the lake. Louie was next. He counted two splashy push-ups and sprinted for shore.

Tradition completed, we sprawled on the sun-warmed shoreline boulders like a tribe of archaic proto-humans. Flies and mosquitoes circled, hunting, but for the moment, we were invisible.

When a mosquito finally pricked my neck, I went in again, flipped onto my back, and splashed out four swim strokes. As I stumbled from the water, I forced a smile from my cold-stiff jaw.

"Come on, Louie, do it again."

"Dad, did you see me?" Louie said, proud and smiling as he rose from the water his second time. "I got my head under—I swam!"

FOR FOUR DAYS, WE hiked, sunbathed, journaled, and fished until we were proteined out. The five-star trout meat we consumed every evening now tasted like boot insoles. Time for carbs. Real carbs.

I rummaged through our blue nylon food bag. "I've got a surprise. Lisa, hand me the frying pan."

I broke an eight-inch-long stir-stick off a nearby tree and propped two rocks on each side of the fire, creating a pan-support slot over the flames. A tablespoon of butter hit the pan bottom, melted in seconds, and hissed like frying bacon. While stirring the butter, I dumped in a quarter pound of brown sugar. Lisa and Louie looked on, mystified.

Kneeling next to the campfire, I blew until flames shot high. The sugar caramelized into a chocolate-toned, Chernobyl molten mass. I stirred fast, attempting to heat it evenly lest thin spots burn.

"Louie, quick, grab the peanuts," I said. "Dump the whole bag in here while I stir. Do it fast."

In moments, the nuts and molten sucrose flowed around the pan bottom like fresh concrete. I removed the pan from the flames and placed it on the ground to cool.

Controlled by the sugar lust written into every human's genes, my wife and son observed with brain-surgeon focus as I inverted the pan over a flat rock and tapped it a few times with my stir stick. Out fell a peanut-brittle pizza. This was not the factory-pure candy your grandparents sent you for Christmas. It was darker, with a whiff of burned butter.

My family was skeptical. "Try it," I said. "I've loved this stuff ever since NOLS."

Lisa snatched the first chunk and took a cautious nibble. Her face lit up. She reached for more before I could fend her off with my cooking stick. Meanwhile, Louie guarded a giant shard with his life. At that moment, after four days of fish and pasta, we each had a single purpose: devour the disaccharide.

I laughed, electrified by the outdoor skills Paul Petzoldt had gifted me so long ago—skills now reincarnated for the family I had hardly dreamed of.

Lisa, Wind River Range   ©Dawson

The following day, we moved camp. A bulky mountain rose west from our new digs. According to the map, a gentle climb would gain the summit via moderate slopes on the north side. But something better caught my attention.

Facing camp, a wall of clean, off-white Wind River granite swept upward to the summit plateau. It appeared not to be a full-on roped climb but a scramble hike, with a few sections where an unroped climber might fall off the mountain—similar to the harder Colorado fourteeners.

As we lounged during breaks between fishing and exploring, I studied the "White Wall." In my mind's eye, a route popped from the mountain like the dotted line on a guidebook photo. *Go left at the bottom, up over that ledge. There's some fall potential, but clean rock, no rubble—we can spot each other like we're bouldering.*

The plan: we'd ascend "fourth class." This climbing style involved the most experienced climber dragging a rope and top-roping those below. We'd bring the six-millimeter-diameter "bear rope" we used to hang food away from animals. It was strong enough if kept tight while belaying. We had zero climbing gear, such as carabiners and rock-anchor devices. I liked the idea of a minimalist adventure. *But was my desire for the ultimate family outing impeding common sense?*

I broached my ideas over dinner.

"Let's climb the mountain before we pack to our next camp. We can wander up through that cliffy area, find a route. It'll be a lot more fun than hiking the grass slopes. There's some danger, but we can handle it."

When Lisa saw Louie's eyes ignite, she was all in. As in the old days with Kennedy, the only word was "When?"

Morning dawned cloudless. A brisk wind hissed through the trees next to camp, surging to thirty-mile-per-hour gusts that sprinkled sandy grit into our oatmeal. Such blasts could be twice as strong on the mountain. But the blows pumped from the east; our route faced west. The mountain would protect us while we climbed—until we reached the lower-angled area below the summit where the jetstream gale might curl into roiling vortices. In that event, we could climb through the wind or turn and escape via the easy route down.

Whatever happened, we'd have a noble adventure.

To begin, we scrambled a few hundred feet of steep, grassy ground leading to a broad ledge. Here, the mountain became real, steeper. Yet nothing drastic—*easy ground* in the climber's vernacular.

We soon locked into a team rhythm. When the route was uncertain, I climbed ahead, checking it out.

"Come on up, careful," I shouted. "Move one leg or foot at a time. Make your own security."

When the climbing eased, I sent Louie ahead.

"Follow that obvious crack, stop on the ledge, and stand back so you're safe from tripping and falling off. Mom and I will climb after you."

A few pitches were a grade harder. On those, I tossed the rope down and wedged myself into a crevice or behind a boulder, so that the rope wrapped behind my back could hold a fall without jerking me off the mountain. My charges tied in with knots we'd practiced in camp. I belayed them up one at a time.

As we scrambled the last of the hand-and-foot climbing, the gale spit pebbles in our faces and hacked the air above with odd rending sounds that resembled tearing cardboard.

"Let's get our jackets and hats on," I shouted. "It's easy hiking from here—this isn't a storm, just wind. We can make the summit. Crawl until we're away from the cliffs."

As we lurched up the final slopes, sixty-plus-mile-per-hour gusts blew us to the ground every five minutes, but we managed. At one point, Lisa crawled next to me, looked into my eyes as her hair whipped across her face like a palm frond in a hurricane, and laughed, "Dawsonized!"

Skinny eleven-year-old Louie kept his eyes on the peak above. I should have considered he was the most likely to be plucked from the mountain by a rogue wind.

At the summit, we hid from the gale behind a waist-high rock outcrop, dug out our snacks, and sat with our shoulders pressed together. Our shelter wall blocked the western view, but the remaining panorama was all we needed to relish the sublime: turquoise lakes by the dozen, granite buttresses swooping to spiked summits, and Wyoming's vast Red Desert hazy in the eastern expanse. As we sat together in a group hug, it occurred to me I'd sought this melding in the Aspen of my youth, and the union was never complete. Today, on the mountaintop, it was.

39 | FIFTEEN TURNS, 2005-2007

IMPOSTER SYNDROME—IT'S A REAL thing, I realized as I stood on the stage at the Denver Marriott in October 2005—a freshly minted Colorado Snowsports Hall of Famer.

The ceremony was over. The speeches spoken. We'd gathered for group photos of attending inductees, past and present.

Olympian Billy Kidd was there, sporting his trademark feather-festooned cowboy hat. And Cindy Nelson stood with us, the first American woman to win a World Cup downhill race, 1974 in Grindelwald, Switzerland. Three years my junior, she still sported the lean face of an athlete and the confident voice of a winner. *Me? Sure, I skied the peaks and wrote the books, but I'm just a Colorado mountain boy who likes 14,000-foot rocks and is a tad accident-prone.*

I was so nervous my jaw got sore. But that was okay. A dose of humility kept me on track, as to how this had happened.

Twenty years prior, Lisa Spieler had appeared in my life as a postal letter and become my bride. She had pulled me from the last vestiges of my dark times, rescued me from the hamster wheel, and given me purpose other than summits. Her support of my fourteeners project—her inspiration to focus, to complete something—had made the scattershot mountains of my youth look like insanity.

At the induction gala, Lisa looked the part.

While budget-wary, my sweetheart had fashioned an ensemble worthy of *Vogue*. The off-the-shoulders blouse sparkled with silver sequins and teased with small star-shaped cutouts. Her eyes radiated, framed by her dark chocolate hair.

"Where did you get that rad outfit?" I asked. "I've never seen it."

"Can you believe it? One trip to the consignment store." She smoothed her skirt with one hand. The black sheath fit her mountain-sports-sculpted body like paint.

I was already planning our own private after-party.

"That's next-level shopping!"

"I was discouraged at first," Lisa said. "It's not like we do many black-tie events. But when I need a lift, my mother's spirit sometimes comes to me. I walked into Miser's Mercantile, and she'd picked out something lovely, just like her."

Lisa's mention of her dear mother—who'd been taken by cancer five years prior—brought my family to mind. Louie was with us, a fresh-faced fifteen, shining with pride in a white dress shirt and a dark navy jacket that contrasted his glowing red ears, sunburned from our last alpine outing. My three brothers had dug out their neckties—Craig and Tapley traveled from California, where they ran a construction business, Tomas from Colorado Springs. My mother was aglow, dressed to the nines in a velvet-black gown, three chunky necklaces layered around her neck, clicking when she moved. Without asking, you knew she was an artist and that she loved her children. To have us all in one place, for her it was paradise.

My father, however, was absent.

Every Hall of Fame event references the 10th Mountain Division, and the associated ski museum boasts perpetual exhibits depicting the skiing soldiers. This year's display featured a life-sized diorama, replete with white-camo-cloaked men sitting around a campfire next to their snowbound tent. It cloned my father's winter training campsite at Camp Hale, where the sleeping bag had frozen over his face, and he bent to work under the massive mortar plate. It cloned his nemesis. Did he need to be reminded?

"Would I need to get a hotel?" my father had said when I phoned him before the event. "I can't afford that, but I'm proud of you."

To the best of my memory, my father had never spoken those four words.
Maybe I should pay for the hotel?

But I didn't pay, and he did not attend. Considering my improving feelings about my dad, I was ashamed I'd not pushed harder—yet I was relieved. I couldn't see an upside. Awkward would have been a weak word for him sharing the banquet hall and maybe a table with his jilted comrades.

By 2005, SKI MOUNTAINEERING was exploding in popularity. Better gear sprouted like fertilized wheat: comfortable yet powerful boots, a revolutionary lightweight binding out of Austria. Ski technique had evolved as well, with resorts providing ever-gnarlier terrain, and the continued popularity of movies depicting big-mountain skiing. Hundreds of people were now capable of skiing the fifty-four peaks. Yet, despite all this—as well as my completing the project fourteen years prior, publishing the recipe for success in two guidebooks, and receiving the nod from the Hall of Fame—no one else had skied the entire list. *Was I a random whackjob with an outlier obsession?*

Consequently, I was ecstatic when, less than a year after my Hall of Fame induction, ski movie star and extreme-skiing champion Chris Davenport announced his goal of skiing the fourteeners. We chatted on the phone.

"You're the man," I said. "I've not heard of anyone as likely to do this as you—I'm excited to watch."

"You should do more than watch," Davenport said.

In late April 2006, I drove five hours south to Great Sand Dunes National Park and Preserve to join "Dav" and his spirited crew of young athletes. Next on their list: Ellingwood Point, the bladelike fourteener above the spot where, sixteen years prior, I had sat under the tutelage of Coyote.

At the top, Dav tapped his ski tails against the summit cairn, popped four elegant turns, and disappeared into the rift of our route.

Time for the oldster. The snow was what skiers understate as "difficult," a breakable shell over damp punk. Five turns in, my quad muscles melted like hot wax. *Thank God this couloir hides me from view,* I thought as I started clocking malformed turns. Rounding a corner, I encountered Dav's cinematographer, Ben Galland, wedged between two boulders with his camera to his eye.

As this was the only Brad Pitt moment I'd ever get, I dug deep and found the Kodachrome inspiration. The turns still felt gross.

Après-ski, I joined Dav's crew on a sun-washed granite slab next to a small lake. Above us, the southerly wall of Ellingwood hid our ski route in its gray, rocky folds. I lounged on my sleeping pad, snacking on Snickers minis and sipping coffee.

Bearded and muscular, well-suited for hauling cameras to 14,000 feet, Galland planted his tripod and began his on-camera interview. He pointed to Dav and his friends, packing their camp gear for the hike out, said, "Look what you started Lou—you're the father of fourteener skiing."

I laughed. "I guess that's true. But this isn't the parenting I envisioned. I've got the real thing at home."

Levity aside, as Galland and I chatted, I sensed we were part of something beyond ourselves—something that produced immense value in many lives. Contributing to that had been my top mountain-culture goal since my Highland Bowl avalanche. Witnessing the next generation take the torch was as much a blessing as my summit turns off Kit Carson Peak.

The following winter, Dav finished his fourteeners with a descent of Longs Peak—on day 362 of his project. Finally, someone else had done it—and in less than a year, record time!

And the movie? Would I have my fifteen turns of fame? Dav and his crew had filmed on U.S. Forest Service land without a commercial filming permit. Showing or distributing their film was of questionable legality, and it was never widely viewed. *The one modern ski flick I'm in, and it's outlaw fringe? What's that sound, my father laughing?* I joined him.

THE MONTH AFTER SKIING with Dav and his crew, the Trooper Traverse again worked its magic. This time, there was no doubt—it was about fathers and sons.

The son of an original Trooper Traverse soldier had contacted me a year prior.

"My dad Neil Christie was on the original traverse," David Christie had said. "Since seeing your Traverse slideshow, I've been trying to do the trip. I keep getting turned back. Weather, not sure of the route."

"How about I guide you?" I replied. "Skiing the Traverse with the son of an original participant—how can I resist?"

Christie emailed me a photo of his soldier father hanging with his foxhole buddy in the Italian mountains in 1945. The young men hold impossibly white cigarettes in their dirt-dark fists, a stack of hand grenades within reach. A dark monochrome sky bodes grim. Neil Christie's eyes are badass, and he boasts a cynical half-smile. He must have been an asset in the mountains and on the battlefield. I looked forward to imagining him as we skied the Traverse.

Neil Christie (left), WWII Italy, 1945

image courtesy David Christie

When I told Christie that Louie would be my assistant, I didn't mention the boy was just sixteen. And, in the shadow of Christie's warrior dad, I wasn't keen on explaining we'd have two generations of 10th Mountain soldier descendants. That could lead to embarrassing details: my father's jail time, and so on. But I liked how this multigenerational aspect played into the 2001 re-creation of the route, when I'd joined with spirits of soldiers past, understood more of my dad, and brought the hill song home to my family. Might such blessings continue?

This time, we stretched the forty-mile trek over five days, with our last night at the McNamara Hut (one of the 10th Mountain Division ski hostels). Huts Association founder Fritz Benedict had started this whole thing when he'd given me that old newspaper in 1988. Eighteen years later, I was with a trooper's son and a deserter's grandson at one of Benedict's inspired huts. Glory.

The McNamara is an unpretentious frame-built box with a dull red gable roof and the footprint of a four-car garage. It's situated on the edge of a meadow next to a conifer forest. From the door, five square miles of moderate terrain awaits your skis. But rather than a skier's base camp, I'd always seen the "Mac" as a Valhalla of contemplation—a refuge where one might forgo the day's powder quest in favor of sipping tea while watching jaybirds feast on scattered cracker crumbs.

Upon our arrival, Christie and I pulled cold beers from the snow in front of the hut—a friend had hauled a sixer up from Aspen—and claimed two spots on the front porch bench. Warm air rose from the sun-heated deck boards. Waking spring surrounded us: the faint maritime scent of melting snow, a woodpecker's hollow, staccato knocks. There was always a woodpecker.

While mentioning that my father could have been on the Trooper Traverse, I broached the short version of his foibles: "Psychological problems; he didn't make it to Europe. That's always bothered me compared to guys like your dad."

"It was a hard time for everyone," Christie said. "My father abandoned our family when I was seven. I hardly remember him or anything he said about the war."

I set my beer at my feet and shrugged off my jacket. "You must have heard things as you grew up, family legends and such?"

"My mom told me he was a bit of a scoundrel. He faked appendicitis during Hale to get a few weeks off," Christie said. "Some years after the war, my younger brother was struggling. Long-gone dad showed up and helped him get it together. Good and bad, nobody's perfect."

I pulled my hat brim over my sunburned nose. We sipped our cold brews and fell into a nature-soaked silence.

As during my first Traverse, I again pictured the soldiers, Bud "Rugged" Winter and now David's father, Neil. Though he wasn't on the original trip, I again pictured my father. A flood of love and acceptance filled me—the brotherhood of rope, skis, and snow.

I'd grabbed another rung on my wobbly emotional ladder: our fathers' actions were theirs, just theirs, nothing for the shame of sons.

At that, positive memories of my father pushed their way to the surface: bouncing our old Jeep up the four-by-four trails near Aspen; exploring for lost silver mines in Big Bend National Park; rattlesnakes; even his Kerouwhackian, LSD-fueled, Ram Dass be-here-now persona, when we partied like maniacs in 1960s Aspen. And the three wonderful houses he'd built for his family. I saw so much of him in myself: trailer-house improvements, my year of hands-on renovations of the home Lisa, Louie, and I now lived in.

With five decades behind me, sitting in the woods with another son of a vet, I saw my father clearly, saw him for who he was, the totality of his gifts and flaws. Something had damaged him. Affluenza? Clinical depression? Both? Smothered, he'd done his best. I'd not understood things until that moment. My obsession with improving on my father's failings, my striving for excellence, and my love of adventure—all were gifts, his gifts to me.

The Trooper Traverse had again delivered the goods. And the avalanches—those of emotion and those of snow—did not stop.

David Christie on Darling Pass, 2006, arrow indicates Trooper Boulder
©Dawson

40 | BATTLEFIELD VISIT, 2008

CORY BRETTMANN WAS A hulk of a man: six-foot-seven inches, 250 pounds. A ski patroller, father, husband.

He'd climbed Denali.

I wished I'd known him.

In December 2008, Brettmann chose to backcountry ski solo behind the Aspen Mountain ski area. As with Meta Burden thirty-six years prior (though in a different spot), a minor avalanche took Brettmann's life. The slide fell 200 vertical feet and ran about the length of a soccer field.

You'd think a guy that strong could battle such a dinky snowslide. But as history teaches, when human and avalanche meet, no slide is dinky. The lethal meld of snow and gravity had mowed Brettmann down like he was a grass stem.

The rescuers spotted a ski on the snow surface. They found Brettmann's booted foot just underneath.

DAWSON FAMILY LIFE WAS ticking along. Our smart, athletic, eighteen-year-old mountain-boy son was in college, his first year. I'd published several books, picked up a few high-dollar guiding clients, and our website was thriving. And Lisa? She was my angel in human disguise, or so I liked to joke with her—though I couldn't help but wonder ...

Yet angels aside, since my first years in Aspen, I'd continued a pattern of denial regarding the avalanches, the climbing falls, and the victims.

Granted, I'd done better regarding my foibles. I'd honored my vow to play by the mountains' rules, and the personal growth after my Highland Bowl escapade was a real thing. Yet within my sphere of alpine sports enthusiasts, the tragedies had continued unabated—young, old, expert, novice. And that's where denial continued its work. Other than initial bouts of hindsight intellectualizing, I thought little about the accidents and said less.

Sometimes, after a few months, I'd forget the fatalities like I'd undergone a brain wipe. There's nothing like denial to disguise denial.

I rarely attended the funerals; we called them "memorials" or "celebrations of life," which was denial in and of itself. In the early days, I'd skipped Meta Burden's. Later, when one of my high school friends died in an avalanche in China and another of altitude sickness in Nepal, I treated their memorials like I was skirting war zones. In their twisted way, such events were precisely that.

And then we had a son who came to love the wild snow. My fortress of denial collapsed. Each time someone perished in the mountains—most often by avalanche—I could not forget. Instead, there were the dreams, sweaty nightmares of body-breaking snow. The visions often depicted Louie in the wrong place at the wrong time—or doing something stupid, as had I.

Since his young teens, we'd enrolled him in the avalanche safety classes. We'd shoveled the snow study pits; had the safety talks.

The day after Brettmann didn't come home, the newspaper screamed a gut-wrenching headline: "Avalanche Claims Former Ski Patroller."

Such wording was more than enough to trigger a conversation.

"You know Louie's going for it when he's out there with his college friends," Lisa said. "He's probably the first down those slopes, like you when you're in guide mode. Are safety classes enough?"

We both knew the answer. Knowledge wasn't attitude; measuring the size and shape of the snow crystals was a far cry from deciding to ski them or not. What any backcountry skier needed was preemptive caution. Didactics perhaps helped, but I wasn't convinced. I'd heard that attaining certification in avalanche safety might predict risky behavior.

I had my Highland Bowl experience to guide me—my understanding of the "other Lou," the lunatic. Lisa had her innate wisdom and maturity. Louie? He had mentors and avalanche safety classes. He was visiting from college. Was it time for a reality check?

Two days after Brettmann's slide, Louie and I ducked under the red boundary rope at the top of Aspen Mountain. A ten-minute hike and a short downhill ski broached the tiny clearing where Brettmann had passed. We slid and dropped over the two-foot high fracture where the avalanche had cracked from the snowpack. A few turns later, we found the lidless sarcophagus tucked next to a half dozen pine saplings. The hole was some three feet deep, sized for a large man, snow from the digging heaped to the sides.

Leaning on my ski poles, I offered a banal, "This is it."

Louie was silent.

As we gazed uphill at the fracture line, I imagined the irresistible cascade. My chest tightened. Without thinking, I moved my skis to the start position for escape—pointed down and across the slope to the forest.

Picturing Brettmann's final ride was too easy: Staccato flashes of dark and sky stab his eyes as he tumbles. He makes swimming motions and struggles to pop back to his feet and out-ski the slide. Then, he's buried, trapped, his boot and ski above the snow.

Had Brettmann somehow wriggled the ski as the slide debris settled over him like quick-hardening cement? Had he a moment of hope that a fellow powder-seeker would happen along, see the evidence, and dig him out? Did that hope soon give way to heartbreaking thoughts of his wife and children?

We followed the recovery team's tracks through a thick pine forest to the ski area. The trail was a curved, scooped-out half tube, made by the loaded patrol toboggan plowing through loose snow—the same snow that experienced ski patroller Cory Brettmann had known could kill.

"What do you think?" I asked during the drive home.

"Pretty scary," Louie murmured, eyes straight ahead. Then silence.

A few days later, our family of three attended the memorial. A fine man, gone before his time.

That night, I dreamed again of avalanches.

41 | HE WILL SKI BETTER, 2009

"Exactly one day in your life your kid will ski as good as you do. The next day, he'll ski better than you." — Warren Miller

I HAD FIRST HEARD Miller's axiom in the 1970s while attending his annual ski movie—a big event when it came to town. The prolific auteur-raconteur recited his wisdom while narrating clips of knee-high groms ripping the slopes like they were born to it—because they were.

Still many years from fatherhood, I stored Miller's words for later neuronal retrieval and turned my attention to the beers we'd smuggled into the funky Aspen theater. Per tradition, we rolled the empty cans under the seats in front of us, where they clanked and banged down the slanted concrete floor to the front.

As did the beers, the years rolled, the kid came. And I never forgot Miller.

Louie was our little ripper. I don't remember his first steps, and we don't have the video. But I possess a vivid mental image of his first time on skis.

December 1991—he was almost two years old. We strapped his red plastic snow-play boots onto a borrowed pair of orange-lacquered toy skis, and pushed him off a suitcase-sized hump of snow we'd shoveled from our walkway. When he fell backward on his butt, Lisa tossed a handful of snow on his chest. He laughed, said, "Again!" and soon shuffled around solo.

A day later, he was dropping the west face of the deck stairs: *kerchunk, kerchunk.*

After that, Dawson family winters were all about the glisse. On stormy nights, we dashed out our front door and twirled under the bright cone of a nearby streetlight; necks bent, eyes to the crystal tornado swirling from the heavens. Come the day, we swarmed the hill with our posse and celebrated the powder as a feast of kings.

My mountain friends might not believe this, but tennis-dad pushing the kid into ski alpinism was not a goal. In fact, should the young man have chosen any viable avocation, Lisa and I would have been delighted.

Still, osmosis is natural; I adventure-parented by default. Commercially equipped boot-fitting and ski-repair shop in the garage, nearly every friend a backcountry skier, school cut for ski days. It was impossible not to catch the fever, and I reveled in it, the alpinist father of a mountain-loving child.

Louie's first uphill ski, 4 years old, 1994

April 2009. Seventeen years after we'd scooted Louie through our snowy yard for his first time on skis, he visited from college. When we picked him up at the airport, I noticed the changes: the straightened, more confident posture, the deep-green eyes shining brighter, somehow combining my blues with Lisa's browns. We hugged. He felt solid. His college freshman experience looked to be a net positive.

"You look great," I said. "The spring snow is ripe, ready for skiing."

I tossed his bag into the back of our pickup. He was traveling light, just a change of street clothing, his orange Scarpa ski boots strung from his neck with a blue climbing sling. Over the years, I'd told him, "Never check boots as baggage." He'd listened.

As we pulled onto the highway, the second sentence out of his mouth was, "Let's ski a fourteener."

I kept my eyes on the road and nodded. We'd skied fourteeners over the years, some difficult. Those runs were about mentoring. This request was different. Louie was an adult, way past the deck stairs, past my lecturing.

"We can do that," I replied. "Castle? Climb the easy north face route, ski the steep east face, the line I first descended in 1999. It's popular these days."

"Cool. But unless we go super early, won't that get first-sun, be too slushy, avalanchy? I don't want to get up at midnight."

I laughed—typical nineteen-year-old. "Trust me, we'll go as late as possible. How does one o'clock sound?"

"Aw, Dad ..."

But I knew he'd rally.

The next morning, if you could call it that, we greeted the sun at Castle's 14,279-foot summit. The last time we'd skied Castle, in 2005, I'd rope belayed fourteen-year-old Louie off the top. After that, we'd skied the broad, low-angled North Couloir. Ultra safe. Today, I left the rope in my pack.

We carved our first turns into the east face, over a steep, fifty-degree wind swale. Though the morning sun was softening the snow, it remained solid and slick enough for an unstoppable sliding fall. Not a pleasant thing with a thousand feet of cliffy mountainside below—if you fall, you ...

The swale dropped us to the rock-lined couloir, where a steep, ten-foot-wide choke allowed just enough space for nimble turns.

The snow soon began its daily sun-softening, making it safer and more fun, yet with the challenge of pushing through a layer of slush. Louie turned into the crux, stopped, and waited for me to leapfrog past him. I'd skied nothing like this for several years. My soft-flex touring boots and stale legs worked against me. Each turn threw me off my stance, forcing an awkward recovery as I almost fell on my butt. I stopped below the crux and fiddled with my camera to hide my embarrassment.

Louie was magnificent. He sprang each turn with cat-like grace, flew for a moment, then sprayed a sheaf of slush from his edges as he set up for his next move. He'd been doing more than school work—Mount Baker ski area was a short drive from Bellingham, and when the lifts got boring, the Cascade mountain range went on forever. As he made the last few carves to my stance, he was singing.

Louie, Castle Peak east face, 2009   ©Dawson

SOON AFTER CASTLE PEAK, my father died. He was eighty-seven. Despite my newfound understanding and forgiveness, we'd never actively reconciled; I'd never made the leap. I felt a niggling of shame. Yet there'd been progress. When I'd visited him in the hospital, I dropped the conversation back to his Army days. In drug-slurred confessional words, he shared how he could not handle things and thought running was the solution. Then, to my surprise, he launched into praise for his Leavenworth cellmate: "Black man, older than me, didn't have any teeth. He taught me the ways of prison. Best friend I've ever had."

That threw me. My entire adult life, I'd pictured my dad suffering through his hard labor incarceration, hunched in shame, defending himself from shiv-wielding convicts. Instead, he had grasped for life, found positivity, or at least a friend. I wished I'd known the man.

We spread my father's ashes in the surf off Virginia Beach. That he lived in the East Coast rat race had saddened me—Charles Dawson had always preferred places high and wild.

Back home, I climbed a mountain by myself and took a summit moment in my dad's memory. As I swept my gaze over Capitol Peak and a hundred lifetimes' worth of the Elk Mountains, I thought of my father's life journey, and prayed that, wherever he was, it was good. I was now the patriarch. *What to do about that? Bigger mountains?*

42 | DENALI PATRIMONY, 2010

IT WAS A SUNNY spring day. Temperature: five below zero. Location: a glaciated shelf at 14,200 feet, known as the 14-Camp. To the southwest, 17,400-foot Mount Foraker floated against the sky like a fever dream. A quarter mile east, just beyond our barrio of seventy brightly colored tents, rose Denali's west face—one vertical mile of rock, snow, and a lot of gray and blue ice.

After 37 years away from the High One, I was back.

Along with our new best friends—about a hundred other climbers—my team of seven was staged for a summit attempt, counting days while we acclimated to the altitude. (Geographic and climatic factors cause 14-Camp air pressure to match about 16,000 feet in ranges such as the Himalayas.) Despite our being fourteener-seasoned Colorado boys, the rare air required a mandatory acclimation layover. Should we cheat, climb too soon, we could die when our brains swelled too large to fit our skulls or our lungs filled with fluid.

We'd had an active morning: snow-block wind-wall construction, melting snow for water, and satellite live-blogging the adventure. Resting, we lounged on couches we'd carved in the snow next to our red half-dome Hilleberg tents. While sipping sweet tea, we chatted up the celebrity alpinists camped next door. Twelve hours ago, they'd returned from the first ascent of an Alaskan-scale alpine big-wall. Listening between the words, you knew they'd danced with death.

Just then, a faint rumble sounded from far above. Distant thunder? Not a chance. Seconds later, the sound surged to a thumping bellow as unmistakable as a train highballing a yard from your face. All eyes tilted toward Denali. A familiar clawing sensation started deep in my chest and rippled into my groin.

Denali, as viewed during shuttle flight   ©Caleb Wray

"A big one," one of our new friends muttered, as if observing ocean waves from high ashore. "Don't worry. A couple of huge crevasses eat the avalanches before they hit camp."

Fat chance. With avalanches, worry was my middle name.

"That's a really, really big one—might jump the crevasse!" my expedition mate Caleb yelled as the white hurricane impacted the glacier at the base of the face, and shot a boiling 300-foot-high powder cloud directly toward us.

Someone jumped from their tent and sprinted. Mass psychology ensued. In an instant, a hundred climbers were storming through camp like escapees from a tsunami. Me included.

As I ran in my floppy camp booties like a barefoot drunk, a recent camp arrival—still in her crampons—sped by to my right, holding her ice axe high as if preparing to turn and battle the beast.

To my left, seeming to float in midair on each of his vast strides, Caleb held his big-lensed camera in one hand, pointing it behind, combat style. *If someone's gonna die, document it!*

Within twenty seconds, we'd crossed the camp boundary, and were headed for a field of crevasses that could swallow our entire riot and not even burp.

Reason overcame the madness. As one organism, the mob stopped and turned toward the mountain. Per our neighbor's prediction, the avalanche had spent itself in the crevasses. Above us, the powder cloud rapidly dissipated in a fairy dust shimmer. When the pulverized crystals sifted down, they smelled of the coldest blizzard you could ever imagine.

As we skulked back to our tents, our Denali-veteran neighbors smirked and laughed. "We watched that whole thing while sipping whisky—you guys can run pretty good!"

What was I doing, running from supersized avalanches, having sworn off expeditionary mountaineering thirty years ago?

WHEN I MET JORDAN White in 2006, he had been through hell. Less than a year before, he and his father were climbing the Maroon Bells fourteeners outside Aspen. They somehow fell from the mountain. All Jordan remembers is waking, badly injured, sprawled at the bottom of the famous burgundy-colored cliffs to find his father nearby, tangled in their rope, dead. Jordan was nineteen.

You'd assume an experience like that would end a mountaineering career. But instead of leaving the hills he and his dad had loved, Jordan embraced them. He became the youngest to ski all the Colorado fourteeners, worked as a mountain guide, and joined Aspen's mountain rescue team.

The *Aspen Times* profiled Jordan, and when I read the article, one of the quotes made me smile: "I read Lou's guidebooks when I was a kid, dreaming of the fourteeners."

Jordan White, Denali, 2010
©Caleb Wray

We welcomed Jordan into our family, and during the spring of 2009, he visited my office to talk about climbing. From the fourteeners, the conversation soon moved north.

"Wouldn't mind skiing Denali, Lou. West Buttress route next spring. You and Louie should join."

Fried crisp after a long day of blogging, I leaned back in my office chair.

"Not sure I could do it, carry the heavy pack and all. I'm a beat-up old guy. I'll be fifty-eight by then."

"You're no ordinary old guy," Jordan replied, reminding me of what I'd accomplished and that the Muldrow route of my past was forty-two miles round trip and 18,000 vertical.

"West Buttress is half that distance," he said, "and a few thou' less gain. No reason you can't do it."

There it was, a vibrant young man appealing to my ego. My distrust of "big" expeditions evaporated like desert rain. Another chance at Denali, the soul-gnawing missed ski descent of my lifetime, this time with my son? *When does life give you a retry like this?*

"Come on, Jordan, you really think I can climb that hulk and ski down?" Jordan laughed, said, "Don't worry. If you fall apart, I'll carry you."

At six-foot-four inches and 210 lean pounds, Jordan could do just that. I needed his backstop—the consequences of my lifestyle had not abated: a knee problem, back issues, and my partially fused ankle—substantial impediments. Still, I had one thing going for me: purpose. Perhaps I could fake it so long as I covered my bald spot.

As I pondered Jordan's proposal, I remembered my father when he was near my present age. He'd bought a parcel of rural land west of Crested Butte. I visited. He was living rough in a leaky-roofed pickup truck camper. I'd never seen him worse: sickly, with a scraggly beard and long, uneven hair. He offered a bathtub-sized mug of red wine from the jug he kept on a peeling plywood table outside his door. I waved it off and left.

I'm doing a lot better than my father was when he was living in that camper. Yet, is Denali the epitome of foolishness? Is my life just a leaky-roofed hovel disguised by pretty mountains? How will Lisa feel about this?

I sprang the question while loading a slice of Lisa's warm apple pie onto my plate. With awkward conversations, it helps to be doing something with your hands.

"So ... Jordan is putting together this Denali expedition—he invited Louie and me."

Lisa reached across the table and stroked my hand, saying nothing.

"Yeah," I continued, "It's a big departure from our life together, and Louie skipping college for months isn't great. But it feels right, so different from my early days ..." As I continued to justify it to Lisa, I knew I had already convinced myself. "It'll be great for the website and Louie. He needs to do this stuff with competent guys around his age."

346 LOUIS W. DAWSON

"I heard you and Jordan talking about this and knew it was coming," Lisa replied, her eyes moistening. "I love the father you are to our son. Denali isn't for me—but it bums me out to miss an adventure like that. I guess climbing that mountain is what mountain men do. And I love my mountain men."

Lisa: "Go."

Louie: "When?"

Me: *How much stupid was still inside this old climber?*

JORDAN INVITED TOO MANY guys. I cried, "Stop!" at seven—*at least it wasn't nine this time.* The final roster beyond Jordan, Louie, and me: Joe Brannan, twenty-six, was the sixth person to ski all the fourteeners. Tyler Christoff, twenty-six, and his brother Colby, twenty-three, were both engineers who'd grown up ski racing. Caleb Wray, thirty-three, was my voice-of-reason counterpart—a self-described hillbilly raised on a Tennessee mountaintop. "Like Davy Crockett," he told me, "but I ended up in Colorado." Caleb's southern drawl buoyed a wicked sense of humor—an essential expeditionary skill. He'd attempted Denali eight years earlier and "learned lessons" I hoped he'd share with our crew.

Wherever my father was in the firmament, I figured he was also in on this. Who else but the part of me that was him would have brought his young son along on such an adventure? Also, my dad's rebel side must have liked our ideas for freshening a standard Denali climb. We'd attempt a ski descent (most climbers traveled on foot) and execute the trip as a do-it-yourself project: no hired guides. And, I intended to live blog our climb via a low-budget satellite phone system—with no idea if we could pull it off. Failure would have consequences.

WildSnow.com was a hit; I'd finally found success as a writer. Along with innumerable Colorado ski tours, I'd been spending a month or more each year in the Alps, covering ski-touring gear and culture in the land where it all began. Now, I'd promised near-live coverage of a Denali climb and ski. If I didn't deliver, my business could take a brutal hit.

The time came for leaving: a sunny day in May. Lisa and I retreated to our bedroom two hours before departure and nested under our down comforter. As the sounds of last-minute packing sifted through our open window, we said our goodbyes, slow and sweet. After, my dear wife cried, gave me a hint of a smile, and gently admonished, "Bring my boys back." I pulled her closer and kissed her, reflecting on my years of struggle with relationships versus climbing. Was I up to my old tricks? I knew one thing: so long as we came back alive, whatever happened on that big hill of ice would be a nexus experience. It would be so for me, the grizzled alpinist. And how could it not be so, for the young man who'd turn twenty years old on the mountain bigger than the world?

LIKE MOST EXPEDITIONS, AFTER a bush plane landing on the Kahiltna Glacier, we traveled the enormous ice river's ten-mile upper section as a four-day series of back-and-forth portages to a camp at 11,000 feet. It was here the low-angled glacier ended, and the real (though technically easy) climbing began. We skinned our uphill portages at odd hours, around two a.m.—when the so-called night was a dim Alaskan twilight, and the slushy snow firmed. The skiing return to the lower camp was the reward: skimming the Kahiltna on our planks, reversing the four-hour uphill in a half hour.

One crystal-clear night, Louie and I were partway down a Kahiltna descent and noticed a moonrise brightening the sky behind the sea of peaks extending south from Denali. We stopped and stood silent on our skis. Now below the horizon, the midnight sun bathed everything in a shadowless luminescence. An icy breeze blew at my back and wrapped around my cheeks. I pulled my neck gaiter over my mouth and wiggled my chilled hands—yet I felt no desire to move. Louie, the same. Soon, a plump moon oozed from the peaks. As I stood in a gobsmacked trance, moonglow and twilight merged, transmuting the glacier into a watery-blue fluorescent ribbon, winding twenty miles from our ski tips to the distant horizon.

Later, as I lay with my sleeping bag cinched around my face, listening to Louie's sleepy breaths, I knew that moonlit stop on the glacier, with my son, had been the best ten minutes of my entire career as an alpinist. I vowed to remember it forever.

Son Louie,
20th birthday
Denali, 2010

©Dawson

TEN DAYS IN, we were finally lodged at the 14-Camp, nestled under Denali's mile-high west wall. All was splendid. By now, I'd filed a slew of blog posts. Lisa had replied that the "site was hopping, tons of comments." We'd had our little jog from the avalanche, acclimated well, and adjusted to the cold. One more day, and we'd go for the summit.

Of course, when the mountain gods learned of our plan, a snow-pumping howl of a storm slammed in, tattered our cooktent, and painted the mountain with a layer of skiable white. As we waited the requisite twenty-four hours for the avalanche danger to subside, another storm slid in. And after that, another. Two days. Three. It was the proverbial waiting game all alpinists detest.

As we cooked, ate, slept, and cooked again, ghost figures staggered through the sideways-streaking snow outside our tents. Climbers returning from storm-beaten summit attempts. They spoke through cracked lips, grimacing under frostbite-scabbed noses:

"Wind. Crawled from wand to wand ... To the summit ... Got lost in the storm, circled, and found the markers."

I wondered about their truth.

These desperate summiteers had lodged above us, at the 17,200-foot high camp—a slum of altitude-sick climbers and murderous temperatures. The advantage? Provided they survived the thin air and cold, climbers at the seventeen were positioned 3,000 vertical feet below the top, able to summit during shorter weather windows. We planned to skip camping at the seventeen, and climb the total 6,000 vert in one push from 14-Camp. This approach worked well for fit, experienced climbers but demanded a reliable weather window, preferably at least 24 hours. In turn, this required a bomber weather forecast. That we had.

Jordan's friend, Joel Gratz, was a meteorological savant who published the *OpenSnow.com* skiers' weather site. He'd agreed to provide personalized Denali-specific weather reports we received as satphone emails. So far, his forecasts were so accurate one might have wondered if he were psychic.

We gathered in our cooktent. The subject: how to summit during this string of storms; should we move to the high camp? I gave my expedition mates the lowdown of the latest weather report I'd gotten from Joel, which predicted a window opening in about forty-eight hours.

"We'll need to race out of here early that morning. Tagging the summit and skiing down, estimate twelve hours. It's too soon to predict how long the break will last. My bet: we'll have time to do the deed."

Brannan spoke through the steam rising from his soup mug.

"That sounds iffy. How about we cancel the one-day plan and move camp to the seventeen today or tomorrow? We can get there while it's storm-ing. Those other guys made the summit from there and climbed through the weather. They didn't ski, but they got it."

"I wouldn't believe all those climbers," I said. "Some of them probably stood on a hump of ice in a ninety-mile-an-hour wind with their goggles iced over and figured they'd done it."

Wray shifted the foam pad he was sitting on—our icy benches were a constant annoyance.

"I camped at the seventeen during my other try," he said. "Miserable. A bunch of coughing, altitude-sick, guided clients who aren't strong enough to climb to the summit from the fourteen. Even taking a crap up there is epic—adult diapers would help, and I didn't bring my nappies. I want to do this safe, with nobody getting sick."

"You guys could be the strongest West Butt team this entire spring," I said, reminding them of what we'd done so far—hauling all our gear while staying healthy and friendly. I also reminded them I was the weak link, that carrying a load to the seventeen would be a lot harder for me than the single-push strategy. "If we move to the seventeen, maybe we can storm-climb without skis. But Caleb's right; that's likely the highest we'll climb. Let's bet on Joel's window and do it from here."

The mood shifted. A round of nods and comments sealed the deal.

"There's one other thing," I said. "The key is how icy it'll be up there. These storm-winds might scrub a lot of snow off the mountain, especially from the Autobahn, that thousand-vertical-foot slope above the seventeen. With snow, it's like an easy ski run at a resort, but when it gets icy, it's a tilted hockey rink, a hassle to climb. Unskiable."

"How did it get the name?" Wray asked.

I explained that a German climbing team had once fallen down the Autobahn—and about a dozen people had perished there since. The name harkened to the German word for their sometimes speed-limitless highways. Plunging down a steep, icy mountainside had similar issues with velocity.

When I poked my head out our tent door the following morning, a blast of wind-powered snow bearded my face like a mall Santa. I cursed, ducked inside, zipped the door, dragged a food duffle against my back so I could sit up, and downloaded Gratz's weather report:

"You'll have the predicted window. If it's clearing tomorrow morning, go for it. Another storm follows, and it's a biggie. Get down before it hits."

AT SIX A.M., SCATTERED scud clung to the slopes above, hiding Denali's upper reaches. But the sky was otherwise blue with a hint of haze, the occasional wind just a stiff breeze. Gratz had been right. It was go time.

While Louie brewed sugary Lipton tea and warmed a few wads of precooked bacon, I fretted over our gear. Unlike climbers who brought almost nothing to the summit—sometimes not even a backpack—I wanted us to follow the mountain's rules. So, along with the usual day gear, I designated a half-pound of food, a bivvy sack, stove, and cook pot. One last thing: I zipped open my personal first aid kit—I'd leave it behind—and pulled out Louie's yellow baby sock, the talisman I'd packed during my fourteeners project and carried during every subsequent day in the backcountry. The scrap of fabric fit perfectly into my parka's breast pocket, three inches from my heart.

Wray poked his head through our half-zipped tent door. "You coming with us? We're gone in a half hour. Let's do this."

"Hard to get my locked ankle into this frozen boot. And making sure we eat enough. We'll follow you guys. I'm not strong enough to break trail. Thanks for going ahead."

When I finally threw my pack out the tent door, our advance team was an hour ahead of us and moving fast. They'd already scaled the steep headwall above camp and were disappearing one by one behind Washburn Ridge, the narrow, rocky highlands connecting to the high camp.

Something was odd. On a typical summit-worthy day, climbers would swarm the mountain above us like ants on a sugary picnic treat. Instead, just two figures followed our team's broken trail.

As I clipped into my skis, I queried a neighbor who was shoveling out his tent.

"Why aren't you guys climbing? There's a window."

"Report we got from the Park Service said stormy today—thought we'd wait."

They didn't have a Joel Gratz. *But what if he was wrong and the Park Service was right?*

I WAS FITTER THAN most men of fifty-eight, yet ten minutes out of camp I felt like I was hiking up a sand dune. The sedentary, high-altitude storm days had taken their toll. Louie could have climbed twice as fast, but he followed, allowing me to set the pace. He exuded an invisible, elemental competence that pushed me from behind, that kept me moving up the first 2,000 feet of vert, then along the narrows of Washburn Ridge to the slumped group of tents and wind-eroded snow-wall kivas at 17,200 feet.

A would-be climber stood in the center of the high camp, inert, blimpy in his goose-down expedition attire, staring upland as if second-guessing his guide's decision not to climb. He looked like a snowman carved by frustrated climbers.

It was a weird scene, but the mountain above interested me more—the doom-dealing Autobahn section. Today, it shined white.

I turned to Louie and grinned. "That thing looks totally skiable. If we can ski off the summit, it's the connector!"

An hour later, we stood at Denali Pass, 18,200 feet, where the storm had pinned our 1973 expedition. There wasn't much to see, just a few dark rocks protruding from unbroken snow next to a wrinkled patch of crevasses.

"This is where the storm stranded us for a week," I said. "Let's stop for a few minutes."

I leaned on my ski poles, closed my eyes, and let the slideshow run:

Pimmy's snow-caked ass. Whisnant kneeling inside our fetid snow cave, voicing the options, grim-faced, knowing the reaper was near. Wading the deep snow down the Harper and Karstens. Ward and Caffrey taking off down the Muldrow, leaving us wondering if they'd make it home alive.

The back of my neck tingled like a sniper had me cross-haired. A bank of gray and white clouds had built off the mountains to the south—Gratz's forecasted storm.

Taking solace that the route markers and our GPS would return us home if the storm blew early, I rested my terrors. A mantra popped into my head, a nod to the transcendence of alpinism: *go with it, choose the now, do your best.*

A half mile of flats, the Football Field, brought us to the base of Pig Hill, a steep, thousand-vertical-foot beat-out leading to the summit ridge.

We called another stop.

I sat on my backpack, opened my thermos, and poured a slug of tea. Some of it splashed onto a mitten and flash-froze to an icy sheen. It was at least fifteen below zero.

"Let's get going," Louie said. "Those clouds are getting closer. I'll carry your thermos so you've got less weight."

Twenty steps up Pig Hill, it hit me. And "it" was not the lightness of being you expect of such a sublime location, but a horse standing on my chest as my lungs gulped for missing oxygen.

Despite the brain-numbing hypoxia, I remembered Paul Petzoldt's words from my first NOLS course: "The rest step. Pause a few seconds between strides ...Rhythmic breathing ... Don't stop and start, no matter how slow you go."

As we gained the summit ridge, our five teammates had topped out, back-slapping and shooting summit photos, interspersed with a somber moment as Jordan cast his father's ashes. They sensed our moment when they saw Louie and me climbing from below. Later, in a blog post, Wray wrote:

> Seeing that old dog Lou leading his son up the summit ridge brought me to a halt and a tear to my eye. Perhaps it was exhaustion or lack of oxygen, but for some reason, that moment struck me as one of the most beautiful things I have ever seen in the mountains.

The subzero snow squeaked under our crampons as we stepped onto the trampled summit. Team one had already slid away, too chilled to wait. Until a pair of climbers behind us caught up, Louie and I were alone in the immensity of sky and distant horizons. Perfect.

With Louie, Denali summit, 2010.
©Dawson

I looked north over the Muldrow Glacier, where countless summits sliced upward through rafts of undercast clouds. Addled by the altitude, barely comprehending the sublime landscape, I turned to my son. His red hood was pulled up, loose around his face. His glacier-dark sunglasses reflected the sky, as if they were heavenly mirrors. A thumb-length snotcicle dangled from his mustache. The white snow, sky-blue ice, and charcoal cliffs of Mount Foraker backdropped behind him. With our packs still shouldered, skis towering above our heads, I grasped his gloved hand and pulled him in, chest to chest.

"I can't believe this, man, we did it!" I blubbered as we hugged. "Oh, thank you, God, just thank you, thank you!"

I stood back, dropped my pack, and made the last three steps to the exact apex. It was a six-by-ten-foot platform of foot-packed snow decorated with a disk-shaped metallic survey marker the size of a serving spoon. A yard on the wrong side of the marker, Denali's 8,000-vertical-foot easterly reaches plunged to oblivion—equal in scale to the north side of Mount Everest.

We were tempted to linger, but Gratz's storm clouds stalked the edges of the sky. As much as this was a place of fulfillment, it was a place of ruin.

A climber was buried nearby, in the ice, and there were more crypts below us: men who'd disappeared on the mountain, never recovered.

My tears were freezing, stiff in the corners of my eyes, my feet close behind.

I picked up my skis and spun the bindings to downhill mode.

"Weather's getting closer. Better boogie."

We took turns touching a ski tail to the survey marker and skittering a few feet down the boot-packed snow—*exact summit, photos!* We then flipped our ski tips to the vertical, and slid together down the white ice on the west side of the summit ridge. Our planks—those peerless tools of snow—ran us through Denali Pass and down the Autobahn like we were skiing a resort.

On Washburn Ridge, we swung to the right toward the Peters Glacier abyss and linked turns in ankle-deep powder. Drop too far, and we'd ski off the curve of a bowling ball and plunge 2,000 feet to demise—and we'd not be the first.

For a moment, I was a few feet off Louie's ski tails, close enough to hear him singing, seeming to keep time with the tapping sounds his skis made as they struck small chunks of ice mixed with the soft snow.

Skidding sideways to a stop above a rocky area, he pulled down his neck gaiter; white vapor puffed from his mouth. A mile-wide smile split his face.

"We're skiing Denali! We're doing it, Dad, we're skiing Denali!"

WE CONTINUED DOWN THE ridge, skis clattering over ice swatches, seeking softer snow. A turn here, a turn there. The day waned. Chill clawed from the sky. Denali's satellite peaks marched before us, and far beyond them sprawled the tundra where a billion lakes and muskeg ponds mirrored the resting arctic sun. In 1973, seen from the Harper Glacier, that same glittering galaxy had blown my mind. Back then, I'd told whoever would listen that I'd climb until I died—and there were many times I almost did. Here again, thirty-seven years later, I faced that same expanse of earthbound stars. Here, with my son, I climbed to live.

Louie, skiing from Denali summit, 2010   ©Dawson

43 | ICEFIELD CONTINUED, 1995

Skiing Denali with my son had tied up so many life themes: fatherhood, the unrequited summit ski descent, balancing marriage with the call of the wild. And yet, as I put such events to paper, there remained something unsaid, something more of how the hills strengthened the bond between Lisa and myself.

Harkening back, we return to the Columbia Icefield of 1995.

Springtime, a decade into marriage. Five-year-old Louie was a spark plug that never stopped firing—fun, yet exhausting. I was forty-three years old, with creaky knees and the niggles of midlife crises sapping my spirit. Still, I had a modicum of purpose. The American Alpine Club had roped me into writing the entire shebang history of North American ski mountaineering.

History book, why not? Good for the career and all that. And yet, with zero background in writing long-form nonfiction and needing to be a trained historian, I'd forked up a way bigger hunk than I could chew. On top of that, the crucial tenth wedding anniversary was just around the corner. This relational landmark seemed as much a marker of joy as a hint that I could improve as a husband.

"God never gives you more than you can handle" was a favorite message at our church. That seemed a touch sophomoric considering the challenges a significant portion of humanity faced, but I prayed it often. And the book project was an excuse for a road trip. A time of renewal, I figured. Leave the kid with my mother, who was living across the street from our home. Pack the skis, subzero sleeping bags, ropes, and tent, and hop into the truck with Lisa. We'd road-trip to Canada, love on each other, enjoy a glacier ski tour, and romance the snow while Grandma Patricia taught the kid how to hold a paintbrush.

As for a goal, I'd honed in on one of Canada's most impressive zones: the Columbia Icefield, an immense, ninety-square-mile glacial cap, the largest in the Rockies, splayed like a titanic starfish on a high plateau in Jasper National Park. Eleven of Canada's twenty-two highest peaks surround the icefield: hulks such as ice-shrouded Mount Columbia and Mount Kitchener, where I'd ventured with Don Peterson so long ago it was another lifetime. According to guidebook author Chic Scott, the Columbia is "One of the premier ski mountaineering locations ... A huge icefield surrounded by mountain giants, between which glaciers wind their way." The crown of the icefield is the aptly named Snow Dome, a low-angled, humped summit in marked contrast to the jagged peaks that characterize the area.

....

Lisa: *I lounge in shorts and a tank top on our back deck, soaking in the warmth of a spring morning. Our garden is bright with sweet peas, red poppies, and butterflies flitting among fragrant lilacs. After each season of avalanche safety decisions, storms, and sometimes brutal ski tours, I welcome summer when I risk nothing more than a scraped knee during a hike or blisters from my garden hoe. All is peace.*

Then my husband sits beside me, tea in hand, and says, "Jeez, it's hot out here. I can't wait until winter ... Come to think of it, let's head north and find some snow."

....

Lou: The gonzo-scale Canadian Rockies smack me like a small-town teen's first drive in city traffic. Mount Whyte, bulking thousands of feet above deep-blue Lake Louise. Lefroy, with its thick, white glacier hanging from the summit. Mount Temple—just the name is enough. They look twice as big and deadly as anything back home—and they nearly are. As the beautiful behemoths fly by our windows like a tourist promotional movie, the burger I'd had for lunch becomes an immovable lump in my stomach. Nothing we can't handle, right?

....

Lisa: *The scenery along the Icefields Parkway astounds me. Rock buttresses plunge and soar, regal snowcapped peaks preside over the deep forest, and clouds* *dot the cerulean sky. But all that becomes mere entertainment when I open the truck door at the parking lot below the Athabasca Glacier.*

As a girl in the Alps, I'd smelled the glacier wind. When gusts of that same eye-watering ether hit my face, I know the mountaineering Lou has planned for me has taken a new turn. I'm calmed by my faith in his skills, and the naivety I've always felt with the unknown. But this is adult stuff; I've backcountry adventured enough to know you can't control everything. If something happens, will I be a worthy partner?

....

Lou: After our first night on the Columbia Icefield, we're well above our camp, near the summit of Snow Dome Mountain. Our string of marker wands and gear-festooned blocks of snow will lead us (I hope) back to the door of our tent.

We pause, gulp the dregs from our thermos, and then jam it in the snow as a final marker for our return route. The whiteout tightens. Icy wind gnaws my face. I think about hypothermia and worry about Lisa. I pray, silently. There's nothing to do but keep moving.

After a hundred feet and a few more steps, the angle eases and I'm skiing down a slight incline. Is this the summit? I shout to Lisa to stop, and I ski a half-circle. All is flat or downhill. We've summited.

The black cadaver of a raven juts from the snow, head buried as if the poor thing had dive-bombed to its fate. Omen? I bring in the rope as Lisa steps up to me. For a moment we stand dazed. Then, before the wind can blow away the socks, candy wrappers, and other assorted detritus we've left behind to mark our path, we snowplow down through the clouds.

....

Lisa: *The summit doesn't feel like the top of a mountain; there's no view, nothing steep dropping from a treacherous edge. It's just a place to turn around. As I ski behind Lou, my partners are numbing cold and endless white. We're moving at a crawl to control the rope between us. Without uphill work, the cold sinks in. I switch to autopilot. Over and over, I stop, retrieve Lou's markers, shout for him to continue, and wait as our cord snakes in front of me. A thousand vertigo-inducing turns later, our tent emerges from the gray ghost of the glacier.*

Lou turns and smiles at me as he brings in the last yards of rope. His blue eyes shine, welcome stars in the murk. His hug and kiss revive me. In the circle of that moment, it's clear how a backcountry adventure completes our relationship, even more than perfect snow or nights in a grand hotel.

With Lisa,
Columbia Icefield, 1995

Lou: We wake early, eager to descend, to complete. The clouds churn—sometimes the sun punches through. I check my map and write compass bearings on my hand. That same queasy feeling hits my stomach, born of fears I haven't known for years: serac, crevasse, injury, weather.

We ski direct and fast to the saddle at the head of the Athabasca Glacier. As a ground blizzard curls behind us, we find one critical marker wand. Unpassable icefalls block either side of the route; if we'd lost viz and strayed just a few hundred feet, the glacier would have had us for lunch. A close shave.

....

Lisa: *We rush down the glacier, solving its intricacies by interminable weaving, creeping over tenuous bridges, dark crevasses below, then skiing in fear below the icefall. The gear sled pushes from behind like a truck bumper, demanding a thigh-burning snowplow wedge to hold control. I can handle it* *for just a few hundred feet, then give the harness to Lou, who soon hands it back. We alternate for what seems like hours.*

Water gurgles under the snow, a sign we're near the end. Soon, we're stepping over tiny rivers of runoff flowing over raw glacier ice. The loamy smell of spring earth pushes away the nose-clearing dryness of altitude. Birds chirp. I think of my garden, what seeds and weeds have sprouted, what mudpies our son will make, and I leave our icy sojourn with awe and appreciation for the extremes of my full life.

....

Lou: At the finish, Lisa retrieves our truck while I wait with the sled, feet touching the asphalt of the access road and my hands in the gravel of the Athabasca moraine. I raise my gaze. Stubby clouds roll over the peaks. Another whiteout up there—I'm glad we're here.

For a minute, the Columbia Icefield had defined our lives—the roar of the stove, the next step of a ski, the simplicity of a tent. During the process, I'd seen a new side of my bride, one with unexpected strength and ease in the face of danger.

Now, we'd head back to the complexity of work, parenting, and bills. It is a noble challenge—joyful—yet sometimes a trudge that can wear you down like an endless climb. But Lisa and I had worked hard and, more importantly, together on the ice. Rather than the desperate nature of my youthful adventures, this time was a melding, a smoothness, a sense of special care. More than ever, I know our love is beyond heat; it is total confidence in each other, whether tied to the ends of a climbing rope or our child's heart.

As I wait, I slip a glacier-rounded pebble into my pocket. I'll use it to remember.

CHAPTER NOTES

SPRING 1995, COLUMBIA ICEFIELD

— Song referenced: Eno, B. & Talking Heads (1981). "Once in a Lifetime." Sire Records.

— Here and epilogue, Lisa Dawson authored the parts attributed to her voice.

— Our guidebook: Scott, C. (1994). *Summits and Icefields* (1st ed.). Rocky Mountain Books.

— Portions of this chapter and the closing chapter first appeared in *Couloir* magazine, November, 1997.

1 - BEGINNINGS

— My father's full name is Charles Craig Dawson, and he went by Craig. To avoid confusion with my brother of the same name, in this book I use the name "Charles" for my father.

— The Colorado Rocky Mountains boast between fifty and sixty named peaks that punch the air above 14,000 feet. The exact number of "fourteeners" isn't official (there is perpetual debate about what defines a mountain when it's attached to another mountain). Yet conventional wisdom holds that fifty-four peaks fit the bill. Roughly a third of the peaks are easy hikes, while a third are moderately difficult, and a third, while nontechnical, require advanced climbing skills. Likewise, skiing.

2 - ASPEN LIFE

— Camp Hale was open for only two winters of training, and many soldiers did not arrive until the second summer/winter. Also, the "10th Mountain Division" did not receive its official naming until November 1944. When writing of times before that, I use the "10th Mountain" designation as a term of convenience. A brief chronology:

1942 - summer, Camp Hale constructed. 1942-43 was Hale's first operational winter.

1943, July 15 - 10th Light Division (Alpine) is activated at Hale.

1943 - 1944, troops' second and last winter at Hale.

1944 - February, soldiers ski Trooper Traverse. March-May, D-Series training. June, soldiers move to Camp Swift, Texas.

1944 - November, "10th Mountain Division" officially named.

1945 - January, 10th Mountain Division begins combat in Northern Italy.

Source: Chronology of the 10th Mountain Division, Mountain-Division.com.

— Comprehensive 10th Mountain Division history: *The Winter Army* by Maurice Isserman (2019).

3 - ASHCROFTERS

— Lead climbing, "leading," in the 1960s and early 1970s was significantly different than modern climbing. The gear wasn't as dependable, and the lower-angled nature of most climbs increased the likelihood of a falling leader hitting a ledge or outcrop before the rope came tight. Thus, until better gear appeared and climbs became steeper, the adage, "the leader shall not fall" was gospel. Yet even today, one must be circumspect about the consequences of falling, especially on easier, less-steep routes.

— Ashcrofters school, described in the book *Climb*, by Achey-Chelton-Godfrey (second edition, 2002).

4 - MOUNTAIN HIPPIES

— In what became known as the "Summer of Love," in 1967 something like 100,000 hippies converged on San Francisco, California. They concentrated in the streets and parks of the Haight-Ashbury district. That same summer the counterculture came on strong in Colorado. The college town of Boulder was a prime destination, as was Aspen. With its libertine atmosphere and fine alpine environment, the ski town became known as the Haight-Ashbury of the Rockies. Seemingly overnight, brightly dressed pot-puffing hipsters filled Aspen's parks and sidewalks. One disconcerted shop owner took to spraying water on hippies when they lounged on a wall outside his establishment. The time was radical, an upheaval, like someone threw a match into a puddle of gasoline.

5 - MY FIRST TIME

— Trailbreaking, on skis with human power, often involves sinking through the surface enough to make the task of "trailbreaking" (i.e., creating a track) an exhausting activity. Sans skis, on foot, trailbreaking in snow is known as "boot packing" or "post holing."

6 - PETZOLDT

— All our campfires, even Petzoldt's infamous infernos, were built to "leave no trace" by locating them on bare spots of mineral soil, or better, on flat boulders or stone outcrops.

— No deaths occurred during the NOLS survival expeditions. Nonetheless, by 1988 the practice had fallen out of favor. In my view, the value far exceeded the risks.

7 - ENTER CHAOS

— Climbing skins are essential to ski mountaineering. Attached to the base of the skis they eliminate the hassles of waxing, and allow skiers to climb steep angles without back-slipping. The bottom of the skin is covered with short-nap fur, angled to slide forward and grip backward, thus enabling uphill travel. The concept isn't new—the name derives from animal skins used in this fashion, long into the past. Modern skins attach with adhesive rather than straps and buckles.

10 - AVALANCHES

—The Loveland Pass avalanche occurred January 7, 1967, during our first winter in Aspen. The second victim died from suffocation brain damage several months after the incident.

— Gretl's restaurant did not exist in 1961, at the time of the Loretta Thorpe avalanche. It was built in 1966, eventually renamed as Bonnie's. The accident occurred on the ski run named North American.

— Numerous rating systems are used for climbs. The Yosemite Decimal System (YDS)—used in this book—was conceived in 1950s as a scale of 5.1 to 5.9 (pronounced five-one, etc.). The 5 refers to the climbing being "fifth class," requiring a rope and technical expertise, while the second numeral is the relative difficulty rating. As rock climbing evolved, the YDS required grades exceeded 5.9. Thus, 5.10 and so on (pronounced five-ten). Consequently, the term "decimal system" became a misnomer. Eventually the difference between the grades was too great. So climbers of the early 1970s began dividing the harder grades into four sub-grades: a; b; c; d. When modern climbing began in Yosemite, 5.9 was considered difficult. The first Yosemite Valley 5.11s were established in 1972: New Dimensions and Hourglass Left. As of the this book's publication, 5.15 was the top grade.

— Work cited: Williams, K. & USDA Forest Service. (1975). *The Snowy Torrents - Avalanche Accidents in the U.S. 1967–71.* Also articles in newspapers.

— With today's highways and automobiles, you can drive from Aspen to Yosemite Valley in about eighteen hours.

13 - THE PITON

—"Crazy Streak," from *Vertigo Games* by Glenn Randall (1983)

— In partnership with German alpinist Fritz Stammberger, Harvey Carter founded *Climbing* magazine in 1970. In 1974, Michael Kennedy was employed as the magazine's editor, later to become owner-publisher.

— Along with aid and free climbing, we were keenly aware of another form as well: free—without a rope. Free-solo, also known as third-classing, was a reasonable endeavor on routes well below our maximum ability level. But free soloing routes near one's limit of ability was another matter. Thus, while respected—and spectated as something of a gladiatorial event (such as Alex Honnold's 2017 free solo of El Capitan)—free soloing at the edge of difficulty was for most climbers not the ideal.

14 - CADAVERS

— We later learned the unfortunate man's name was Robert Allen. On August 25, 1972, age 26, he'd fallen from the exposed final section of the Gannett climb. His friends had attempted to drag his body down the glacier, but without rescue equipment and requisite manpower, they'd given up and descended.

16 - SPIN THE WHEEL

— Published source: *The Snowy Torrents: Avalanche Accidents in the United States, 1910-1966* (1967). Meta Burden's fatal route is now an avalanche-controlled inbounds run known as "Kristi." Some accounts of this tragedy say the argument was about where Meta was planning on skiing, or just a breakup squabble. A trusted source person claims the late Tim Howe never shared, with anyone, what the fight was about.

17 - WINTER EPICS

— The first winter ascent of Capitol is documented in a 1966 *Aspen Times* newspaper article. Karl "Bernie" Arndt and Skip Hamilton both went on to live as Aspenites. Bill Roos and Matthew Wells hailed from the eastern part of the state.

— 1972-1973, I'd obsessively tracked the story of the Uruguayan Air Force Flight 571 plane crash on a South American glacier. After the authorities canceled the search—having overflown the crash site without spotting it, the survivors lived for two months in the crumpled fuselage while cannibalizing their refrigerated fellow passengers. When an avalanche struck and their plight went from desperate to hopeless, two passengers, outfitted with soccer shoes and random clothing, climbed over an icy mountain to seek a rescue. The survivors were finally rescued around December 22, 1972.

18 - DENALI WAS ALIVE

— In his book *On The Road* (1957), Kerouac wrote, "You drive and drive and you're still in Texas tomorrow night." This in reference to road tripping across the "great Texas plain."

— Numerous books cover the 1967 mountaineering disaster on the Muldrow route, among them: *The Hall of the Mountain King,* by H. H. Snyder (1973). *White Winds,* by J. Wilcox (1981). *Forever on the Mountain,* by J. Tabor (2008). *Denali's Howl,* by A. Hall (2014).

— Our march to McGonagall Pass totaled 25 miles (not counting load relays, which more-or-less tripled the approach march to 75 miles). The National Park road to Wonder Lake was still closed by snow, so we flew into a bush landing strip that added about five miles to the trek.

19 - THEN CAME THE WIND

— The Harper Icefall is similar in scale to the Khumbu Icefall on Mount Everest, but steeper, and unclimbable due to constant avalanches.

— At the time, we did not know Tsuyoshi Ueki and Kazuo Hoshikawa had skied off the summit a few years prior, in July of 1970. For many years I thought we'd missed being first, though claiming the second summit ski descent would have been sweet.

— We had barometric altimeters, but they were not useful for finding exact locations on the somewhat flat glacier, especially during storms when the air pressure might vary rapidly.

20 - MONSTER TOWER

— Because it's an acronym (Realized Ultimate Reality Piton), the word rurp is often written as RURP. In the interest of sentence flow, I chose not to capitalize.

— A Jumar Ascender (brand/model name, also a generic term in lower case) is a mechanical rope ascender that pinches the rope when weighted, while otherwise free to slide upwards. Using such equipment for rope climbing is often called "jumaring" or "jugging." The generic term "jumar" denotes any type of mechanical rope-climbing device. Today's climbers use a variety of such devices, often called "ascenders."

— Portions of this story (here heavily revised) were originally published in the anthology *Desert Towers,* 2010, Sharp End Publishing, and *Alpinist* magazine #8, 2004.

21 - THE WORD IS WHEN

— The Capitol Peak climb details in this chapter are sourced from personal memory, stimulated by Glenn Randall's book, *Vertigo Games* (1983). Randall was a prolific Alaskan alpinist, and is presently a fine-art photographer.

22 - FRIENDS OF JARDINE

— Today's climbers will laugh out loud when they read we made a goal out of climbing thirty named 5.10 rated climbs. There are now thousands. The guidebook we used was *Climber's Guide to Yosemite Valley*, by Steve Roper (1971).

— This first Yosemite use of Friends is documented in Jardine's and my climbing logs. To be clear, I used a few pieces of normal protection gear (chocks) as well, where the crack fit them. But I didn't place any backup pieces and protected a long section with just the Friends.

— As to the future of Friends—and cams in general—I was immediately convinced they would revolutionize rock climbing. And that's what happened. While the new devices didn't always make climbs athletically easier—as would sticky-rubber-soled shoes a few years later—they often made climbing safer, faster, and more fun. And sometimes they shattered the paradigm, as with parallel-sided cracks where in the past the lead climber had to hammer pitons or drill bolt-holes for protection.

— Full Ansel Adams quote: "The great rocks of Yosemite, expressing qualities of timeless, yet intimate grandeur, are the most compelling formations of their kind. We should not casually pass them by for they are the very heart of the earth speaking to us." *My Camera in Yosemite Valley,* by A. Adams (1949).

23 - DAY OF THE NIAD

— "Mayor" of the Valley climbers, Jim Bridwell, whom I was told had watched our speed attempt from El Cap meadow (a traditional El Cap viewing spot), teamed up a year later (spring 1975) with John Long and Billy Westbay for the first NIAD, at about eighteen hours for the ascent. While they reportedly may have pre-placed a few pieces of gear on the first pitches, they did not use the fixed ropes. The year before our effort, Jim Donini & Pete Minks had made a little known first two-day ascent in 1973, see Donini biography: *Survival is Not Assured*, by Geoff Powter (2024). I've never been sure, down to the minute, what our total time on the wall was, but 28 or 29 hours is what sticks in my head. To avoid overstating, I changed "28" to "29" in later printings, and added the word "about."

24 - TRIPS WITH PETERSON

— The controversial article's first publication: "Tis-sa-ack," by Royal Robbins. *Ascent* (1970). The article has been published in at least one anthology, and is available online.

— Regarding the Mad Arab climb, Michael and I did not come up with the route name out of cultural conflict or bias. The moniker alludes to a character in the H. P. Lovecraft horror/fantasy novels we enjoyed, as the route had a dangerous runout.

— Hourglass Left's reputation as the "first" unrehearsed 5.11 wasn't entirely accurate—there were doubtless a handful of pitches of equal difficulty, of which at least several had probably been climbed without rehearsal. Still, Hourglass was the first unrehearsed climb to receive the badge of the new grade. The others had been called hard 5.10, or 5.10-d.

— Climb ratings change over the years. When we hit Outer Limits it was said to be 5.11, the consensus now appears to be 5.10-c.

— In the early 1970s, rehearsing a short-hard climb by repeatedly top roping it was not unheard of, but was not as common as it is in modern climbing. Likewise, it's common for today's climbers to take dozens if not hundreds of leader falls while attempting a route, hang on the rope after each fall, rest, regain the rock, and try the move again. This practice is known as "hang dogging." There are numerous variations: leading a route without ever trying it, and without falls, is known as "on-sighting," while leading a route after rehearsing it is known as "red-pointing." On-sighting was my ideal, and still is.

— The next fall, Colorado alpinists Jeff Lowe and Mike Weiss made the first ascent of the Grand Central Couloir. I was Colorado proud for them, yet envious, thinking Don and I should have pushed on. Years later, I was surprised and delighted to learn Don had returned in 1980 and climbed the route. "It's good we quit," he told me. "The top section was too radical, verglas-coated limestone, for the weather and gear you and I had. We'd probably still be up there, frozen inside a crevasse."

25 - TOOTH DECAY

— I'm not sure it has any significance, but Larry Bruce and I had probably pulled off the first guided ascent of El Capitan.

26 - ICE

— Glenn Randall's book, *Vertigo Games* (1983), includes an account of our Ames climb I used as a source for this chapter.

— Among his many first ascents, Steve Shea went on to establish a new ice-climbing route in the Alps near Chamonix, France (with partner Dick Jackson), and played the protagonist in the first commercial "extreme skiing" movie made in North America: *Fall Line*, 1978.

— Fritz Stammberger married Playboy centerfold Janice Pennington in 1974. He attempted a solo ascent of Tirich Mir, Pakistan, during the summer of 1975, and never returned. It was assumed he fell from the climb or was lost in a glacier crevasse.

— Our Half Dome speed climb did not set a record, yet was one of the faster ascents to date. We bivouacked part way up the approach trail.

27 -SKI TO DIE

— The accident description is based on my original *Powder* magazine article: "Out of Bounds and Out of Luck," November, 1977.

28 - OUTWARD BOUND

— The Friend's Hut, a backcountry ski-touring shelter situated on a twenty-mile ski route between

Crested Butte and Aspen, was completed in 1985 as a memorial to the midair collision victims.

— Some of my internet postings state a 1980 date for the ski descents I made with Bruce Adams, La Plata Peak and French Mountain. As stated in my narrative, our descents were made in spring 1979.

— Paul Ramer introduced his eponymous ski touring binding around 1975. It was lighter than any other binding of similar function, had a heel lifter/elevator to help with foot and leg angles while uphill striding, and would accept some models of heavy-duty hiking boots. I helped with testing the Ramer binding. After the first pre-retail prototype broke during my first run, Ramer quickly improved the binding, and for a few years it was a standard of the sport. Every ski touring binding on the present market uses several of Ramer's design concepts.

29 - IF YOU FALL

— Paraphrased from personal conversations with Landry, as well as his writings in *Couloir* magazine 1993.

— In 1981, while interviewing Landry for an article about his descents, *Sports Illustrated* magazine journalist Oscar Johnson asked how he would define extreme skiing. Verbally and via correspondence with *Couloir Magazine*, Landry later clarified that he'd explained that the French might say, "It's when you fall, you die." Landry then told Johnson that this pithy slogan was the worst definition. As I came to understand it, for Landry steep skiing was an evolution combining his two favorite disciplines: climbing and skiing. Extreme skiing was not about dying. It was about skiing to live, about experiencing the extremes of human potential.

— The *Sports Illustrated* article lead either misquoted or paraphrased Landry thusly: "The definition of extreme skiing is pretty simple—if you fall, you die." Landry was appalled at how the magazine had hacked his effort at relating what the French might say. "It was expedient, not to mention spectacular, and ultimately disappointing, for *Sports Illustrated* to lead the story with their version of that near-bizarre phrase. "I hated it," Landry wrote in *Couloir* Magazine.

— Work cited: Johnson, O. J. (1981, March). "It's Got Its Ups and Downs." *Sports Illustrated.*

30 – IN A WINTER SEA

— The indigenous peoples Udall referred to go by a variety of names, one of which is Inuit.

31 - AVALANCHE RAGDOLL

— In the years around 1999, with an extensive avalanche control program, Highland Bowl was opened to ski-area ticket holders. Rather than the runs extending to the valley bottom and Castle Creek Road, the bowl is egressed via a catwalk that traverses to the base of a ski lift.

— The naming of Highland Bowl is an ongoing question. The ski resort is Aspen Highlands, and the bowl is sometimes referred to as "Highlands" rather than "Highland." I use "Highland Peak/Bowl" in this narrative because that's the way we spoke it. Moreover, the USGS quadrangle map covering the peak is called "Highland Peak," and on that map the mountain is named the same singular. The B1 line in Highland Bowl was eventually named Ozone and Beone.

— Portions of this chapter were inspired by my first account of the avalanche, published in the *Denver Post* as an "as told to," written by Ted Kerasote after he interviewed me in my hospital bed. The vast majority of the text is entirely new, while any fragments from the *Post* article are heavily revised and rewritten in my memoir voice.

32 - POSITIVE POWER

— Perhaps the best known scripture passage regarding knowing God through creation is Romans 1:19,20: "What may be known of God is manifest in them for God has shown it to them. For since the creation of the world His invisible attributes are clearly seen, being understood by the things that are made, even His eternal power and Godhead, so that they are without excuse." I always took this to mean that not only was God both harsh and beautiful, but that our free will was practiced within the confines of physical law—except when it was not, as in the case of miracles. How that all worked I made no profession to understand, and I never thought anyone else did, either. Other than Jesus.

— My first ski touring guidebook was *Colorado High Routes*, published in 1986 by The Mountaineers.

— On March 31, 1984, Chris Kessler, Craig Soddy, and Tom Snyder were doing avalanche control and research work in Highland Bowl. The three ski patrollers set off explosive charges while standing in what was assumed to be a safe area. A gigantic white flood fell from above. All three men perished. Tom Snyder had been with the team that rescued me.

— By the late 1990s, Highland Bowl had become part of the public-accessed resort, albeit with intensive avalanche control, along with strict openings and closures based on avalanche conditions.

— My aunt and uncle's copy of *The Power of Positive Thinking*, by Norman Vincent Peale, was the 29th printing, December 1966. In the preface, Peale writes of his timeless book's two millionth copy anniversary—it has sold many more in the ensuing years.

33 - PEN PALS

— Our bicycle route's mountain passes: Schofield, Kebler, Ohio, Slumgullion, Engineer. Over the years I've lost track of our Mount Hood trips, suffice it to say we were indeed enjoying Hood soon after our marriage.

34 - FOURTEENER SKIER

— Obsession with climbing all the fourteeners began in 1923, when climbers Carl Blaurock and Bill Ervin were first to complete the list, then counted as forty-six peaks.

— In the late 1980s, Aspen locals skied Stammberger's North Maroon Peak route several times every spring. Backcountry skiers didn't make light of this descent—you could still fall down it—but it had become a trade route.

— Mountaineering has no official rules. Thus, there is always some question about who first "skied" a peak. My personal ethic held that in most cases the peak had to be skied from the exact summit, several exceptions being peaks that had cliffy, rocky, normally unaskable summit caps. Also, my style had to match previous successful descents accomplished during the snow coverage of a normal winter.

35 - PEAK EXTREME
— Over ensuing years, *Blizzard* film style skiing came to be called "free skiing" or "big-mountain skiing" and the "extreme" moniker returned to its rightful place as the term for steep ski mountaineering. To be fair to Hattrup, Plake, and Schmidt, they were powerful skiers who throughout their media careers, and after, were passionate ski mountaineers.

36 - THE KID & THE LIST
— While skiing the fourteeners as a list project was not something on the cultural radar of the early 1990s, throughout the 1980s and 90s, brothers Howie and Mike Fitz and their friend Bob Pfeiffer had been skiing fourteeners as a list goal. They halted their quest with a handful of remaining descents, because they were unable to complete them as a trio of friends. They provided me with their journals and photographs while I was completing my project, for which I'm forever grateful.

— Kit Carson's highest summit as well as the entire massif is officially named Kit Carson *Mountain.* Climbers often refer to it as *Peak*, and I use that convention here.

— Glen Randall's book: *Vertigo Games* (1983).

37 - TALES OF THE 10TH
— I acquired my father's military records in 2009. There were no great revelations, though the details helped verify the facts I'd been privy to, as well as my subsequent feelings. Portions of this chapter are based on my previous writings, including "Trooper Traverse," in *Skiing* magazine (2002).

38 - BORN AGAIN NOLSIE
— This chapter conflates several family backpacking trips.

— Swimming can contaminate pristine waters.

39 - FIFTEEN TURNS
— Before Davenport, a few skiers had come close to completing the project.

40 - BATTLEFIELD VISIT
— Based on newspaper reports and those of the Colorado Avalanche Information Center.

41 - HE WILL SKI BETTER
— Warren A. Miller (October 15, 1924 – January 24, 2018) created and narrated his movies until 1988. By some accounts, his body of work comprises more than 750 films.

42 - DENALI PATRIMONY
— The satphone transmitted blog writing and photos were curated by Lisa and several others back in Colorado.

43 - ICEFIELD CONTINUED
— History book: *Wild Snow* (1st ed.) (paperback, 1998). The AAC Press.

Acknowledgements

I thank Fritz Barthel, Andrew Bisharat, Deborah Bradford, Eva Breton, Art Burrows, Jim Carnes, Harvey Carter, Chris Clark, David Clark, Cindy Conolly, David Christie, Richard Compton, Chris Davenport, my wife Lisa Dawson, son Louie Dawson, my mother Patricia Dawson, father Charles Craig, grandfather Louis Dawson, uncle Franklin Pillsbury III, aunt Sue Pillsbury, cousin Franklin Pillsbury IV, and brothers Craig, Tapley, Tomas. Also James Engelhardt, Kellan Eisenhardt, Dave & Sherry Farny, Howie & Mike Fitz, Albert Fiorello, Manasseh Franklin, Agustin Goba, Joel Gratz, Pauli Hayes, John "Izzo" Isaacs, Rich Jack, Dick Jackson, Ray Jardine, Michael and Julie Kennedy, Ted Kerasote, Peter Kray, Bob Limacher, Brian Litz, Catherine Lutz, Mike Marolt, Scott Messina, Kim Miller, Jim Milstein, Denise Moss, Chris Overacker, Bob Perlmutter, Julie Peters, Don Peterson, Bob Pfeiffer, Robert "Pimmy" Pimentel, Ken Pletcher, John Quinn, Glenn Randall, Doug Rhinehart, Jerry Roberts, David Rothman, Sandy Sandusky and her family, Steve Shea, Doug Stenclik, Kristina Thorpe, Randall Udall, Kris Walker, Jon Waterman, John Whisnant, Jordan White, Kendall Williams, Robert "Kritz" Wilson, Mark Worley, the 10th Mountain Division Hut Association, Aspen Historical Society, Denver Public Library, National Archives, and the many other institutions and individuals who helped with image contributions, beta-reads, editorial feedback, backstory and more. As for the three laws of fishing, a grizzled guy wearing a mosquito headnet told me they're something like: 1)Every chance you get. 2)It doesn't matter how. 3)Never promise.

About the Author

Louis "Lou" Dawson is among North America's best-known ski mountaineers. He has been inducted into the Colorado Snowsports Hall of Fame, and named by *Powder Magazine* in 2006 as one of "The Most Influential Skiers of the Past 35 Years." He was a top rock and ice climber of the 1970s, and went on to become the first person to ski down all fifty-four of Colorado's 14,000-foot mountains. He's authored numerous magazine articles and award-winning books, and is founder and publisher emeritus of W *ildSnow.com*. Lou has climbed and skied throughout the world, and lives in Colorado with his wife Lisa.

LouDawson.com
AvalancheDreams.com
Facebook.com/Lou.Dawson.writer
X: DawsonMountains

Made in the USA
Thornton, CO
12/12/24 16:49:13

45175bbf-c399-4288-9cd8-ce5cdfb15c7aR01